School Rumble

⑧

Jin Kobayashi

TRANSLATED AND ADAPTED BY
William Flanagan

LETTERED BY
Michaelis/Carpelis Design

BALLANTINE BOOKS ● NEW YORK

School Rumble volume 8 is a work of fiction. Names, characters, places, and incidents are the products of the author's imagination or are used fictitiously. Any resemblance to actual events, locales, or persons, living or dead, is entirely coincidental.

A Del Rey Manga/Kodansha Trade Paperback Original

Publication rights arranged through Kodansha Ltd.

Published in the United States by Del Rey Books, an imprint of The Random House Publishing Group, a division of Random House, Inc., New York.

DEL REY is a registered trademark and the Del Rey colophon is a trademark of Random House, Inc.

Publication rights arranged through Kodansha Ltd.

First published in Japan in 2005 by Kodansha Ltd., Tokyo

ISBN 978-0-345-50143-1

Printed in the United States of America

www.delreymanga.com

9 8 7 6 5 4 3 2 1

Translated and adapted: William Flanagan
Lettered: Michaelis/Carpelis Design

Honorifics Explained

Throughout the Del Rey Manga books, you will find Japanese honorifics left intact in the translations. For those not familiar with how the Japanese use honorifics and, more important, how they differ from American honorifics, we present this brief overview.

Politeness has always been a critical facet of Japanese culture. Ever since the feudal era, when Japan was a highly stratified society, use of honorifics—which can be defined as polite speech that indicates relationship or status—has played an essential role in the Japanese language. When addressing someone in Japanese, an honorific usually takes the form of a suffix attached to one's name (example: "Asuna-san"), is used as a title at the end of one's name, or appears in place of the name itself (example: "Negi-sensei," or simply "Sensei!").

Honorifics can be expressions of respect or endearment. In the context of manga and anime, honorifics give insight into the nature of the relationship between characters. Many English translations leave out these important honorifics and therefore distort the feel of the original Japanese. Because Japanese honorifics contain nuances that English honorifics lack, it is our policy at Del Rey not to translate them. Here, instead, is a guide to some of the honorifics you may encounter in Del Rey Manga.

-san: This is the most common honorific and is equivalent to Mr., Miss, Ms., or Mrs. It is the all-purpose honorific and can be used in any situation where politeness is required.

-sama: This is one level higher than "-san" and is used to confer great respect.

-dono: This comes from the word "tono," which means "lord." It is an even higher level than "-sama" and confers utmost respect.

-kun: This suffix is used at the end of boys' names to express familiarity or endearment. It is also sometimes used by men among friends, or when addressing someone younger or of a lower station.

-chan: This is used to express endearment, mostly toward girls. It is also used for little boys, pets, and even among lovers. It gives a sense of childish cuteness.

Bozu: This is an informal way to refer to a boy, similar to the English terms "kid" and "squirt."

Sempai/Senpai: This title suggests that the addressee is one's senior in a group or organization. It is most often used in a school setting, where underclassmen refer to their upperclassmen as "sempai." It can also be used in the workplace, such as when a newer employee addresses an employee who has seniority in the company.

Kohai: This is the opposite of "sempai" and is used toward underclassmen in school or newcomers in the workplace. It connotes that the addressee is of a lower station.

Sensei: Literally meaning "one who has come before," this title is used for teachers, doctors, or masters of any profession or art.

Onee-san/Onii-san: Normally older siblings are not called by name but rather by the title of older sister (Onee-san) or older brother (Onii-san). Depending on the relationship, "-chan" or "-sama" can also be used instead of "-san." However, this honorific can also be used with someone unrelated when the relationship resembles that of siblings.

-[blank]: This is usually forgotten in these lists, but it is perhaps the most significant difference between Japanese and English. The lack of honorific means that the speaker has permission to address the person in a very intimate way. Usually, only family, spouses, or very close friends have this kind of permission. Known as *yobisute*, it can be gratifying when someone who has earned the intimacy starts to call one by one's name without an honorific. But when that intimacy hasn't been earned, it can be very insulting.

Cultural Note

To preserve some of the humor found in *School Rumble*, we have elected to keep Japanese names in their original Japanese order—that is to say, with the family name first, followed by the personal name. So when you hear the name Tsukamoto Tenma, Tenma is just one member of the Tsukamoto family.

School Rumble 8

Jin Kobayashi

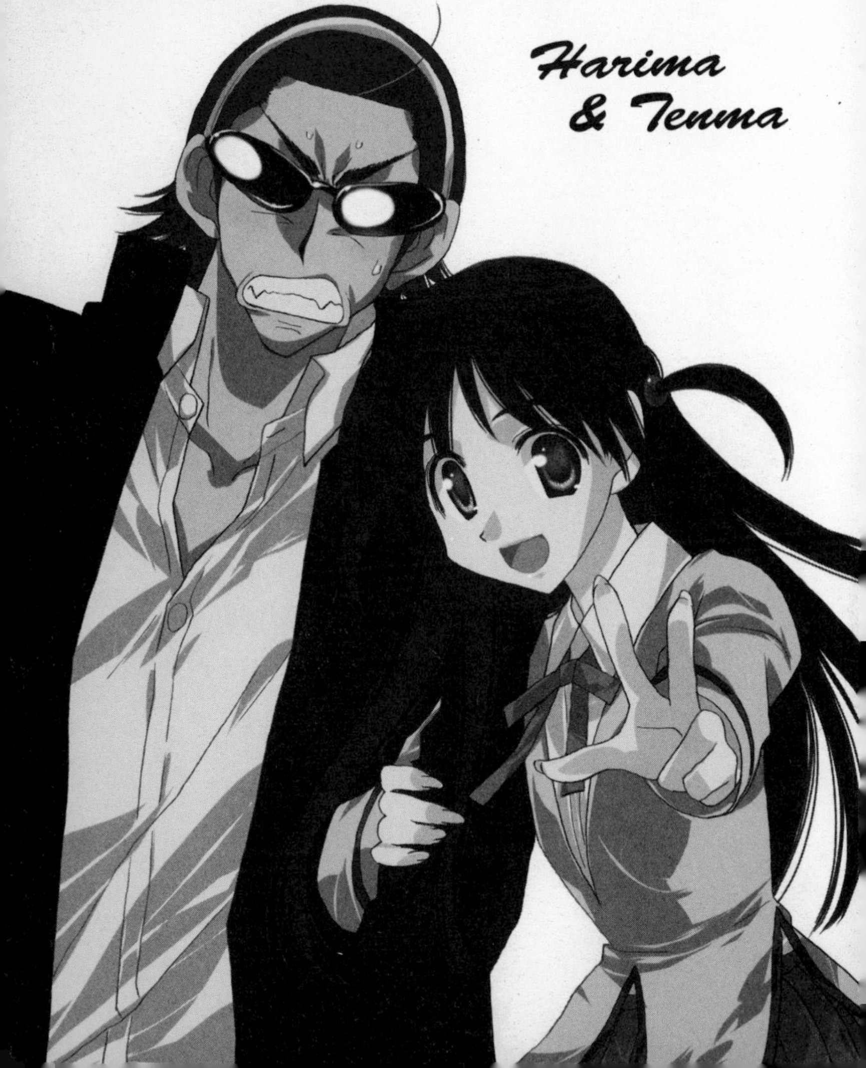
Harima
& Tenma

Contents

#97 TWO FOR THE ROAD 003

#98 THE BIRTHDAY PARTY 013

#99 THE TRUE-HEARTED 023

#100 GELOSIA 030

#101 TOO HOT TO HANDLE 038

#102 JOHNNY GOT HIS GUN 049

#103 THE DOGS OF WAR 059

#104 THE ULTIMATE THRILL 073

#105 QUICK 085

#106 LA TRAVESTIE 096

#107 WHISPERS IN THE DARK 106

#108 TRULY, MADLY, DEEPLY 117

♭21 NUIT DOCILE 129

♭22 THE SECRET GARDEN 137

♭23 CALIFORNIA MAN 145

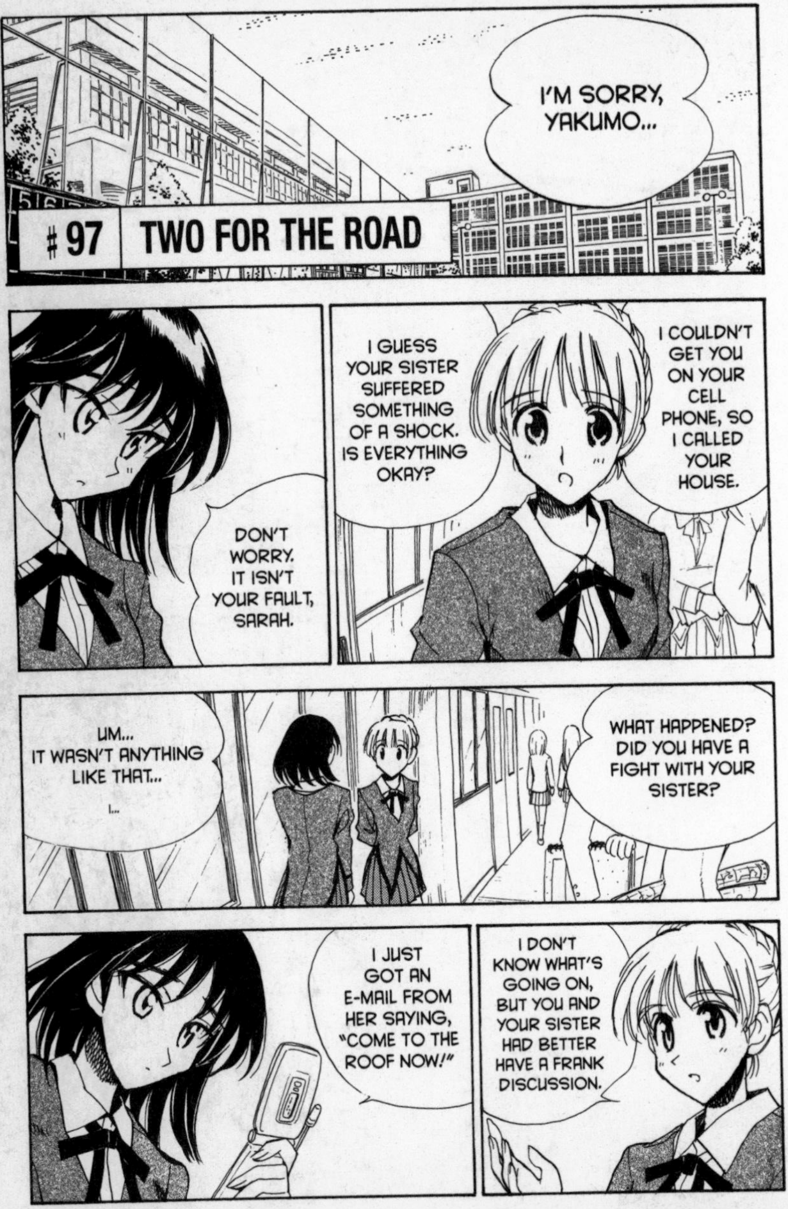
I'M SORRY, YAKUMO...
#97 TWO FOR THE ROAD
I COULDN'T GET YOU ON YOUR CELL PHONE, SO I CALLED YOUR HOUSE.
I GUESS YOUR SISTER SUFFERED SOMETHING OF A SHOCK. IS EVERYTHING OKAY?
DON'T WORRY. IT ISN'T YOUR FAULT, SARAH.
WHAT HAPPENED? DID YOU HAVE A FIGHT WITH YOUR SISTER?
UM... IT WASN'T ANYTHING LIKE THAT... I...
I DON'T KNOW WHAT'S GOING ON, BUT YOU AND YOUR SISTER HAD BETTER HAVE A FRANK DISCUSSION.
I JUST GOT AN E-MAIL FROM HER SAYING, "COME TO THE ROOF NOW!"

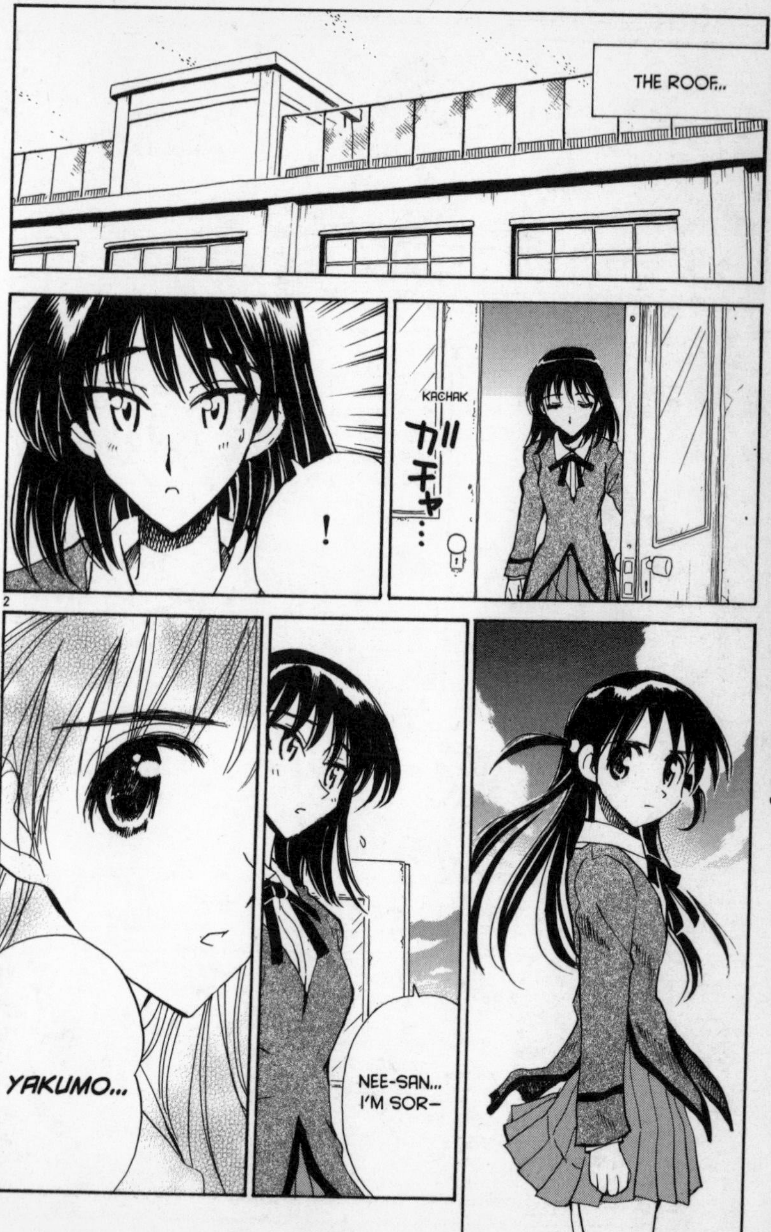
THE ROOF...
KACHAK
ガチャ…
!
NEE-SAN... I'M SOR–
YAKUMO...

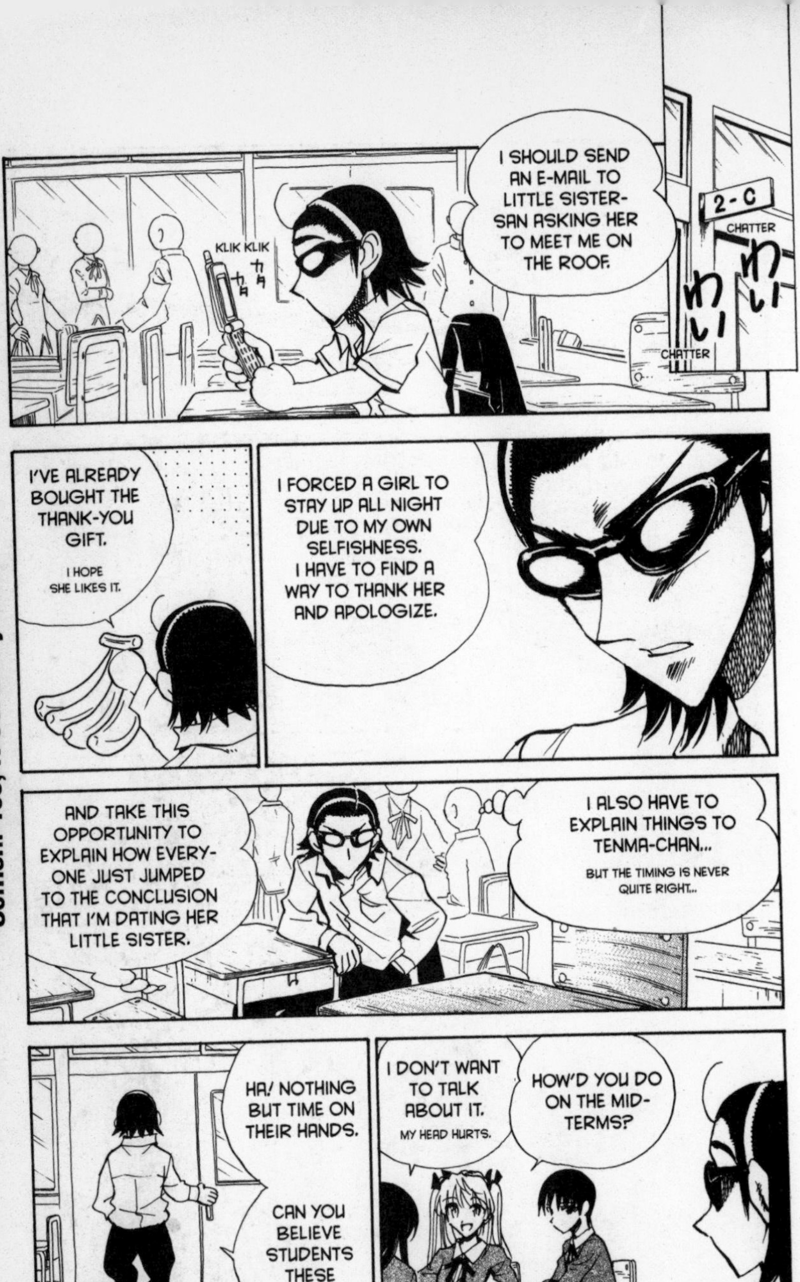
2-C
CHATTER
CHATTER
I SHOULD SEND AN E-MAIL TO LITTLE SISTER-SAN ASKING HER TO MEET ME ON THE ROOF.
KLIK KLIK
I FORCED A GIRL TO STAY UP ALL NIGHT DUE TO MY OWN SELFISHNESS. I HAVE TO FIND A WAY TO THANK HER AND APOLOGIZE.
I'VE ALREADY BOUGHT THE THANK-YOU GIFT.
I HOPE SHE LIKES IT.
I ALSO HAVE TO EXPLAIN THINGS TO TENMA-CHAN...
BUT THE TIMING IS NEVER QUITE RIGHT...
AND TAKE THIS OPPORTUNITY TO EXPLAIN HOW EVERY-ONE JUST JUMPED TO THE CONCLUSION THAT I'M DATING HER LITTLE SISTER.
HOW'D YOU DO ON THE MID-TERMS?
I DON'T WANT TO TALK ABOUT IT.
MY HEAD HURTS.
HA! NOTHING BUT TIME ON THEIR HANDS.
CAN YOU BELIEVE STUDENTS THESE DAYS...

Selfish: Yes, it certainly was.

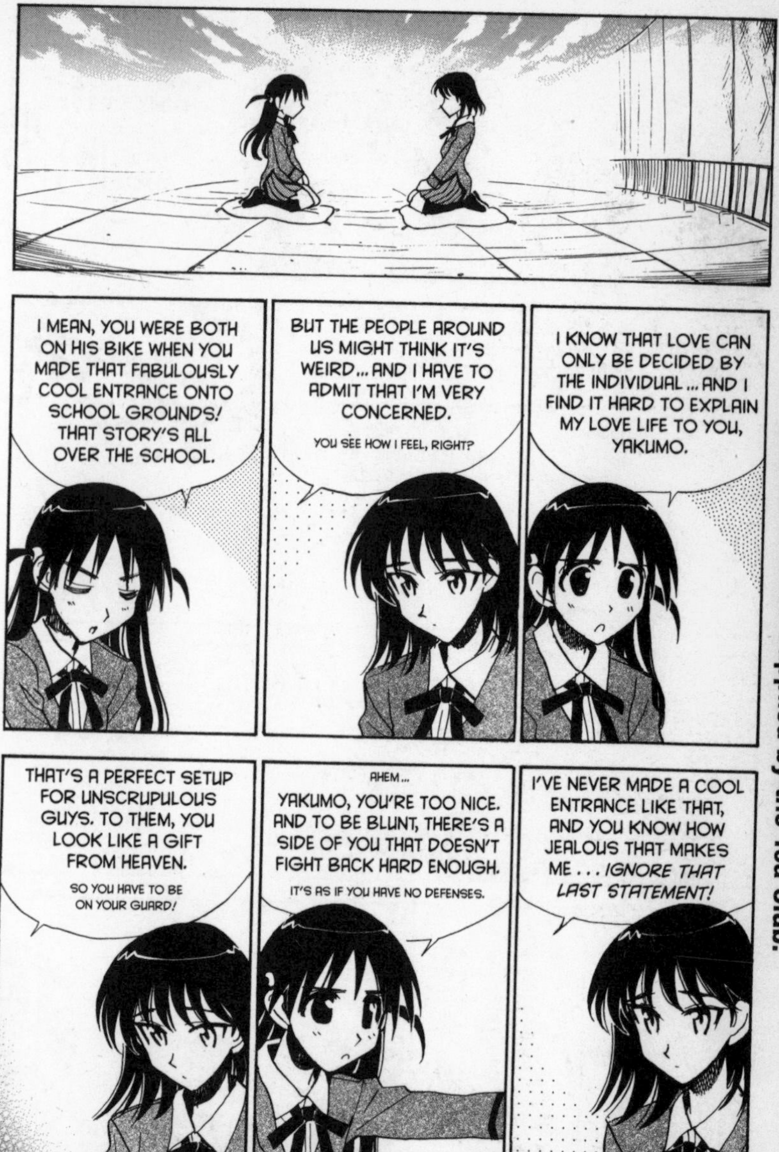
I KNOW THAT LOVE CAN ONLY BE DECIDED BY THE INDIVIDUAL ... AND I FIND IT HARD TO EXPLAIN MY LOVE LIFE TO YOU, YAKUMO.
BUT THE PEOPLE AROUND US MIGHT THINK IT'S WEIRD... AND I HAVE TO ADMIT THAT I'M VERY CONCERNED.
YOU SEE HOW I FEEL, RIGHT?
I MEAN, YOU WERE BOTH ON HIS BIKE WHEN YOU MADE THAT FABULOUSLY COOL ENTRANCE ONTO SCHOOL GROUNDS! THAT STORY'S ALL OVER THE SCHOOL.
I'VE NEVER MADE A COOL ENTRANCE LIKE THAT, AND YOU KNOW HOW JEALOUS THAT MAKES ME . . . *IGNORE THAT LAST STATEMENT!*
AHEM ...
YAKUMO, YOU'RE TOO NICE. AND TO BE BLUNT, THERE'S A SIDE OF YOU THAT DOESN'T FIGHT BACK HARD ENOUGH.
IT'S AS IF YOU HAVE NO DEFENSES.
THAT'S A PERFECT SETUP FOR UNSCRUPULOUS GUYS. TO THEM, YOU LOOK LIKE A GIFT FROM HEAVEN.
SO YOU HAVE TO BE ON YOUR GUARD!

Zabuton Cushions Supplied by the Tea Club.

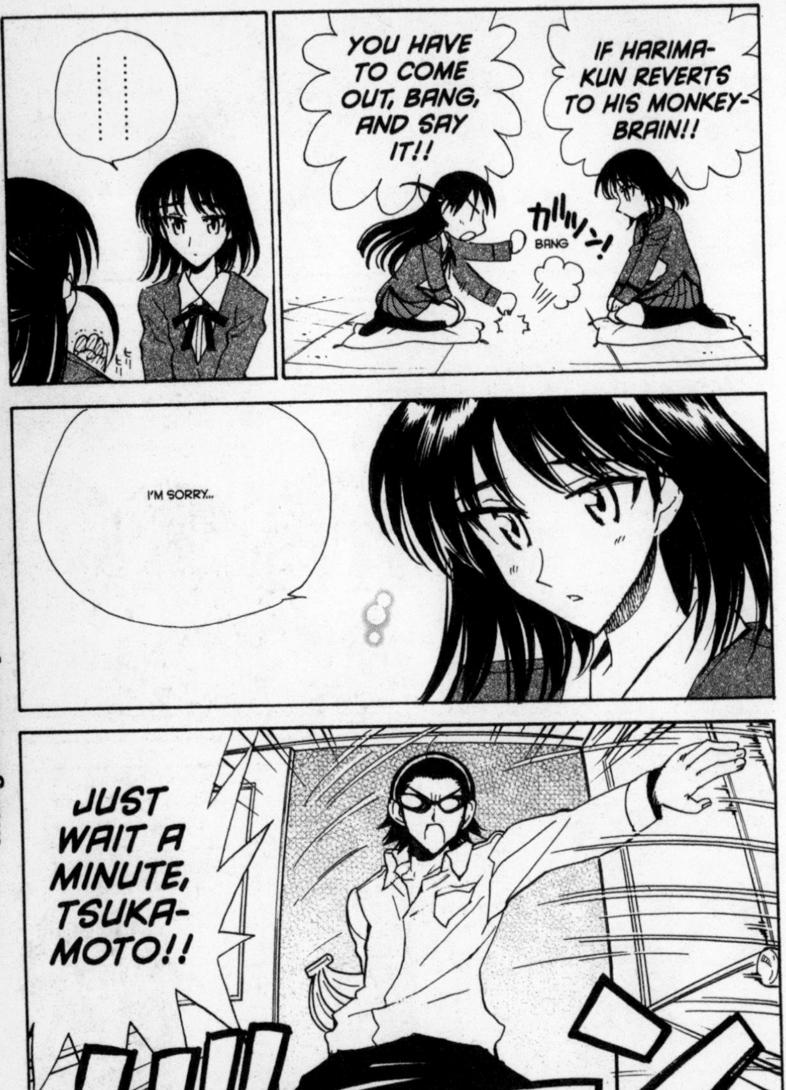
IF HARIMA-KUN REVERTS TO HIS MONKEY-BRAIN!!
YOU HAVE TO COME OUT, BANG, AND SAY IT!!
BANG
……
I'M SORRY...
JUST WAIT A MINUTE, TSUKA-MOTO!!
BAMM

Manga Monkey: Bursts on the scene.

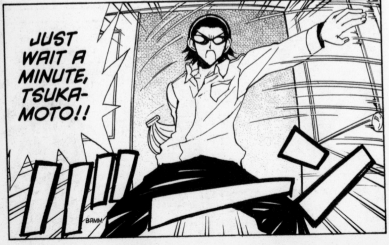

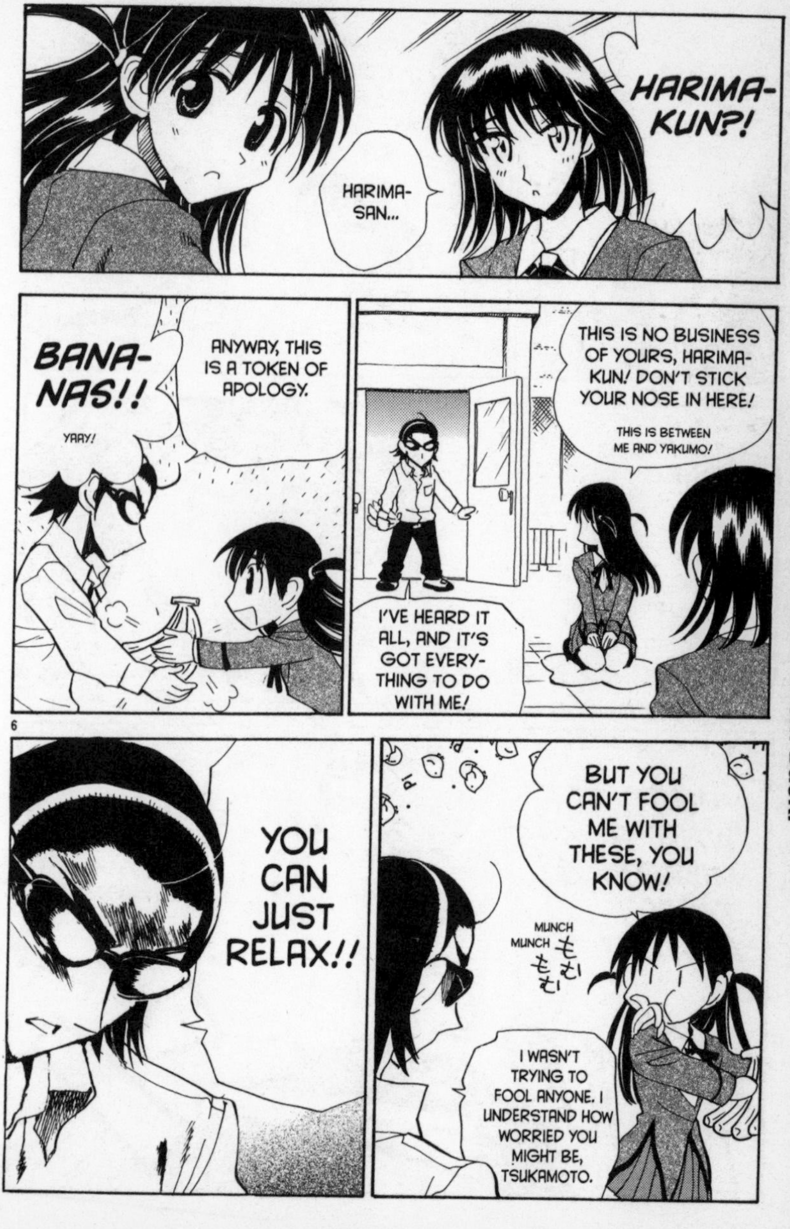
HARIMA-KUN?!
HARIMA-SAN...
THIS IS NO BUSINESS OF YOURS, HARIMA-KUN! DON'T STICK YOUR NOSE IN HERE!
THIS IS BETWEEN ME AND YAKUMO!
I'VE HEARD IT ALL, AND IT'S GOT EVERYTHING TO DO WITH ME!
ANYWAY, THIS IS A TOKEN OF APOLOGY.
BANANAS!!
YAAY!
6
BUT YOU CAN'T FOOL ME WITH THESE, YOU KNOW!
MUNCH MUNCH もむもむ
I WASN'T TRYING TO FOOL ANYONE. I UNDERSTAND HOW WORRIED YOU MIGHT BE, TSUKAMOTO.
YOU CAN JUST RELAX!!

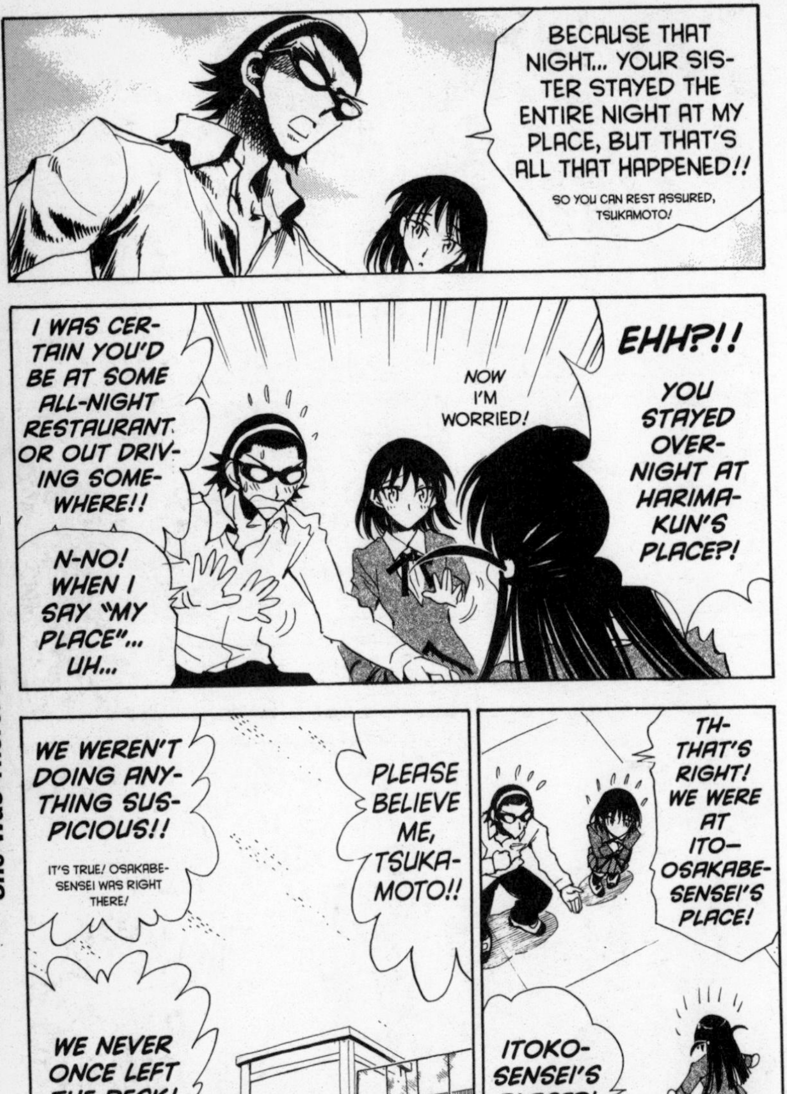
BECAUSE THAT NIGHT... YOUR SISTER STAYED THE ENTIRE NIGHT AT MY PLACE, BUT THAT'S ALL THAT HAPPENED!!
SO YOU CAN REST ASSURED, TSUKAMOTO!
EHH?!!
YOU STAYED OVERNIGHT AT HARIMA-KUN'S PLACE?!
NOW I'M WORRIED!
I WAS CERTAIN YOU'D BE AT SOME ALL-NIGHT RESTAURANT OR OUT DRIVING SOMEWHERE!!
N-NO! WHEN I SAY "MY PLACE"... UH...
TH-THAT'S RIGHT! WE WERE AT ITO-OSAKABE-SENSEI'S PLACE!
ITOKO-SENSEI'S PLACE?!
THAT SOUNDS LIKE A LIE!
PLEASE BELIEVE ME, TSUKAMOTO!!
WE WEREN'T DOING ANYTHING SUSPICIOUS!!
IT'S TRUE! OSAKABE-SENSEI WAS RIGHT THERE!
WE NEVER ONCE LEFT THE DESK!
YEAH, NEVER LEFT THE DESK!!

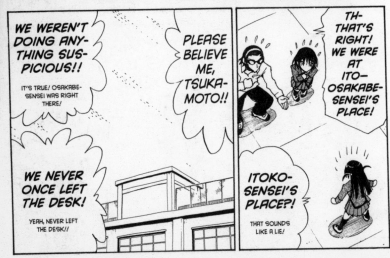

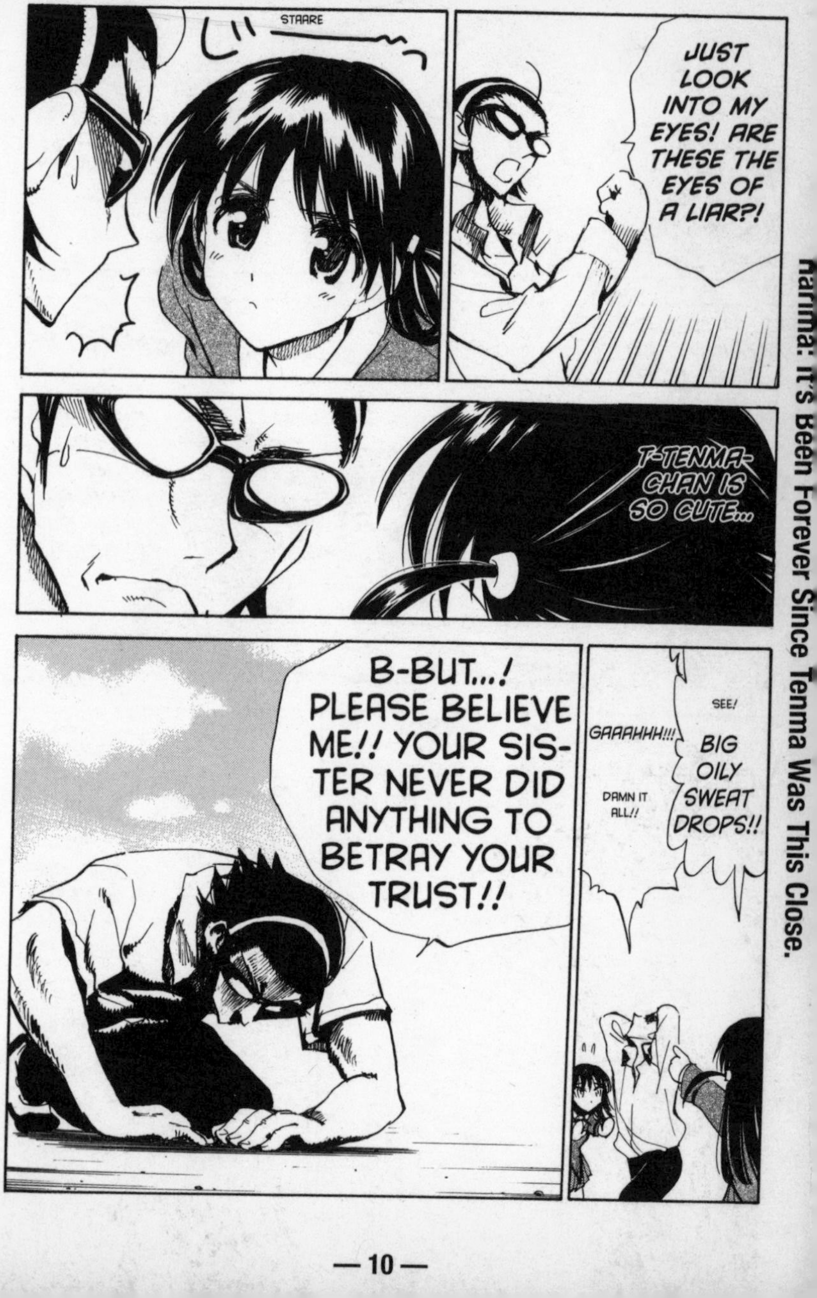
JUST LOOK INTO MY EYES! ARE THESE THE EYES OF A LIAR?!
STAARE
T-TENMA-CHAN IS SO CUTE...
SEE!
BIG OILY SWEAT DROPS!!
GAAAHHH!!!
DAMN IT ALL!!
B-BUT...! PLEASE BELIEVE ME!! YOUR SISTER NEVER DID ANYTHING TO BETRAY YOUR TRUST!!

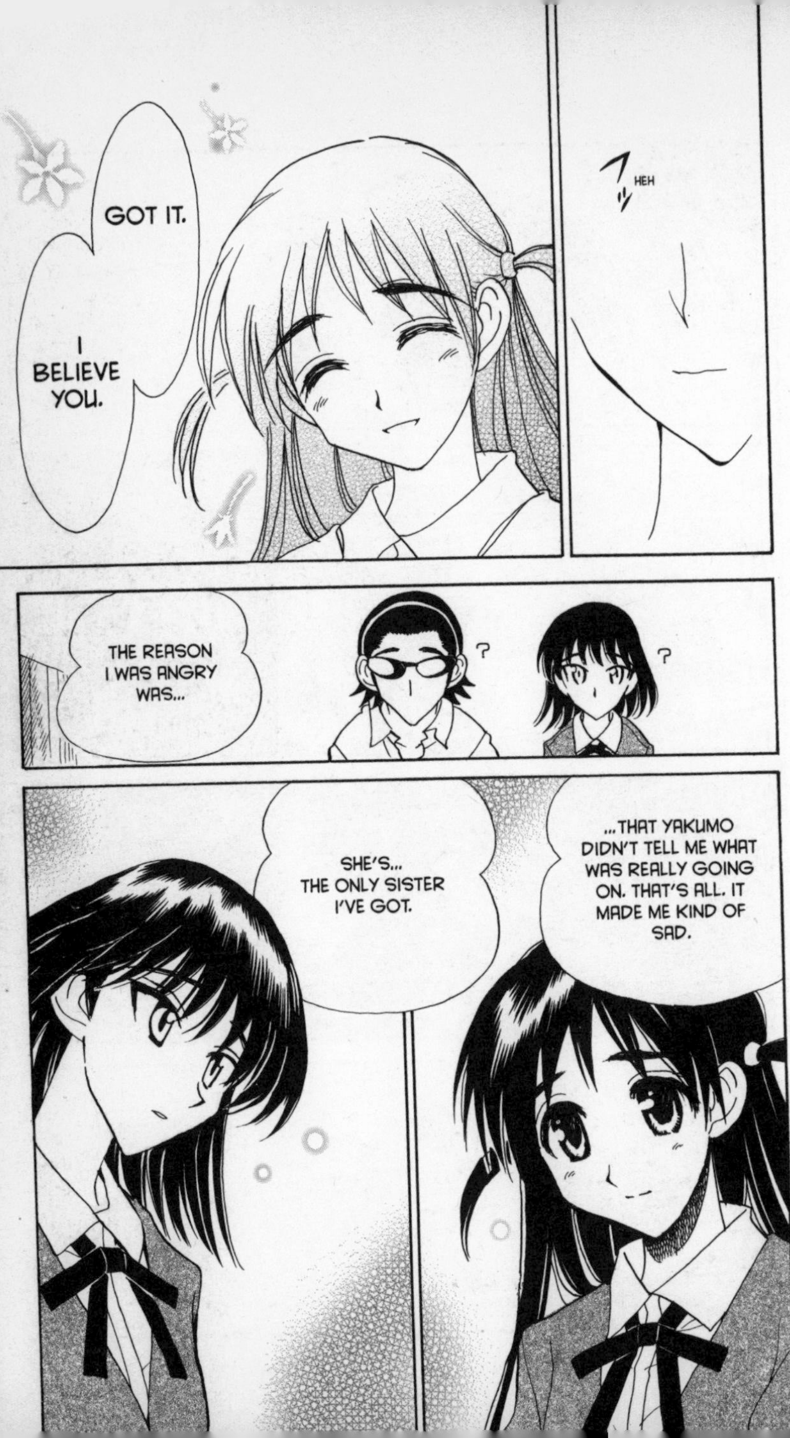
HEH
GOT IT.
I BELIEVE YOU.
THE REASON I WAS ANGRY WAS...
?
?
...THAT YAKUMO DIDN'T TELL ME WHAT WAS REALLY GOING ON. THAT'S ALL. IT MADE ME KIND OF SAD.
SHE'S... THE ONLY SISTER I'VE GOT.

And the Misconception Triangle Is Complete.

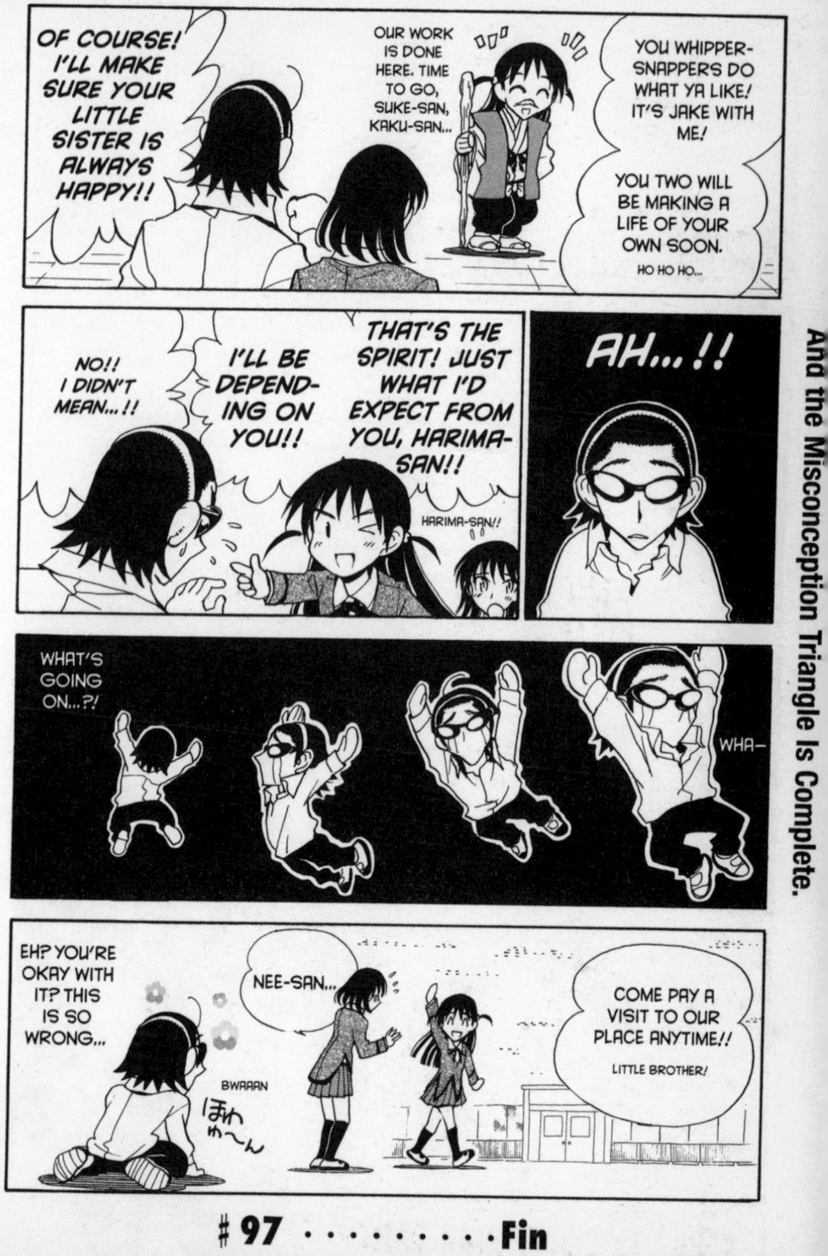
YOU WHIPPER-SNAPPERS DO WHAT YA LIKE! IT'S JAKE WITH ME!
YOU TWO WILL BE MAKING A LIFE OF YOUR OWN SOON.
HO HO HO...
OUR WORK IS DONE HERE. TIME TO GO, SUKE-SAN, KAKU-SAN...
OF COURSE! I'LL MAKE SURE YOUR LITTLE SISTER IS ALWAYS HAPPY!!
AH...!!
THAT'S THE SPIRIT! JUST WHAT I'D EXPECT FROM YOU, HARIMA-SAN!!
HARIMA-SAN!!
I'LL BE DEPENDING ON YOU!!
NO!! I DIDN'T MEAN...!!
WHA-
WHAT'S GOING ON...?!
COME PAY A VISIT TO OUR PLACE ANYTIME!!
LITTLE BROTHER!
NEE-SAN...
BWAAAN
ほわゎ〜ん
EH? YOU'RE OKAY WITH IT? THIS IS SO WRONG...

97 .... Fin

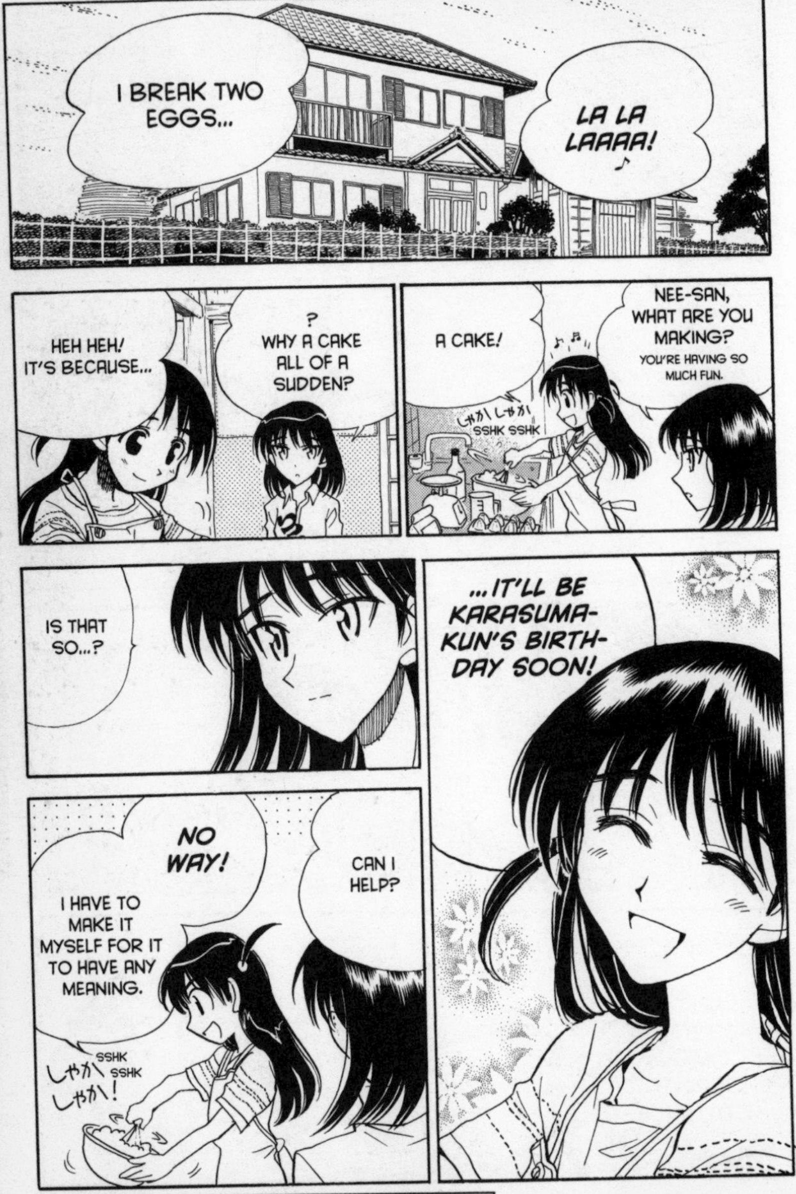
LA LA LAAAA! ♪
I BREAK TWO EGGS...
NEE-SAN, WHAT ARE YOU MAKING? YOU'RE HAVING SO MUCH FUN.
A CAKE!
しゃかしゃか SSHK SSHK
? WHY A CAKE ALL OF A SUDDEN?
HEH HEH! IT'S BECAUSE...
...IT'LL BE KARASUMA-KUN'S BIRTH-DAY SOON!
IS THAT SO...?
CAN I HELP?
NO WAY!
I HAVE TO MAKE IT MYSELF FOR IT TO HAVE ANY MEANING.
しゃかしゃか! SSHK SSHK

#98 THE BIRTHDAY PARTY

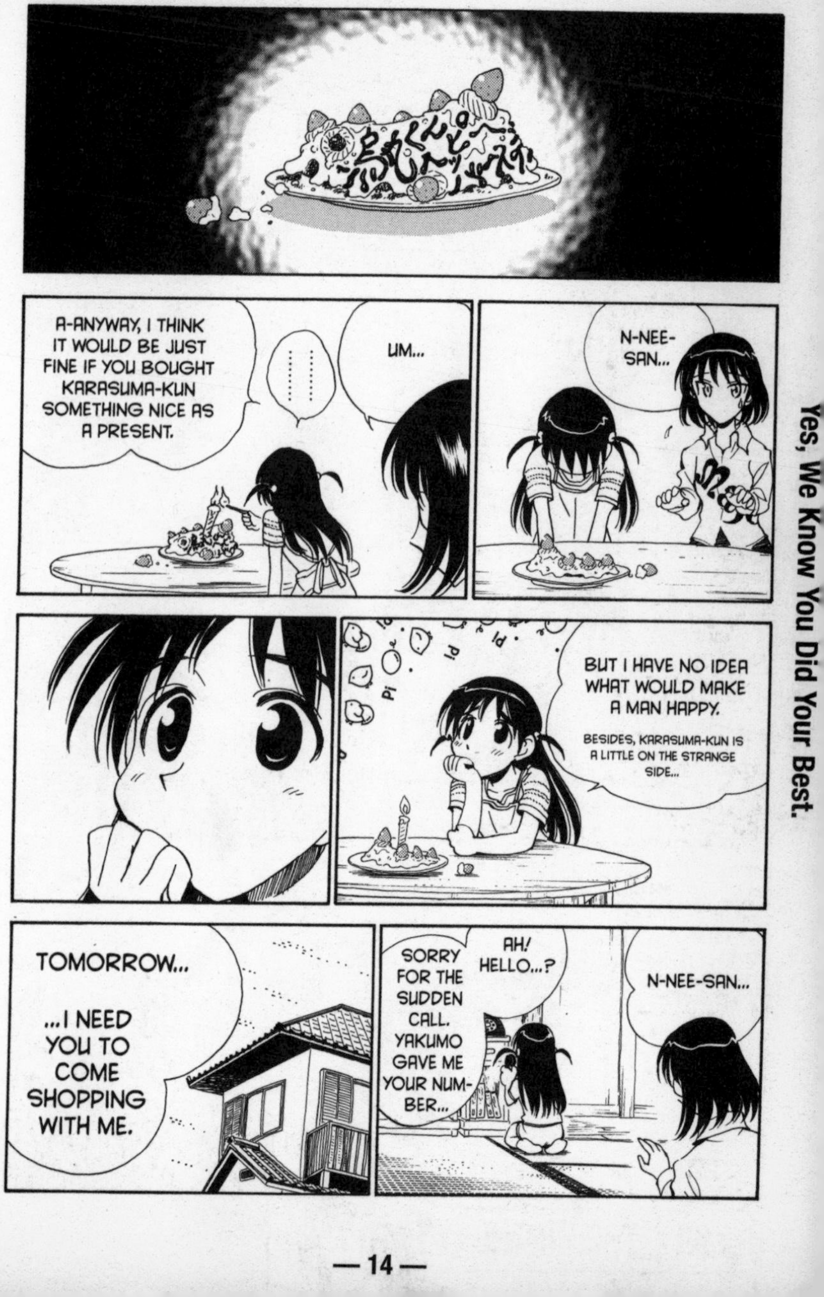
N-NEE-SAN...
UM...
......
A-ANYWAY, I THINK IT WOULD BE JUST FINE IF YOU BOUGHT KARASUMA-KUN SOMETHING NICE AS A PRESENT.
BUT I HAVE NO IDEA WHAT WOULD MAKE A MAN HAPPY.
BESIDES, KARASUMA-KUN IS A LITTLE ON THE STRANGE SIDE...
Pi Pi Pi Pi
N-NEE-SAN...
AH! HELLO...?
SORRY FOR THE SUDDEN CALL. YAKUMO GAVE ME YOUR NUMBER...
TOMORROW...
...I NEED YOU TO COME SHOPPING WITH ME.

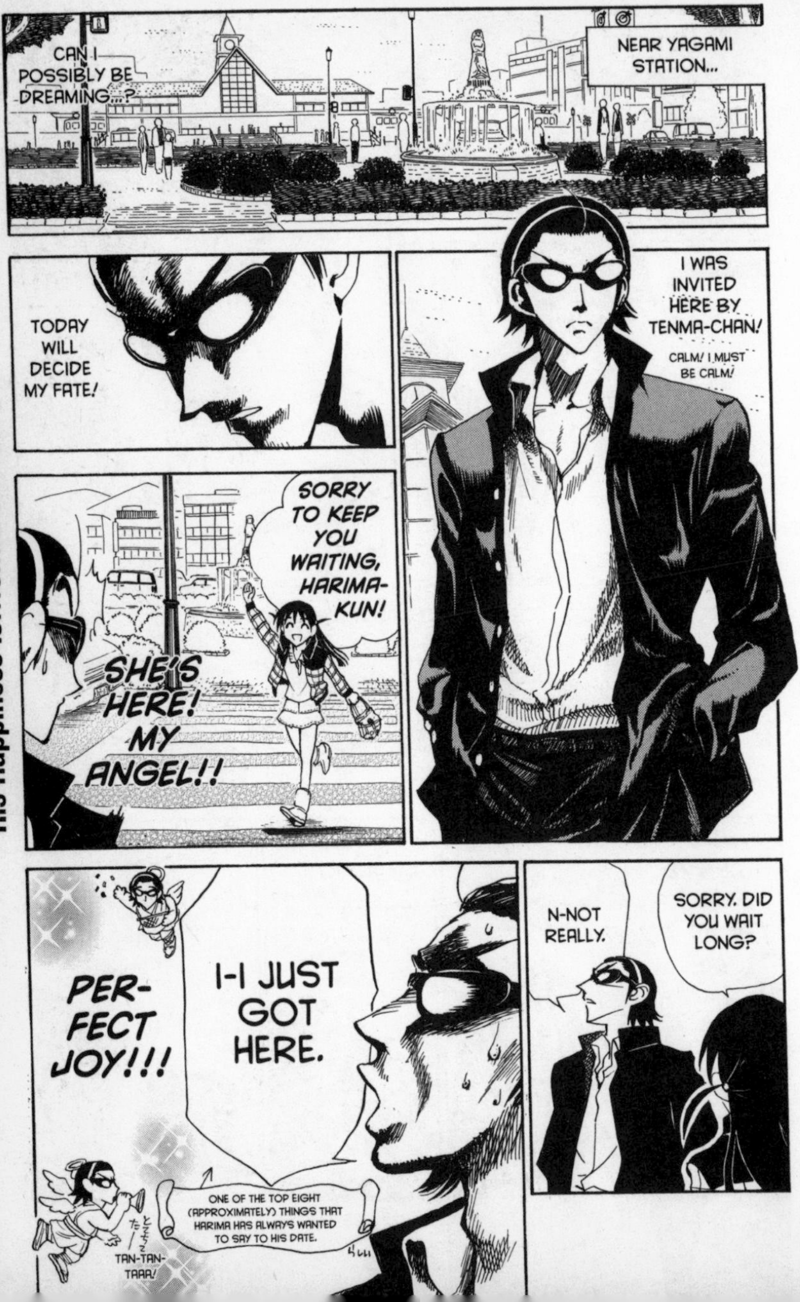
NEAR YAGAMI STATION...
CAN I POSSIBLY BE DREAMING...?
I WAS INVITED HERE BY TENMA-CHAN!
CALM! I MUST BE CALM!
TODAY WILL DECIDE MY FATE!
SORRY TO KEEP YOU WAITING, HARIMA-KUN!
SHE'S HERE! MY ANGEL!!
SORRY. DID YOU WAIT LONG?
N-NOT REALLY.
I-I JUST GOT HERE.
PER-FECT JOY!!!
ONE OF THE TOP EIGHT (APPROXIMATELY) THINGS THAT HARIMA HAS ALWAYS WANTED TO SAY TO HIS DATE.
TAN-TAN-TARA!

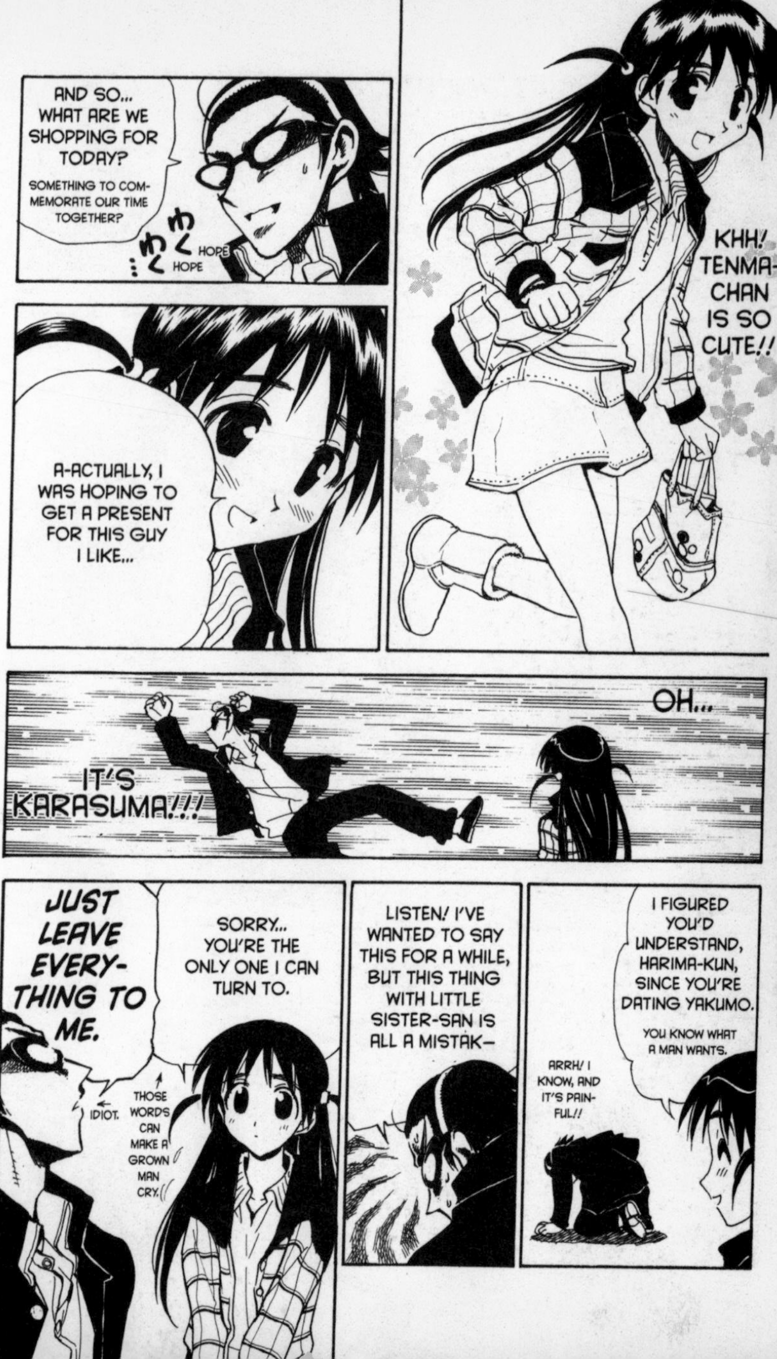
KHH! TENMA-CHAN IS SO CUTE!!
AND SO... WHAT ARE WE SHOPPING FOR TODAY?
SOMETHING TO COMMEMORATE OUR TIME TOGETHER?
わくわく…
HOPE HOPE
A-ACTUALLY, I WAS HOPING TO GET A PRESENT FOR THIS GUY I LIKE...
OH...
IT'S KARASUMA!!!
I FIGURED YOU'D UNDERSTAND, HARIMA-KUN, SINCE YOU'RE DATING YAKUMO.
YOU KNOW WHAT A MAN WANTS.
ARRH! I KNOW, AND IT'S PAINFUL!!
LISTEN! I'VE WANTED TO SAY THIS FOR A WHILE, BUT THIS THING WITH LITTLE SISTER-SAN IS ALL A MISTAK—
SORRY... YOU'RE THE ONLY ONE I CAN TURN TO.
JUST LEAVE EVERYTHING TO ME.
IDIOT.
THOSE WORDS CAN MAKE A GROWN MAN CRY.

Tenma: Loves Karasuma-kun. In Case You Didn't Know.

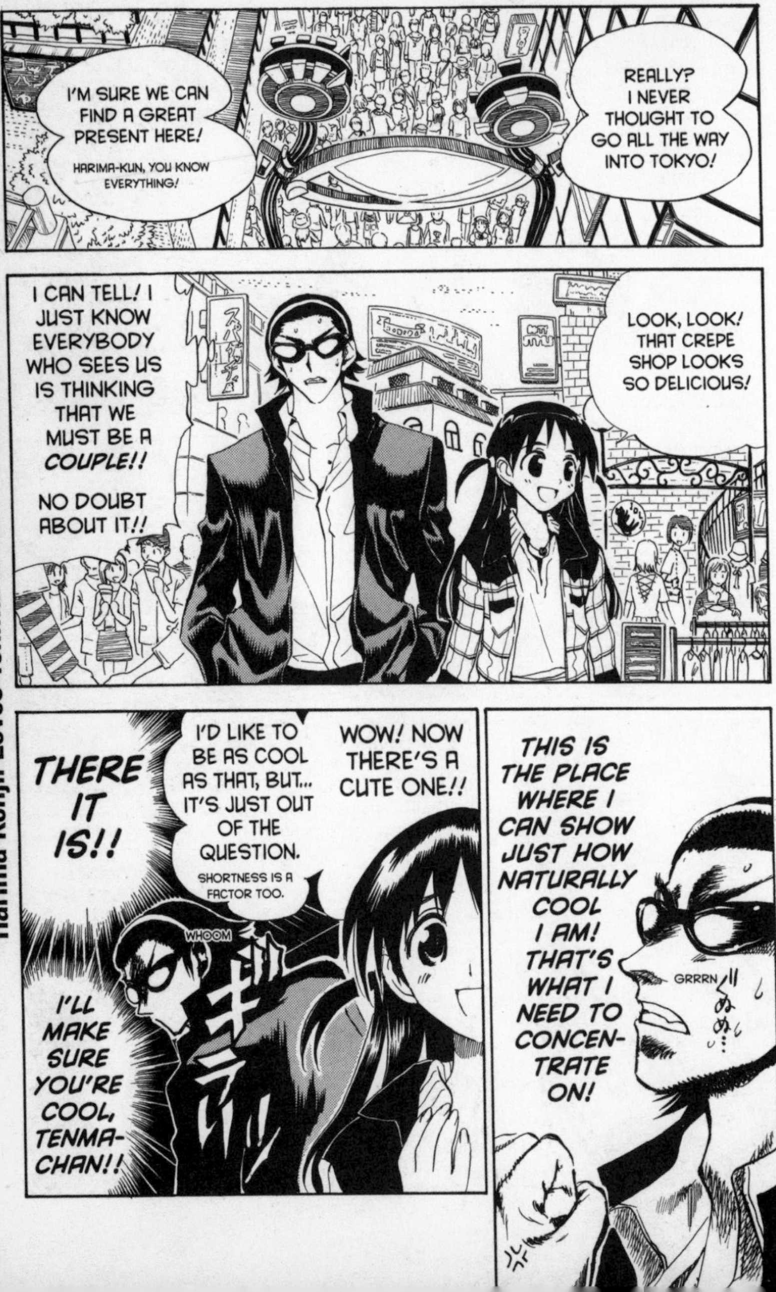
REALLY? I NEVER THOUGHT TO GO ALL THE WAY INTO TOKYO!
I'M SURE WE CAN FIND A GREAT PRESENT HERE!
HARIMA-KUN, YOU KNOW EVERYTHING!
LOOK, LOOK! THAT CREPE SHOP LOOKS SO DELICIOUS!
I CAN TELL! I JUST KNOW EVERYBODY WHO SEES US IS THINKING THAT WE MUST BE A COUPLE!!
NO DOUBT ABOUT IT!!
THIS IS THE PLACE WHERE I CAN SHOW JUST HOW NATURALLY COOL I AM! THAT'S WHAT I NEED TO CONCEN-TRATE ON!
GRRRN
WOW! NOW THERE'S A CUTE ONE!!
I'D LIKE TO BE AS COOL AS THAT, BUT... IT'S JUST OUT OF THE QUESTION.
SHORTNESS IS A FACTOR TOO.
THERE IT IS!!
WHOOM
I'LL MAKE SURE YOU'RE COOL, TENMA-CHAN!!

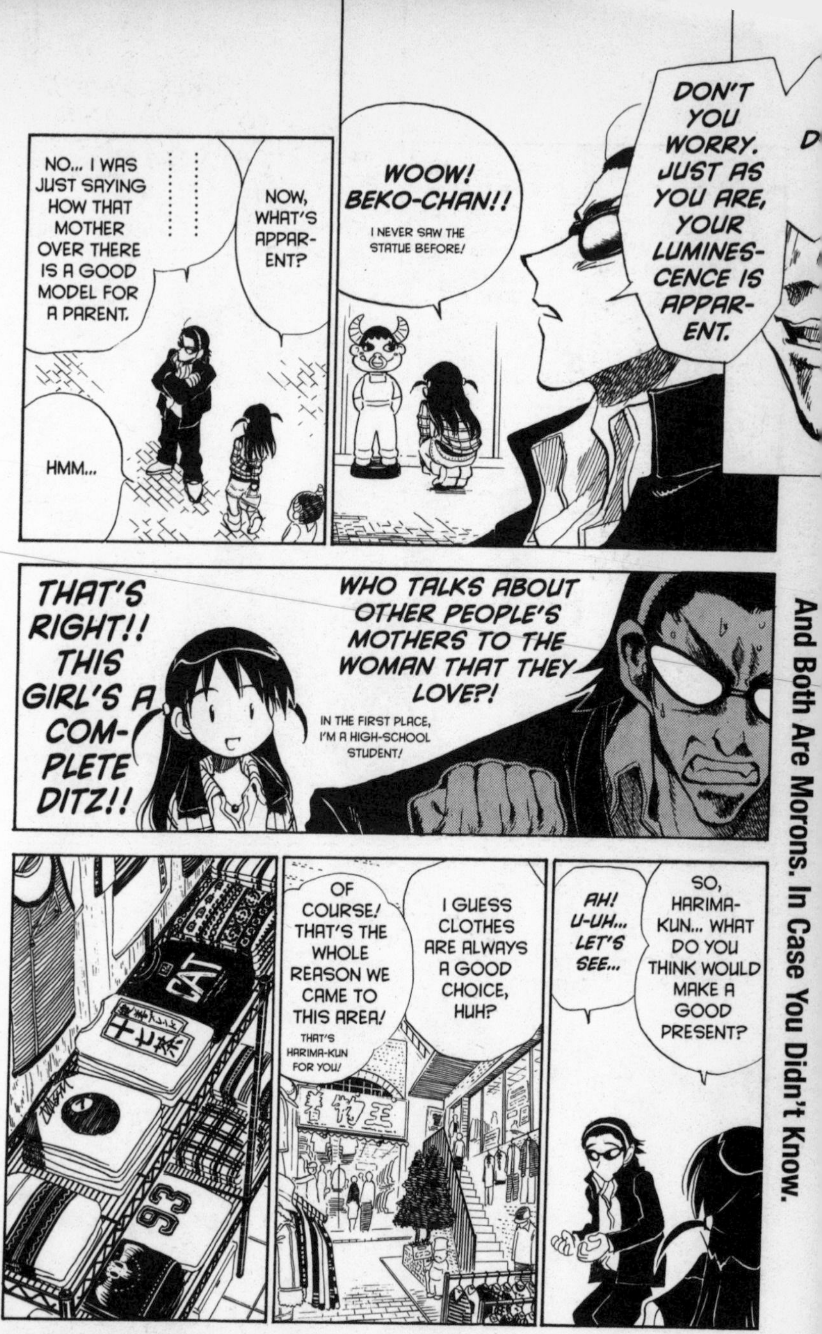
DON'T YOU WORRY. JUST AS YOU ARE, YOUR LUMINESCENCE IS APPARENT.
D
WOOW! BEKO-CHAN!!
I NEVER SAW THE STATUE BEFORE!
NOW, WHAT'S APPARENT?
......
NO... I WAS JUST SAYING HOW THAT MOTHER OVER THERE IS A GOOD MODEL FOR A PARENT.
HMM...
WHO TALKS ABOUT OTHER PEOPLE'S MOTHERS TO THE WOMAN THAT THEY LOVE?!
IN THE FIRST PLACE, I'M A HIGH-SCHOOL STUDENT!
THAT'S RIGHT!! THIS GIRL'S A COMPLETE DITZ!!
SO, HARIMA-KUN... WHAT DO YOU THINK WOULD MAKE A GOOD PRESENT?
AH! U-UH... LET'S SEE...
I GUESS CLOTHES ARE ALWAYS A GOOD CHOICE, HUH?
OF COURSE! THAT'S THE WHOLE REASON WE CAME TO THIS AREA!
THAT'S HARIMA-KUN FOR YOU!
CAT

And Both Are Morons. In Case You Didn't Know.

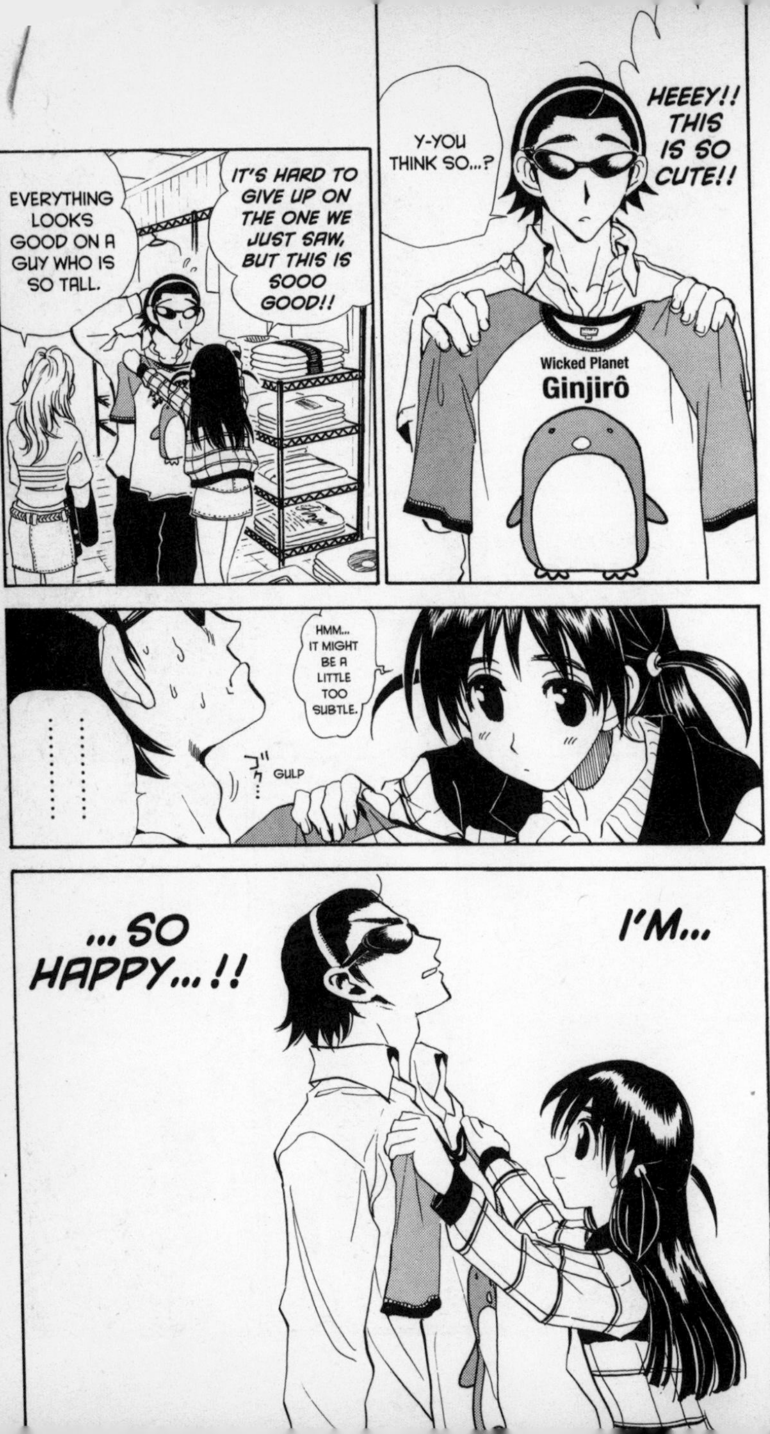
HEEEY!! THIS IS SO CUTE!!
Y-YOU THINK SO...?
Wicked Planet Ginjirô
IT'S HARD TO GIVE UP ON THE ONE WE JUST SAW, BUT THIS IS SOOO GOOD!!
EVERYTHING LOOKS GOOD ON A GUY WHO IS SO TALL.
HMM... IT MIGHT BE A LITTLE TOO SUBTLE.
GULP
I'M...
...SO HAPPY...!!

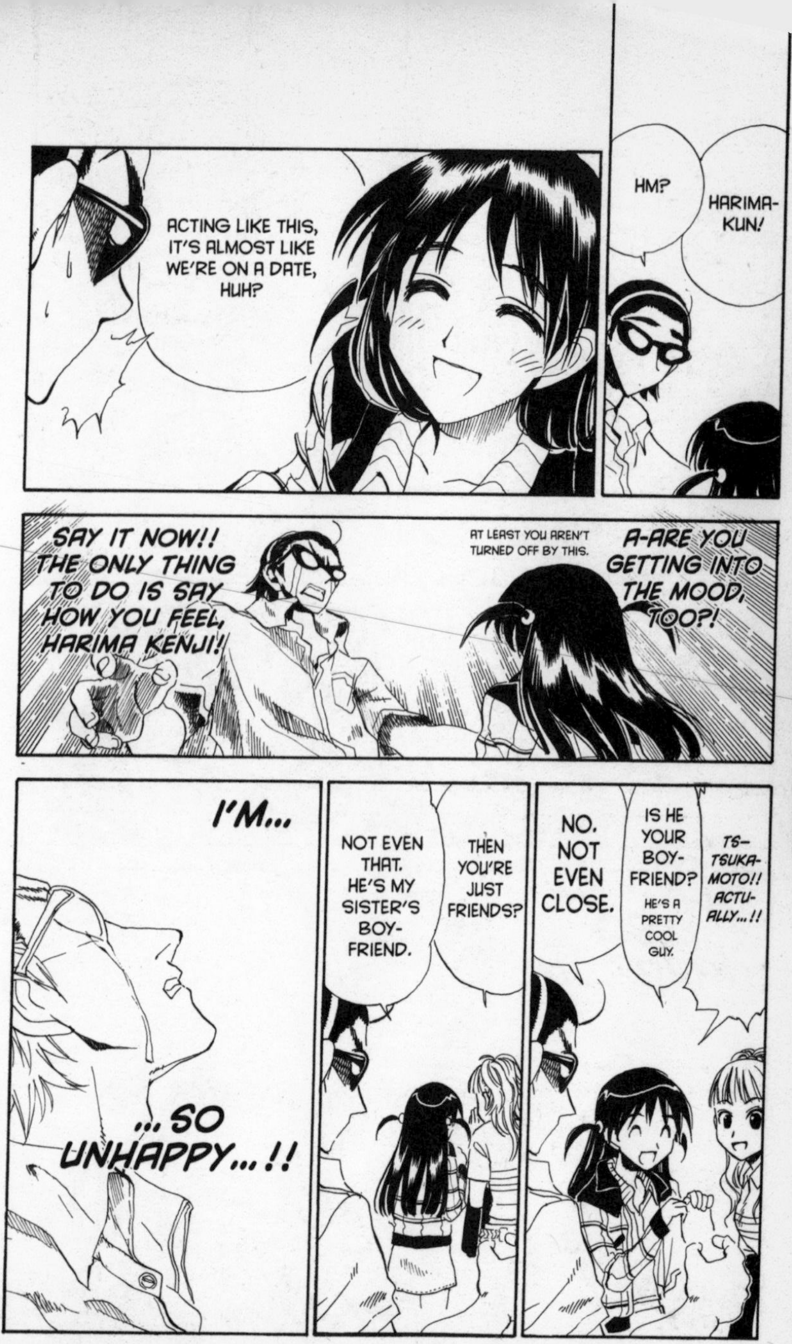
HARIMA-KUN!
HM?
ACTING LIKE THIS, IT'S ALMOST LIKE WE'RE ON A DATE, HUH?
A-ARE YOU GETTING INTO THE MOOD, TOO?!
AT LEAST YOU AREN'T TURNED OFF BY THIS.
SAY IT NOW!! THE ONLY THING TO DO IS SAY HOW YOU FEEL, HARIMA KENJI!
TS-TSUKAMOTO!! ACTU-ALLY...!!
IS HE YOUR BOY-FRIEND?
HE'S A PRETTY COOL GUY.
NO. NOT EVEN CLOSE.
THEN YOU'RE JUST FRIENDS?
NOT EVEN THAT. HE'S MY SISTER'S BOY-FRIEND.
I'M...
...SO UNHAPPY...!!

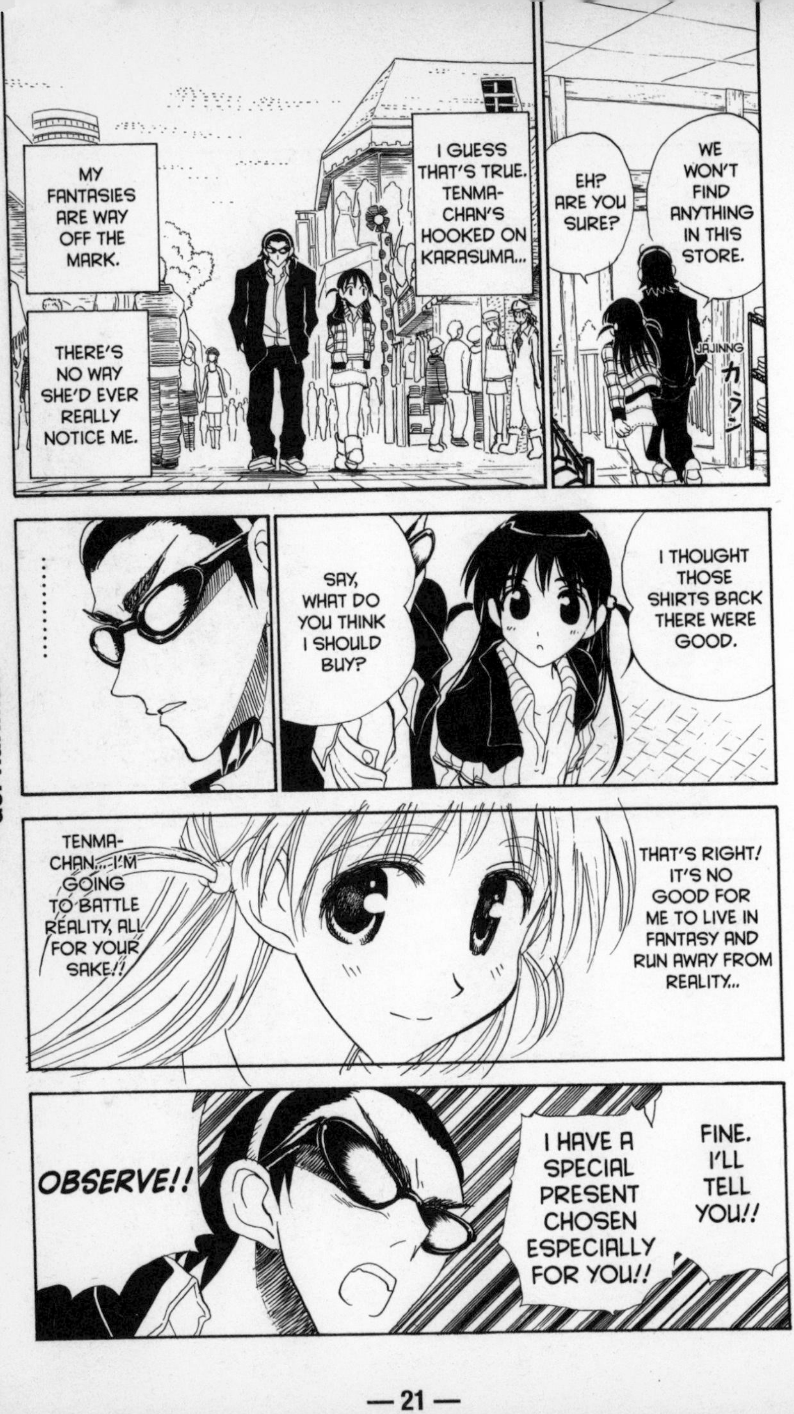
WE WON'T FIND ANYTHING IN THIS STORE.
EH? ARE YOU SURE?
JAJINNG
カラン
I GUESS THAT'S TRUE. TENMA-CHAN'S HOOKED ON KARASUMA...
MY FANTASIES ARE WAY OFF THE MARK.
THERE'S NO WAY SHE'D EVER REALLY NOTICE ME.
I THOUGHT THOSE SHIRTS BACK THERE WERE GOOD.
SAY, WHAT DO YOU THINK I SHOULD BUY?
THAT'S RIGHT! IT'S NO GOOD FOR ME TO LIVE IN FANTASY AND RUN AWAY FROM REALITY...
TENMA-CHAN... I'M GOING TO BATTLE REALITY, ALL FOR YOUR SAKE!!
FINE. I'LL TELL YOU!!
I HAVE A SPECIAL PRESENT CHOSEN ESPECIALLY FOR YOU!!
OBSERVE!!

Who Needs That...?

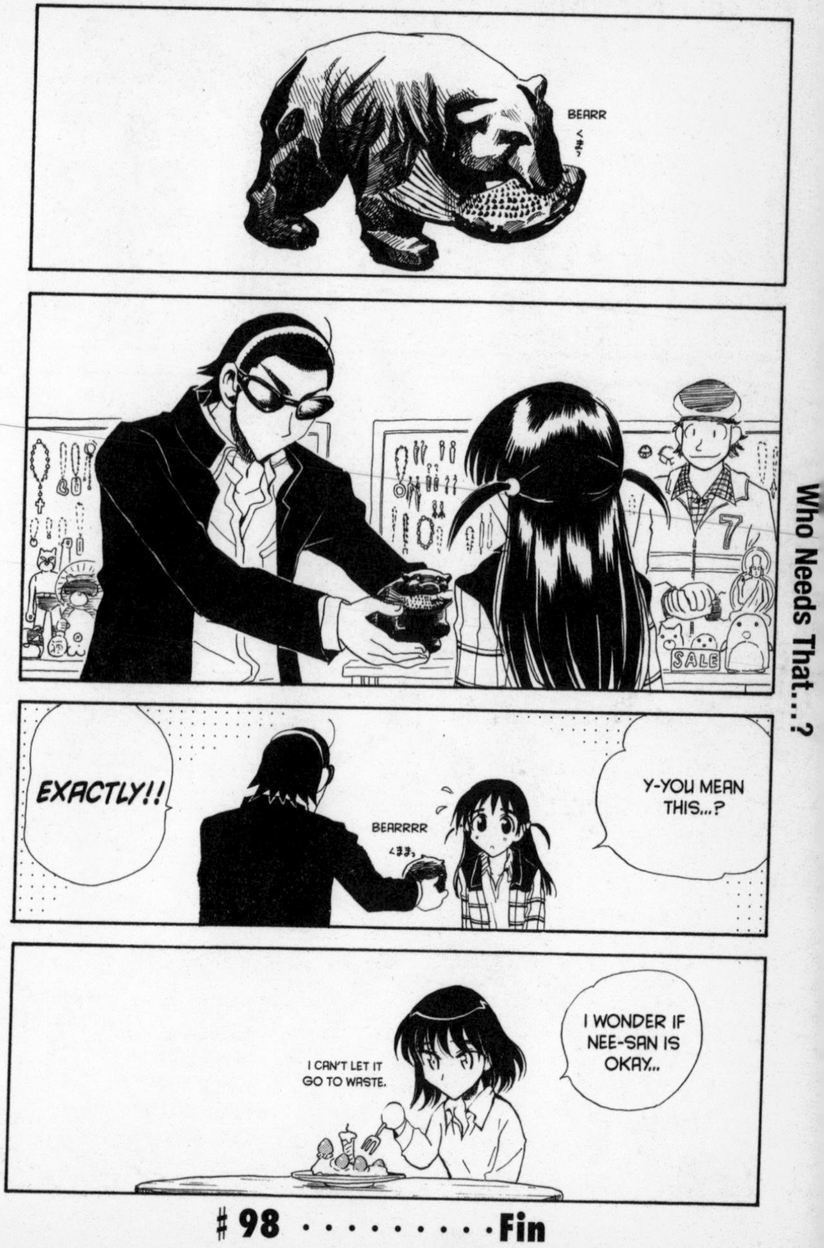
BEARR
Y-YOU MEAN THIS...?
BEARRRR
EXACTLY!!
I WONDER IF NEE-SAN IS OKAY...
I CAN'T LET IT GO TO WASTE.

98 . . . . .Fin

99 THE TRUE HEARTED

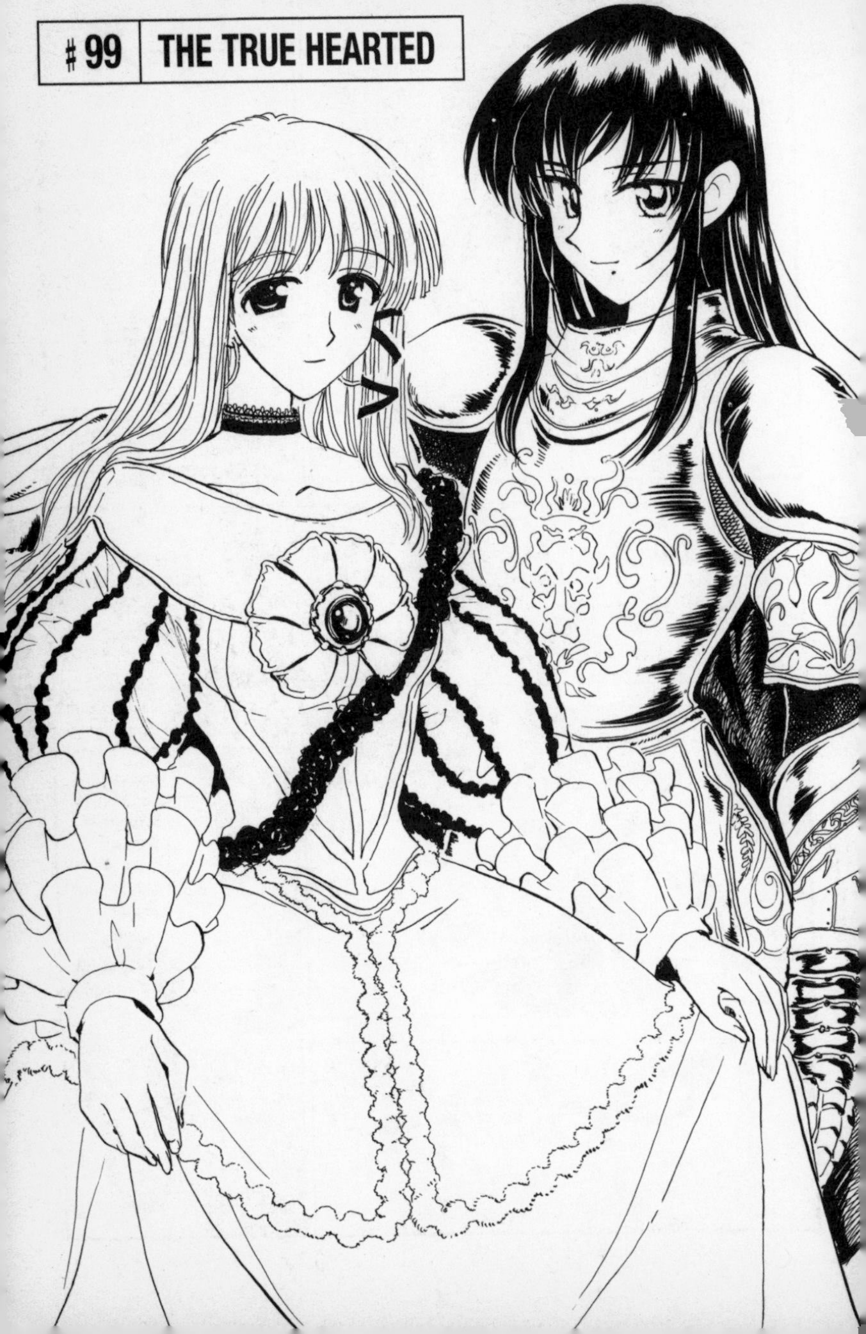

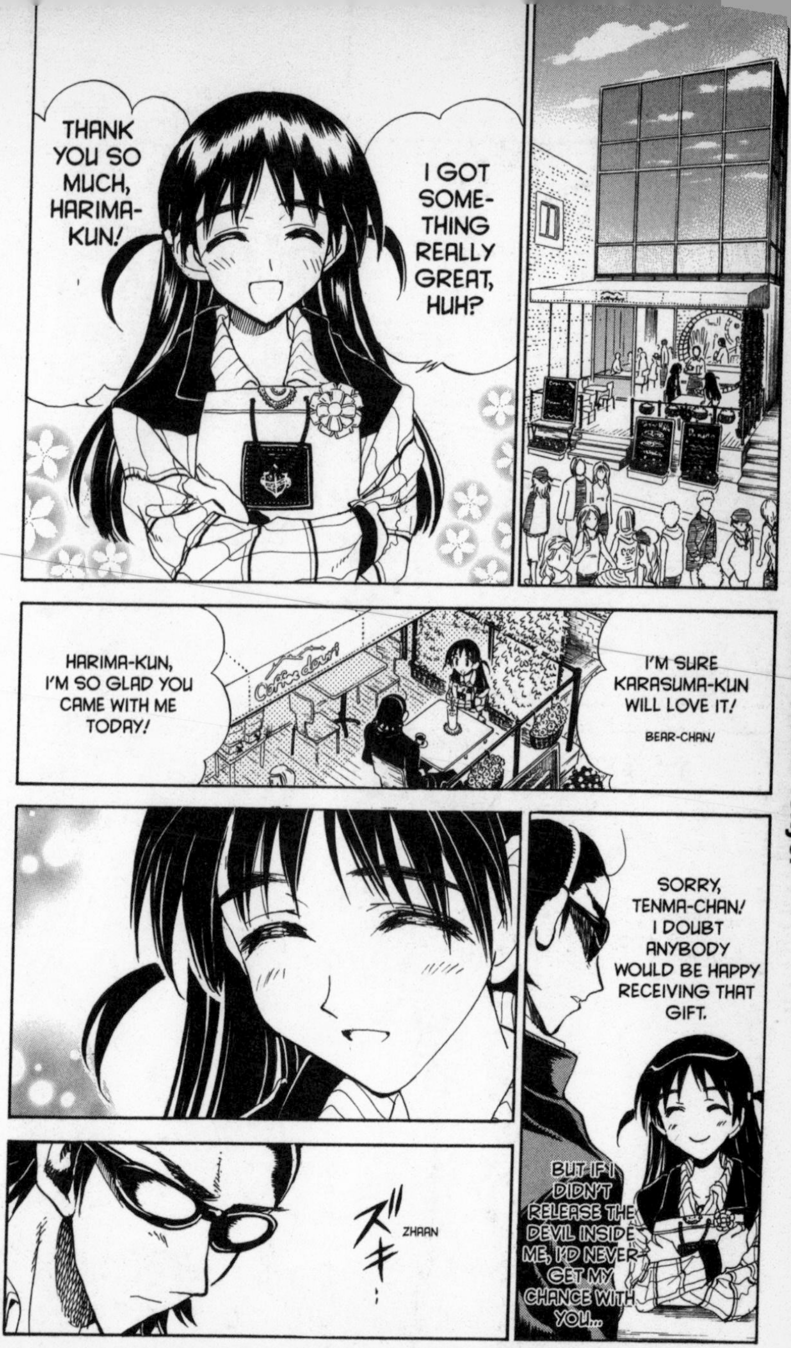
I GOT SOME-THING REALLY GREAT, HUH?
THANK YOU SO MUCH, HARIMA-KUN!
I'M SURE KARASUMA-KUN WILL LOVE IT!
BEAR-CHAN!
HARIMA-KUN, I'M SO GLAD YOU CAME WITH ME TODAY!
SORRY, TENMA-CHAN! I DOUBT ANYBODY WOULD BE HAPPY RECEIVING THAT GIFT.
BUT IF I DIDN'T RELEASE THE DEVIL INSIDE ME, I'D NEVER GET MY CHANCE WITH YOU...
ZHAAN

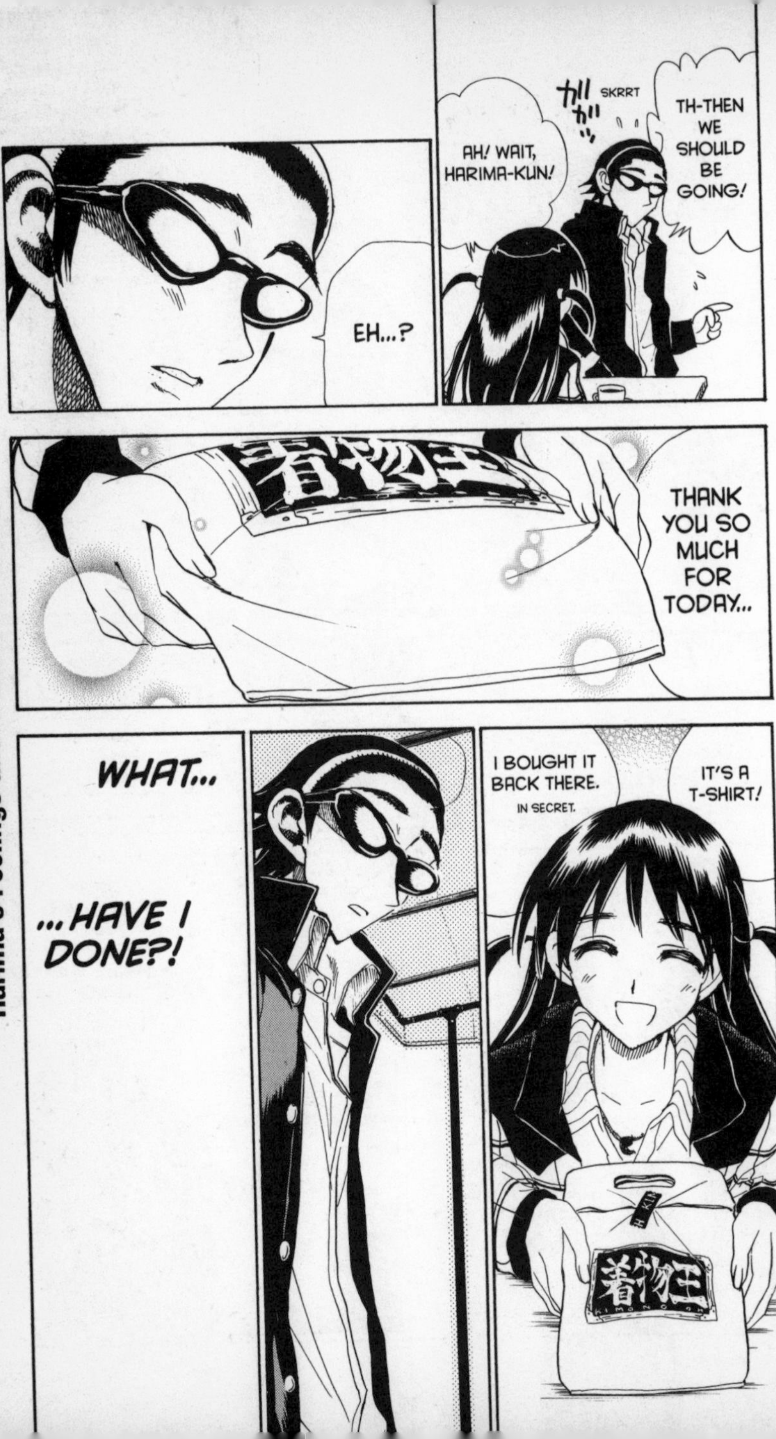
TH-THEN WE SHOULD BE GOING!
SKRRT
AH! WAIT, HARIMA-KUN!
EH...?
THANK YOU SO MUCH FOR TODAY...
IT'S A T-SHIRT!
I BOUGHT IT BACK THERE.
IN SECRET.
WHAT...
...HAVE I DONE?!

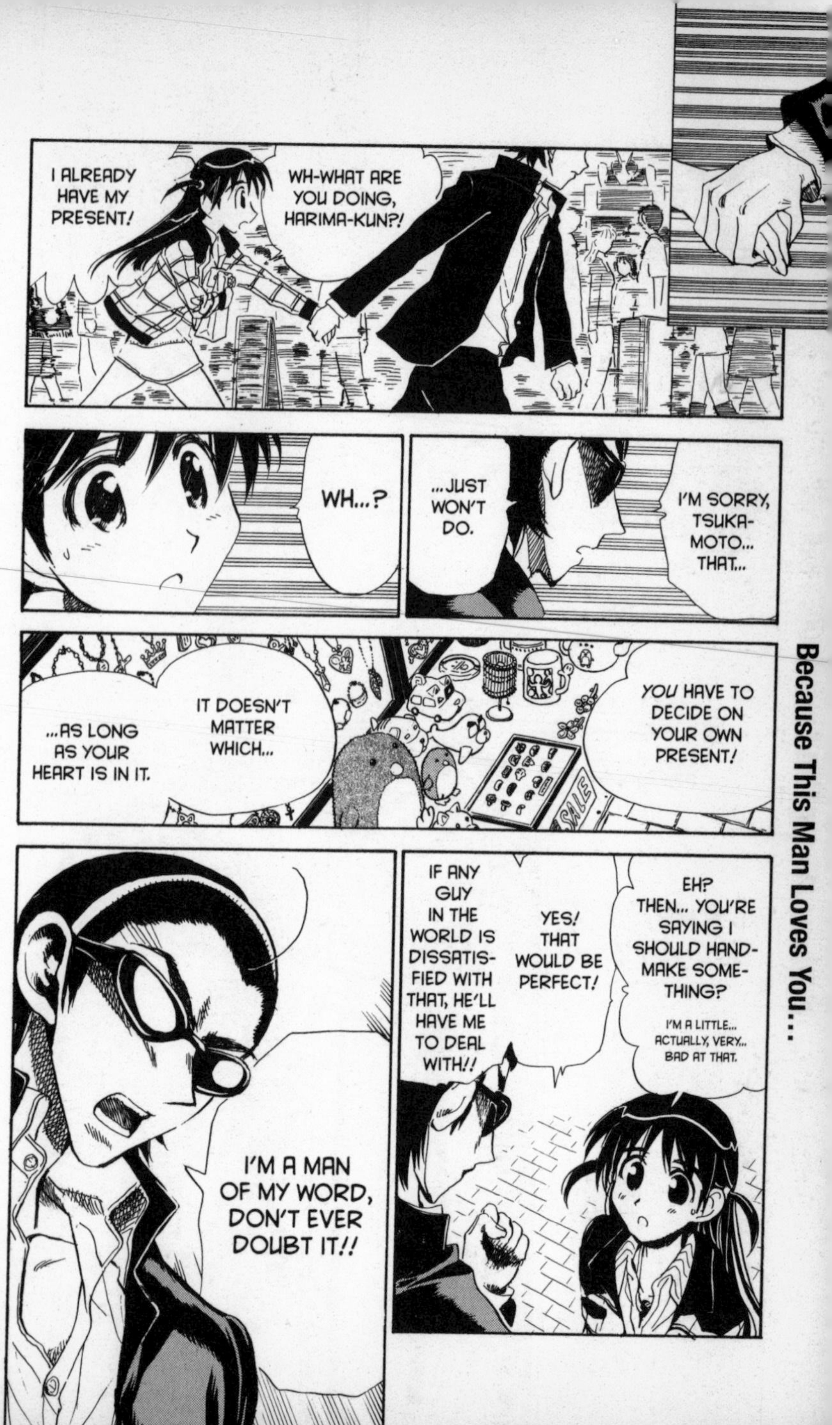
WH-WHAT ARE YOU DOING, HARIMA-KUN?!
I ALREADY HAVE MY PRESENT!
I'M SORRY, TSUKAMOTO... THAT...
...JUST WON'T DO.
WH...?
YOU HAVE TO DECIDE ON YOUR OWN PRESENT!
IT DOESN'T MATTER WHICH...
...AS LONG AS YOUR HEART IS IN IT.
EH? THEN... YOU'RE SAYING I SHOULD HAND-MAKE SOME-THING?
I'M A LITTLE... ACTUALLY, VERY... BAD AT THAT.
YES! THAT WOULD BE PERFECT!
IF ANY GUY IN THE WORLD IS DISSATIS-FIED WITH THAT, HE'LL HAVE ME TO DEAL WITH!!
I'M A MAN OF MY WORD, DON'T EVER DOUBT IT!!

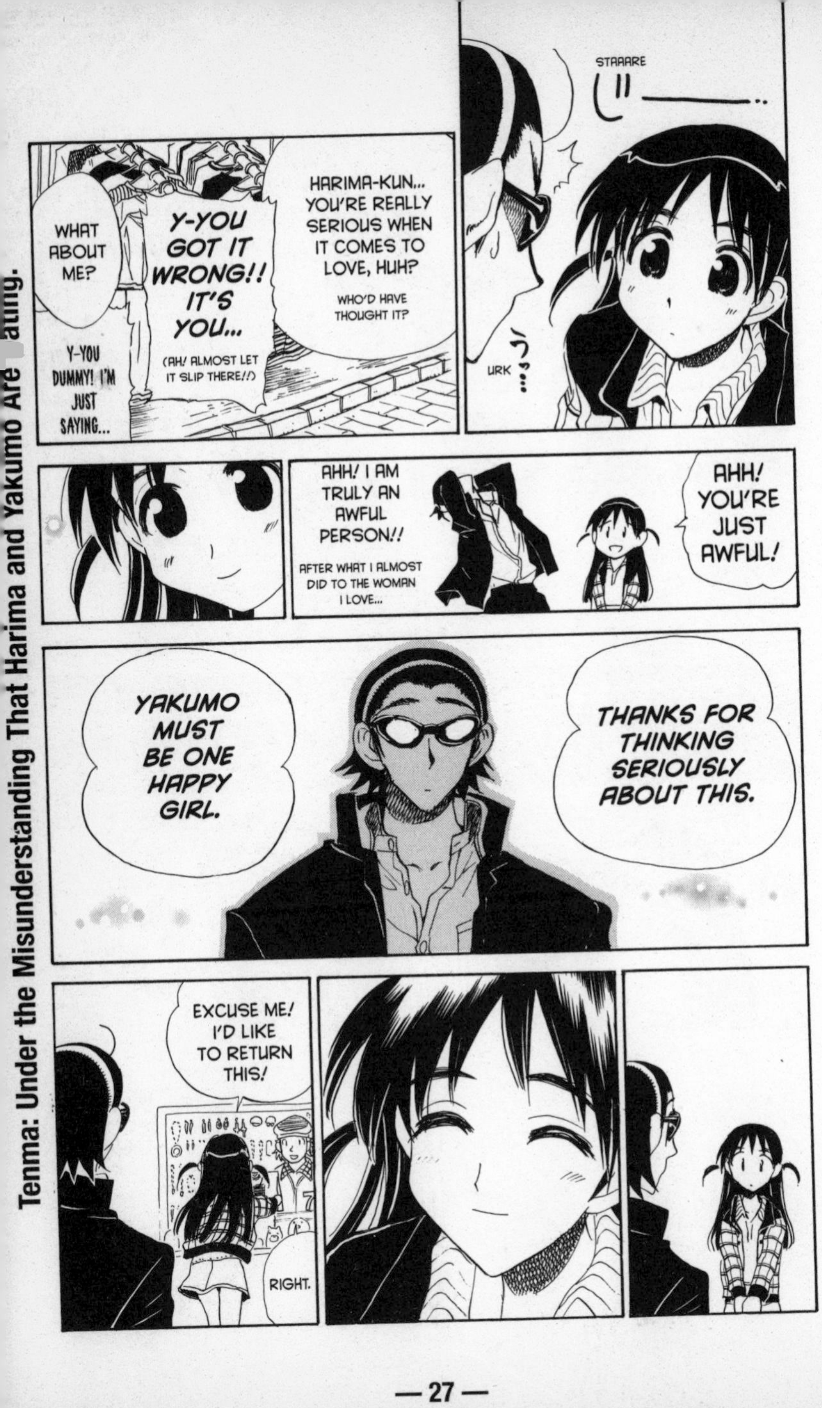
STARRRE
URK
HARIMA-KUN... YOU'RE REALLY SERIOUS WHEN IT COMES TO LOVE, HUH?
WHO'D HAVE THOUGHT IT?
Y-YOU GOT IT WRONG!! IT'S YOU...
(AH! ALMOST LET IT SLIP THERE!!)
WHAT ABOUT ME?
Y-YOU DUMMY! I'M JUST SAYING...
AHH! YOU'RE JUST AWFUL!
AHH! I AM TRULY AN AWFUL PERSON!!
AFTER WHAT I ALMOST DID TO THE WOMAN I LOVE...
THANKS FOR THINKING SERIOUSLY ABOUT THIS.
YAKUMO MUST BE ONE HAPPY GIRL.
EXCUSE ME! I'D LIKE TO RETURN THIS!
RIGHT.

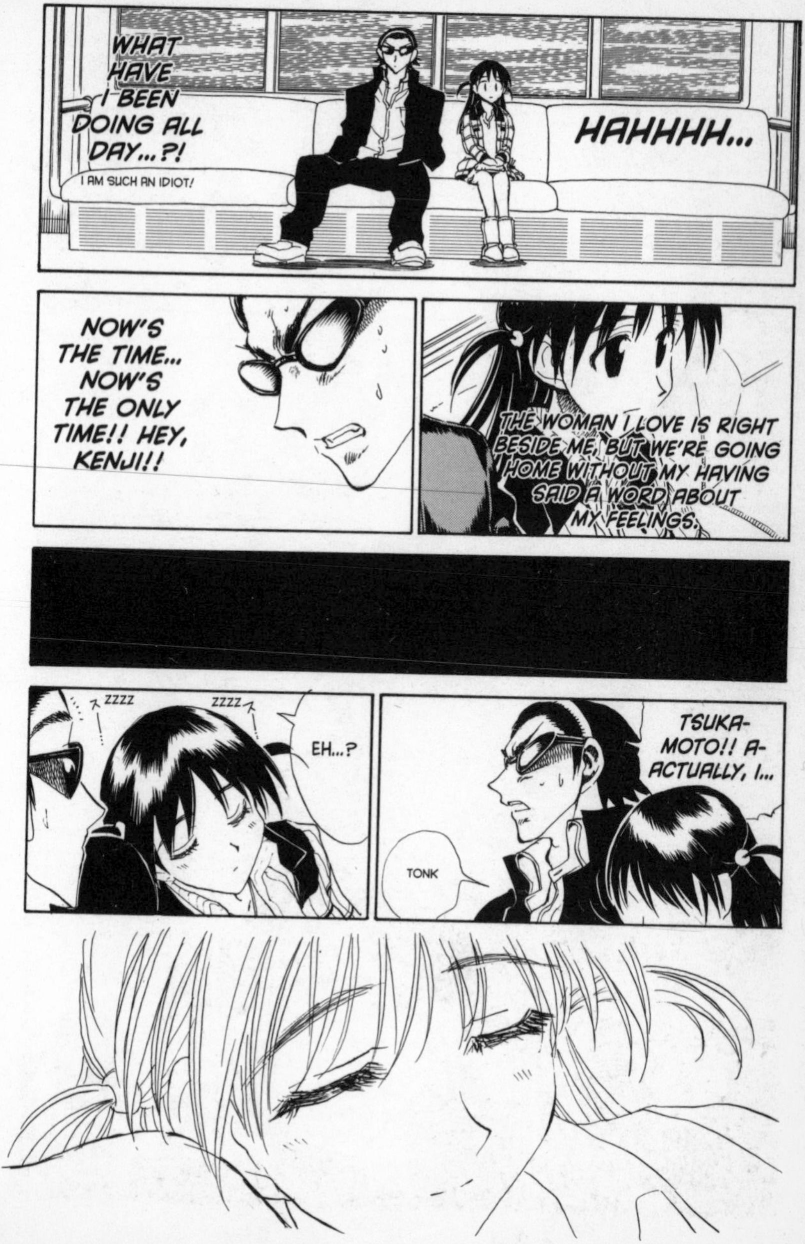
HAHHHH...
WHAT HAVE I BEEN DOING ALL DAY...?!
I AM SUCH AN IDIOT!
THE WOMAN I LOVE IS RIGHT BESIDE ME, BUT WE'RE GOING HOME WITHOUT MY HAVING SAID A WORD ABOUT MY FEELINGS.
NOW'S THE TIME... NOW'S THE ONLY TIME!! HEY, KENJI!!
TSUKA-MOTO!! A-ACTUALLY, I...
TONK
ZZZZ
ZZZZ
EH...?

Bon Voyage!

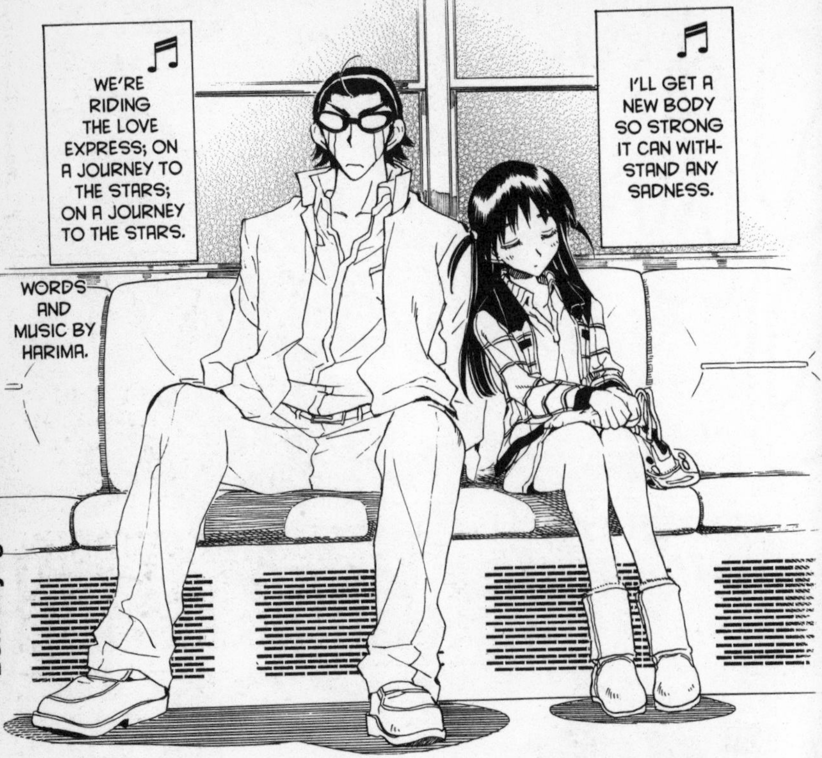
I'LL GET A NEW BODY SO STRONG IT CAN WITH-STAND ANY SADNESS.
WE'RE RIDING THE LOVE EXPRESS; ON A JOURNEY TO THE STARS; ON A JOURNEY TO THE STARS.
WORDS AND MUSIC BY HARIMA.

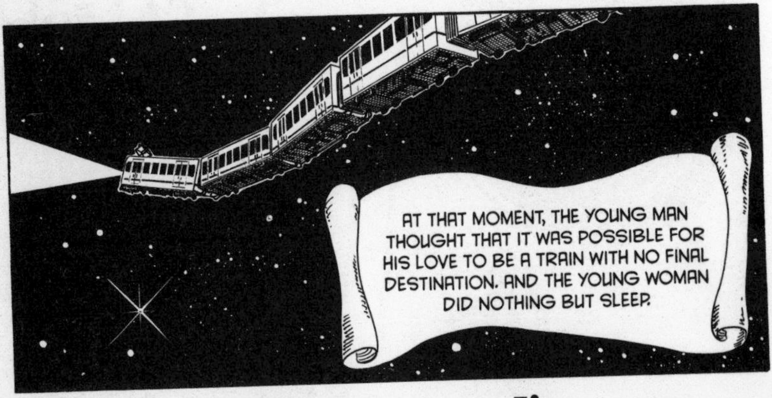
AT THAT MOMENT, THE YOUNG MAN THOUGHT THAT IT WAS POSSIBLE FOR HIS LOVE TO BE A TRAIN WITH NO FINAL DESTINATION. AND THE YOUNG WOMAN DID NOTHING BUT SLEEP.

 # 99 . . . . Fin

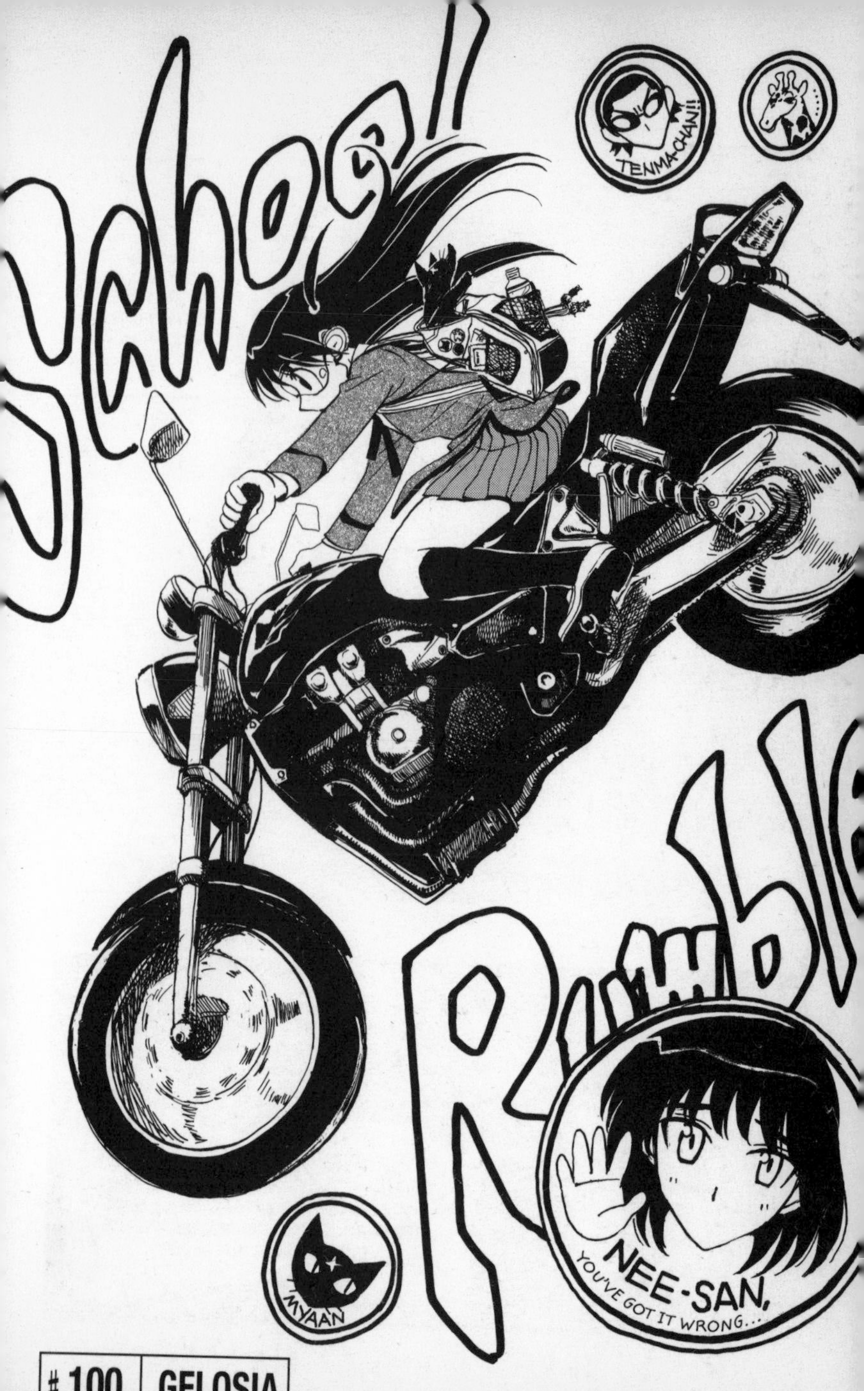
School Rumble
TENMA-CHAN!!
NEE-SAN,
YOU'VE GOT IT WRONG...
MYAAN

#100 GELOSIA

Sawachika Eri: Bad at Japanese Language–Based Subjects. Spent Too Much Time Overseas.

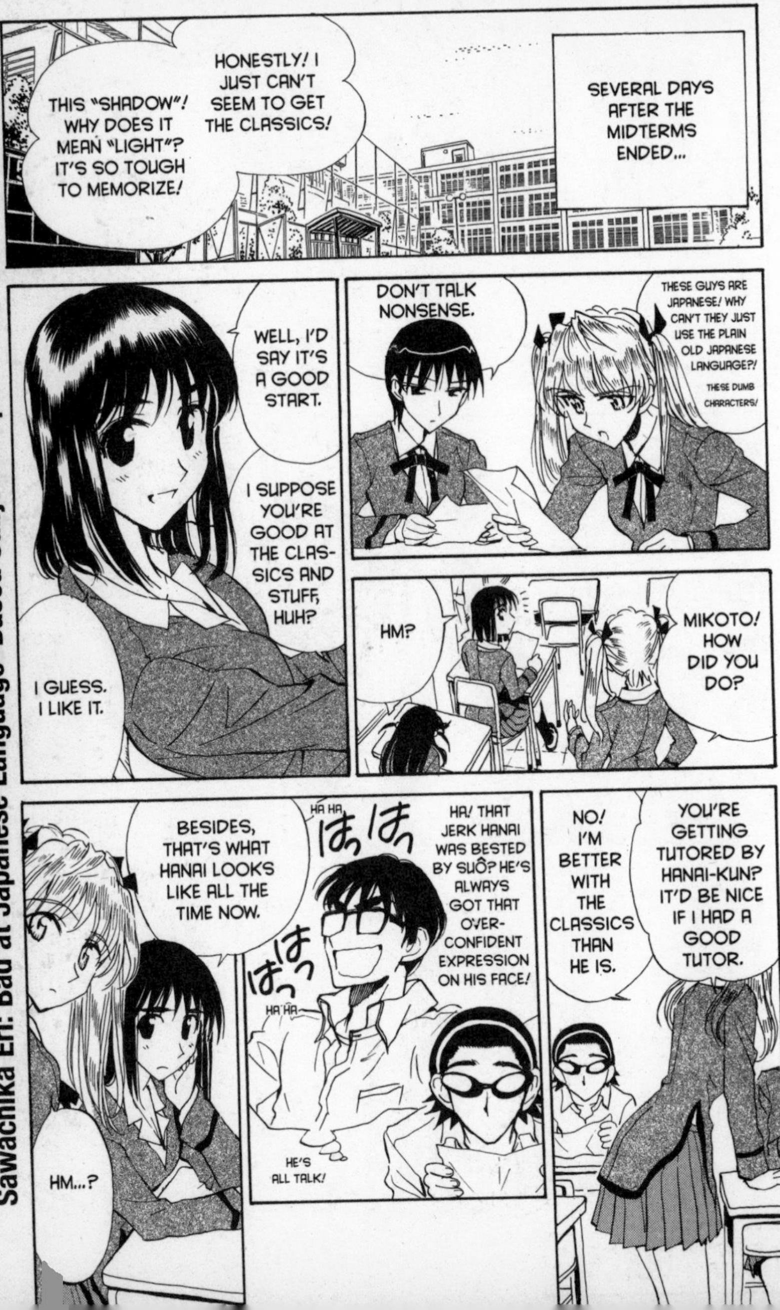
SEVERAL DAYS AFTER THE MIDTERMS ENDED...
HONESTLY! I JUST CAN'T SEEM TO GET THE CLASSICS!
THIS "SHADOW"! WHY DOES IT MEAN "LIGHT"? IT'S SO TOUGH TO MEMORIZE!
THESE GUYS ARE JAPANESE! WHY CAN'T THEY JUST USE THE PLAIN OLD JAPANESE LANGUAGE?!
THESE DUMB CHARACTERS!
DON'T TALK NONSENSE.
MIKOTO! HOW DID YOU DO?
HM?
WELL, I'D SAY IT'S A GOOD START.
I SUPPOSE YOU'RE GOOD AT THE CLASSICS AND STUFF, HUH?
I GUESS. I LIKE IT.
YOU'RE GETTING TUTORED BY HANAI-KUN? IT'D BE NICE IF I HAD A GOOD TUTOR.
NO! I'M BETTER WITH THE CLASSICS THAN HE IS.
HA! THAT JERK HANAI WAS BESTED BY SUÔ? HE'S ALWAYS GOT THAT OVER-CONFIDENT EXPRESSION ON HIS FACE!
はっはっ
HA HA
はっはっ
HA HA
HE'S ALL TALK!
BESIDES, THAT'S WHAT HANAI LOOKS LIKE ALL THE TIME NOW.
HM...?

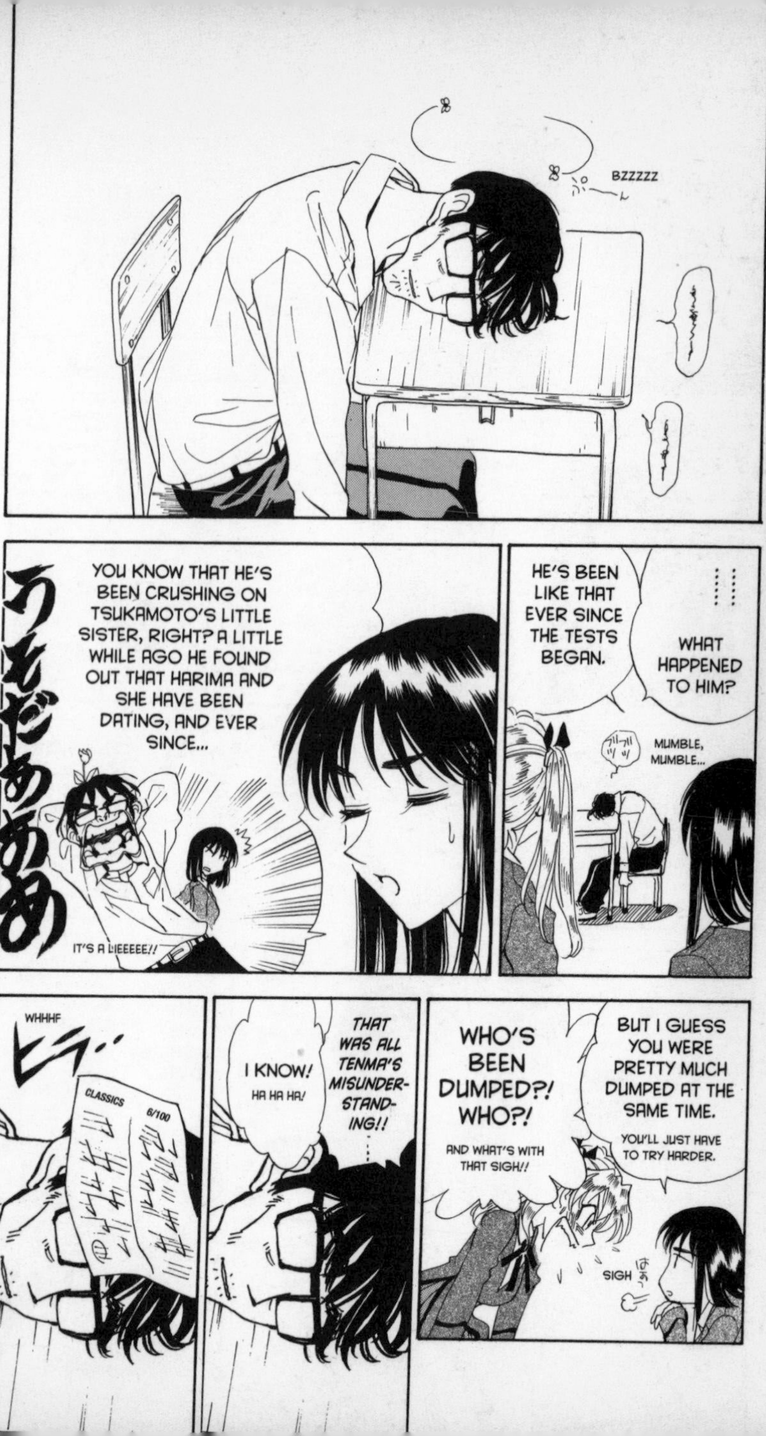
BZZZZZ
ぷ〜ん
......
WHAT HAPPENED TO HIM?
HE'S BEEN LIKE THAT EVER SINCE THE TESTS BEGAN.
ブツブツ
MUMBLE, MUMBLE...
YOU KNOW THAT HE'S BEEN CRUSHING ON TSUKAMOTO'S LITTLE SISTER, RIGHT? A LITTLE WHILE AGO HE FOUND OUT THAT HARIMA AND SHE HAVE BEEN DATING, AND EVER SINCE...
うそだぁぁぁ
IT'S A LIEEEEE!!
BUT I GUESS YOU WERE PRETTY MUCH DUMPED AT THE SAME TIME.
YOU'LL JUST HAVE TO TRY HARDER.
WHO'S BEEN DUMPED?! WHO?!
AND WHAT'S WITH THAT SIGH!!
はぁ
SIGH
THAT WAS ALL TENMA'S MISUNDERSTANDING!!
I KNOW!
HA HA HA!
...
WHHHF
ヒラ…
CLASSICS
6/100

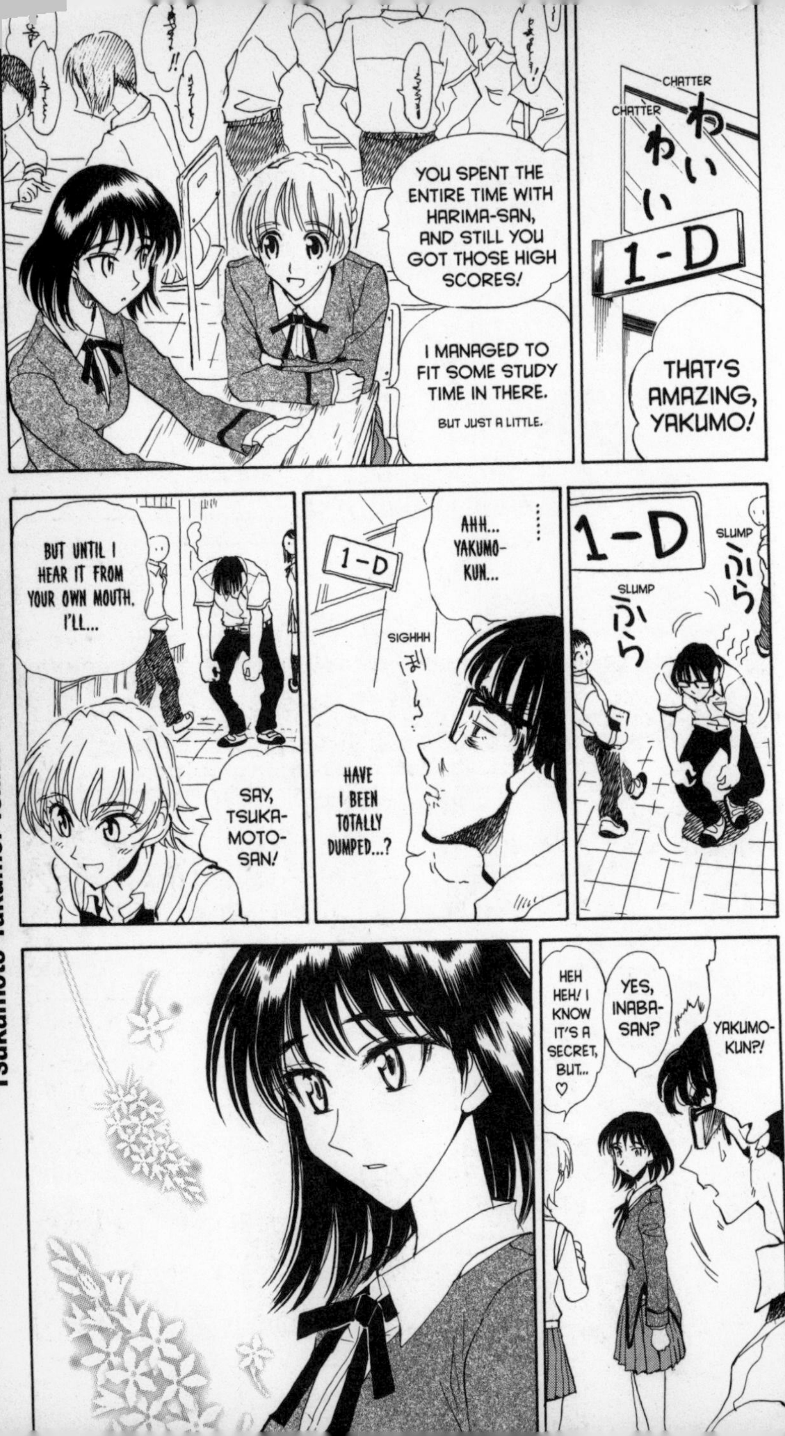
CHATTER
CHATTER
わいわい
1-D
THAT'S AMAZING, YAKUMO!
YOU SPENT THE ENTIRE TIME WITH HARIMA-SAN, AND STILL YOU GOT THOSE HIGH SCORES!
I MANAGED TO FIT SOME STUDY TIME IN THERE.
BUT JUST A LITTLE.
1-D
SLUMP
ふら
SLUMP
ふら
AHH... YAKUMO-KUN...
......
1-D
SIGHHH
HAVE I BEEN TOTALLY DUMPED...?
BUT UNTIL I HEAR IT FROM YOUR OWN MOUTH, I'LL...
SAY, TSUKAMOTO-SAN!
YAKUMO-KUN?!
YES, INABA-SAN?
HEH HEH! I KNOW IT'S A SECRET, BUT... ♡

Tsukamoto Yakumo: Tenma's Sister. Just a Basic Fact.

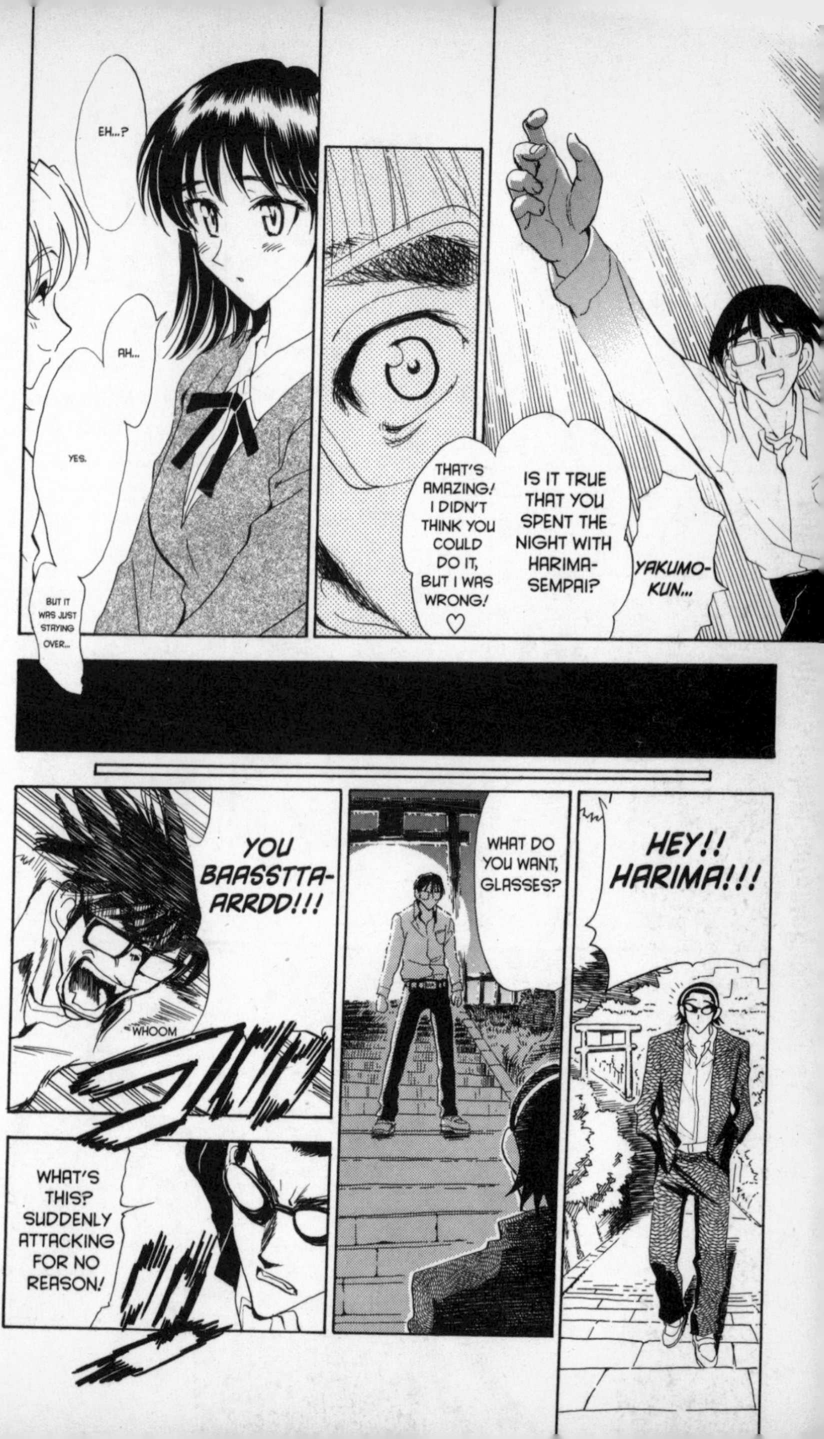
YAKUMO-KUN...
IS IT TRUE THAT YOU SPENT THE NIGHT WITH HARIMA-SEMPAI?
THAT'S AMAZING! I DIDN'T THINK YOU COULD DO IT, BUT I WAS WRONG! ♡
EH...?
AH...
YES.
BUT IT WAS JUST STAYING OVER...
HEY!! HARIMA!!!
WHAT DO YOU WANT, GLASSES?
YOU BAASSTTA-ARRDD!!!
WHOOM
WHAT'S THIS? SUDDENLY ATTACKING FOR NO REASON!

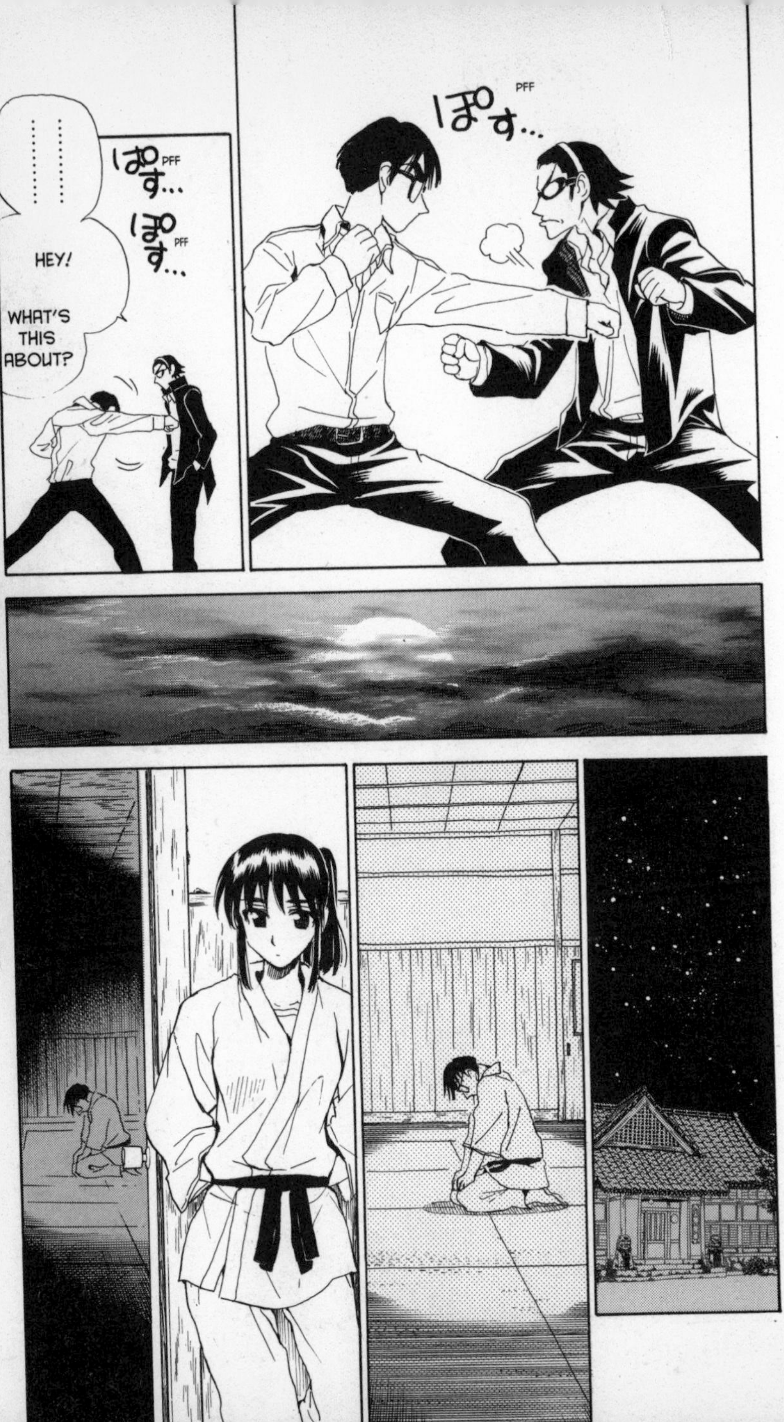

ぽす… PFF
ぽす… PFF
ぽす… PFF
……
HEY!
WHAT'S THIS ABOUT?

Suô Mikoto: Hanai's Childhood Friend.

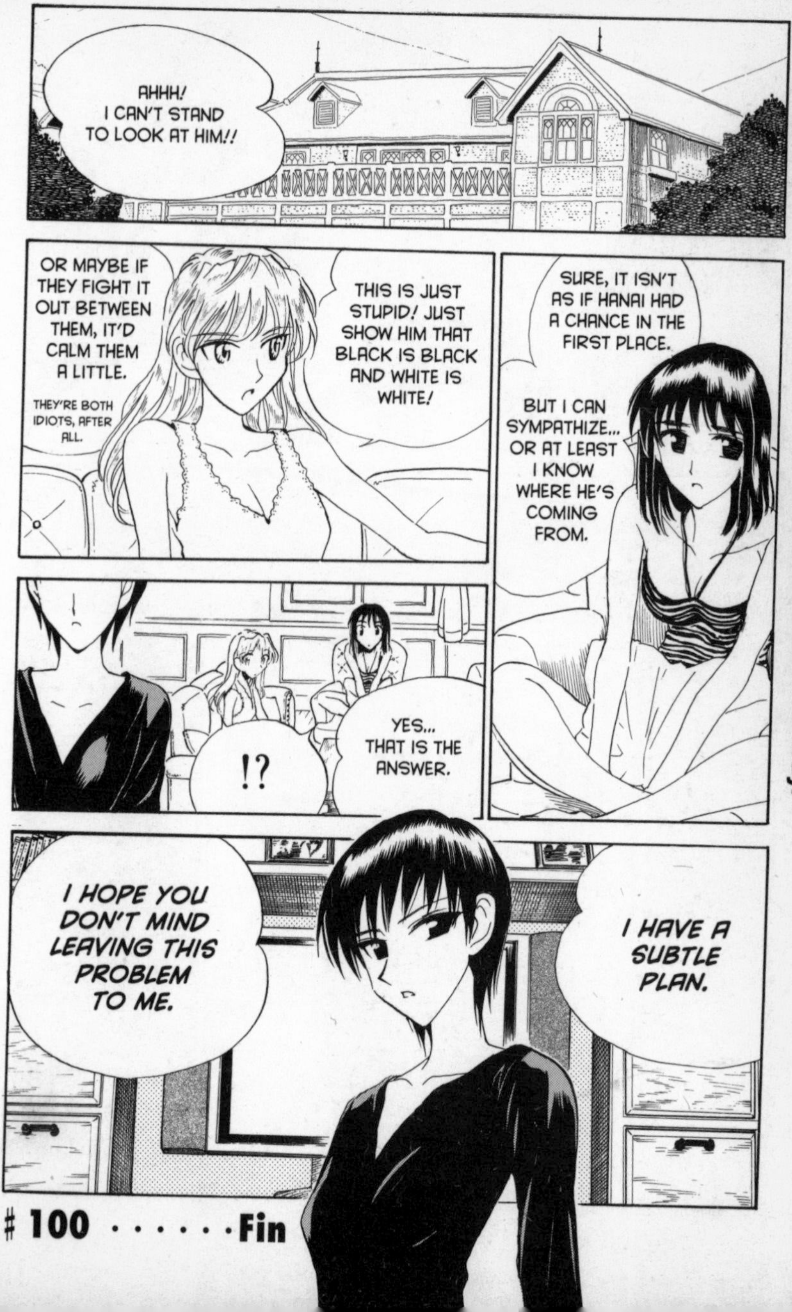
AHHH!
I CAN'T STAND TO LOOK AT HIM!!
SURE, IT ISN'T AS IF HANAI HAD A CHANCE IN THE FIRST PLACE.
BUT I CAN SYMPATHIZE... OR AT LEAST I KNOW WHERE HE'S COMING FROM.
THIS IS JUST STUPID! JUST SHOW HIM THAT BLACK IS BLACK AND WHITE IS WHITE!
OR MAYBE IF THEY FIGHT IT OUT BETWEEN THEM, IT'D CALM THEM A LITTLE.
THEY'RE BOTH IDIOTS, AFTER ALL.
YES... THAT IS THE ANSWER.
!?
I HAVE A SUBTLE PLAN.
I HOPE YOU DON'T MIND LEAVING THIS PROBLEM TO ME.

Takano Akira: Joins the Fray.

 # 100 ······Fin

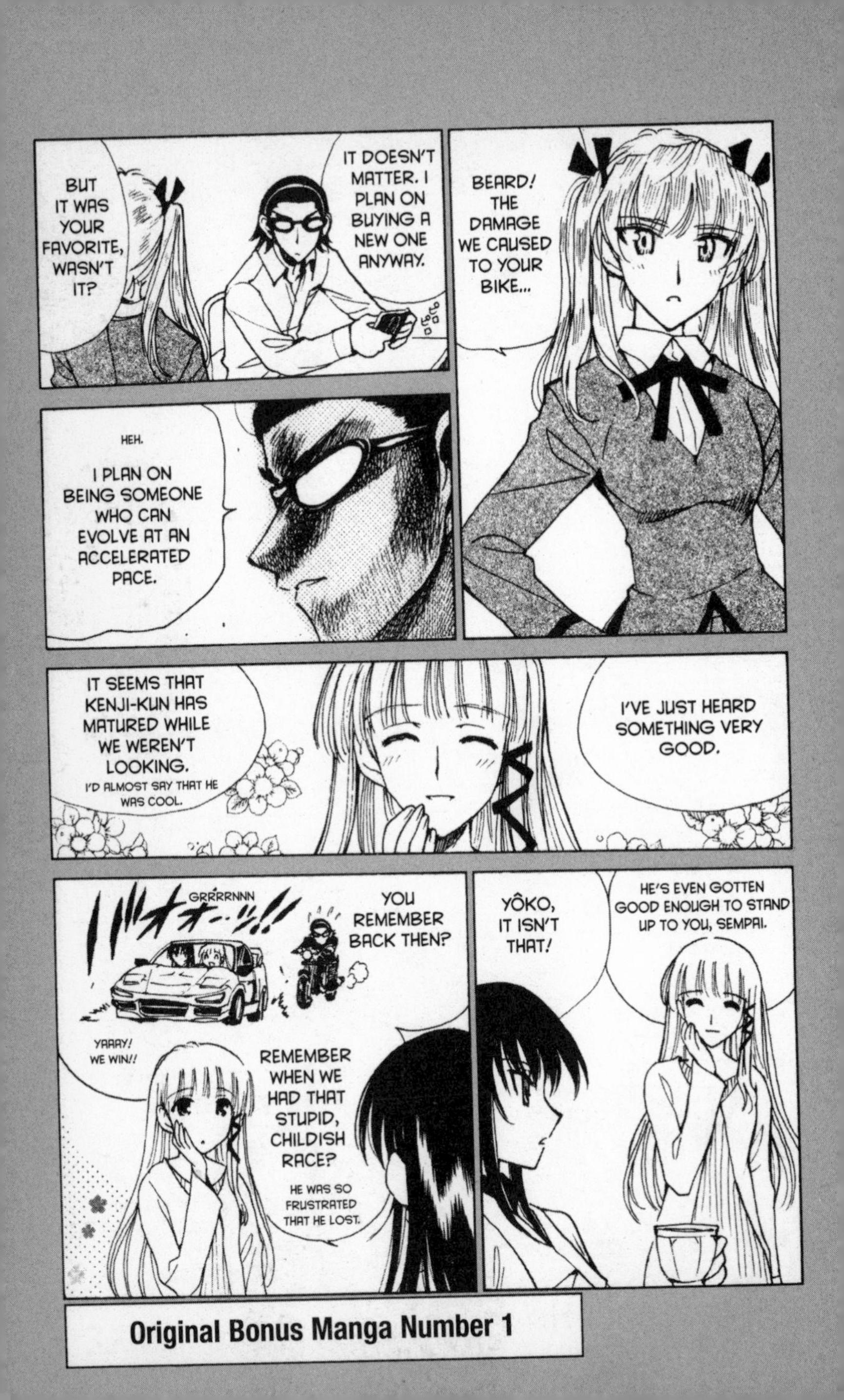
BEARD! THE DAMAGE WE CAUSED TO YOUR BIKE...
IT DOESN'T MATTER. I PLAN ON BUYING A NEW ONE ANYWAY.
BUT IT WAS YOUR FAVORITE, WASN'T IT?
HEH.
I PLAN ON BEING SOMEONE WHO CAN EVOLVE AT AN ACCELERATED PACE.
I'VE JUST HEARD SOMETHING VERY GOOD.
IT SEEMS THAT KENJI-KUN HAS MATURED WHILE WE WEREN'T LOOKING.
I'D ALMOST SAY THAT HE WAS COOL.
HE'S EVEN GOTTEN GOOD ENOUGH TO STAND UP TO YOU, SEMPAI.
YÔKO, IT ISN'T THAT!
YOU REMEMBER BACK THEN?
GRRRRNNN
YAAAY! WE WIN!!
REMEMBER WHEN WE HAD THAT STUPID, CHILDISH RACE?
HE WAS SO FRUSTRATED THAT HE LOST.

Original Bonus Manga Number 1

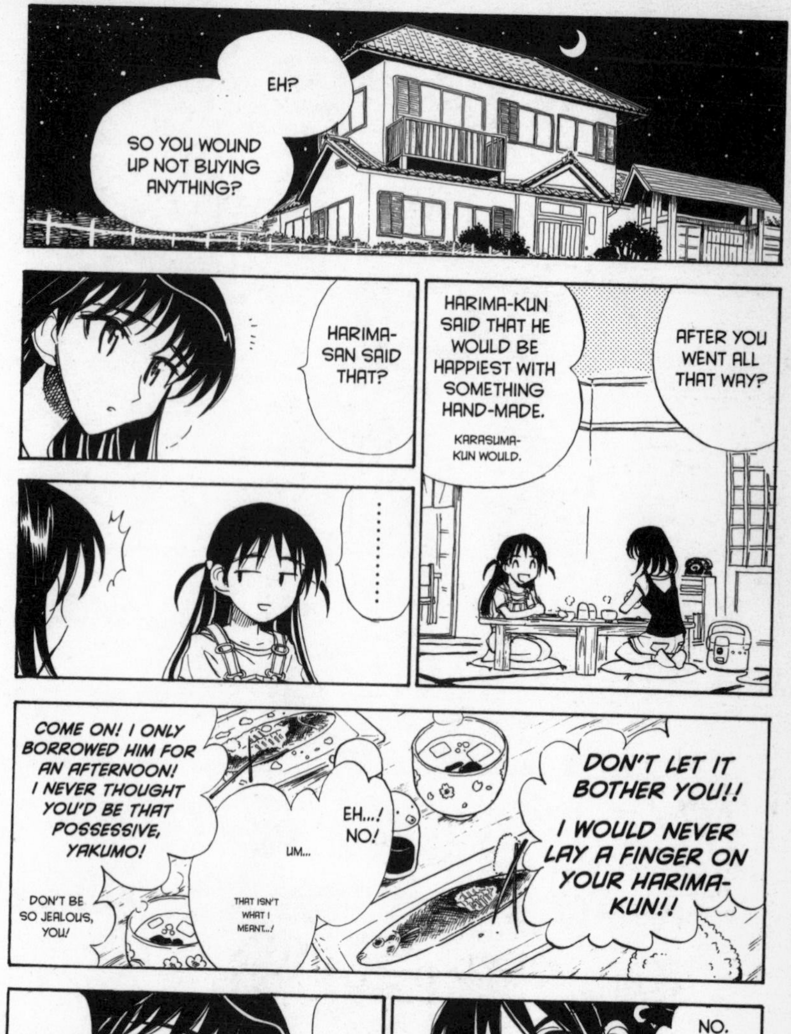
EH?
SO YOU WOUND UP NOT BUYING ANYTHING?
AFTER YOU WENT ALL THAT WAY?
HARIMA-KUN SAID THAT HE WOULD BE HAPPIEST WITH SOMETHING HAND-MADE.
KARASUMA-KUN WOULD.
HARIMA-SAN SAID THAT?
......
DON'T LET IT BOTHER YOU!!
I WOULD NEVER LAY A FINGER ON YOUR HARIMA-KUN!!
EH...! NO!
UM...
THAT ISN'T WHAT I MEANT...!
COME ON! I ONLY BORROWED HIM FOR AN AFTERNOON! I NEVER THOUGHT YOU'D BE THAT POSSESSIVE, YAKUMO!
DON'T BE SO JEALOUS, YOU!
NO. YOU'VE GOT IT WRONG...
I'VE GOT WHAT WRONG?
Y—
YOU'VE GOT...

#101 TOO HOT TO HANDLE

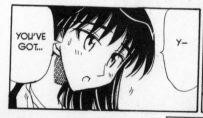

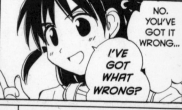

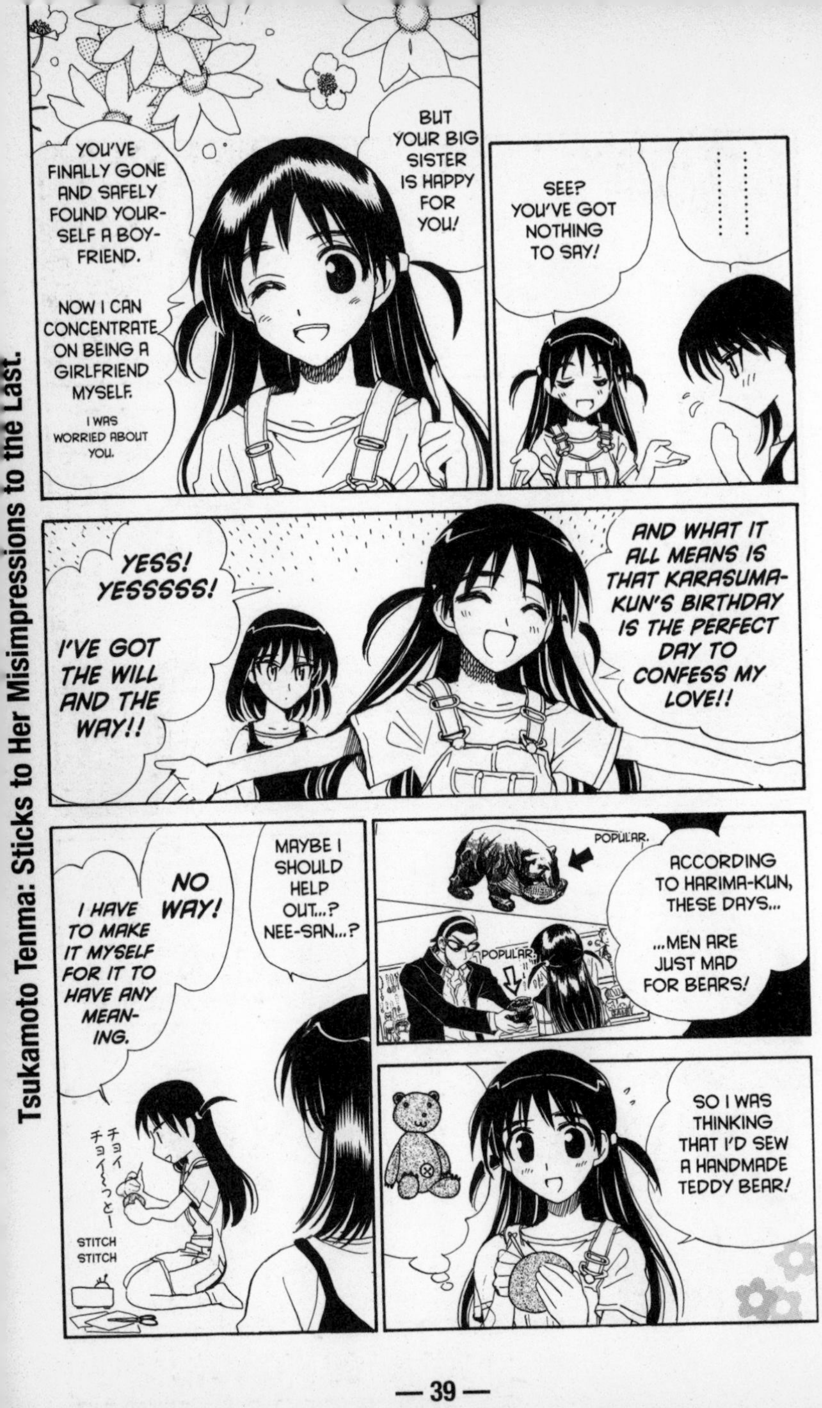
......
......
SEE? YOU'VE GOT NOTHING TO SAY!
BUT YOUR BIG SISTER IS HAPPY FOR YOU!
YOU'VE FINALLY GONE AND SAFELY FOUND YOURSELF A BOY-FRIEND.
NOW I CAN CONCENTRATE ON BEING A GIRLFRIEND MYSELF.
I WAS WORRIED ABOUT YOU.
AND WHAT IT ALL MEANS IS THAT KARASUMA-KUN'S BIRTHDAY IS THE PERFECT DAY TO CONFESS MY LOVE!!
YESS! YESSSSS!
I'VE GOT THE WILL AND THE WAY!!
POPULAR.
ACCORDING TO HARIMA-KUN, THESE DAYS...
...MEN ARE JUST MAD FOR BEARS!
POPULAR.
SO I WAS THINKING THAT I'D SEW A HANDMADE TEDDY BEAR!
MAYBE I SHOULD HELP OUT...? NEE-SAN...?
NO WAY!
I HAVE TO MAKE IT MYSELF FOR IT TO HAVE ANY MEAN-ING.
チョイチョイ～っとー
STITCH STITCH

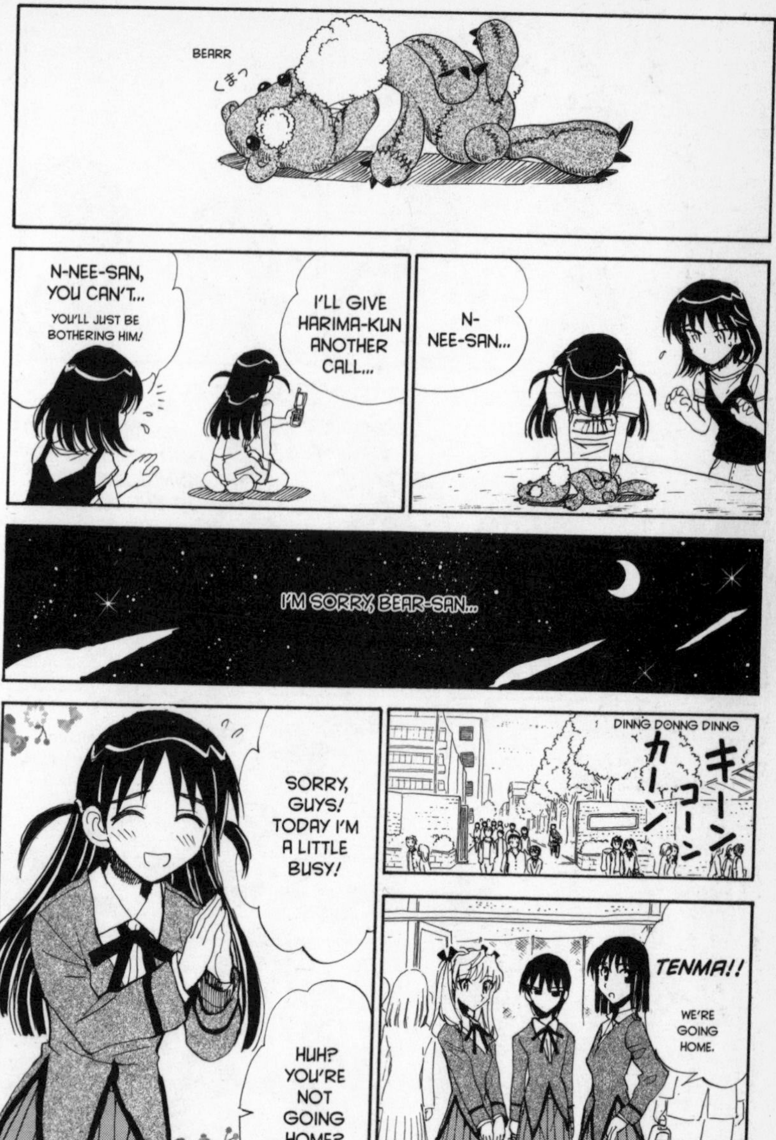
BEARR
くまっ
N-
NEE-SAN...
I'LL GIVE HARIMA-KUN ANOTHER CALL...
N-NEE-SAN, YOU CAN'T...
YOU'LL JUST BE BOTHERING HIM!
I'M SORRY, BEAR-SAN...
DINNG DONNG DINNG
キーンコーンカーン
TENMA!!
WE'RE GOING HOME.
SORRY, GUYS! TODAY I'M A LITTLE BUSY!
HUH? YOU'RE NOT GOING HOME?

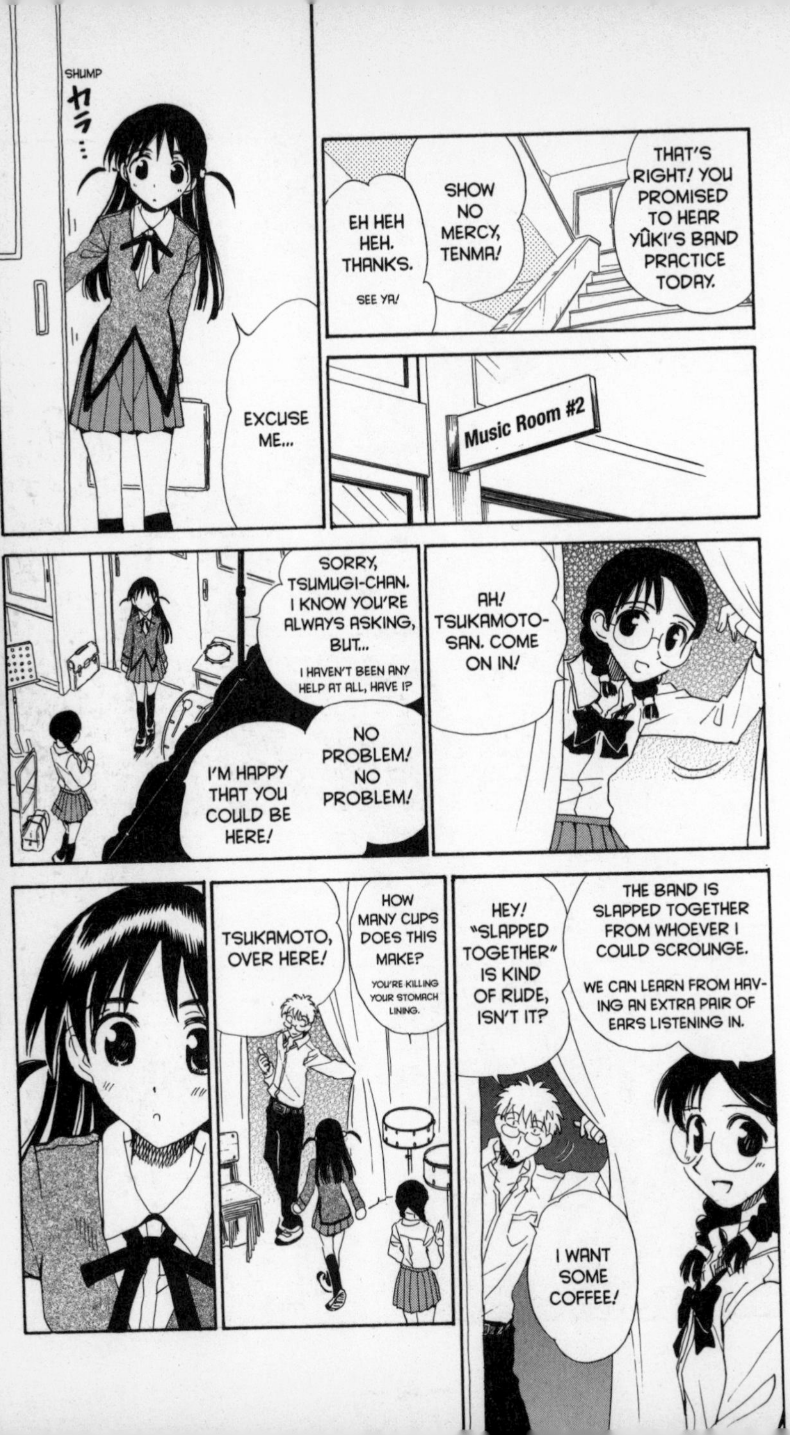
THAT'S RIGHT! YOU PROMISED TO HEAR YÛKI'S BAND PRACTICE TODAY.
SHOW NO MERCY, TENMA!
EH HEH HEH. THANKS.
SEE YA!
Music Room #2
SHUMP
EXCUSE ME...
AH! TSUKAMOTO-SAN. COME ON IN!
SORRY, TSUMUGI-CHAN. I KNOW YOU'RE ALWAYS ASKING, BUT...
I HAVEN'T BEEN ANY HELP AT ALL, HAVE I?
NO PROBLEM! NO PROBLEM!
I'M HAPPY THAT YOU COULD BE HERE!
THE BAND IS SLAPPED TOGETHER FROM WHOEVER I COULD SCROUNGE.
WE CAN LEARN FROM HAVING AN EXTRA PAIR OF EARS LISTENING IN.
HEY! "SLAPPED TOGETHER" IS KIND OF RUDE, ISN'T IT?
I WANT SOME COFFEE!
HOW MANY CUPS DOES THIS MAKE?
YOU'RE KILLING YOUR STOMACH LINING.
TSUKAMOTO, OVER HERE!

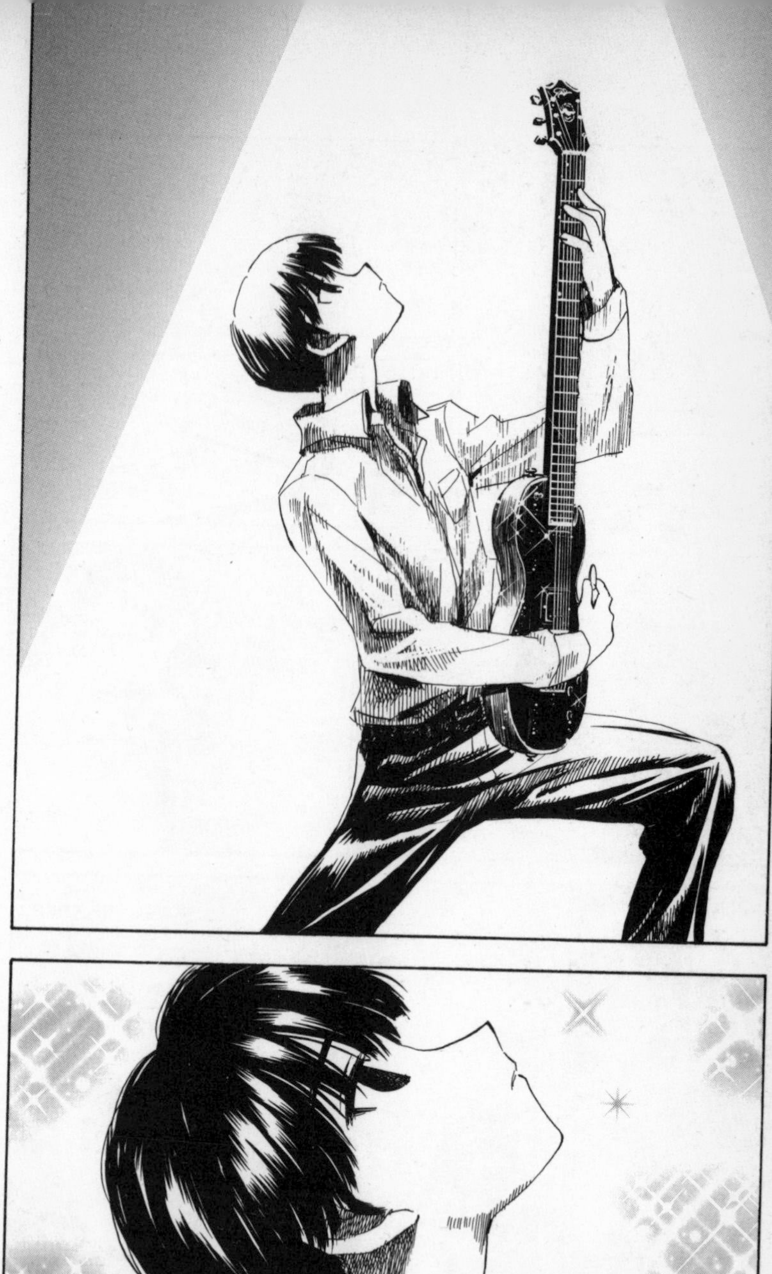

Karasuma Oji: Tenma's Classmate and Love. Just a Basic Fact.

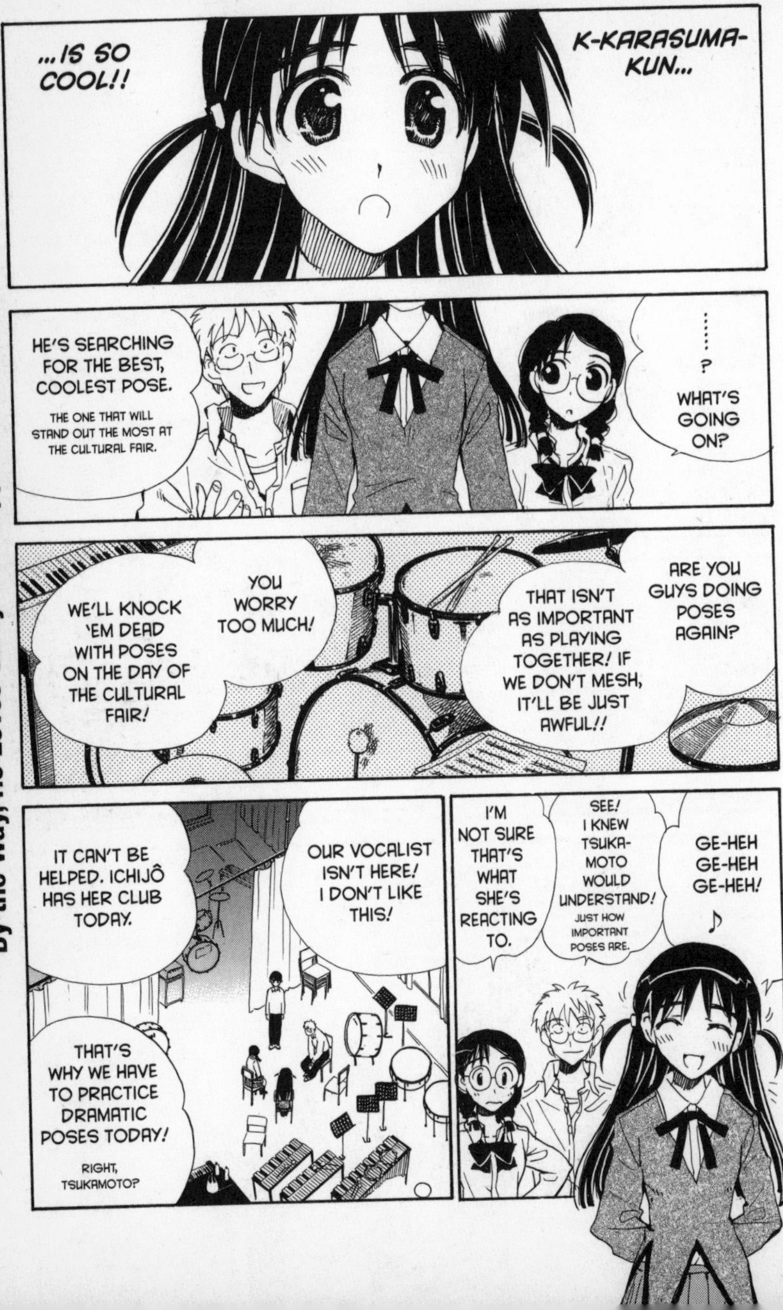
K-KARASUMA-KUN...
...IS SO COOL!!
......? WHAT'S GOING ON?
HE'S SEARCHING FOR THE BEST, COOLEST POSE.
THE ONE THAT WILL STAND OUT THE MOST AT THE CULTURAL FAIR.
ARE YOU GUYS DOING POSES AGAIN?
THAT ISN'T AS IMPORTANT AS PLAYING TOGETHER! IF WE DON'T MESH, IT'LL BE JUST AWFUL!!
YOU WORRY TOO MUCH!
WE'LL KNOCK 'EM DEAD WITH POSES ON THE DAY OF THE CULTURAL FAIR!
GE-HEH GE-HEH GE-HEH! ♪
SEE! I KNEW TSUKA-MOTO WOULD UNDERSTAND!
JUST HOW IMPORTANT POSES ARE.
I'M NOT SURE THAT'S WHAT SHE'S REACTING TO.
OUR VOCALIST ISN'T HERE! I DON'T LIKE THIS!
IT CAN'T BE HELPED. ICHIJÔ HAS HER CLUB TODAY.
THAT'S WHY WE HAVE TO PRACTICE DRAMATIC POSES TODAY!
RIGHT, TSUKAMOTO?

By the Way, He Loves Curry and Kappa Water Sprites.

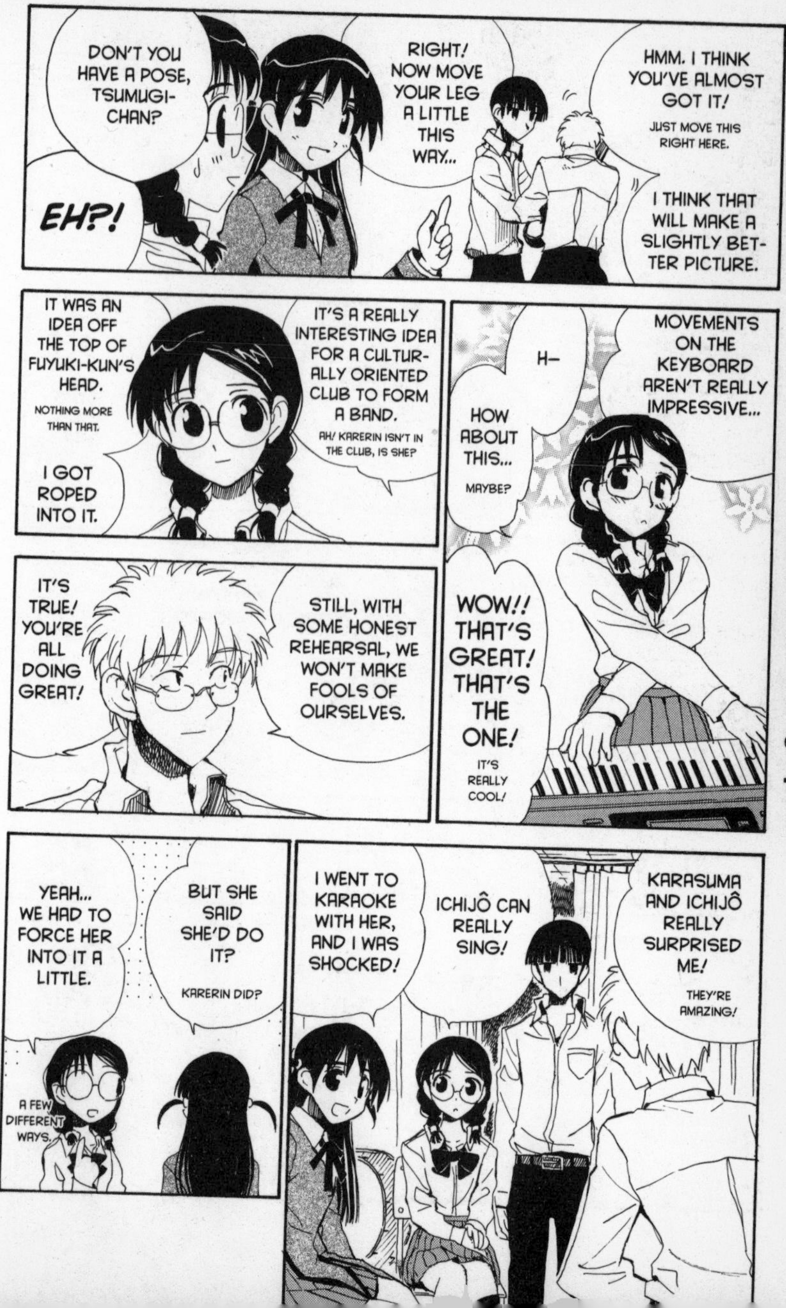
HMM. I THINK YOU'VE ALMOST GOT IT!
JUST MOVE THIS RIGHT HERE.
I THINK THAT WILL MAKE A SLIGHTLY BET-TER PICTURE.
RIGHT! NOW MOVE YOUR LEG A LITTLE THIS WAY...
DON'T YOU HAVE A POSE, TSUMUGI-CHAN?
EH?!
MOVEMENTS ON THE KEYBOARD AREN'T REALLY IMPRESSIVE...
H—
HOW ABOUT THIS...
MAYBE?
WOW!! THAT'S GREAT! THAT'S THE ONE!
IT'S REALLY COOL!
IT'S A REALLY INTERESTING IDEA FOR A CULTUR-ALLY ORIENTED CLUB TO FORM A BAND.
AH! KARERIN ISN'T IN THE CLUB, IS SHE?
IT WAS AN IDEA OFF THE TOP OF FUYUKI-KUN'S HEAD.
NOTHING MORE THAN THAT.
I GOT ROPED INTO IT.
STILL, WITH SOME HONEST REHEARSAL, WE WON'T MAKE FOOLS OF OURSELVES.
IT'S TRUE! YOU'RE ALL DOING GREAT!
KARASUMA AND ICHIJÔ REALLY SURPRISED ME!
THEY'RE AMAZING!
ICHIJÔ CAN REALLY SING!
I WENT TO KARAOKE WITH HER, AND I WAS SHOCKED!
BUT SHE SAID SHE'D DO IT?
KARERIN DID?
YEAH... WE HAD TO FORCE HER INTO IT A LITTLE.
A FEW DIFFERENT WAYS.
Fuyuki Takeichi: Ero-Photographer.

Sagano Megumi Handles the Bass.

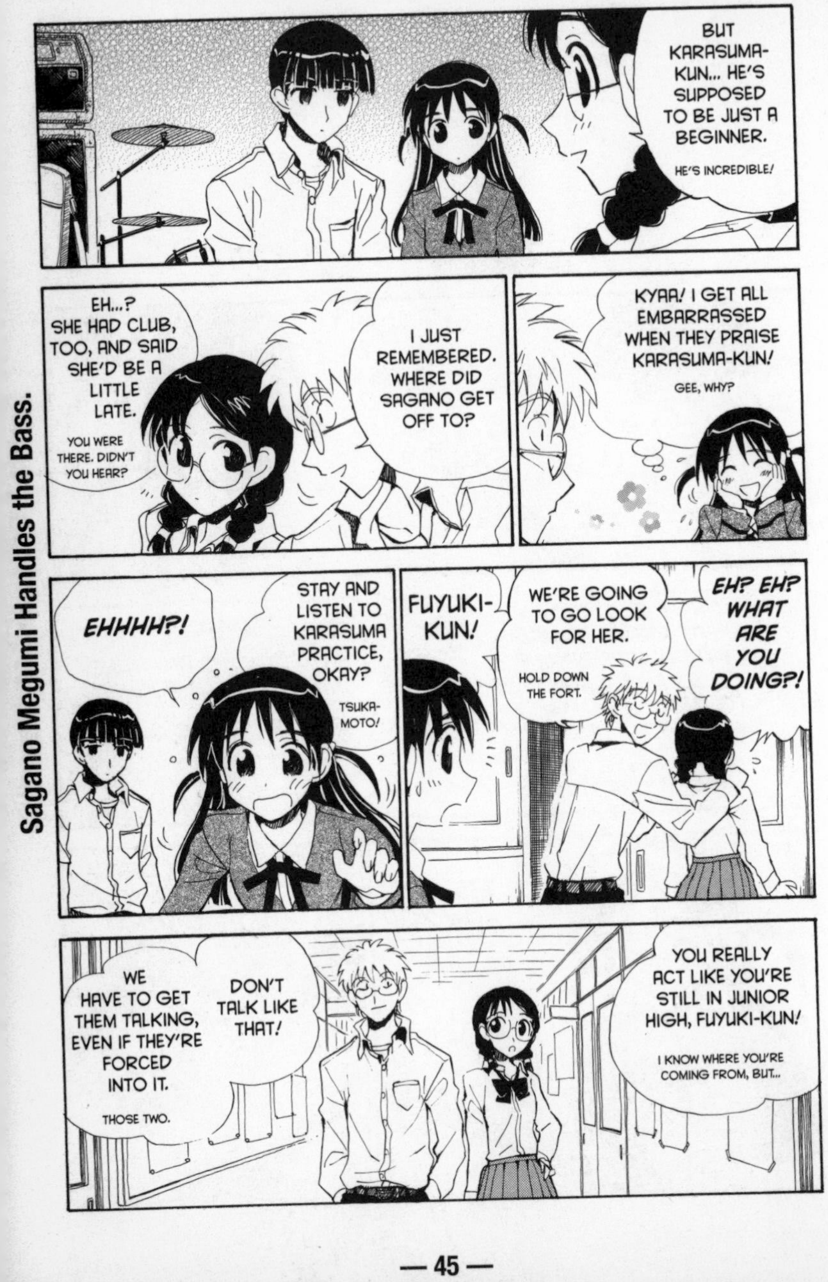
BUT KARASUMA-KUN... HE'S SUPPOSED TO BE JUST A BEGINNER.
HE'S INCREDIBLE!
KYAA! I GET ALL EMBARRASSED WHEN THEY PRAISE KARASUMA-KUN!
GEE, WHY?
I JUST REMEMBERED. WHERE DID SAGANO GET OFF TO?
EH...? SHE HAD CLUB, TOO, AND SAID SHE'D BE A LITTLE LATE.
YOU WERE THERE. DIDN'T YOU HEAR?
EH? EH? WHAT ARE YOU DOING?!
WE'RE GOING TO GO LOOK FOR HER.
HOLD DOWN THE FORT.
FUYUKI-KUN!
STAY AND LISTEN TO KARASUMA PRACTICE, OKAY?
TSUKA-MOTO!
EHHHH?!
YOU REALLY ACT LIKE YOU'RE STILL IN JUNIOR HIGH, FUYUKI-KUN!
I KNOW WHERE YOU'RE COMING FROM, BUT...
DON'T TALK LIKE THAT!
WE HAVE TO GET THEM TALKING, EVEN IF THEY'RE FORCED INTO IT.
THOSE TWO.

Brain Overload: 500 percent

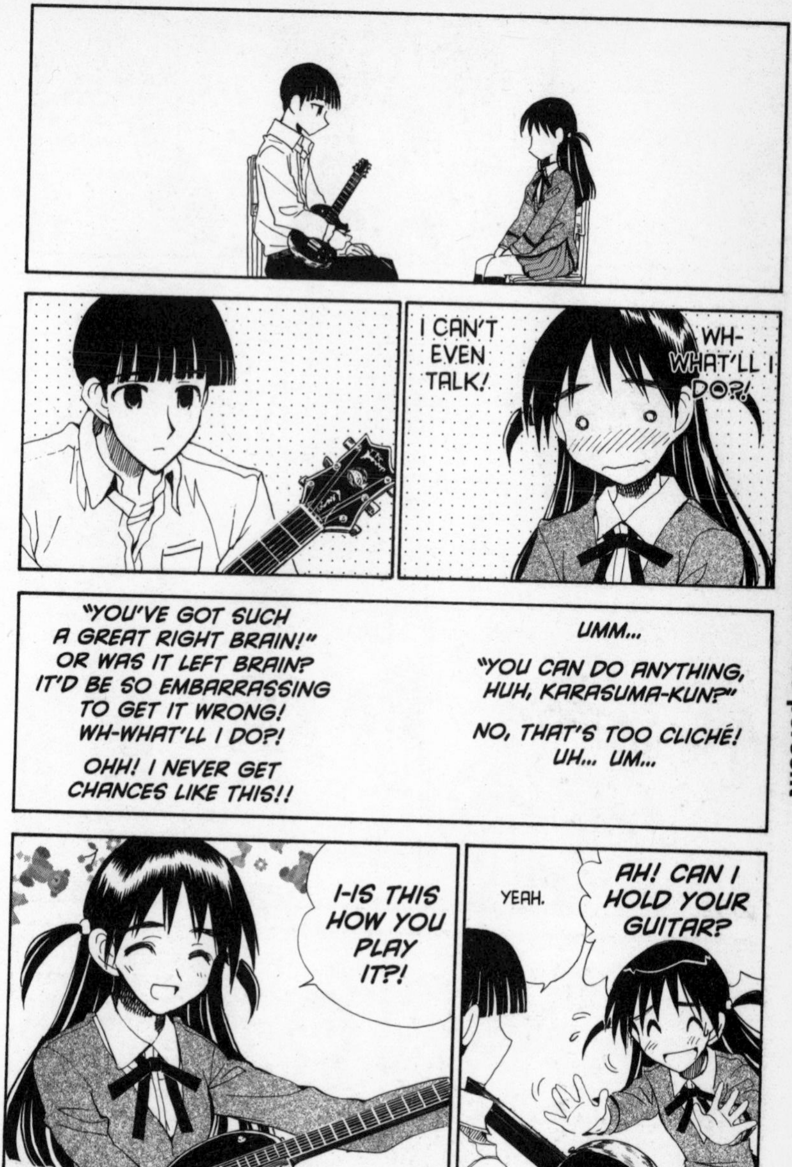
WH-WHAT'LL I DO?!
I CAN'T EVEN TALK!
UMM...
"YOU CAN DO ANYTHING, HUH, KARASUMA-KUN?"
NO, THAT'S TOO CLICHÉ! UH... UM...
"YOU'VE GOT SUCH A GREAT RIGHT BRAIN!" OR WAS IT LEFT BRAIN? IT'D BE SO EMBARRASSING TO GET IT WRONG! WH-WHAT'LL I DO?!
OHH! I NEVER GET CHANCES LIKE THIS!!
AH! CAN I HOLD YOUR GUITAR?
YEAH.
I-IS THIS HOW YOU PLAY IT?!

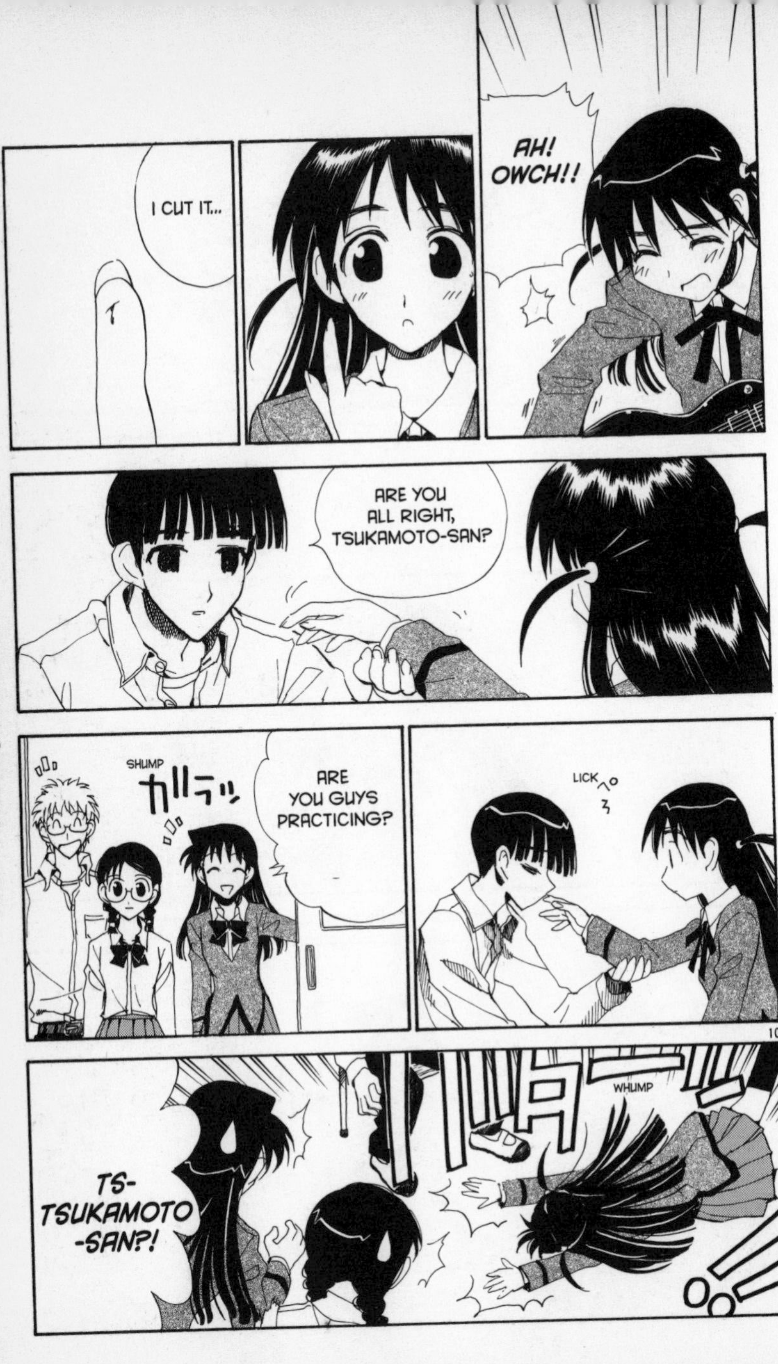
AH!
OWCH!!
I CUT IT...
ARE YOU ALL RIGHT, TSUKAMOTO-SAN?
LICK
ARE YOU GUYS PRACTICING?
SHUMP
WHUMP
TS-TSUKAMOTO-SAN?!

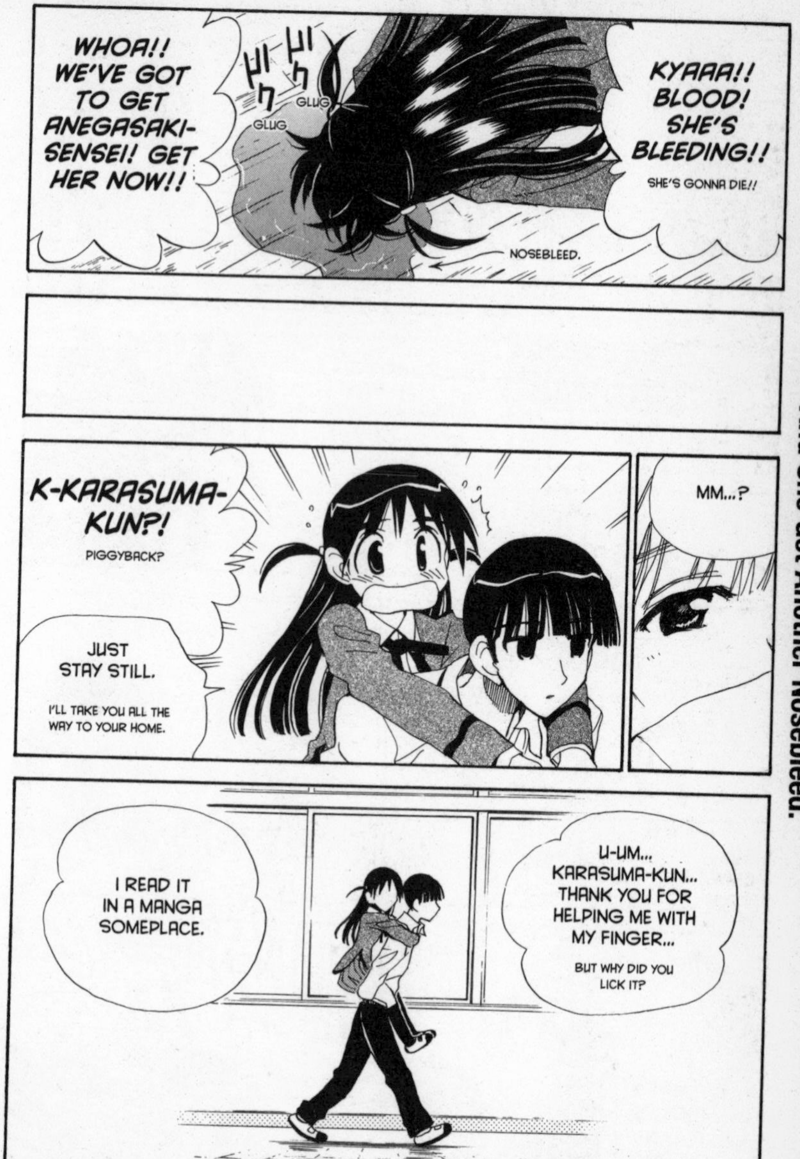
KYAAA!! BLOOD! SHE'S BLEEDING!!
SHE'S GONNA DIE!!
NOSEBLEED.
GLUG
GLUG
WHOA!! WE'VE GOT TO GET ANEGASAKI-SENSEI! GET HER NOW!!
MM...?
K-KARASUMA-KUN?!
PIGGYBACK?
JUST STAY STILL.
I'LL TAKE YOU ALL THE WAY TO YOUR HOME.
U-UM... KARASUMA-KUN... THANK YOU FOR HELPING ME WITH MY FINGER...
BUT WHY DID YOU LICK IT?
I READ IT IN A MANGA SOMEPLACE.

And She Got Another Nosebleed.

101 ....Fin

#102 JOHNNY GOT HIS GUN

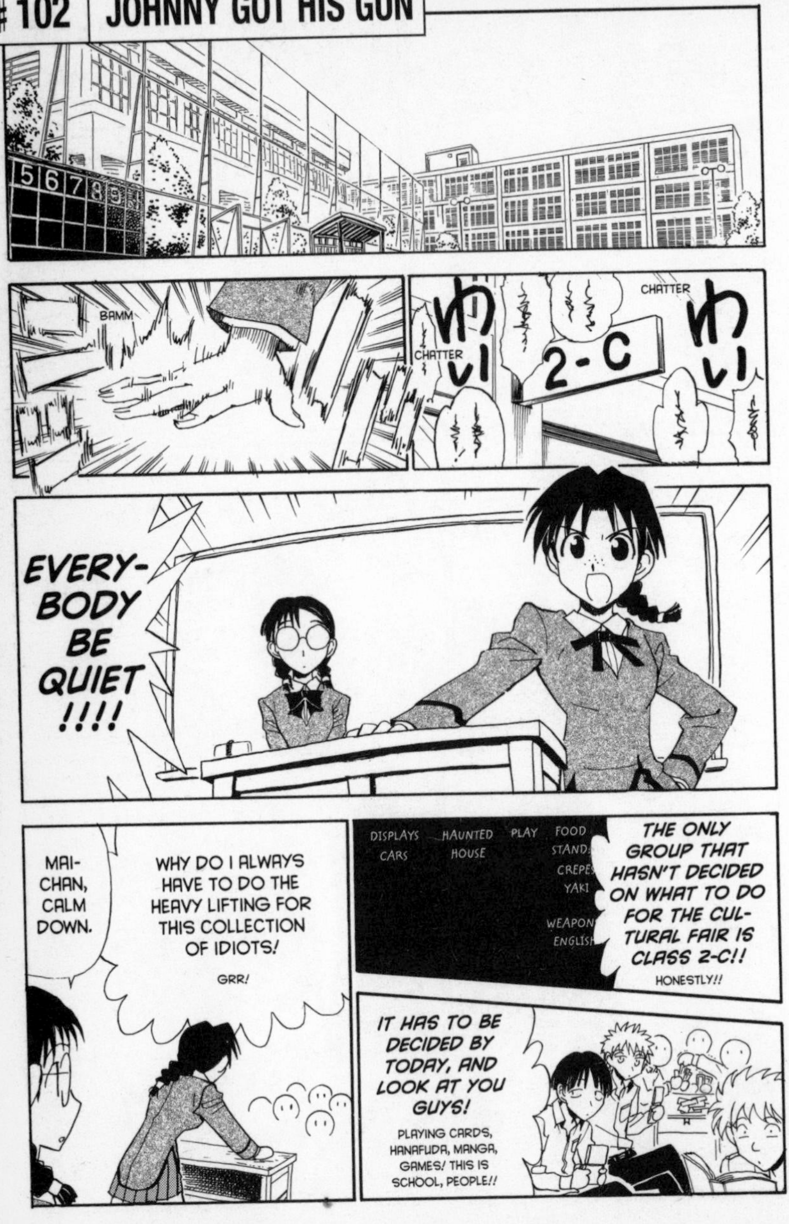

わい
CHATTER
2-C
CHATTER
わい
BAMM
EVERY-BODY BE QUIET!!!!
DISPLAYS CARS
HAUNTED HOUSE
PLAY
FOOD STAND: CREPES YAKI
WEAPON ENGLISH
THE ONLY GROUP THAT HASN'T DECIDED ON WHAT TO DO FOR THE CULTURAL FAIR IS CLASS 2-C!!
HONESTLY!!
IT HAS TO BE DECIDED BY TODAY, AND LOOK AT YOU GUYS!
PLAYING CARDS, HANAFUDA, MANGA, GAMES! THIS IS SCHOOL, PEOPLE!!
WHY DO I ALWAYS HAVE TO DO THE HEAVY LIFTING FOR THIS COLLECTION OF IDIOTS!
GRR!
MAI-CHAN, CALM DOWN.

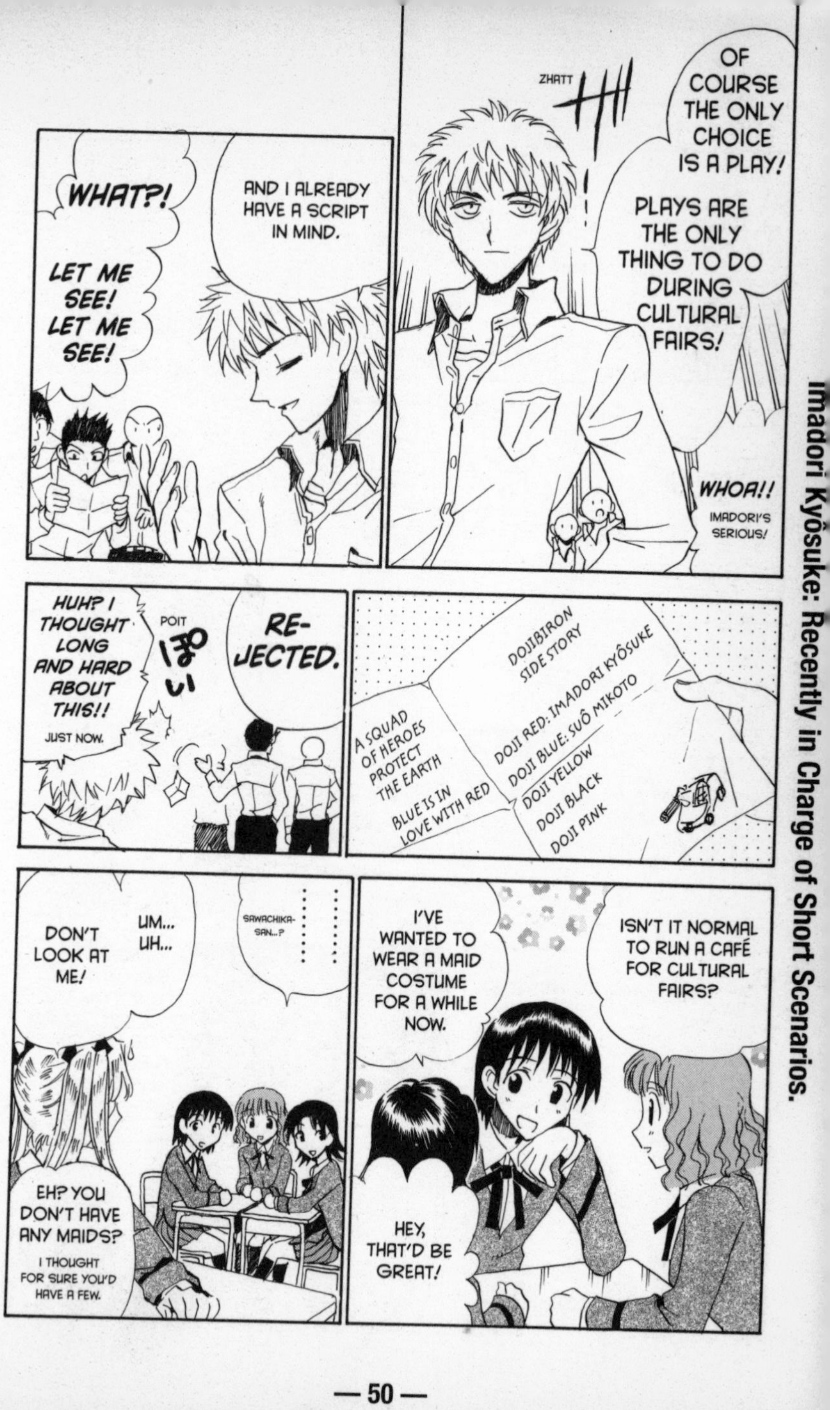
ZHATT
OF COURSE THE ONLY CHOICE IS A PLAY!
PLAYS ARE THE ONLY THING TO DO DURING CULTURAL FAIRS!
WHOA!!
IMADORI'S SERIOUS!
AND I ALREADY HAVE A SCRIPT IN MIND.
WHAT?!
LET ME SEE! LET ME SEE!
DOJIBIRON SIDE STORY
DOJI RED: IMADORI KYÔSUKE
DOJI BLUE: SUÔ MIKOTO
DOJI YELLOW
DOJI BLACK
DOJI PINK
A SQUAD OF HEROES PROTECT THE EARTH
BLUE IS IN LOVE WITH RED
RE-JECTED.
POIT
ぽい
HUH? I THOUGHT LONG AND HARD ABOUT THIS!!
JUST NOW.
ISN'T IT NORMAL TO RUN A CAFÉ FOR CULTURAL FAIRS?
I'VE WANTED TO WEAR A MAID COSTUME FOR A WHILE NOW.
HEY, THAT'D BE GREAT!
......
SAWACHIKA-SAN...?
UM... UH...
DON'T LOOK AT ME!
EH? YOU DON'T HAVE ANY MAIDS?
I THOUGHT FOR SURE YOU'D HAVE A FEW.

Imadori Kyôsuke: Recently in Charge of Short Scenarios.

Harima Kenji: Busy with Make-Up Exams.

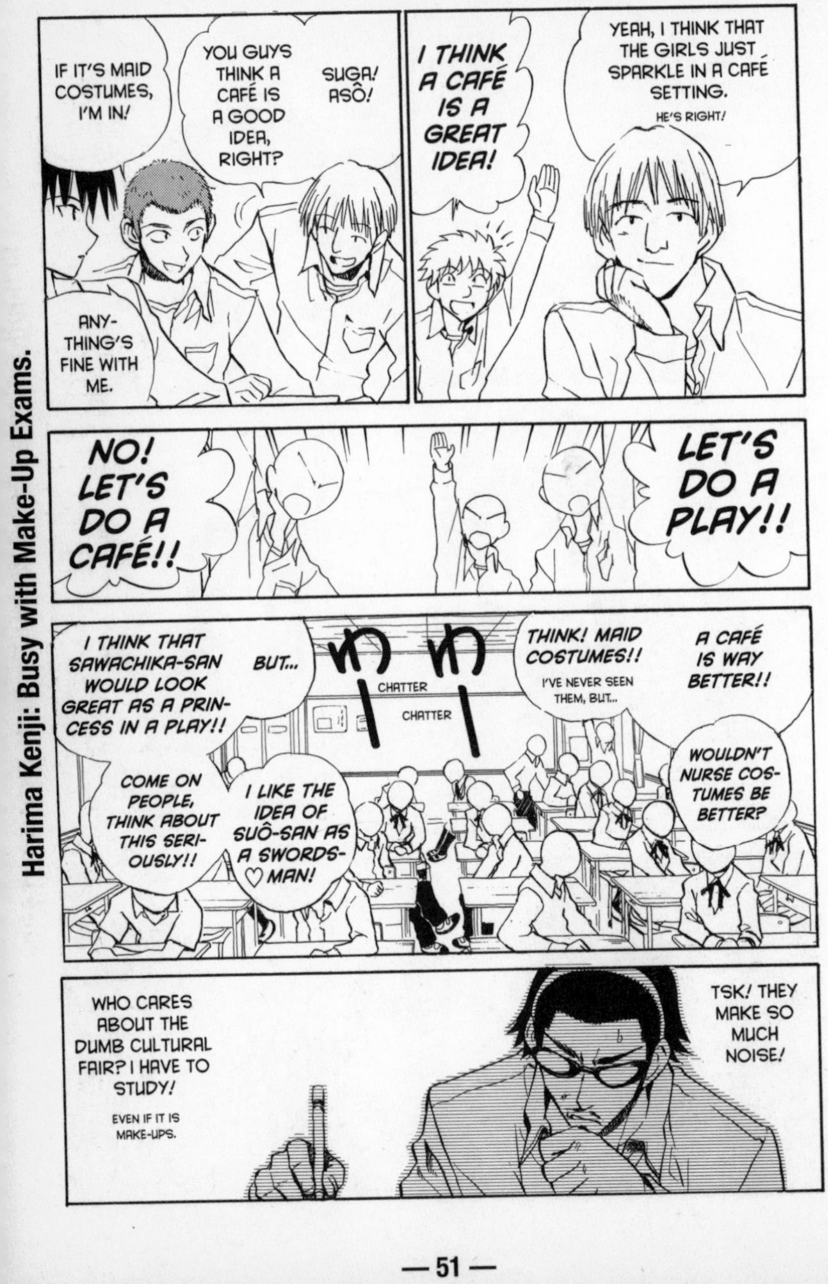

YEAH, I THINK THAT THE GIRLS JUST SPARKLE IN A CAFÉ SETTING.
HE'S RIGHT!
I THINK A CAFÉ IS A GREAT IDEA!
SUGA! ASÔ!
YOU GUYS THINK A CAFÉ IS A GOOD IDEA, RIGHT?
IF IT'S MAID COSTUMES, I'M IN!
ANYTHING'S FINE WITH ME.
LET'S DO A PLAY!!
NO! LET'S DO A CAFÉ!!
A CAFÉ IS WAY BETTER!!
THINK! MAID COSTUMES!!
I'VE NEVER SEEN THEM, BUT...
わー わー
CHATTER
CHATTER
BUT...
I THINK THAT SAWACHIKA-SAN WOULD LOOK GREAT AS A PRINCESS IN A PLAY!!
WOULDN'T NURSE COSTUMES BE BETTER?
I LIKE THE IDEA OF SUÔ-SAN AS A SWORDS-♡MAN!
COME ON PEOPLE, THINK ABOUT THIS SERIOUSLY!!
TSK! THEY MAKE SO MUCH NOISE!
WHO CARES ABOUT THE DUMB CULTURAL FAIR? I HAVE TO STUDY!
EVEN IF IT IS MAKE-UPS.

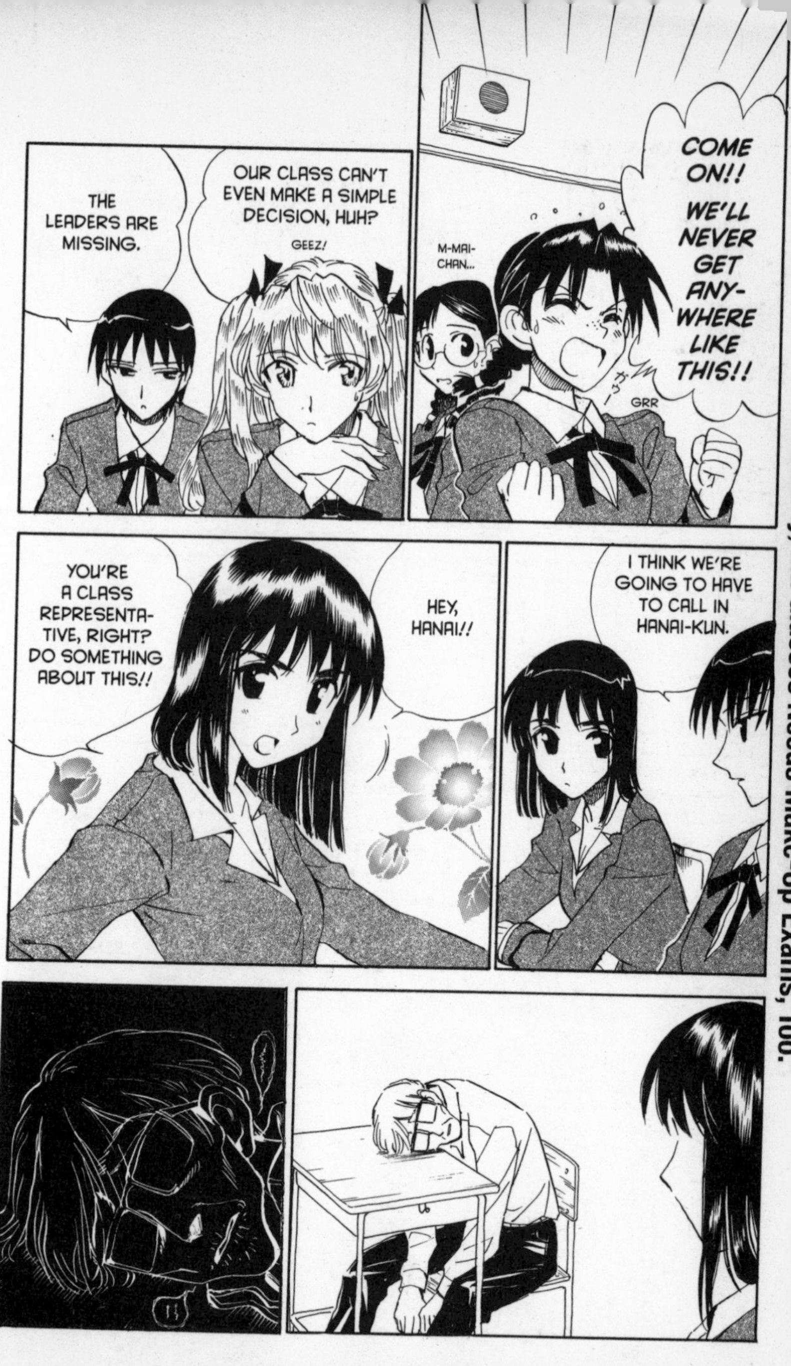
COME ON!! WE'LL NEVER GET ANYWHERE LIKE THIS!!
GRR
M-MAI-CHAN...
OUR CLASS CAN'T EVEN MAKE A SIMPLE DECISION, HUH?
GEEZ!
THE LEADERS ARE MISSING.
I THINK WE'RE GOING TO HAVE TO CALL IN HANAI-KUN.
HEY, HANAI!!
YOU'RE A CLASS REPRESENTATIVE, RIGHT? DO SOMETHING ABOUT THIS!!

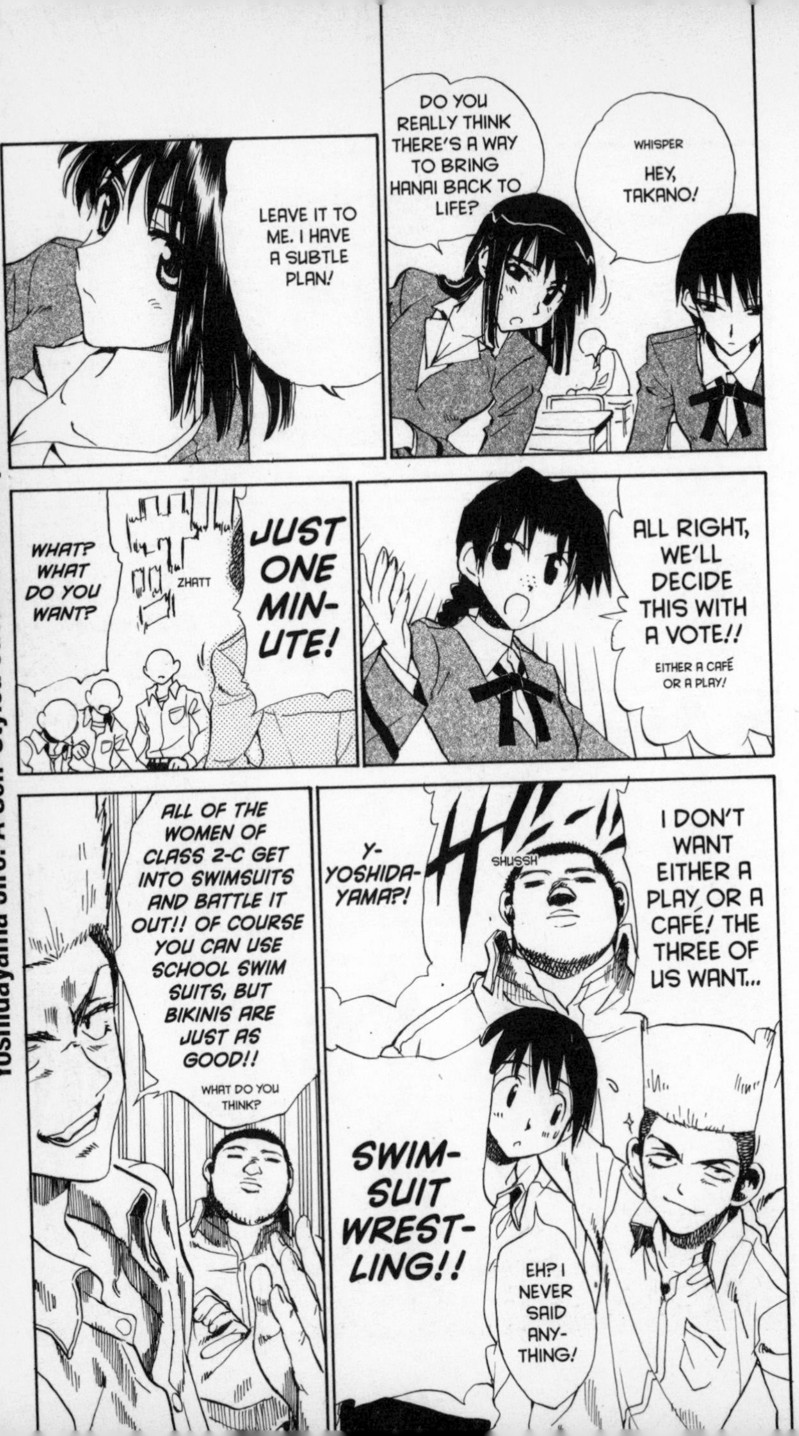
WHISPER
HEY, TAKANO!
DO YOU REALLY THINK THERE'S A WAY TO BRING HANAI BACK TO LIFE?
LEAVE IT TO ME. I HAVE A SUBTLE PLAN!
ALL RIGHT, WE'LL DECIDE THIS WITH A VOTE!!
EITHER A CAFÉ OR A PLAY!
JUST ONE MIN-UTE!
ZHATT
WHAT? WHAT DO YOU WANT?
I DON'T WANT EITHER A PLAY OR A CAFÉ! THE THREE OF US WANT...
SHUSSH
Y-YOSHIDA-YAMA?!
SWIM-SUIT WREST-LING!!
EH? I NEVER SAID ANY-THING!
ALL OF THE WOMEN OF CLASS 2-C GET INTO SWIMSUITS AND BATTLE IT OUT!! OF COURSE YOU CAN USE SCHOOL SWIM SUITS, BUT BIKINIS ARE JUST AS GOOD!!
WHAT DO YOU THINK?

Yoshidayama Jirô: A Self-Styled Juvenile Delinquent.

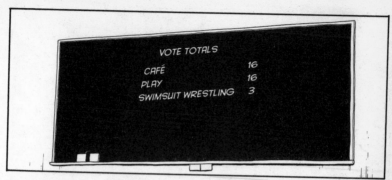

VOTE TOTALS

CAFÉ	16
PLAY	16
SWIMSUIT WRESTLING	3

I WASN'T ALL THAT THRILLED WITH THE IDEA ANYWAY.

AND THE NUMBERS DON'T ADD UP! WHAT'S GOING ON HERE?!

ARE THERE PEOPLE WHO HAVEN'T RAISED THEIR HANDS YET?!

IT'S ANOTHER TIE! HOW ARE WE EVER GOING TO DECIDE THIS!!

PRINCESS: TENMA

PRINCE: HARIMA

JUST TAKE A LOOK AT IT.

DON'T BOTHER WITH ME.

I DON'T CARE.

I'VE BEEN WRITING THE SCRIPT FOR THE PLAY. DO YOU WANT TO SEE?

MM? YEAH, UM...

YOU'RE TSUKAMOTO'S FRIEND, RIGHT?

HARIMA-KUN!

SCRIPT

SST

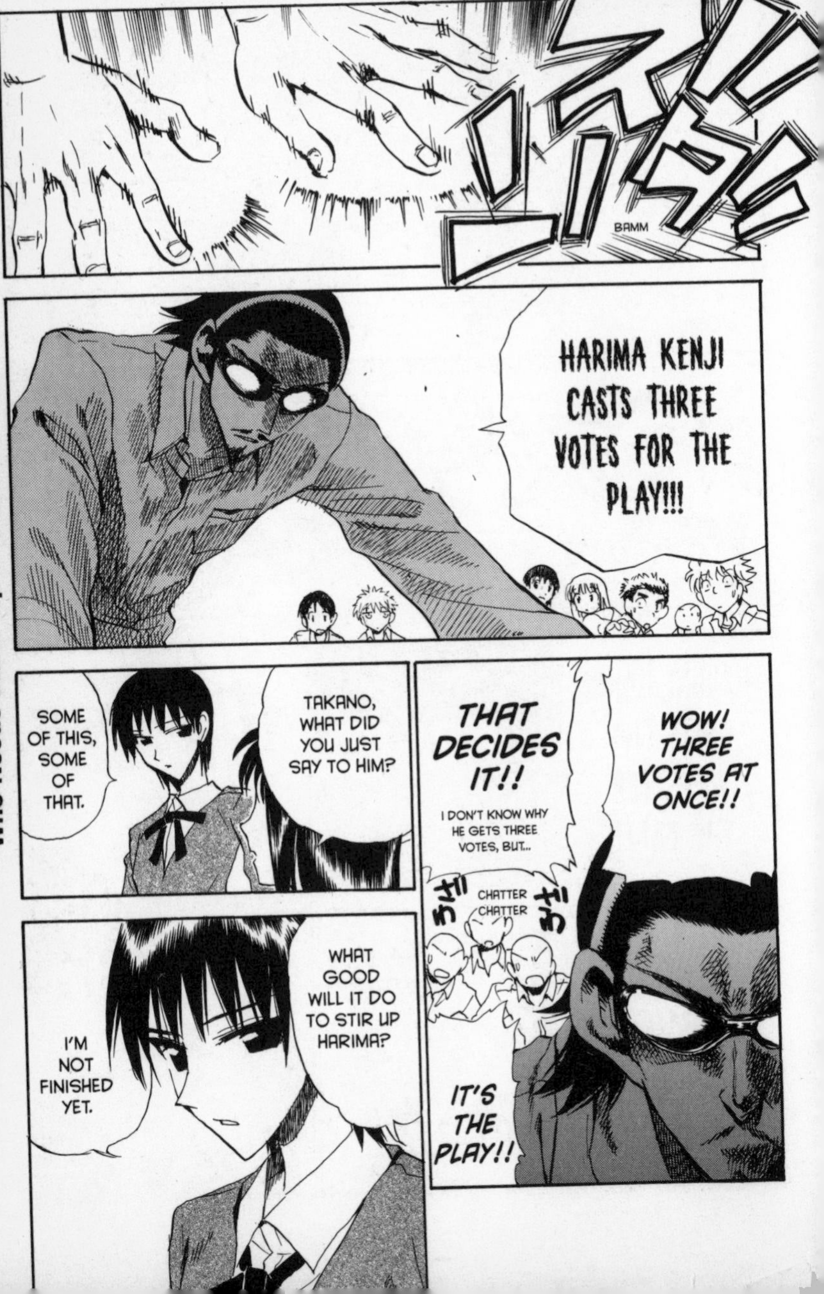
BAMM
HARIMA KENJI CASTS THREE VOTES FOR THE PLAY!!!!
WOW! THREE VOTES AT ONCE!!
THAT DECIDES IT!!
I DON'T KNOW WHY HE GETS THREE VOTES, BUT...
CHATTER CHATTER
IT'S THE PLAY!!
TAKANO, WHAT DID YOU JUST SAY TO HIM?
SOME OF THIS, SOME OF THAT.
WHAT GOOD WILL IT DO TO STIR UP HARIMA?
I'M NOT FINISHED YET.

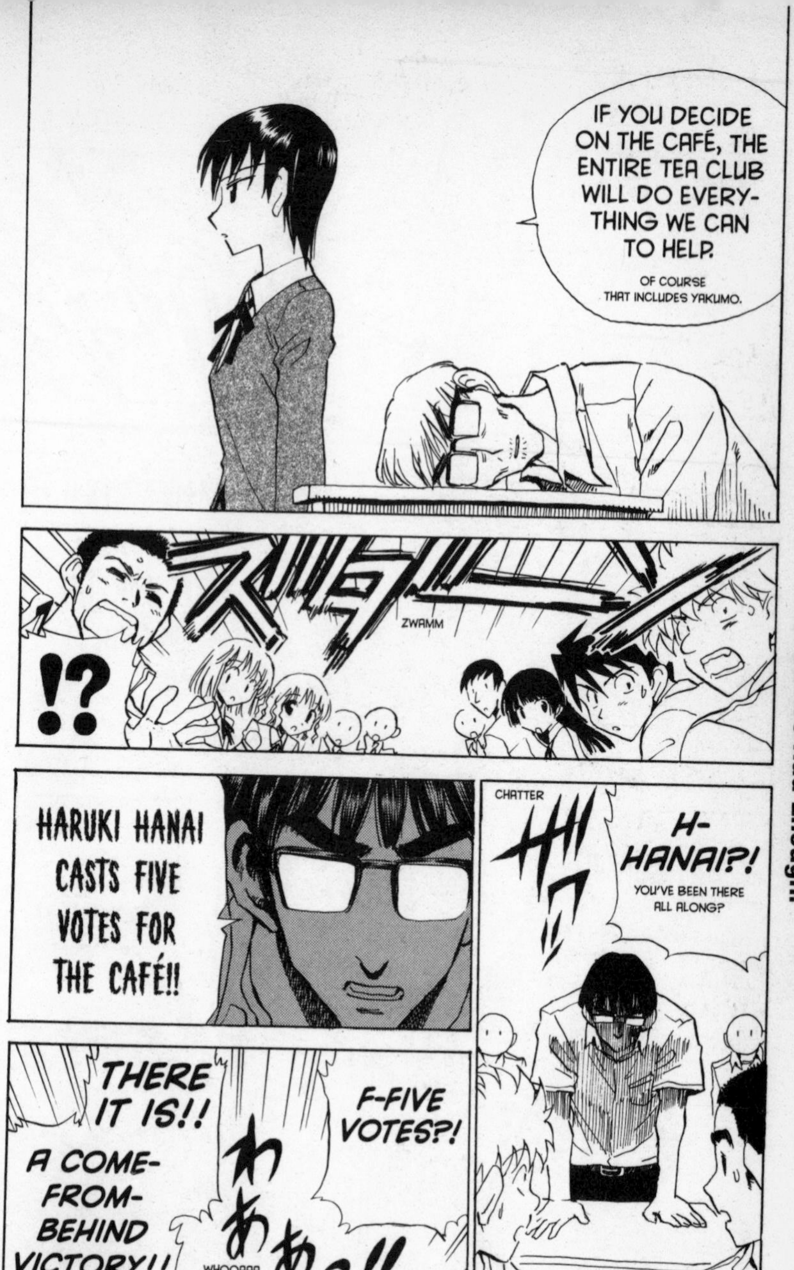
IF YOU DECIDE ON THE CAFÉ, THE ENTIRE TEA CLUB WILL DO EVERY-THING WE CAN TO HELP.
OF COURSE THAT INCLUDES YAKUMO.
ZWAMM
!?
CHATTER
H-HANAI?!
YOU'VE BEEN THERE ALL ALONG?
HARUKI HANAI CASTS FIVE VOTES FOR THE CAFÉ!!
F-FIVE VOTES?!
THERE IT IS!!
A COME-FROM-BEHIND VICTORY!!
わああっ!!
WHOORAA
WHY DOES HE GET TO CAST 5 VOTES?

They're Both Mistaken.

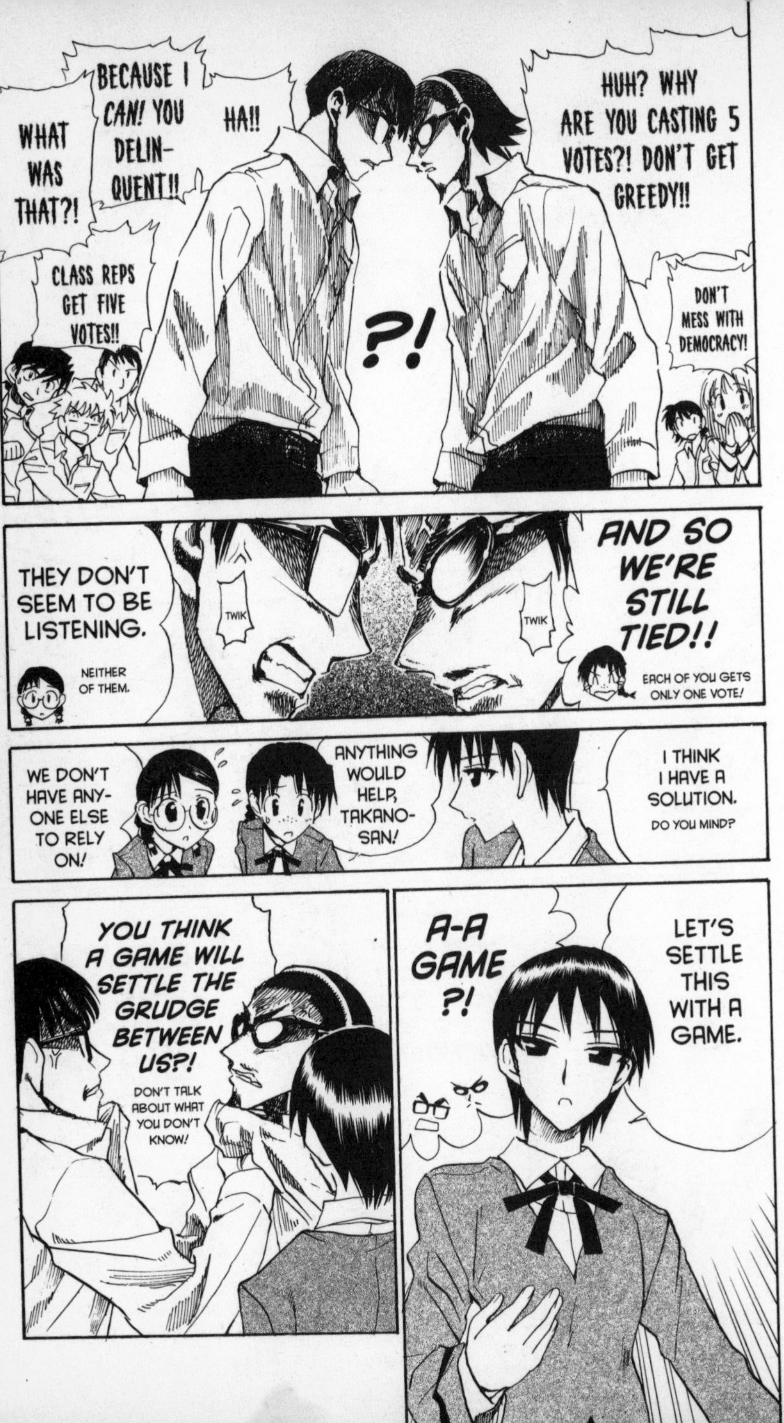

HUH? WHY ARE YOU CASTING 5 VOTES?! DON'T GET GREEDY!!
HA!!
BECAUSE I CAN! YOU DELIN-QUENT!!
WHAT WAS THAT?!
DON'T MESS WITH DEMOCRACY!
?!
CLASS REPS GET FIVE VOTES!!
AND SO WE'RE STILL TIED!!
TWIK
EACH OF YOU GETS ONLY ONE VOTE!
TWIK
THEY DON'T SEEM TO BE LISTENING.
NEITHER OF THEM.
I THINK I HAVE A SOLUTION.
DO YOU MIND?
ANYTHING WOULD HELP, TAKANO-SAN!
WE DON'T HAVE ANY-ONE ELSE TO RELY ON!
LET'S SETTLE THIS WITH A GAME.
A-A GAME?!
YOU THINK A GAME WILL SETTLE THE GRUDGE BETWEEN US?!
DON'T TALK ABOUT WHAT YOU DON'T KNOW!

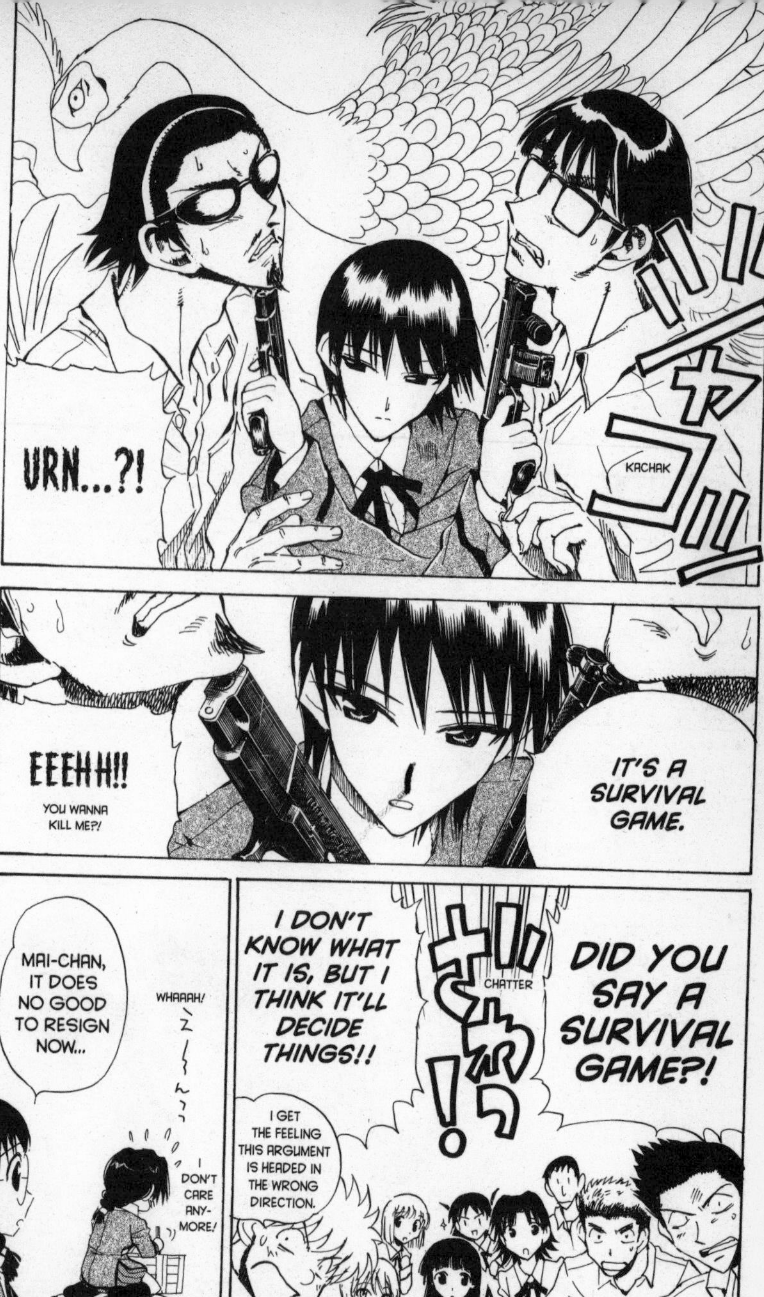
URN...?!
KACHAK
IT'S A SURVIVAL GAME.
EEEHH!!
YOU WANNA KILL ME?!
DID YOU SAY A SURVIVAL GAME?!
CHATTER
I DON'T KNOW WHAT IT IS, BUT I THINK IT'LL DECIDE THINGS!!
I GET THE FEELING THIS ARGUMENT IS HEADED IN THE WRONG DIRECTION.
MAI-CHAN, IT DOES NO GOOD TO RESIGN NOW...
WHAAAH!
I DON'T CARE ANYMORE!

Ah . . . Tenma.

102 . . . . Fin

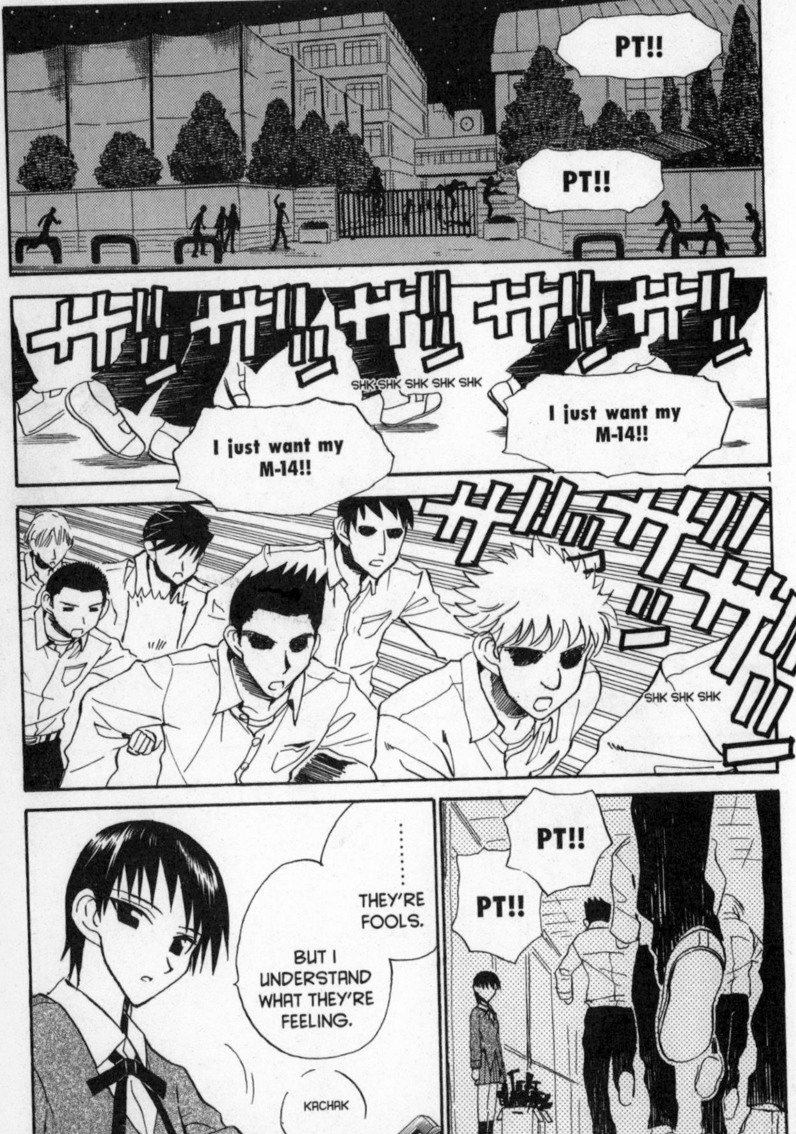
PT!!
PT!!
SHK SHK SHK SHK SHK
I just want my M-14!!
I just want my M-14!!
SHK SHK SHK
PT!!
PT!!
...... THEY'RE FOOLS.
BUT I UNDERSTAND WHAT THEY'RE FEELING.
KACHAK

#103 THE DOGS OF WAR

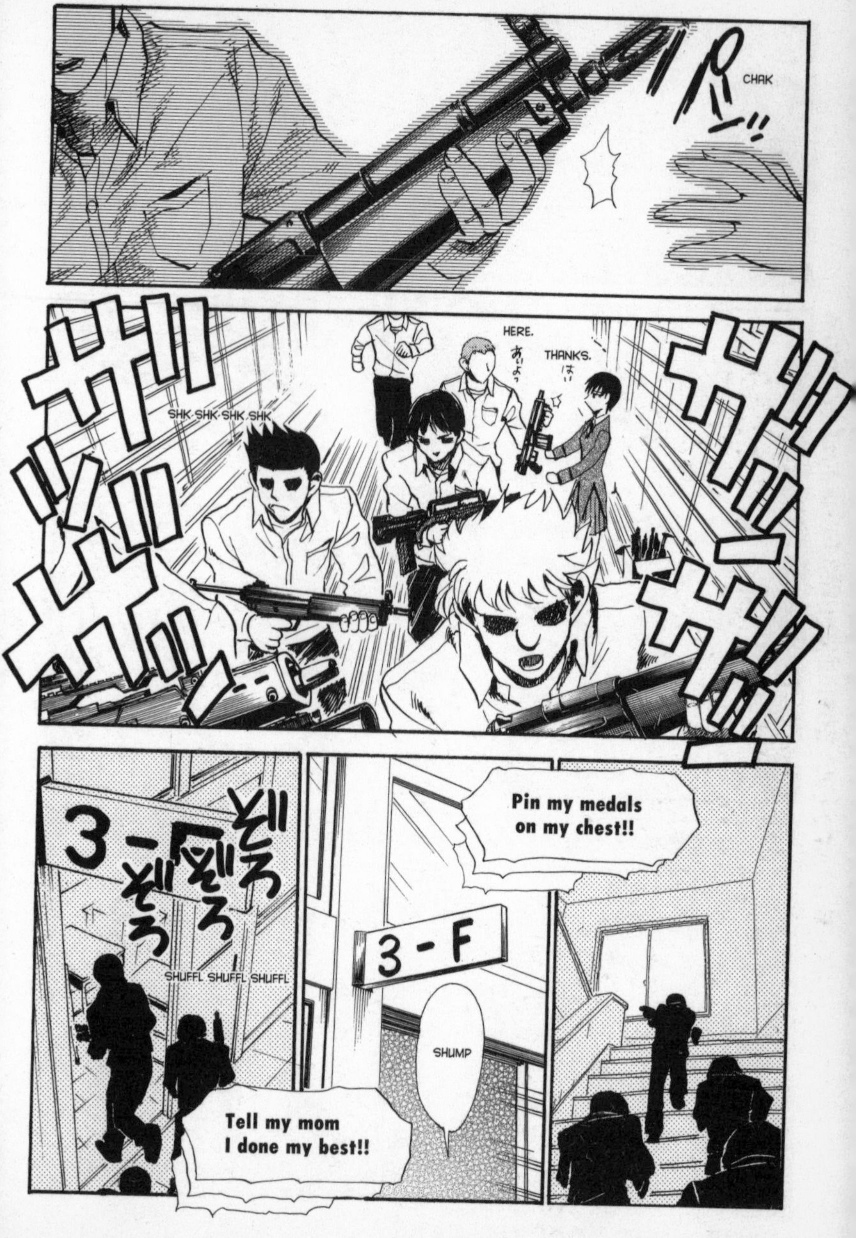
パン!!
CHAK
HERE.
あいよっ
THANKS.
はい
SHK-SHK-SHK-SHK
Pin my medals on my chest!!
3-F
SHUMP
3-F
ぞろぞろぞろぞろ
SHUFFL SHUFFL SHUFFL
Tell my mom I done my best!!

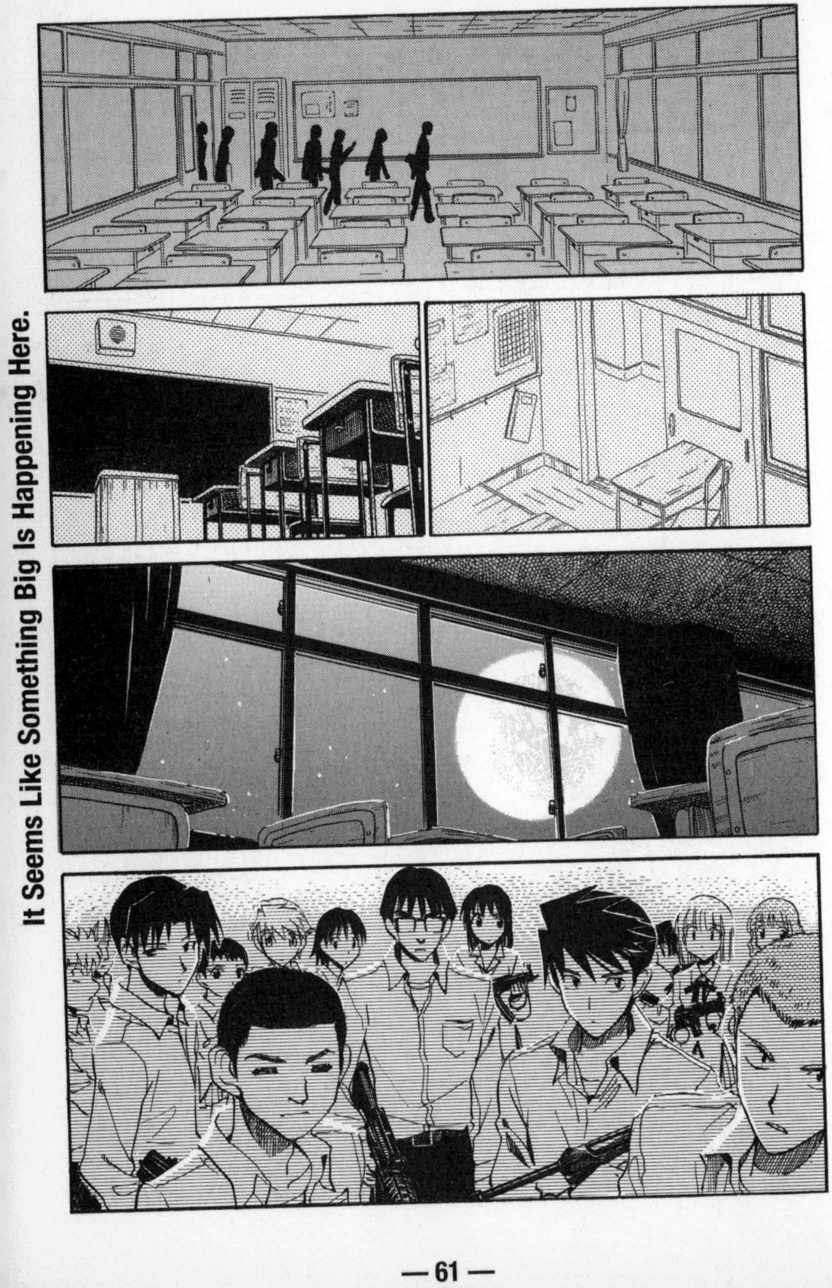

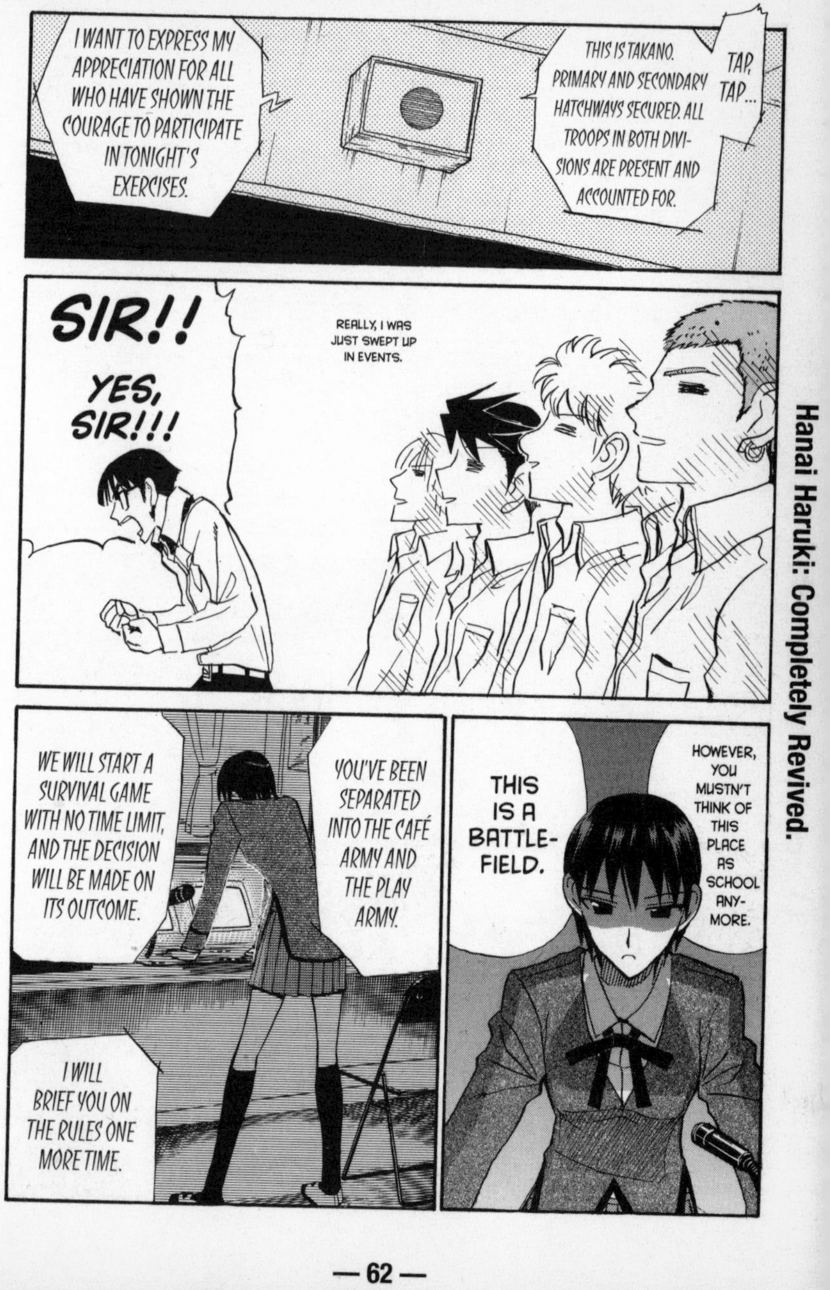

TAP, TAP...
THIS IS TAKANO. PRIMARY AND SECONDARY HATCHWAYS SECURED. ALL TROOPS IN BOTH DIVISIONS ARE PRESENT AND ACCOUNTED FOR.
I WANT TO EXPRESS MY APPRECIATION FOR ALL WHO HAVE SHOWN THE COURAGE TO PARTICIPATE IN TONIGHT'S EXERCISES.
REALLY, I WAS JUST SWEPT UP IN EVENTS.
SIR!!
YES, SIR!!!
HOWEVER, YOU MUSTN'T THINK OF THIS PLACE AS SCHOOL ANYMORE.
THIS IS A BATTLEFIELD.
YOU'VE BEEN SEPARATED INTO THE CAFÉ ARMY AND THE PLAY ARMY.
WE WILL START A SURVIVAL GAME WITH NO TIME LIMIT, AND THE DECISION WILL BE MADE ON ITS OUTCOME.
I WILL BRIEF YOU ON THE RULES ONE MORE TIME.

Hanai Haruki: Completely Revived.

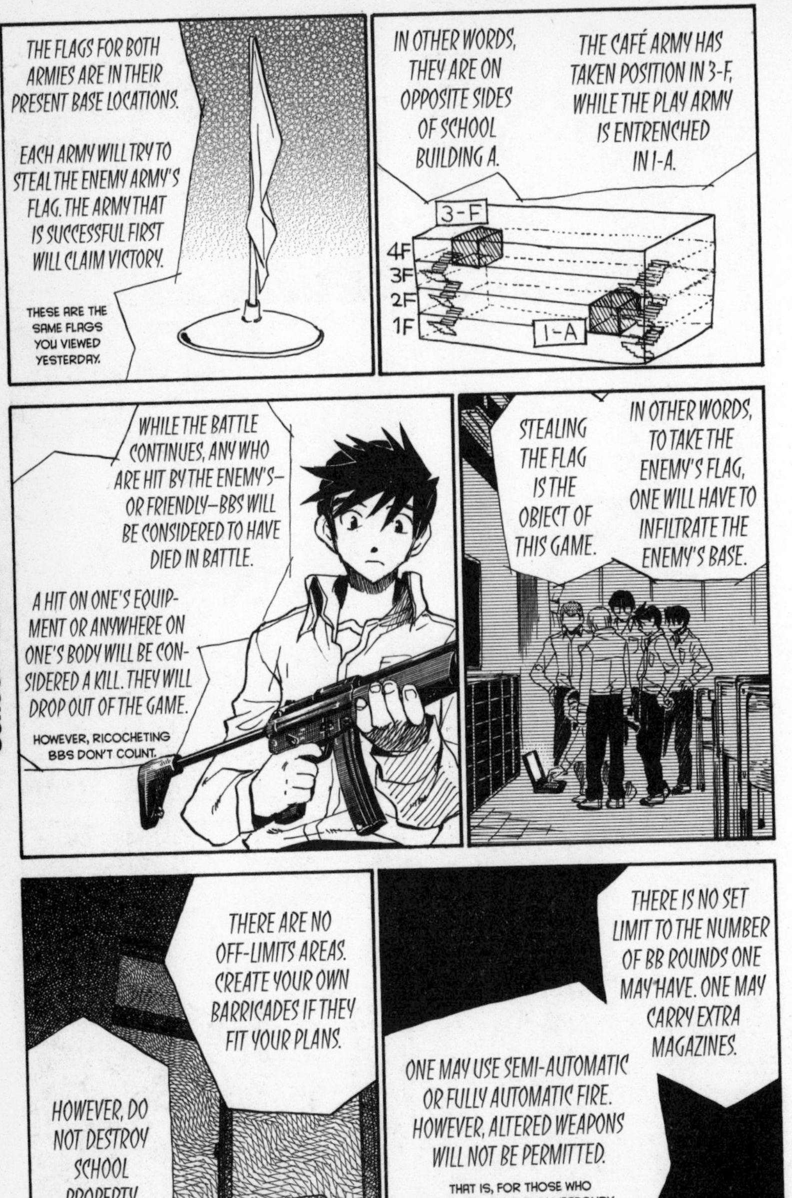
THE CAFÉ ARMY HAS TAKEN POSITION IN 3-F, WHILE THE PLAY ARMY IS ENTRENCHED IN 1-A.
IN OTHER WORDS, THEY ARE ON OPPOSITE SIDES OF SCHOOL BUILDING A.
3-F
4F
3F
2F
1F
1-A
THE FLAGS FOR BOTH ARMIES ARE IN THEIR PRESENT BASE LOCATIONS.
EACH ARMY WILL TRY TO STEAL THE ENEMY ARMY'S FLAG. THE ARMY THAT IS SUCCESSFUL FIRST WILL CLAIM VICTORY.
THESE ARE THE SAME FLAGS YOU VIEWED YESTERDAY.
IN OTHER WORDS, TO TAKE THE ENEMY'S FLAG, ONE WILL HAVE TO INFILTRATE THE ENEMY'S BASE.
STEALING THE FLAG IS THE OBJECT OF THIS GAME.
WHILE THE BATTLE CONTINUES, ANY WHO ARE HIT BY THE ENEMY'S—OR FRIENDLY—BBS WILL BE CONSIDERED TO HAVE DIED IN BATTLE.
A HIT ON ONE'S EQUIPMENT OR ANYWHERE ON ONE'S BODY WILL BE CONSIDERED A KILL. THEY WILL DROP OUT OF THE GAME.
HOWEVER, RICOCHETING BBS DON'T COUNT.
THERE IS NO SET LIMIT TO THE NUMBER OF BB ROUNDS ONE MAY HAVE. ONE MAY CARRY EXTRA MAGAZINES.
ONE MAY USE SEMI-AUTOMATIC OR FULLY AUTOMATIC FIRE. HOWEVER, ALTERED WEAPONS WILL NOT BE PERMITTED.
THAT IS, FOR THOSE WHO BROUGHT THEIR OWN WEAPONRY.
THERE ARE NO OFF-LIMITS AREAS. CREATE YOUR OWN BARRICADES IF THEY FIT YOUR PLANS.
HOWEVER, DO NOT DESTROY SCHOOL PROPERTY.

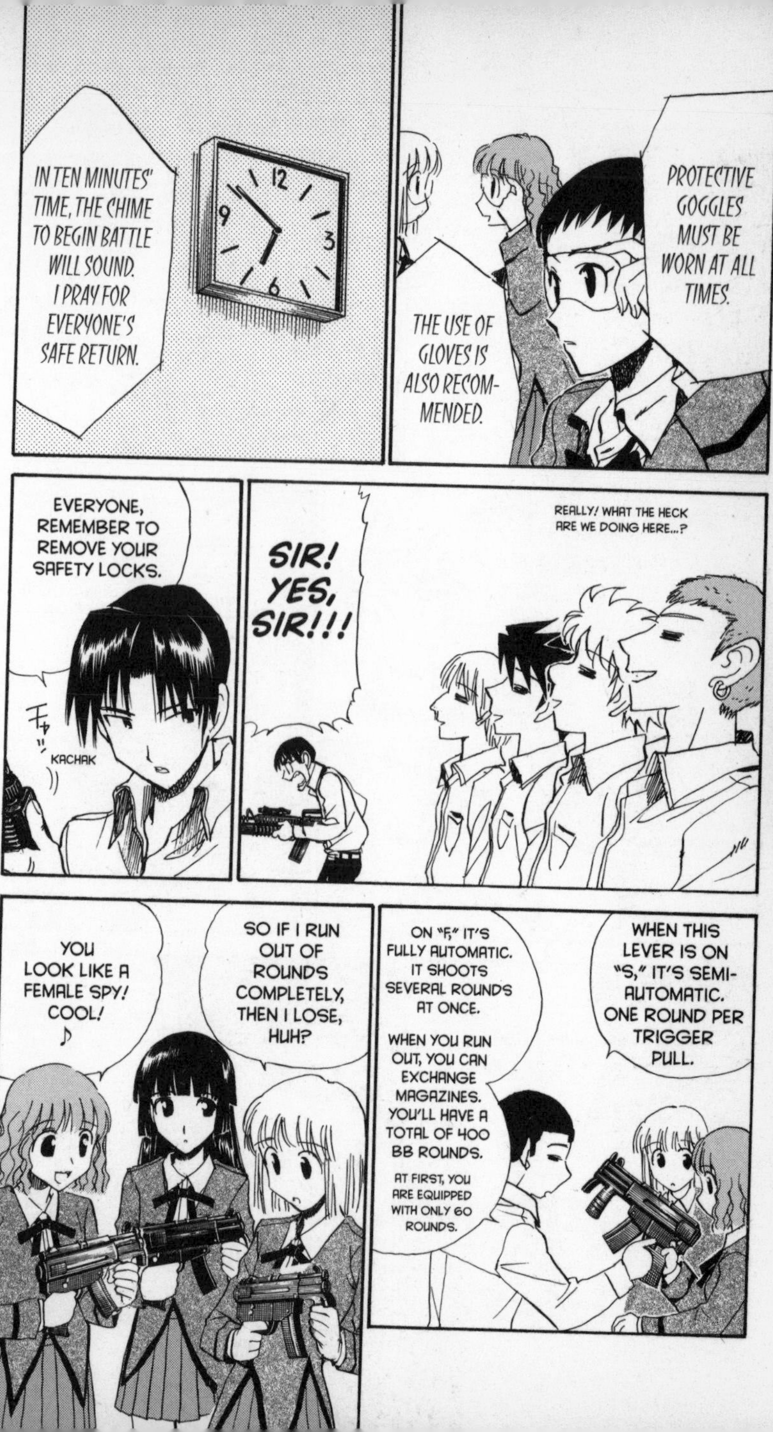
PROTECTIVE GOGGLES MUST BE WORN AT ALL TIMES.
THE USE OF GLOVES IS ALSO RECOM-MENDED.
IN TEN MINUTES' TIME, THE CHIME TO BEGIN BATTLE WILL SOUND. I PRAY FOR EVERYONE'S SAFE RETURN.
REALLY! WHAT THE HECK ARE WE DOING HERE...?
SIR! YES, SIR!!!
EVERYONE, REMEMBER TO REMOVE YOUR SAFETY LOCKS.
KACHAK
WHEN THIS LEVER IS ON "S," IT'S SEMI-AUTOMATIC. ONE ROUND PER TRIGGER PULL.
ON "F," IT'S FULLY AUTOMATIC. IT SHOOTS SEVERAL ROUNDS AT ONCE.
WHEN YOU RUN OUT, YOU CAN EXCHANGE MAGAZINES. YOU'LL HAVE A TOTAL OF 400 BB ROUNDS.
AT FIRST, YOU ARE EQUIPPED WITH ONLY 60 ROUNDS.
SO IF I RUN OUT OF ROUNDS COMPLETELY, THEN I LOSE, HUH?
YOU LOOK LIKE A FEMALE SPY! COOL! ♪

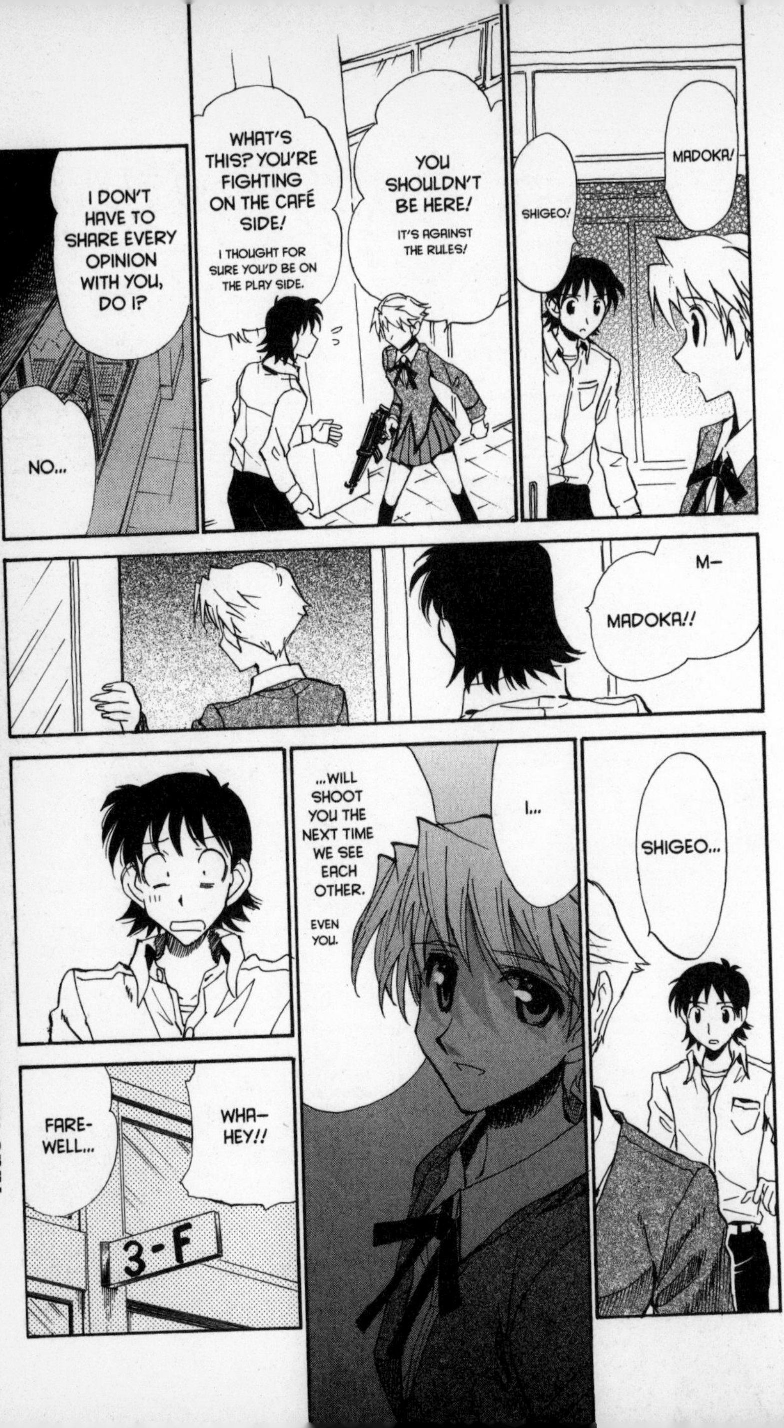
MADOKA!
SHIGEO!
YOU SHOULDN'T BE HERE!
IT'S AGAINST THE RULES!
WHAT'S THIS? YOU'RE FIGHTING ON THE CAFÉ SIDE!
I THOUGHT FOR SURE YOU'D BE ON THE PLAY SIDE.
I DON'T HAVE TO SHARE EVERY OPINION WITH YOU, DO I?
NO...
M— MADOKA!!
SHIGEO...
I...
...WILL SHOOT YOU THE NEXT TIME WE SEE EACH OTHER.
EVEN YOU.
WHA— HEY!!
FARE- WELL...
3-F

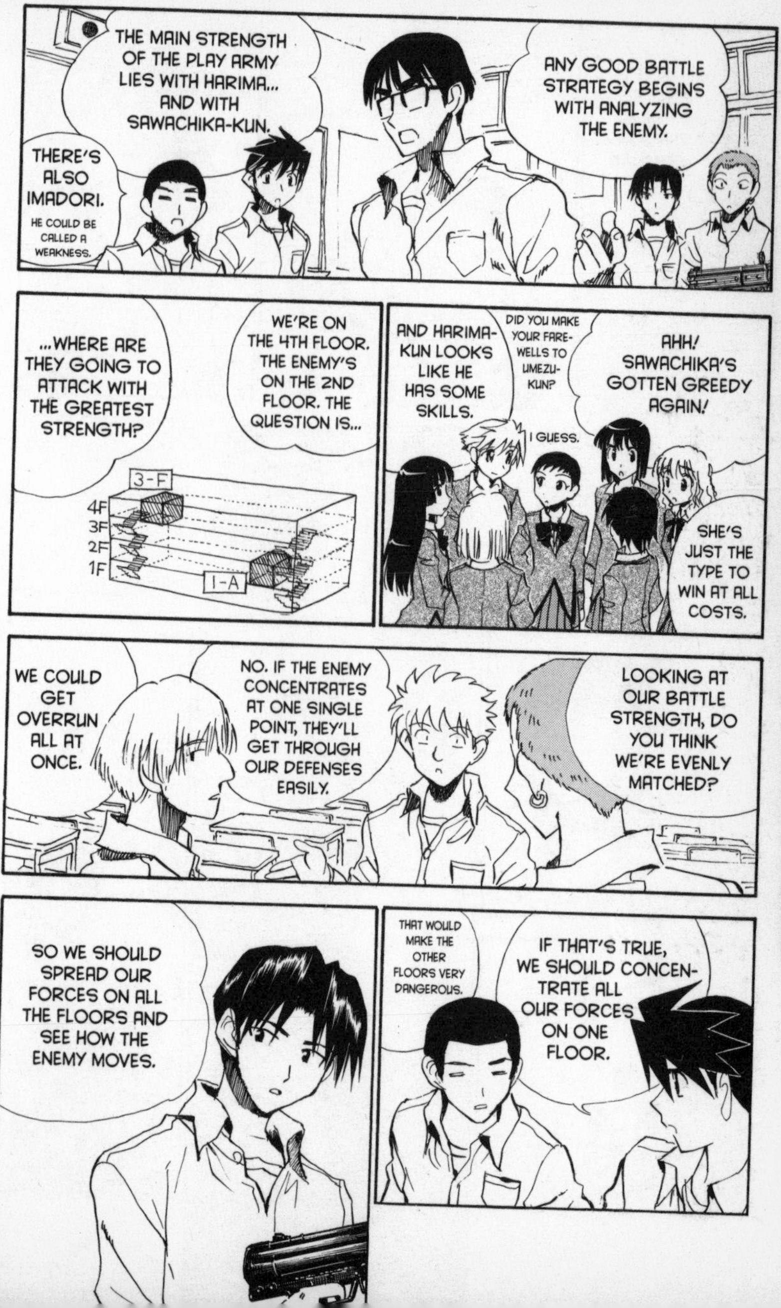
ANY GOOD BATTLE STRATEGY BEGINS WITH ANALYZING THE ENEMY.
THE MAIN STRENGTH OF THE PLAY ARMY LIES WITH HARIMA... AND WITH SAWACHIKA-KUN.
THERE'S ALSO IMADORI.
HE COULD BE CALLED A WEAKNESS.
AHH! SAWACHIKA'S GOTTEN GREEDY AGAIN!
DID YOU MAKE YOUR FAREWELLS TO UMEZU-KUN?
AND HARIMA-KUN LOOKS LIKE HE HAS SOME SKILLS.
I GUESS.
SHE'S JUST THE TYPE TO WIN AT ALL COSTS.
WE'RE ON THE 4TH FLOOR. THE ENEMY'S ON THE 2ND FLOOR. THE QUESTION IS...
...WHERE ARE THEY GOING TO ATTACK WITH THE GREATEST STRENGTH?
3-F
4F
3F
2F
1F
1-A
LOOKING AT OUR BATTLE STRENGTH, DO YOU THINK WE'RE EVENLY MATCHED?
NO. IF THE ENEMY CONCENTRATES AT ONE SINGLE POINT, THEY'LL GET THROUGH OUR DEFENSES EASILY.
WE COULD GET OVERRUN ALL AT ONCE.
IF THAT'S TRUE, WE SHOULD CONCENTRATE ALL OUR FORCES ON ONE FLOOR.
THAT WOULD MAKE THE OTHER FLOORS VERY DANGEROUS.
SO WE SHOULD SPREAD OUR FORCES ON ALL THE FLOORS AND SEE HOW THE ENEMY MOVES.

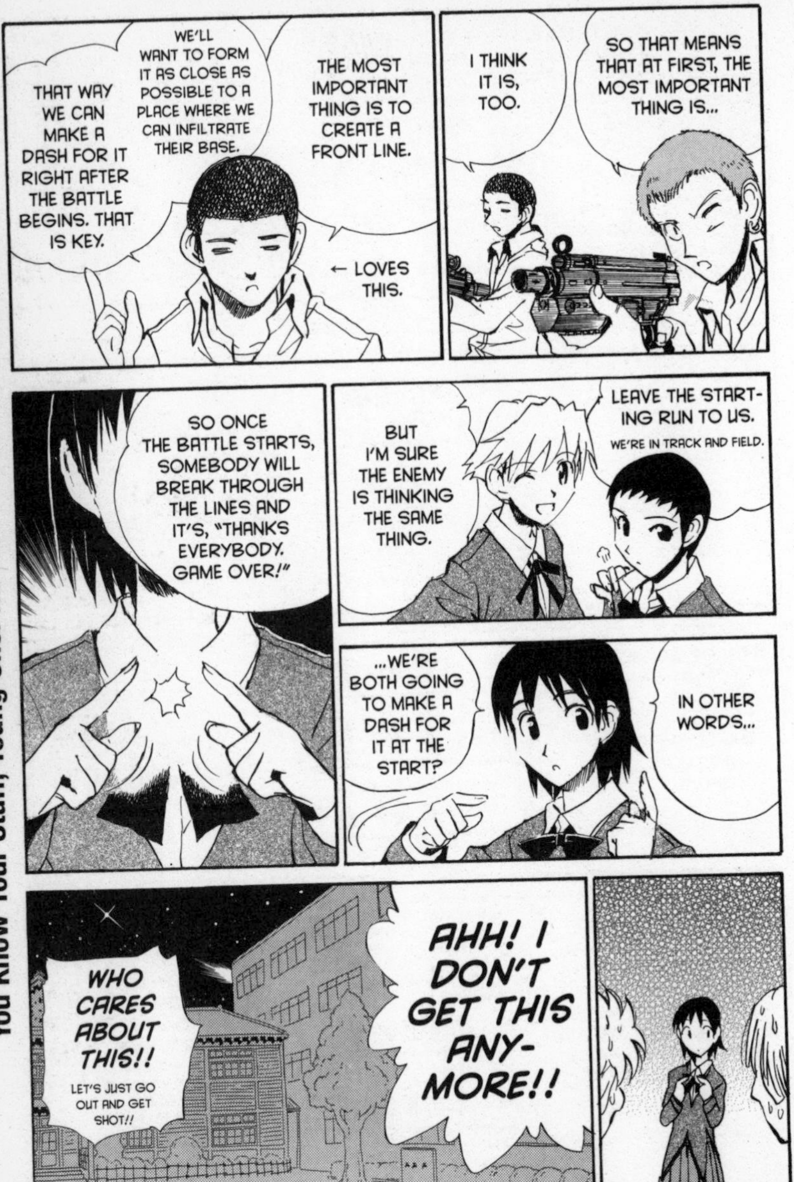
SO THAT MEANS THAT AT FIRST, THE MOST IMPORTANT THING IS...
I THINK IT IS, TOO.
THE MOST IMPORTANT THING IS TO CREATE A FRONT LINE.
WE'LL WANT TO FORM IT AS CLOSE AS POSSIBLE TO A PLACE WHERE WE CAN INFILTRATE THEIR BASE.
THAT WAY WE CAN MAKE A DASH FOR IT RIGHT AFTER THE BATTLE BEGINS. THAT IS KEY.
← LOVES THIS.
LEAVE THE STARTING RUN TO US.
WE'RE IN TRACK AND FIELD.
BUT I'M SURE THE ENEMY IS THINKING THE SAME THING.
IN OTHER WORDS...
...WE'RE BOTH GOING TO MAKE A DASH FOR IT AT THE START?
SO ONCE THE BATTLE STARTS, SOMEBODY WILL BREAK THROUGH THE LINES AND IT'S, "THANKS EVERYBODY. GAME OVER!"
AHH! I DON'T GET THIS ANYMORE!!
WHO CARES ABOUT THIS!!
LET'S JUST GO OUT AND GET SHOT!!

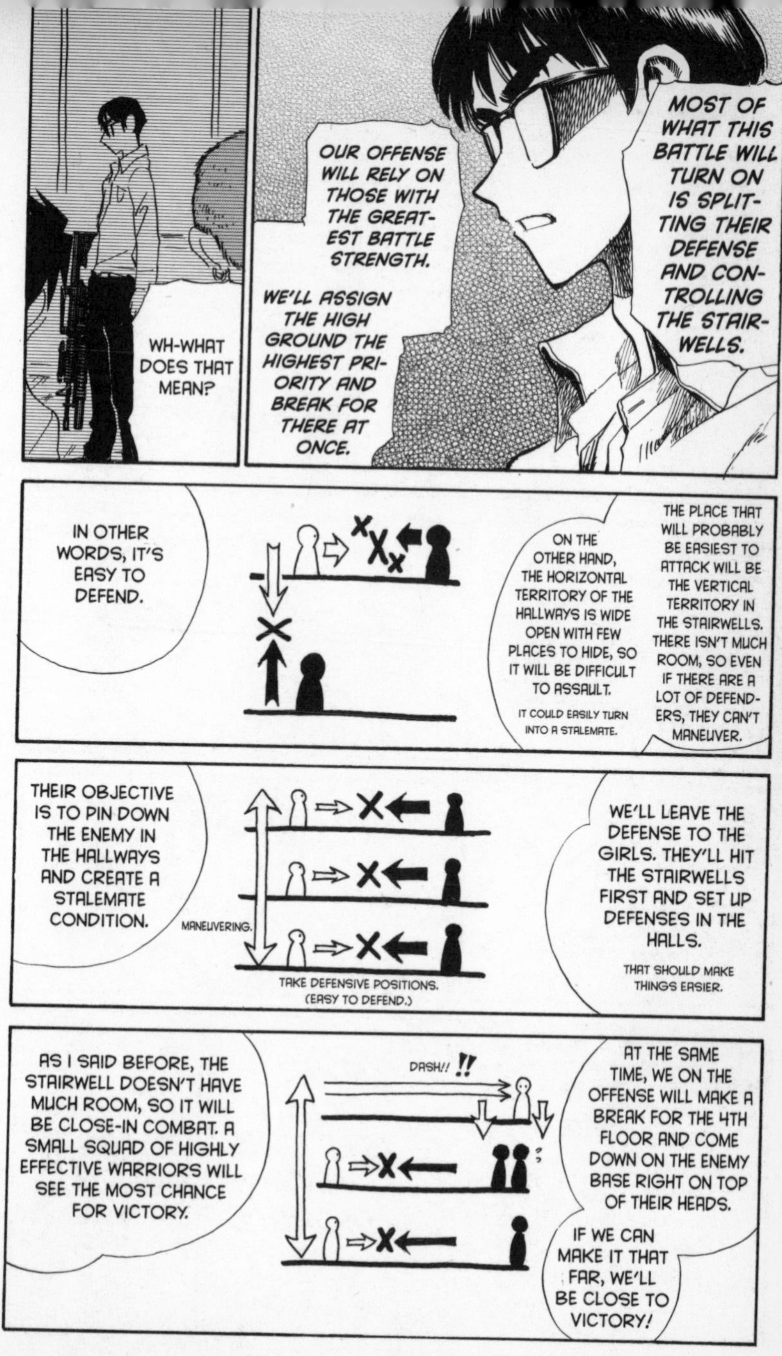

MOST OF WHAT THIS BATTLE WILL TURN ON IS SPLITTING THEIR DEFENSE AND CONTROLLING THE STAIRWELLS.
OUR OFFENSE WILL RELY ON THOSE WITH THE GREATEST BATTLE STRENGTH.
WE'LL ASSIGN THE HIGH GROUND THE HIGHEST PRIORITY AND BREAK FOR THERE AT ONCE.
WH-WHAT DOES THAT MEAN?
THE PLACE THAT WILL PROBABLY BE EASIEST TO ATTACK WILL BE THE VERTICAL TERRITORY IN THE STAIRWELLS. THERE ISN'T MUCH ROOM, SO EVEN IF THERE ARE A LOT OF DEFENDERS, THEY CAN'T MANEUVER.
ON THE OTHER HAND, THE HORIZONTAL TERRITORY OF THE HALLWAYS IS WIDE OPEN WITH FEW PLACES TO HIDE, SO IT WILL BE DIFFICULT TO ASSAULT.
IT COULD EASILY TURN INTO A STALEMATE.
IN OTHER WORDS, IT'S EASY TO DEFEND.
WE'LL LEAVE THE DEFENSE TO THE GIRLS. THEY'LL HIT THE STAIRWELLS FIRST AND SET UP DEFENSES IN THE HALLS.
THAT SHOULD MAKE THINGS EASIER.
THEIR OBJECTIVE IS TO PIN DOWN THE ENEMY IN THE HALLWAYS AND CREATE A STALEMATE CONDITION.
MANEUVERING.
TAKE DEFENSIVE POSITIONS. (EASY TO DEFEND.)
AT THE SAME TIME, WE ON THE OFFENSE WILL MAKE A BREAK FOR THE 4TH FLOOR AND COME DOWN ON THE ENEMY BASE RIGHT ON TOP OF THEIR HEADS.
DASH!! !!
IF WE CAN MAKE IT THAT FAR, WE'LL BE CLOSE TO VICTORY!
AS I SAID BEFORE, THE STAIRWELL DOESN'T HAVE MUCH ROOM, SO IT WILL BE CLOSE-IN COMBAT. A SMALL SQUAD OF HIGHLY EFFECTIVE WARRIORS WILL SEE THE MOST CHANCE FOR VICTORY.

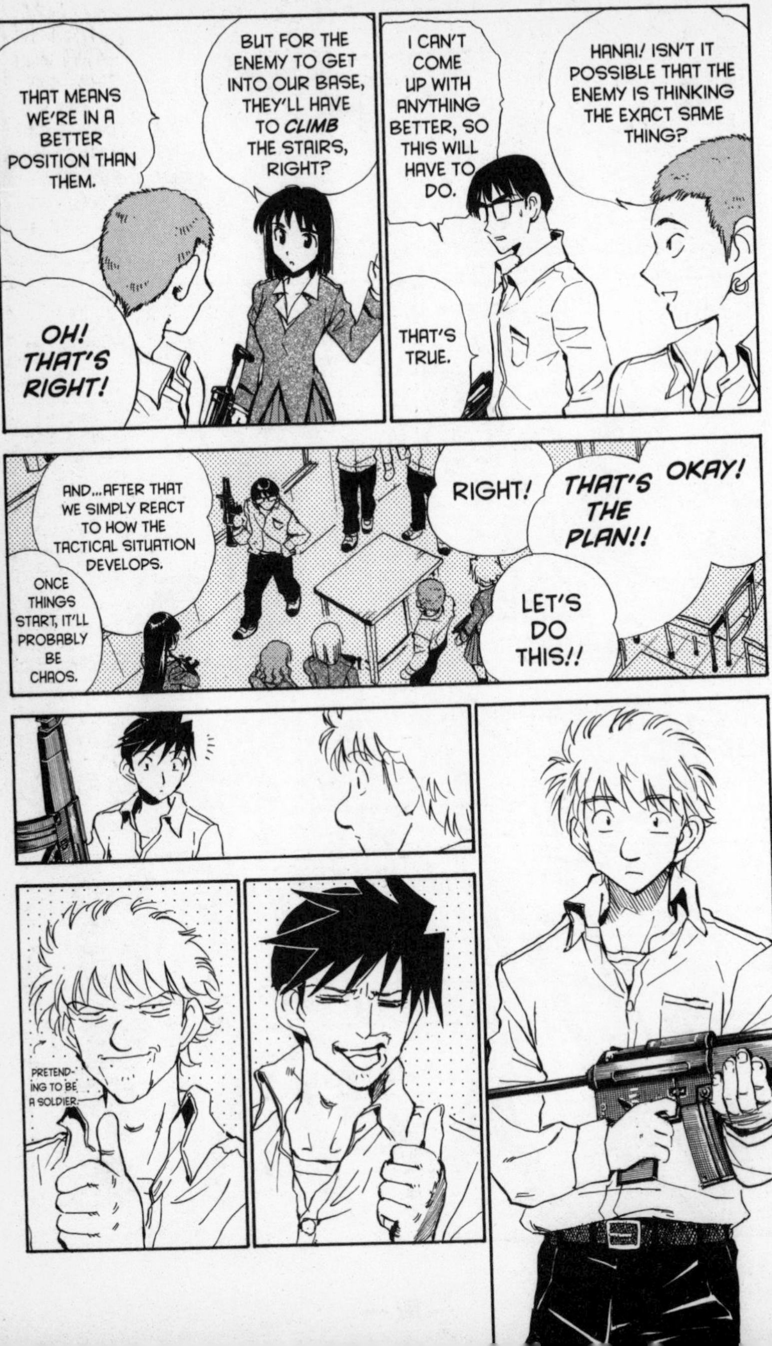
HANAI! ISN'T IT POSSIBLE THAT THE ENEMY IS THINKING THE EXACT SAME THING?
I CAN'T COME UP WITH ANYTHING BETTER, SO THIS WILL HAVE TO DO.
THAT'S TRUE.
BUT FOR THE ENEMY TO GET INTO OUR BASE, THEY'LL HAVE TO *CLIMB* THE STAIRS, RIGHT?
THAT MEANS WE'RE IN A BETTER POSITION THAN THEM.
OH! THAT'S RIGHT!
OKAY!
THAT'S THE PLAN!!
RIGHT!
LET'S DO THIS!!
AND...AFTER THAT WE SIMPLY REACT TO HOW THE TACTICAL SITUATION DEVELOPS.
ONCE THINGS START, IT'LL PROBABLY BE CHAOS.
PRETENDING TO BE A SOLDIER.

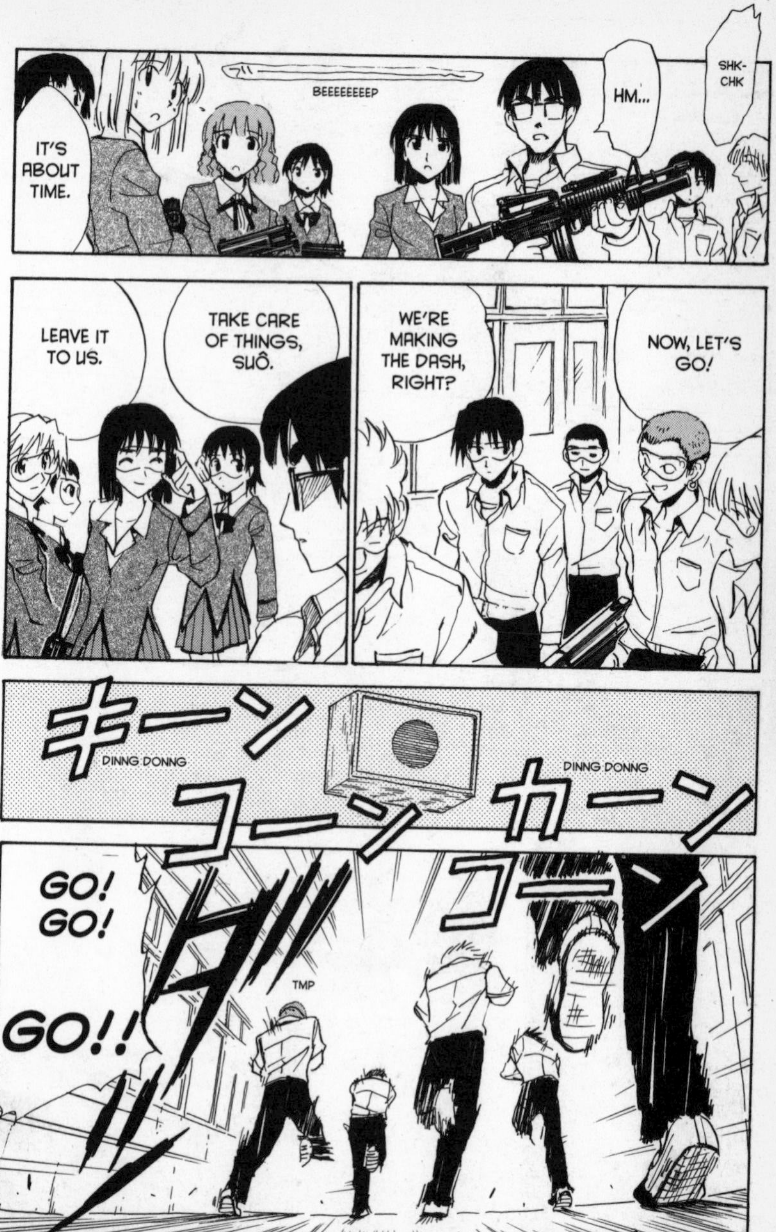
SHK-CHK
HM...
BEEEEEEEEP
IT'S ABOUT TIME.
NOW, LET'S GO!
WE'RE MAKING THE DASH, RIGHT?
TAKE CARE OF THINGS, SUÔ.
LEAVE IT TO US.
キーン
DINNG DONNG
コーン
カーン
DINNG DONNG
コーン
GO! GO!
GO!!
TMP

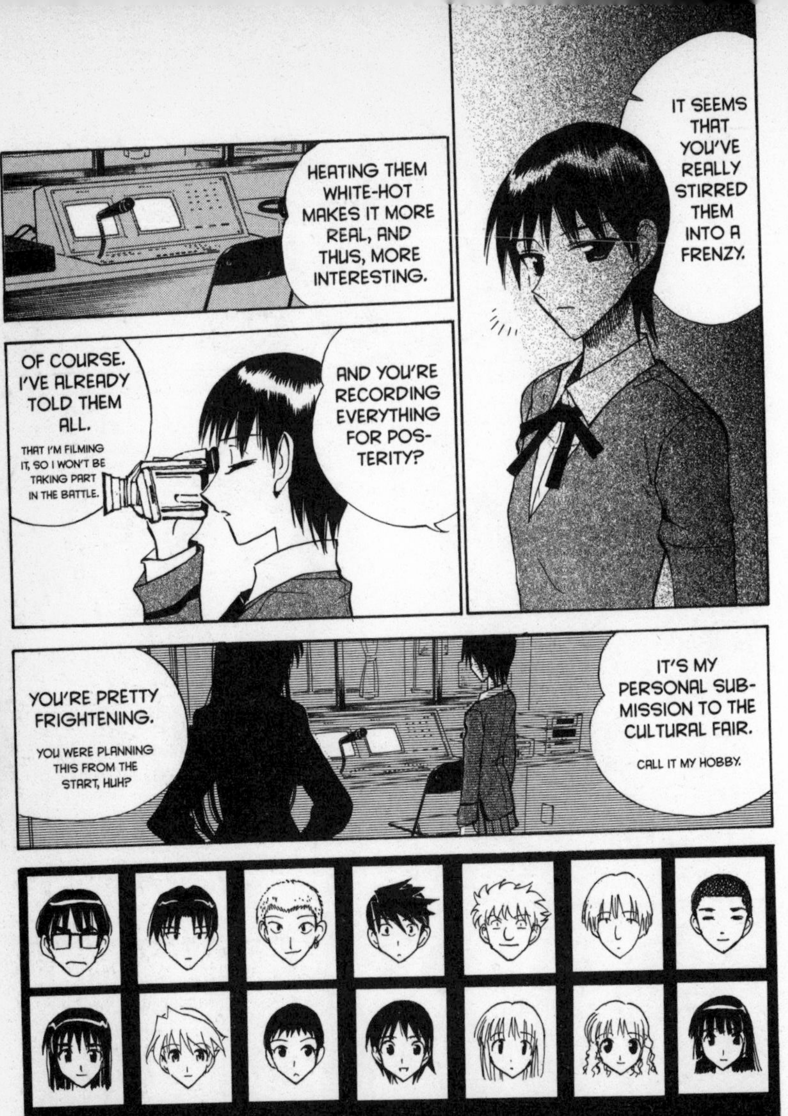
IT SEEMS THAT YOU'VE REALLY STIRRED THEM INTO A FRENZY.
HEATING THEM WHITE-HOT MAKES IT MORE REAL, AND THUS, MORE INTERESTING.
AND YOU'RE RECORDING EVERYTHING FOR POS-TERITY?
OF COURSE. I'VE ALREADY TOLD THEM ALL.
THAT I'M FILMING IT, SO I WON'T BE TAKING PART IN THE BATTLE.
IT'S MY PERSONAL SUB-MISSION TO THE CULTURAL FAIR.
CALL IT MY HOBBY.
YOU'RE PRETTY FRIGHTENING.
YOU WERE PLANNING THIS FROM THE START, HUH?
There are fourteen members of the Café Army! Who will survive? And... who comprises the Play Army?

103 ....Fin

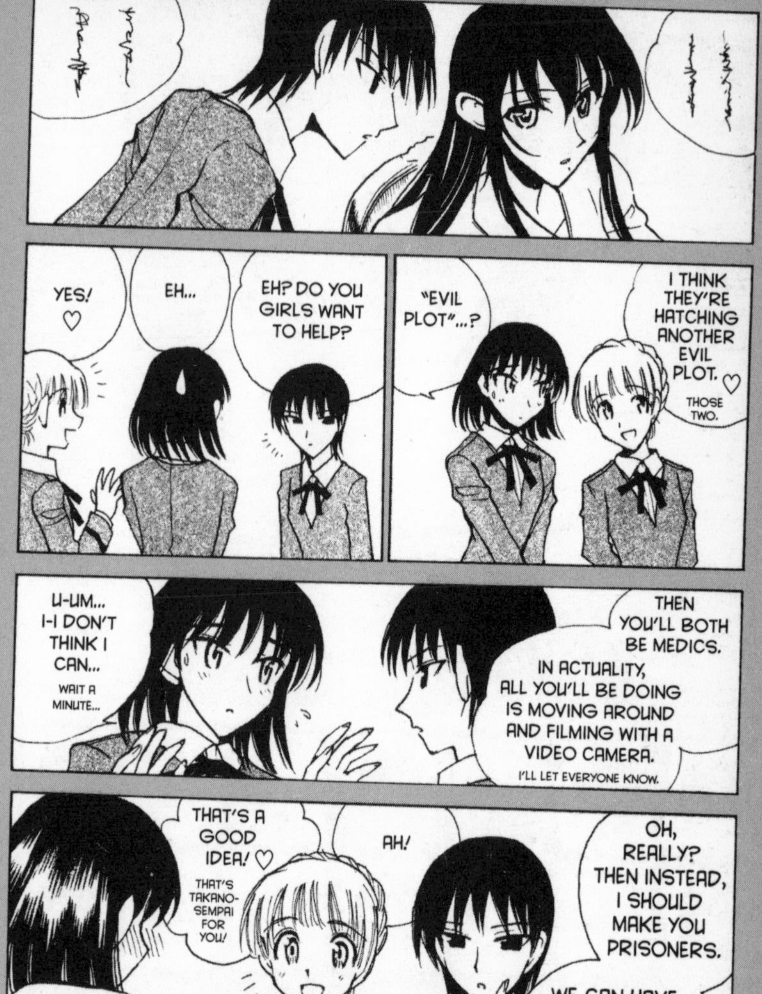
I THINK THEY'RE HATCHING ANOTHER EVIL PLOT. ♡
THOSE TWO.
"EVIL PLOT"...?
EH? DO YOU GIRLS WANT TO HELP?
EH...
YES! ♡
THEN YOU'LL BOTH BE MEDICS.
IN ACTUALITY, ALL YOU'LL BE DOING IS MOVING AROUND AND FILMING WITH A VIDEO CAMERA.
I'LL LET EVERYONE KNOW.
U-UM... I-I DON'T THINK I CAN...
WAIT A MINUTE...
OH, REALLY? THEN INSTEAD, I SHOULD MAKE YOU PRISONERS.
AH!
THAT'S A GOOD IDEA! ♡
THAT'S TAKANO-SEMPAI FOR YOU!
WE CAN HAVE THE ARMIES RESCUE YOU INSTEAD OF CAPTURING THE FLAG...
UM... I'D RATHER BE A MEDIC.

Original Bonus Manga Number 2

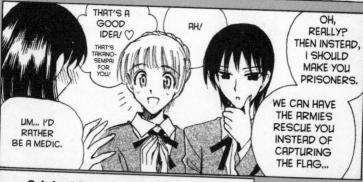

#104 THE ULTIMATE THRILL

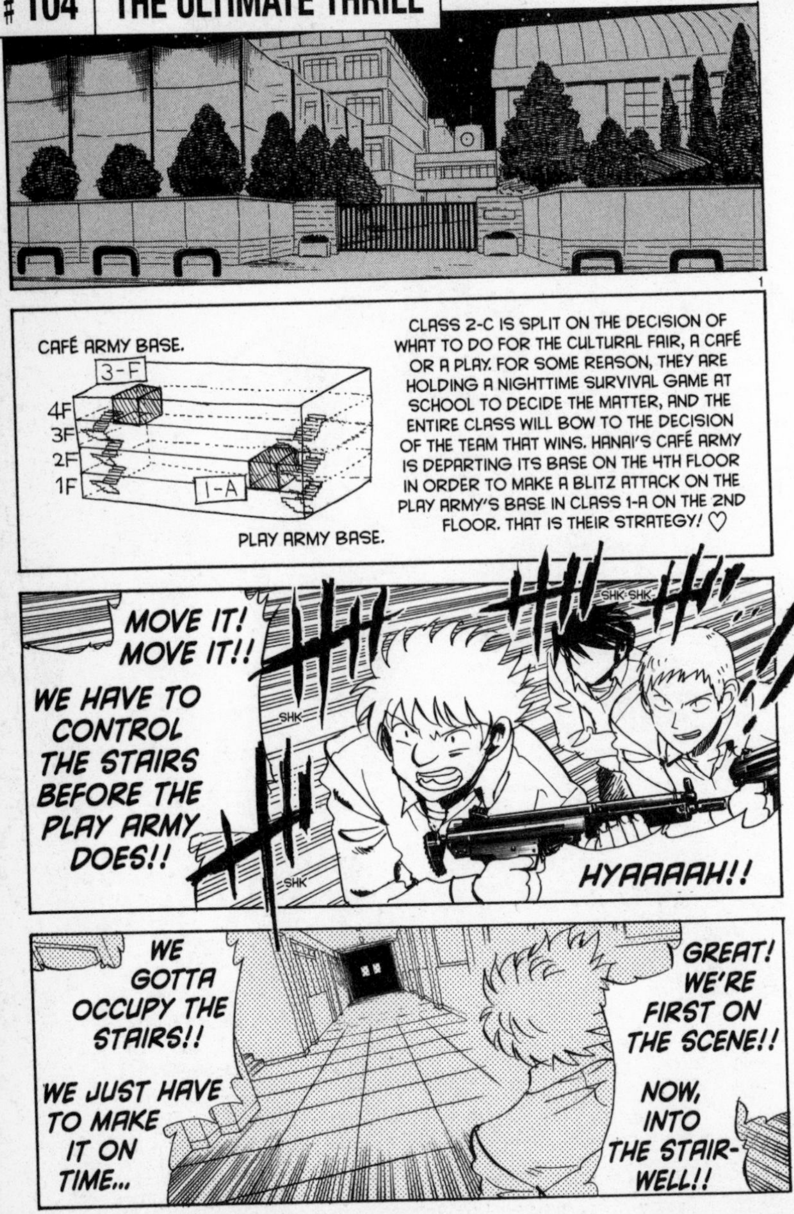

CLASS 2-C IS SPLIT ON THE DECISION OF WHAT TO DO FOR THE CULTURAL FAIR, A CAFÉ OR A PLAY. FOR SOME REASON, THEY ARE HOLDING A NIGHTTIME SURVIVAL GAME AT SCHOOL TO DECIDE THE MATTER, AND THE ENTIRE CLASS WILL BOW TO THE DECISION OF THE TEAM THAT WINS. HANAI'S CAFÉ ARMY IS DEPARTING ITS BASE ON THE 4TH FLOOR IN ORDER TO MAKE A BLITZ ATTACK ON THE PLAY ARMY'S BASE IN CLASS 1-A ON THE 2ND FLOOR. THAT IS THEIR STRATEGY! ♡
CAFÉ ARMY BASE.
3-F
4F
3F
2F
1F
1-A
PLAY ARMY BASE.
SHK SHK
MOVE IT! MOVE IT!!
WE HAVE TO CONTROL THE STAIRS BEFORE THE PLAY ARMY DOES!!
SHK
SHK
HYAAAAH!!
GREAT! WE'RE FIRST ON THE SCENE!!
NOW, INTO THE STAIR-WELL!!
WE GOTTA OCCUPY THE STAIRS!!
WE JUST HAVE TO MAKE IT ON TIME...

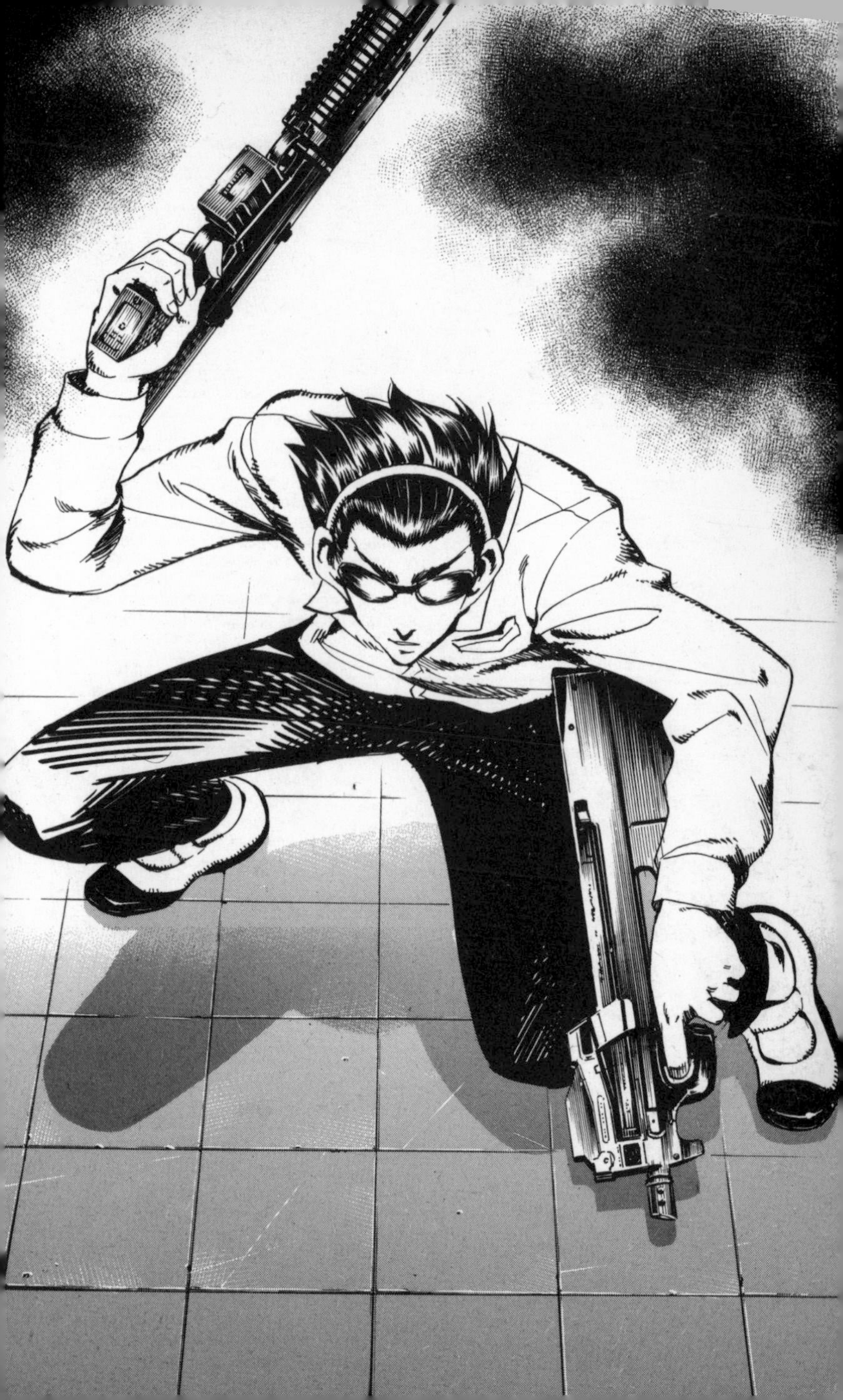

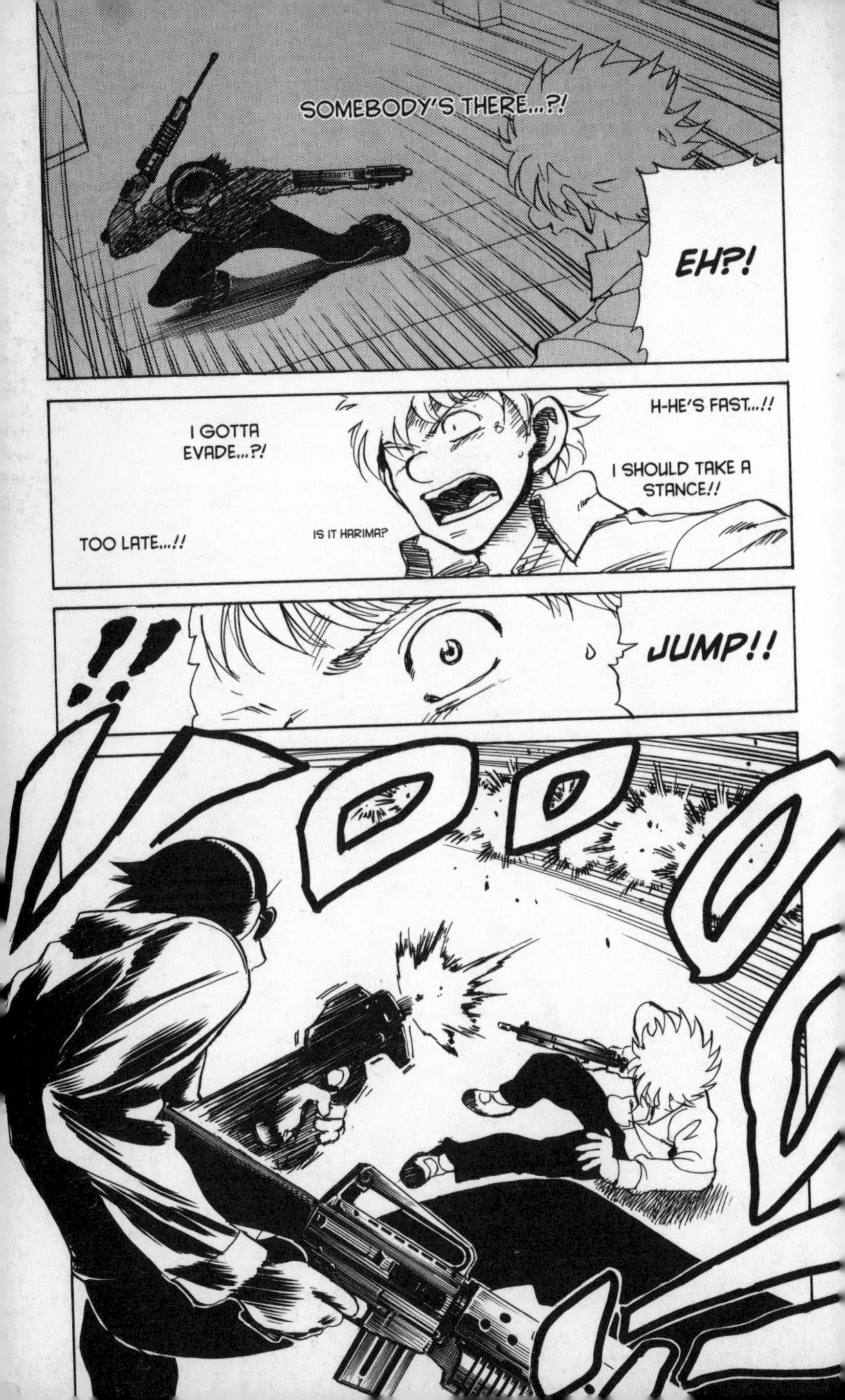

SOMEBODY'S THERE...?!
EH?!
H-HE'S FAST...!!
I SHOULD TAKE A STANCE!!
I GOTTA EVADE...?!
IS IT HARIMA?
TOO LATE...!!
JUMP!!
!!

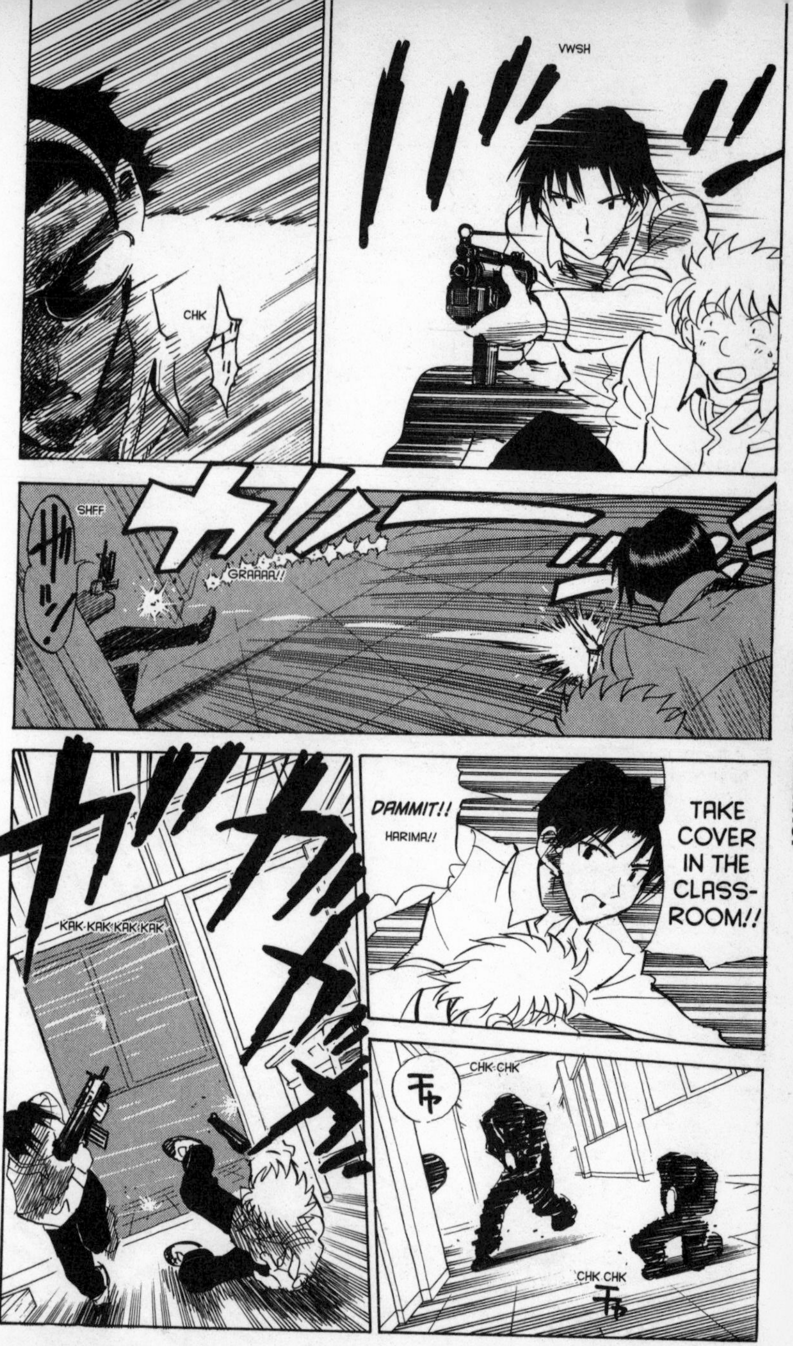
VWSH
CHK
GRAAAA!!
SHFF
TAKE COVER IN THE CLASS-ROOM!!
DAMMIT!!
HARIMA!!
CHK CHK
CHK CHK
KAK KAK KAK KAK

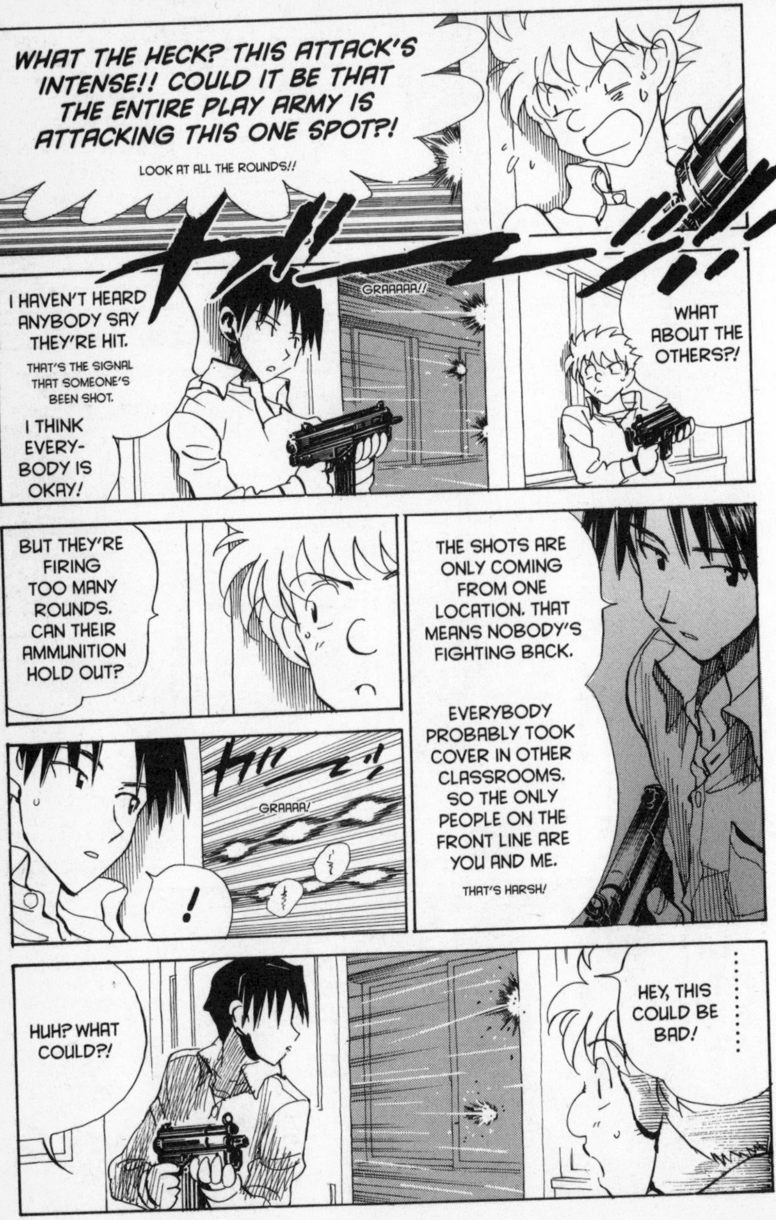
WHAT THE HECK? THIS ATTACK'S INTENSE!! COULD IT BE THAT THE ENTIRE PLAY ARMY IS ATTACKING THIS ONE SPOT?!
LOOK AT ALL THE ROUNDS!!
WHAT ABOUT THE OTHERS?!
GRAAAAA!!
I HAVEN'T HEARD ANYBODY SAY THEY'RE HIT.
THAT'S THE SIGNAL THAT SOMEONE'S BEEN SHOT.
I THINK EVERY-BODY IS OKAY!
THE SHOTS ARE ONLY COMING FROM ONE LOCATION. THAT MEANS NOBODY'S FIGHTING BACK.
EVERYBODY PROBABLY TOOK COVER IN OTHER CLASSROOMS. SO THE ONLY PEOPLE ON THE FRONT LINE ARE YOU AND ME.
THAT'S HARSH!
BUT THEY'RE FIRING TOO MANY ROUNDS. CAN THEIR AMMUNITION HOLD OUT?
GRAAAA!
!
......
HEY, THIS COULD BE BAD!
HUH? WHAT COULD?!

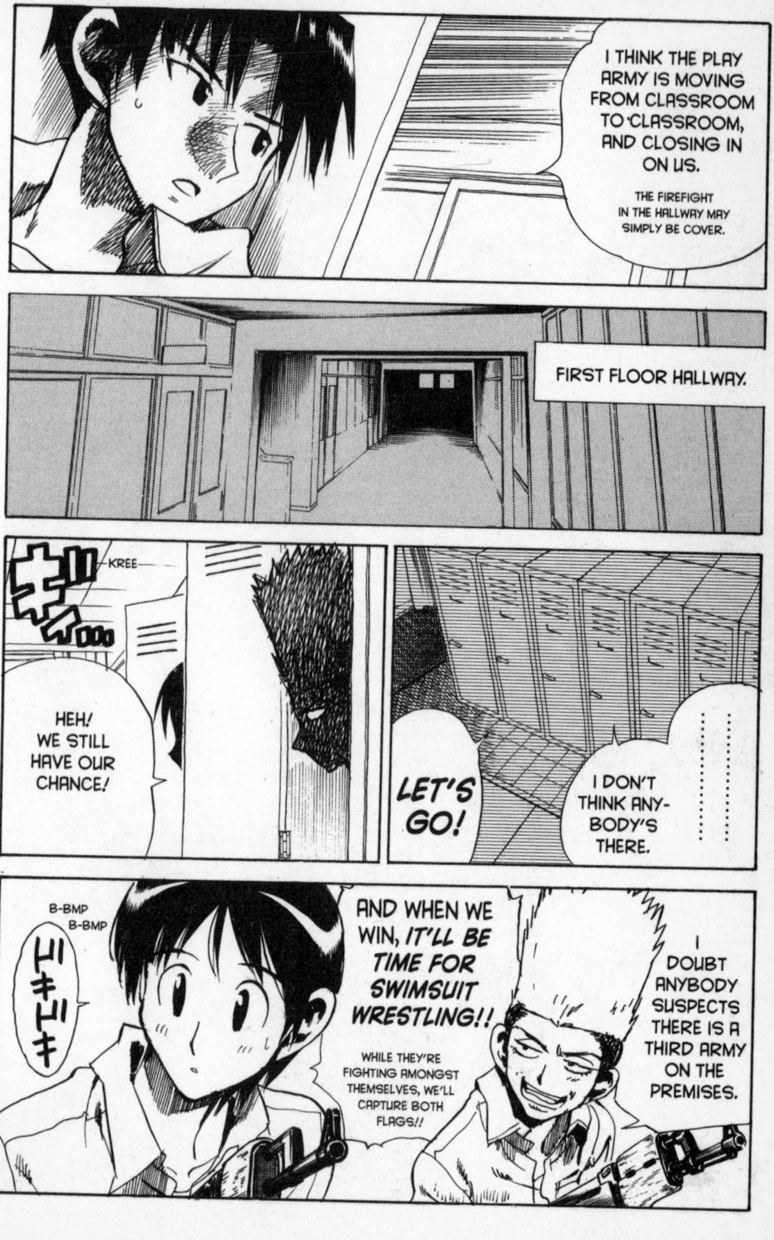
I THINK THE PLAY ARMY IS MOVING FROM CLASSROOM TO CLASSROOM, AND CLOSING IN ON US.
THE FIREFIGHT IN THE HALLWAY MAY SIMPLY BE COVER.
FIRST FLOOR HALLWAY.
......
I DON'T THINK ANYBODY'S THERE.
LET'S GO!
KREE
HEH! WE STILL HAVE OUR CHANCE!
I DOUBT ANYBODY SUSPECTS THERE IS A THIRD ARMY ON THE PREMISES.
AND WHEN WE WIN, *IT'LL BE TIME FOR SWIMSUIT WRESTLING!!*
WHILE THEY'RE FIGHTING AMONGST THEMSELVES, WE'LL CAPTURE BOTH FLAGS!!
B-BMP
B-BMP

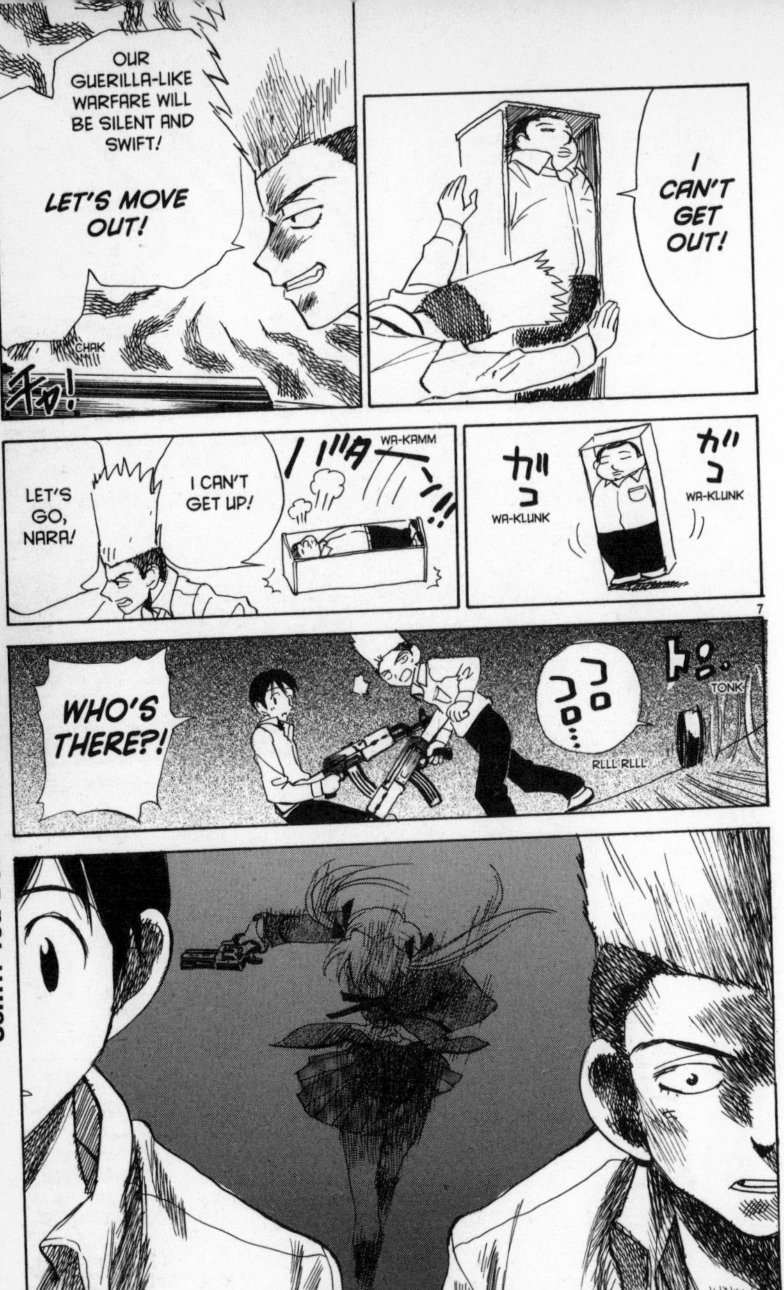
I CAN'T GET OUT!
OUR GUERILLA-LIKE WARFARE WILL BE SILENT AND SWIFT!
LET'S MOVE OUT!
チャ!
CHAK
ガッ
WA-KLUNK
ガッ
WA-KLUNK
バタン!!
WA-KAMM
I CAN'T GET UP!
LET'S GO, NARA!
トン
TONK
コロコロ...
RLLL RLLL
WHO'S THERE?!

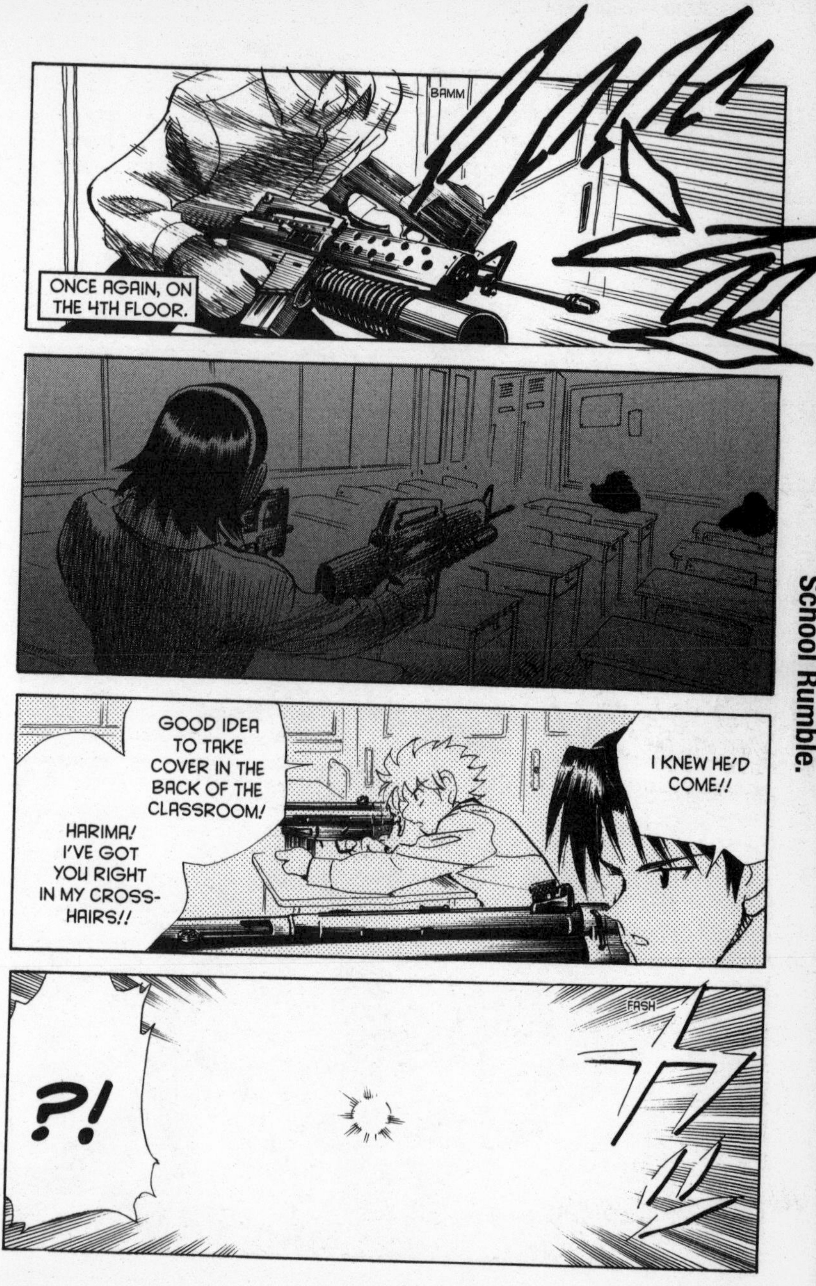
BAMM
ONCE AGAIN, ON THE 4TH FLOOR.
I KNEW HE'D COME!!
GOOD IDEA TO TAKE COVER IN THE BACK OF THE CLASSROOM!
HARIMA! I'VE GOT YOU RIGHT IN MY CROSS-HAIRS!!
FASH
?!

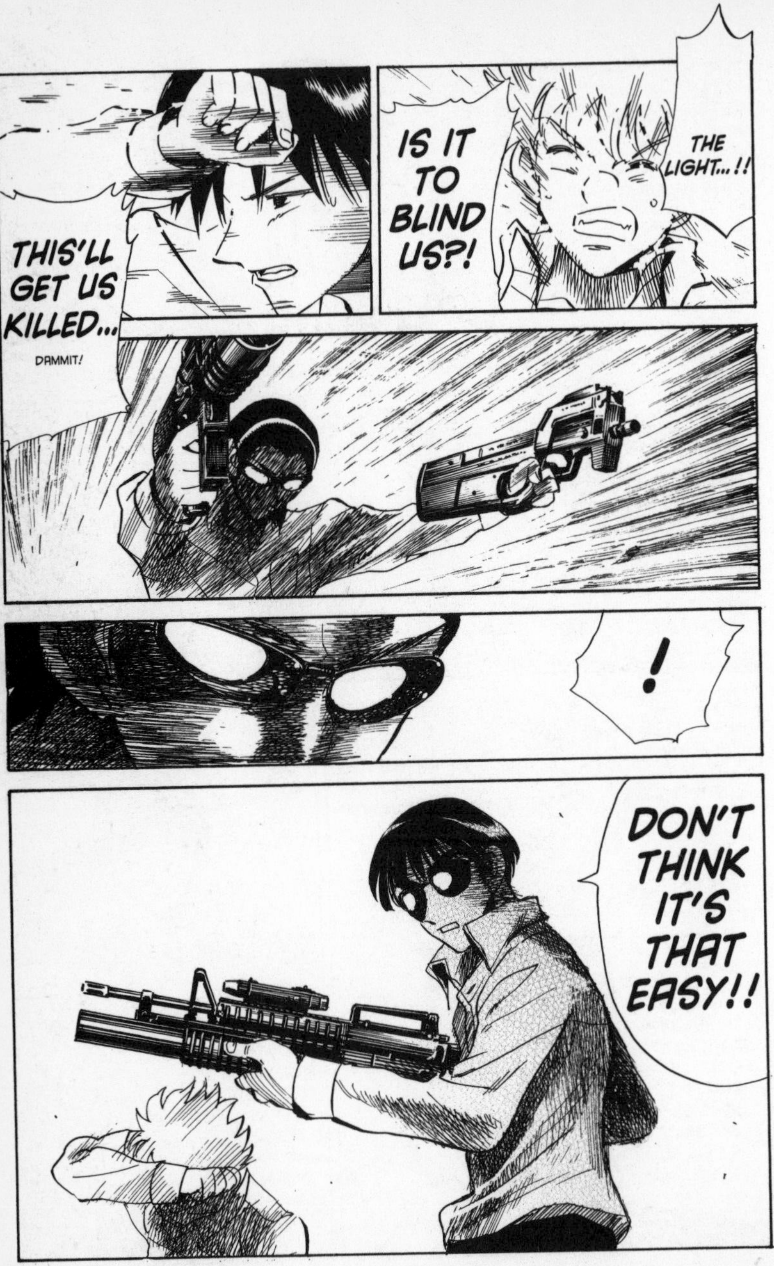
THE LIGHT...!!
IS IT TO BLIND US?!
THIS'LL GET US KILLED...
DAMMIT!
!
DON'T THINK IT'S THAT EASY!!

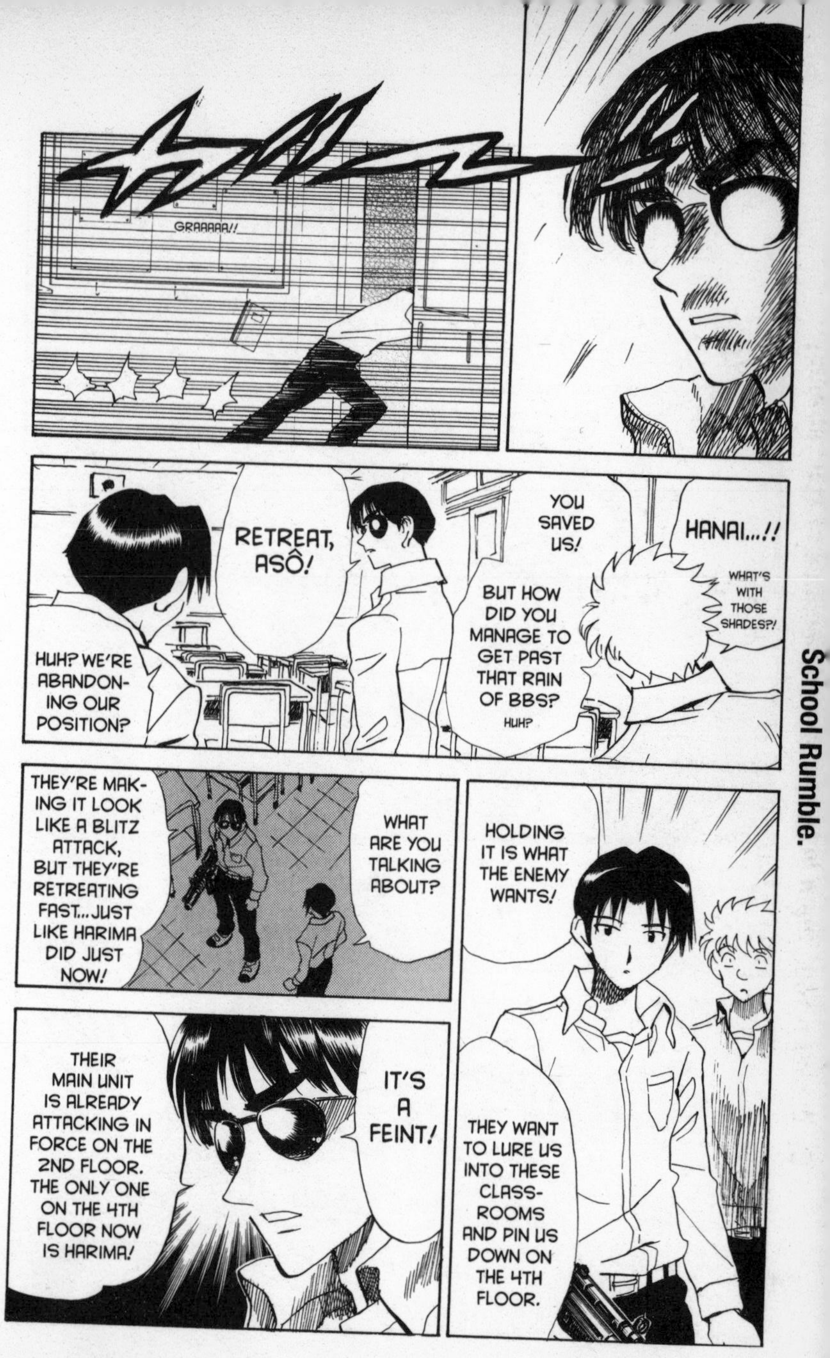
GRAAAAA!!
HANAI...!!
WHAT'S WITH THOSE SHADES?!
YOU SAVED US!
BUT HOW DID YOU MANAGE TO GET PAST THAT RAIN OF BBS?
HUH?
RETREAT, ASÔ!
HUH? WE'RE ABANDONING OUR POSITION?
HOLDING IT IS WHAT THE ENEMY WANTS!
THEY WANT TO LURE US INTO THESE CLASSROOMS AND PIN US DOWN ON THE 4TH FLOOR.
WHAT ARE YOU TALKING ABOUT?
THEY'RE MAKING IT LOOK LIKE A BLITZ ATTACK, BUT THEY'RE RETREATING FAST...JUST LIKE HARIMA DID JUST NOW!
IT'S A FEINT!
THEIR MAIN UNIT IS ALREADY ATTACKING IN FORCE ON THE 2ND FLOOR. THE ONLY ONE ON THE 4TH FLOOR NOW IS HARIMA!

By the Way, Your Team Is Outnumbered Because of Your Strategy!

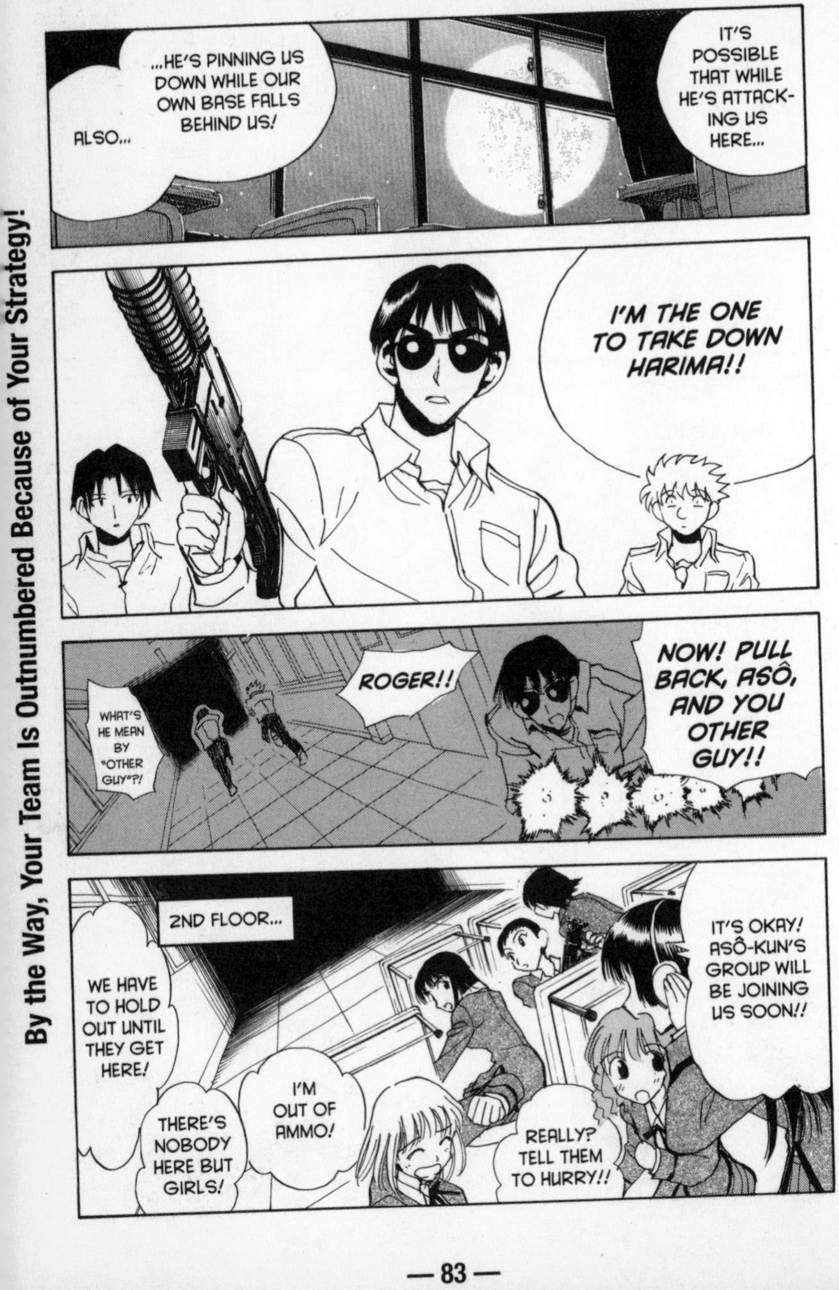
IT'S POSSIBLE THAT WHILE HE'S ATTACKING US HERE...
...HE'S PINNING US DOWN WHILE OUR OWN BASE FALLS BEHIND US!
ALSO...
I'M THE ONE TO TAKE DOWN HARIMA!!
NOW! PULL BACK, ASÔ, AND YOU OTHER GUY!!
ROGER!!
WHAT'S HE MEAN BY "OTHER GUY"?!
2ND FLOOR...
IT'S OKAY! ASÔ-KUN'S GROUP WILL BE JOINING US SOON!!
REALLY? TELL THEM TO HURRY!!
WE HAVE TO HOLD OUT UNTIL THEY GET HERE!
I'M OUT OF AMMO!
THERE'S NOBODY HERE BUT GIRLS!

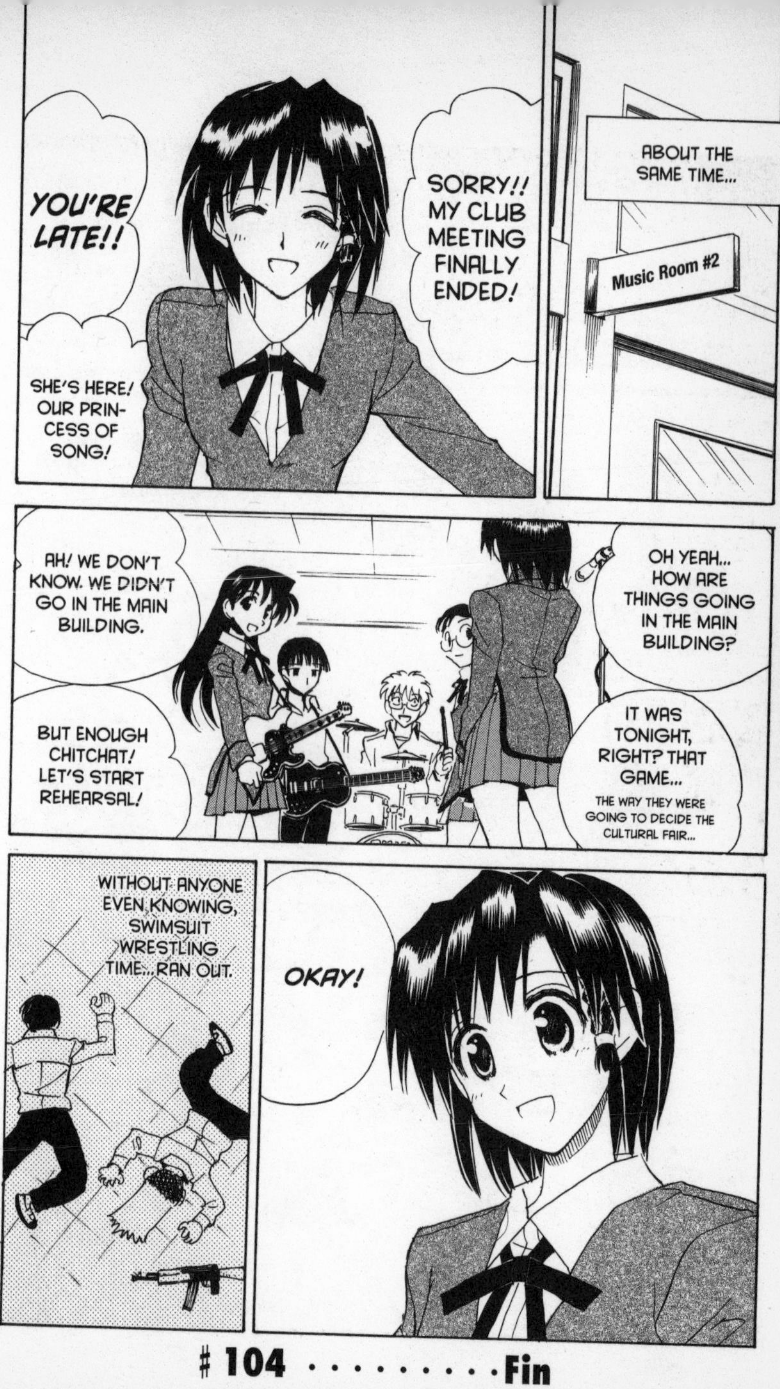
ABOUT THE SAME TIME...
Music Room #2
SORRY!! MY CLUB MEETING FINALLY ENDED!
YOU'RE LATE!!
SHE'S HERE! OUR PRIN- CESS OF SONG!
OH YEAH... HOW ARE THINGS GOING IN THE MAIN BUILDING?
AH! WE DON'T KNOW. WE DIDN'T GO IN THE MAIN BUILDING.
IT WAS TONIGHT, RIGHT? THAT GAME...
THE WAY THEY WERE GOING TO DECIDE THE CULTURAL FAIR...
BUT ENOUGH CHITCHAT! LET'S START REHEARSAL!
OKAY!
WITHOUT ANYONE EVEN KNOWING, SWIMSUIT WRESTLING TIME...RAN OUT.

 # 104 . . . . Fin

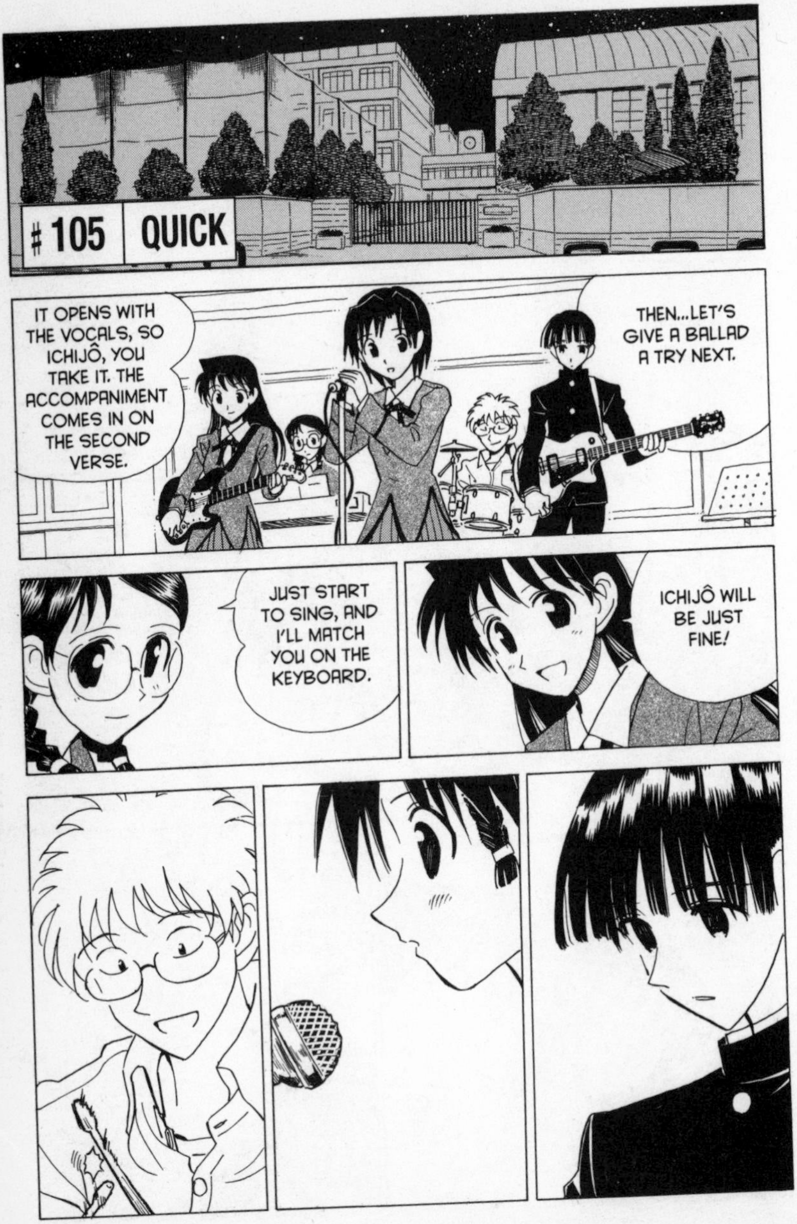
#105 QUICK
THEN...LET'S GIVE A BALLAD A TRY NEXT.
IT OPENS WITH THE VOCALS, SO ICHIJÔ, YOU TAKE IT. THE ACCOMPANIMENT COMES IN ON THE SECOND VERSE.
ICHIJÔ WILL BE JUST FINE!
JUST START TO SING, AND I'LL MATCH YOU ON THE KEYBOARD.

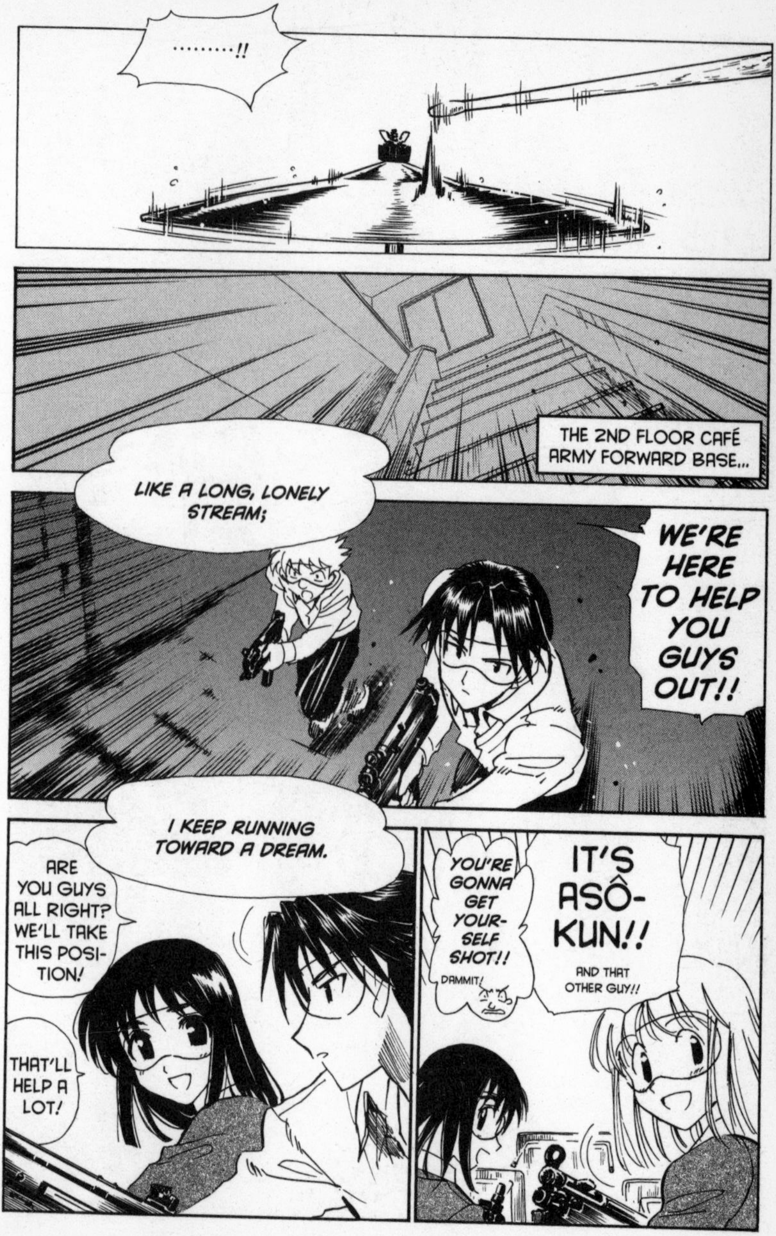
..........!!
THE 2ND FLOOR CAFÉ ARMY FORWARD BASE...
LIKE A LONG, LONELY STREAM;
WE'RE HERE TO HELP YOU GUYS OUT!!
IT'S ASÔ-KUN!!
AND THAT OTHER GUY!!
YOU'RE GONNA GET YOUR-SELF SHOT!!
DAMMIT!
I KEEP RUNNING TOWARD A DREAM.
ARE YOU GUYS ALL RIGHT? WE'LL TAKE THIS POSI-TION!
THAT'LL HELP A LOT!

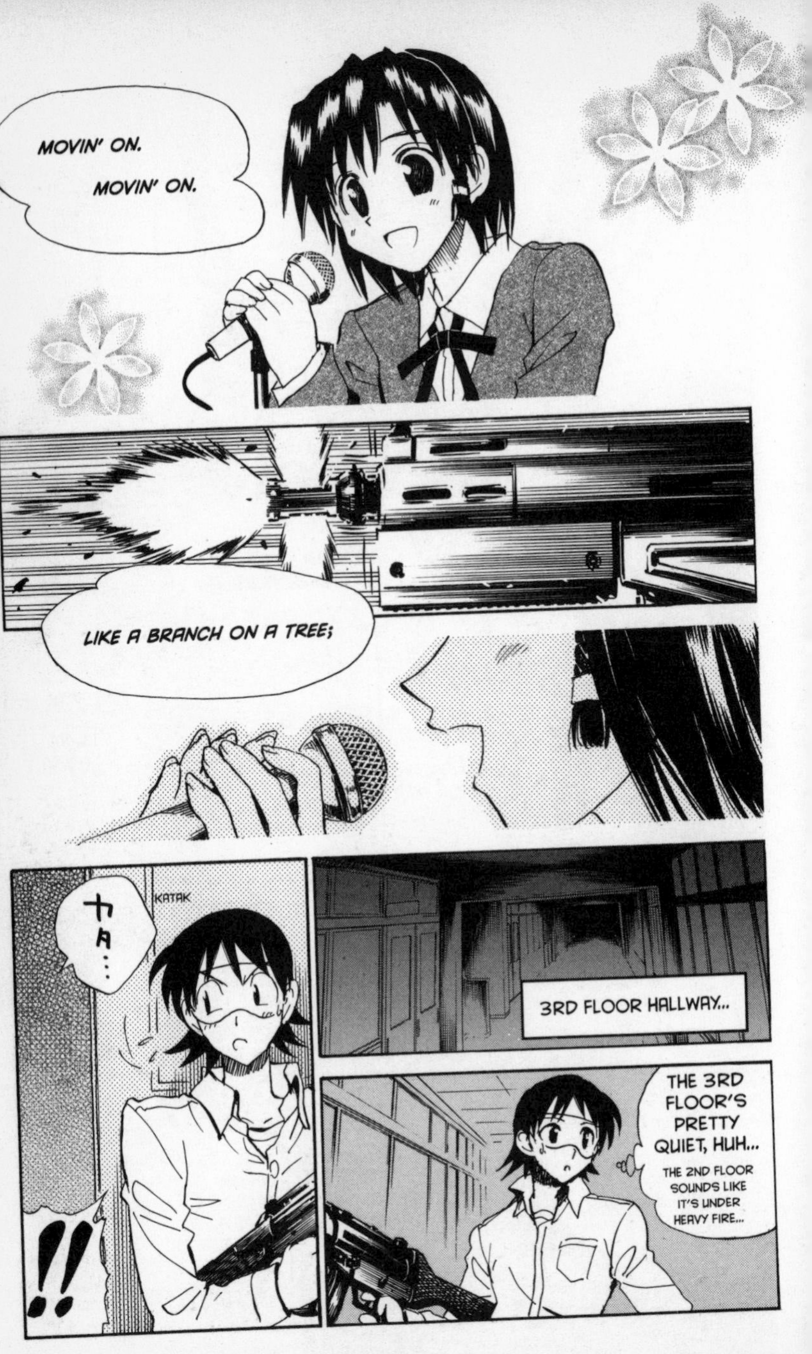
MOVIN' ON. MOVIN' ON.
LIKE A BRANCH ON A TREE;
3RD FLOOR HALLWAY...
THE 3RD FLOOR'S PRETTY QUIET, HUH...
THE 2ND FLOOR SOUNDS LIKE IT'S UNDER HEAVY FIRE...
KATAK
ヤA...
!!

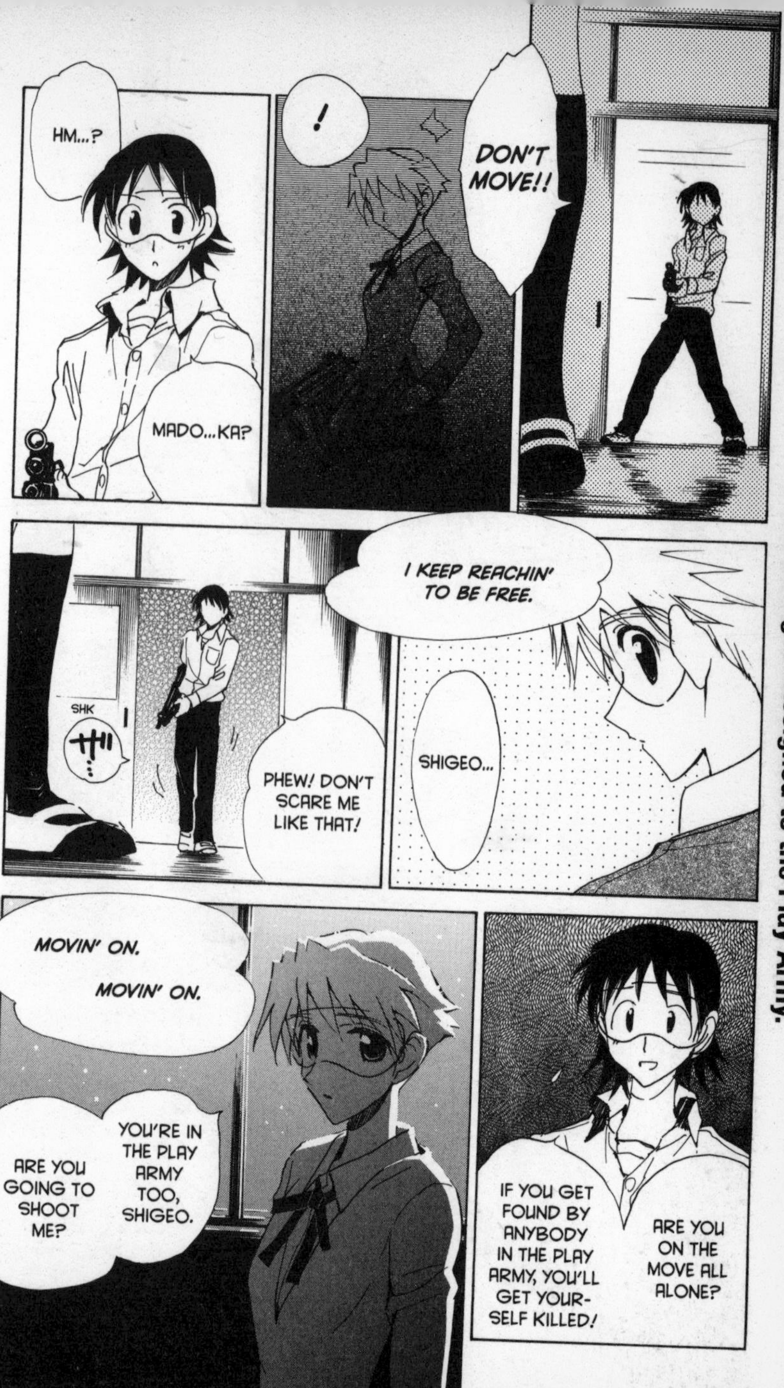
DON'T MOVE!!
!
HM...?
MADO...KA?
I KEEP REACHIN' TO BE FREE.
SHIGEO...
SHK
ザ...
PHEW! DON'T SCARE ME LIKE THAT!
ARE YOU ON THE MOVE ALL ALONE?
IF YOU GET FOUND BY ANYBODY IN THE PLAY ARMY, YOU'LL GET YOURSELF KILLED!
MOVIN' ON.
MOVIN' ON.
YOU'RE IN THE PLAY ARMY TOO, SHIGEO.
ARE YOU GOING TO SHOOT ME?

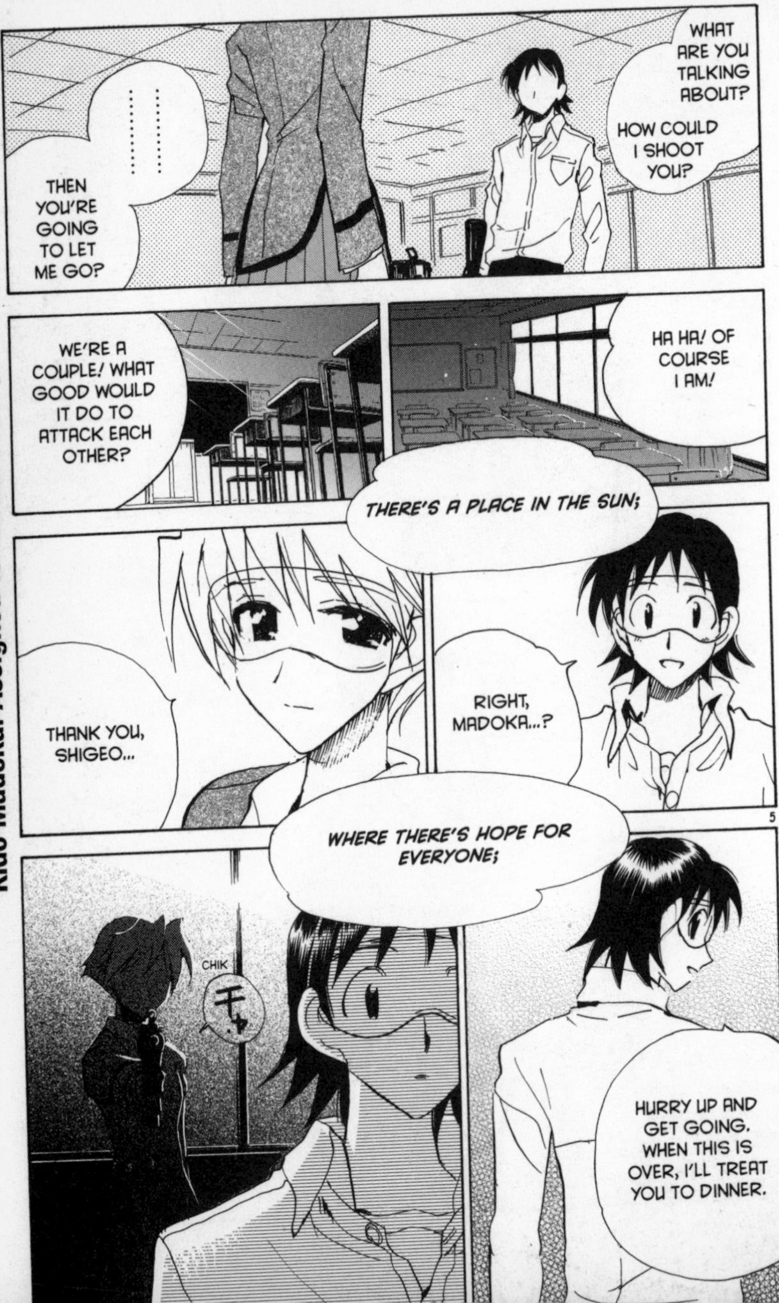
WHAT ARE YOU TALKING ABOUT?
HOW COULD I SHOOT YOU?
……
THEN YOU'RE GOING TO LET ME GO?
HA HA! OF COURSE I AM!
WE'RE A COUPLE! WHAT GOOD WOULD IT DO TO ATTACK EACH OTHER?
THERE'S A PLACE IN THE SUN;
RIGHT, MADOKA...?
THANK YOU, SHIGEO...
WHERE THERE'S HOPE FOR EVERYONE;
HURRY UP AND GET GOING. WHEN THIS IS OVER, I'LL TREAT YOU TO DINNER.
CHIK
チャ

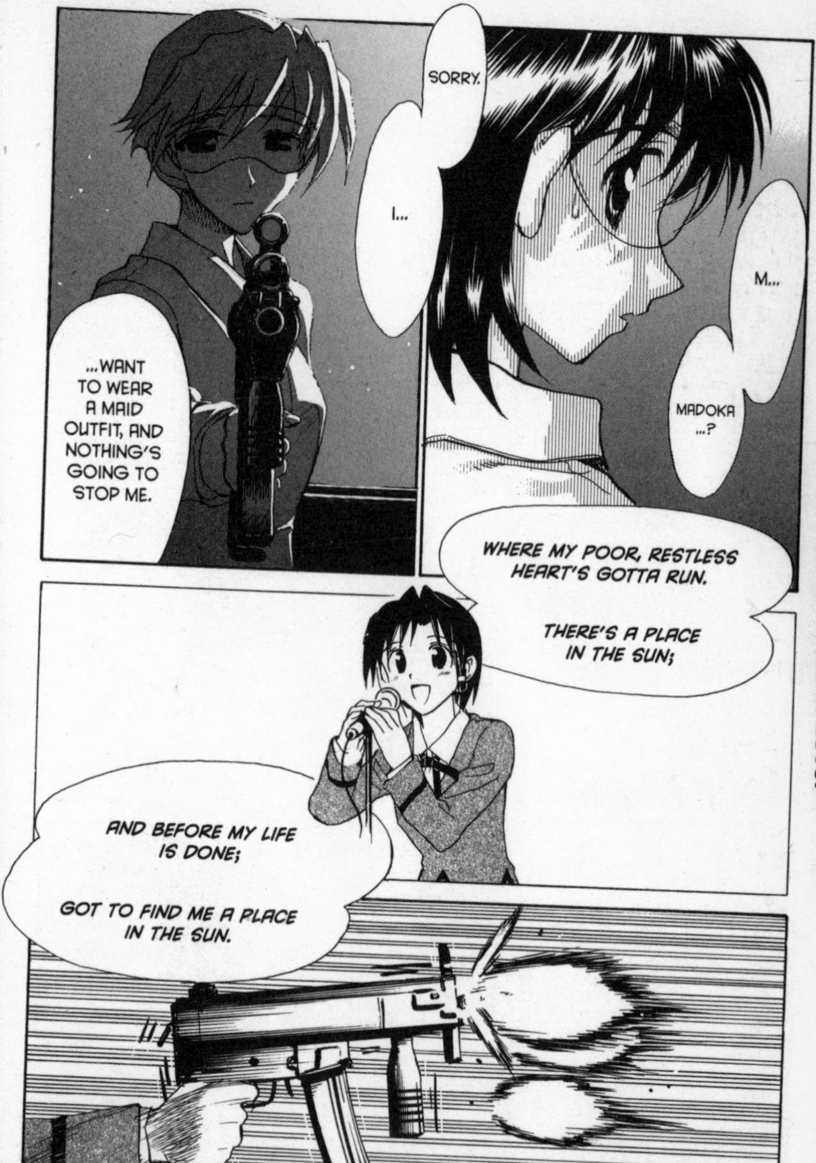
M...
MADOKA ...?
SORRY.
I...
...WANT TO WEAR A MAID OUTFIT, AND NOTHING'S GOING TO STOP ME.
WHERE MY POOR, RESTLESS HEART'S GOTTA RUN.
THERE'S A PLACE IN THE SUN;
AND BEFORE MY LIFE IS DONE;
GOT TO FIND ME A PLACE IN THE SUN.

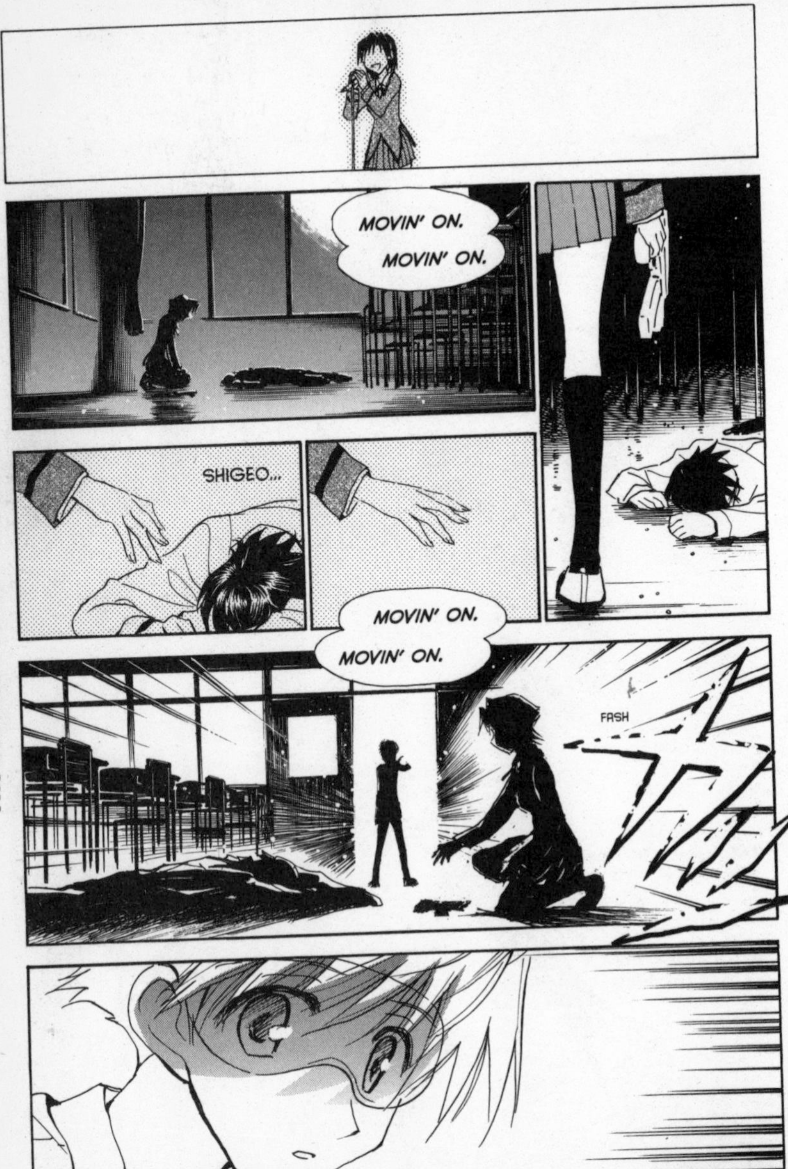
MOVIN' ON.
MOVIN' ON.
SHIGEO...
MOVIN' ON.
MOVIN' ON.
FASH

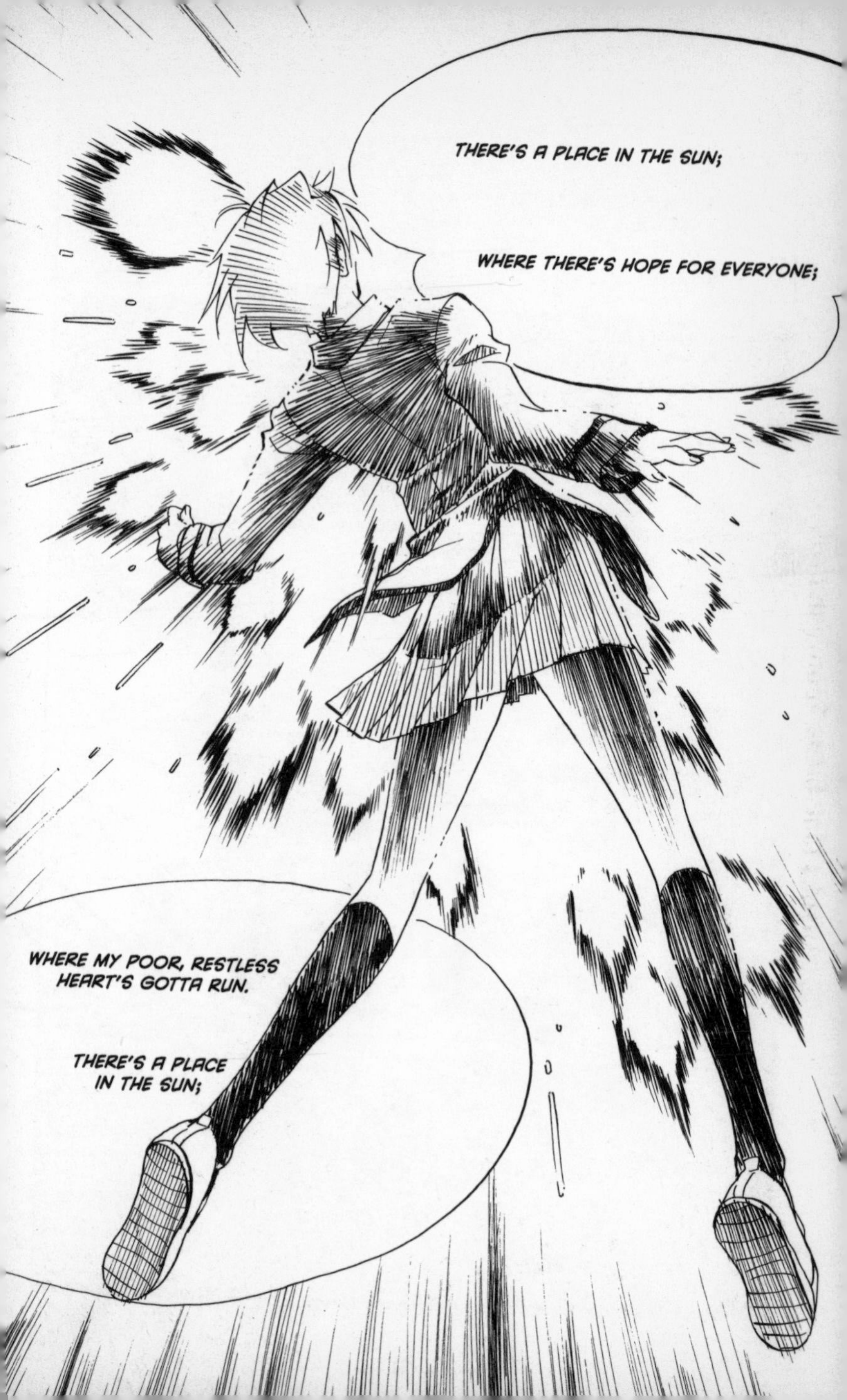
THERE'S A PLACE IN THE SUN;
WHERE THERE'S HOPE FOR EVERYONE;
WHERE MY POOR, RESTLESS HEART'S GOTTA RUN.
THERE'S A PLACE IN THE SUN;

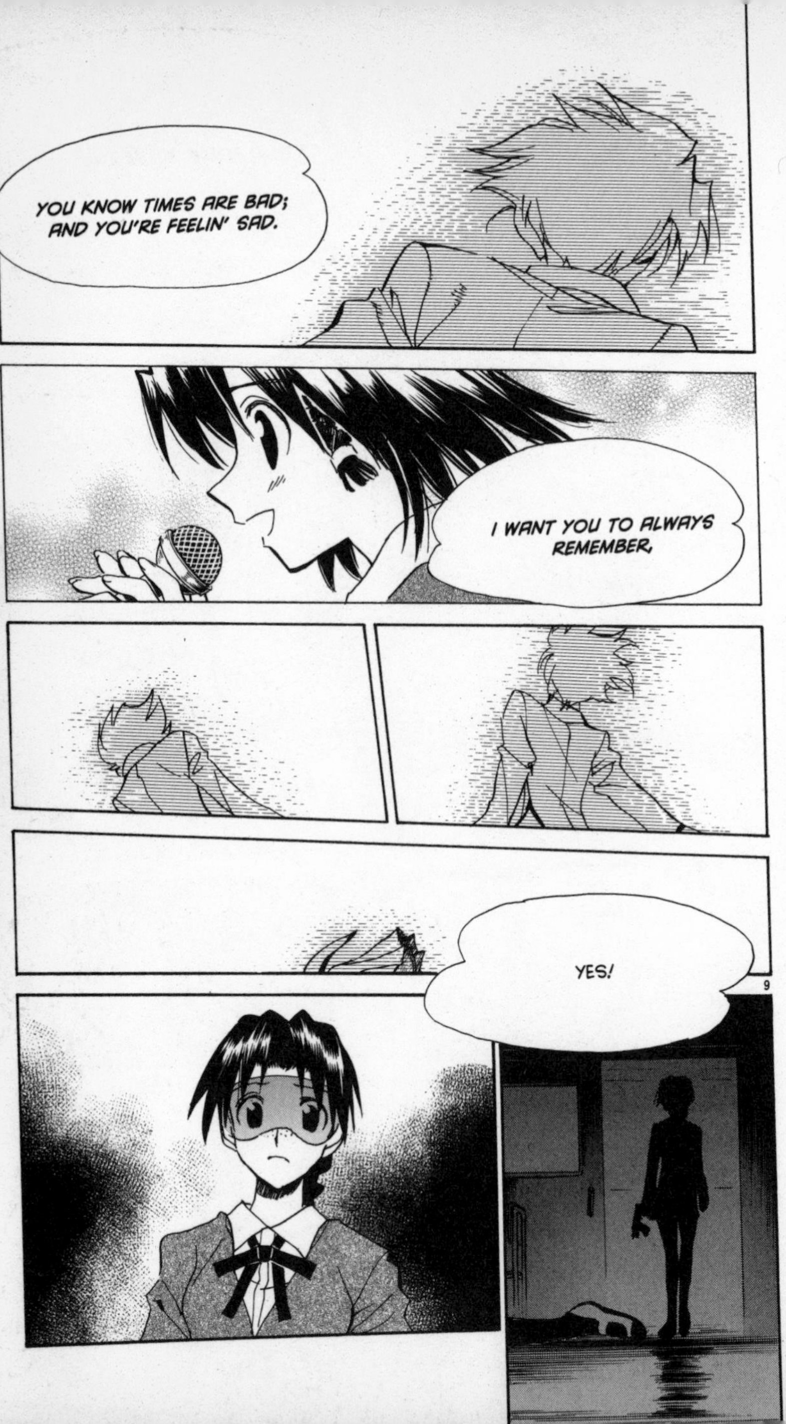
YOU KNOW TIMES ARE BAD; AND YOU'RE FEELIN' SAD.
I WANT YOU TO ALWAYS REMEMBER,
YES!

Ôtsuka Mai: Class Representative.

Too Late Now...

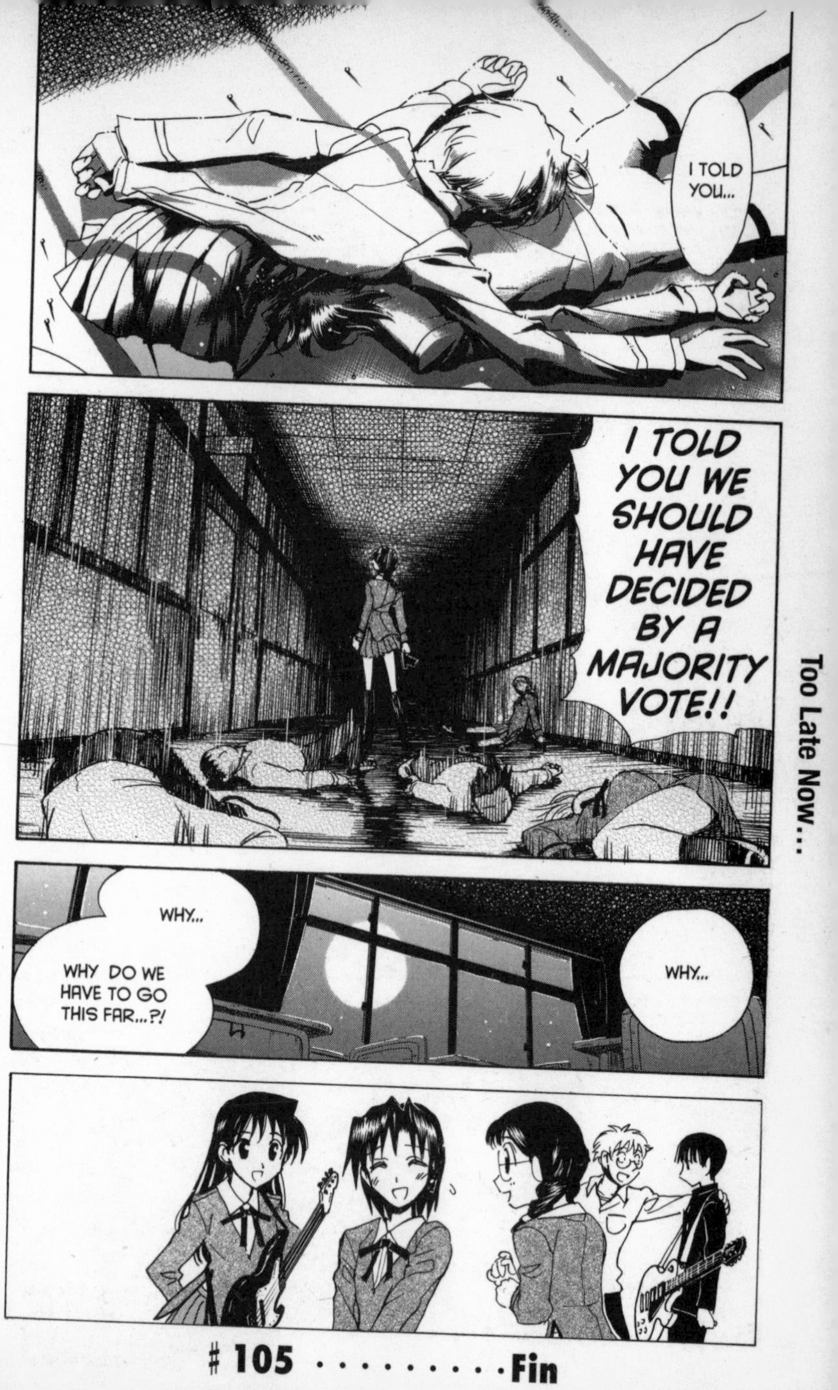
I TOLD YOU...
I TOLD YOU WE SHOULD HAVE DECIDED BY A MAJORITY VOTE!!
WHY...
WHY...
WHY DO WE HAVE TO GO THIS FAR...?!

105 ....Fin

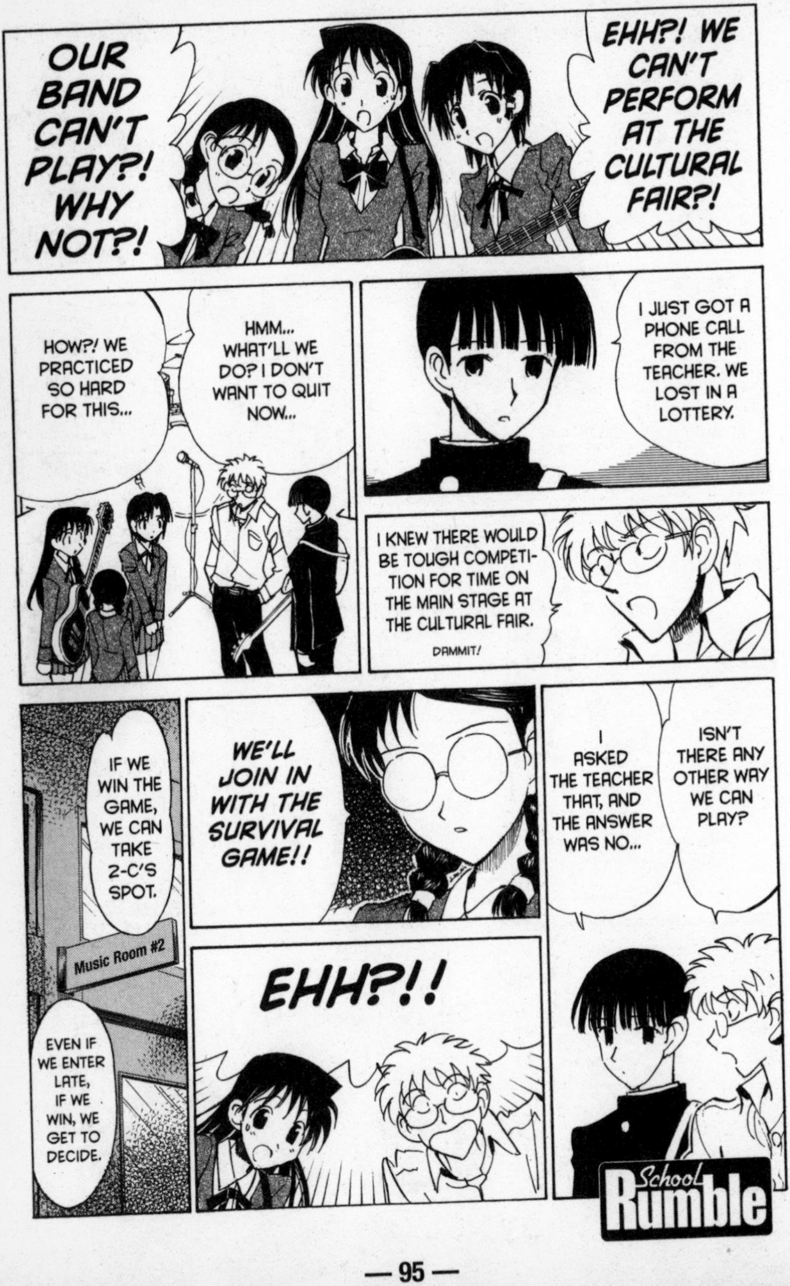

EHH?! WE CAN'T PERFORM AT THE CULTURAL FAIR?!
OUR BAND CAN'T PLAY?! WHY NOT?!
I JUST GOT A PHONE CALL FROM THE TEACHER. WE LOST IN A LOTTERY.
I KNEW THERE WOULD BE TOUGH COMPETITION FOR TIME ON THE MAIN STAGE AT THE CULTURAL FAIR.
DAMMIT!
HMM... WHAT'LL WE DO? I DON'T WANT TO QUIT NOW...
HOW?! WE PRACTICED SO HARD FOR THIS...
ISN'T THERE ANY OTHER WAY WE CAN PLAY?
I ASKED THE TEACHER THAT, AND THE ANSWER WAS NO...
WE'LL JOIN IN WITH THE SURVIVAL GAME!!
EHH?!!
IF WE WIN THE GAME, WE CAN TAKE 2-C'S SPOT.
Music Room #2
EVEN IF WE ENTER LATE, IF WE WIN, WE GET TO DECIDE.
School Rumble

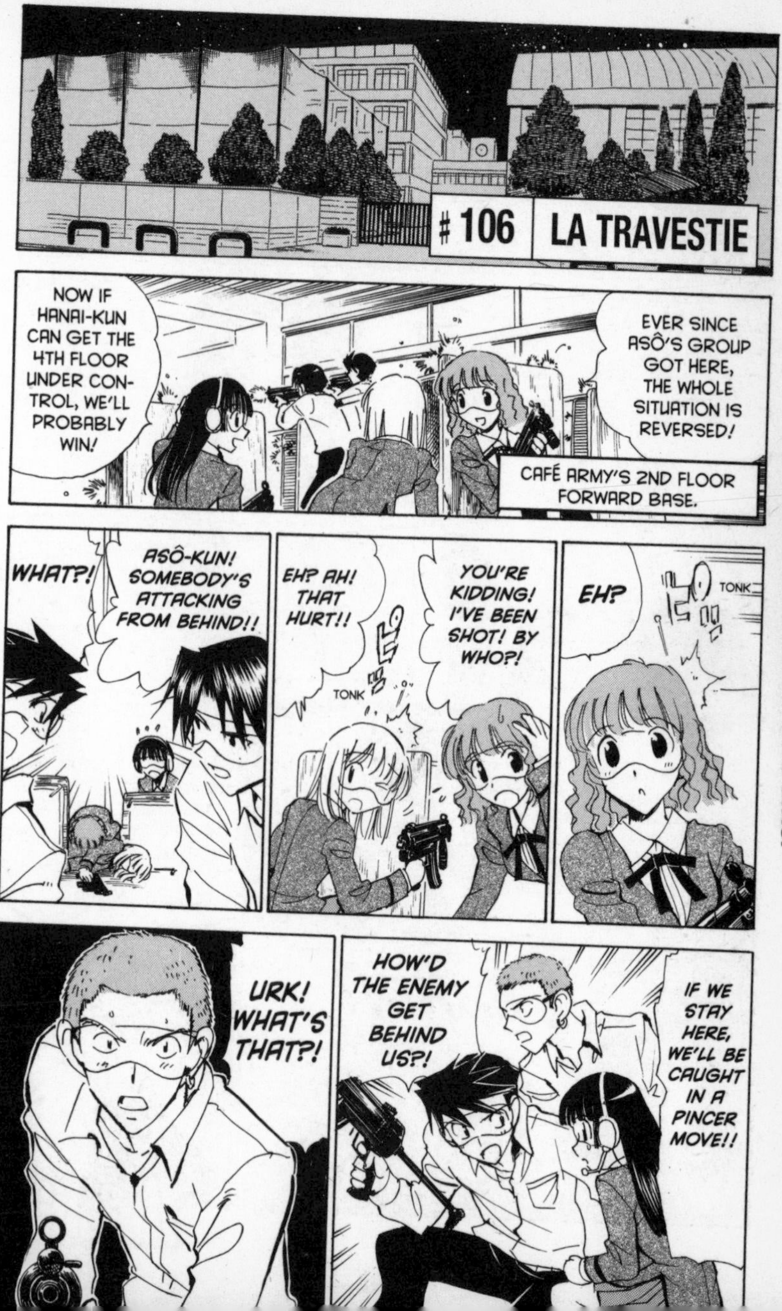

106
LA TRAVESTIE
EVER SINCE ASÔ'S GROUP GOT HERE, THE WHOLE SITUATION IS REVERSED!
NOW IF HANAI-KUN CAN GET THE 4TH FLOOR UNDER CON-TROL, WE'LL PROBABLY WIN!
CAFÉ ARMY'S 2ND FLOOR FORWARD BASE.
TONK
EH?
YOU'RE KIDDING! I'VE BEEN SHOT! BY WHO?!
EH? AH! THAT HURT!!
TONK
ASÔ-KUN! SOMEBODY'S ATTACKING FROM BEHIND!!
WHAT?!
IF WE STAY HERE, WE'LL BE CAUGHT IN A PINCER MOVE!!
HOW'D THE ENEMY GET BEHIND US?!
URK! WHAT'S THAT?!

The Nameless Death-Bound Girls.

The Strongest Ones Are the Girls.

Broadcast Room

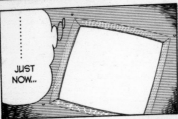

......
JUST NOW...

LET'S GO IN PURSUIT!! WE CAN GET THE FLAG!!

THAT HAIR STYLE! IT'S...

THAT THROWS BOTH ARMIES OUT OF BALANCE.

THAT PERSON ISN'T PLAYING AT THE SAME LEVEL AS THE OTHERS.

2ND FLOOR. AT THE CAFÉ ARMY'S FORWARD BASE...

TMP TMP TMP

KACHAK

I DON'T WANT TO STICK MY NOSE INTO A FIGHT BETWEEN CHILDREN, BUT...

KACHIK

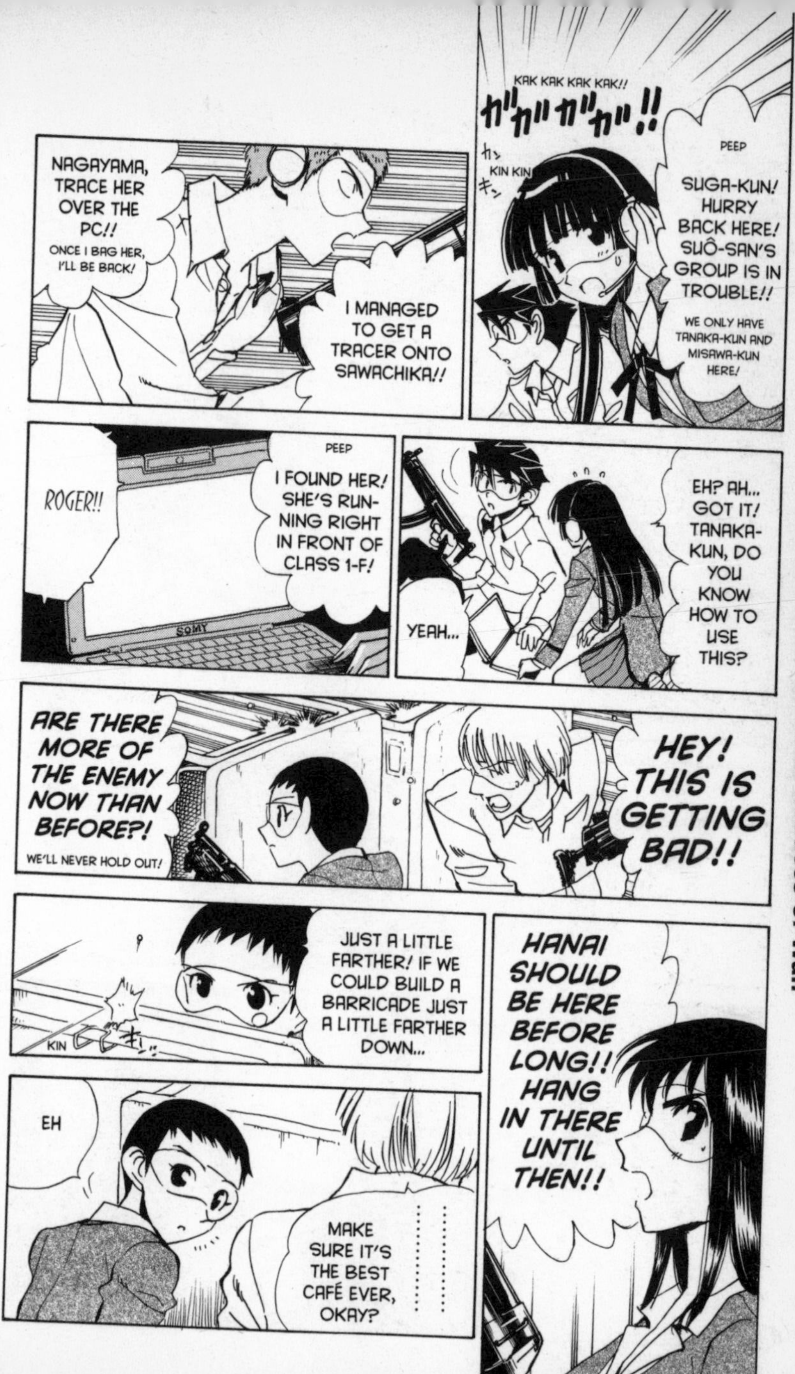

KAK KAK KAK KAK!!
PEEP
SUGA-KUN! HURRY BACK HERE! SUÔ-SAN'S GROUP IS IN TROUBLE!!
WE ONLY HAVE TANAKA-KUN AND MISAWA-KUN HERE!
KIN KIN
I MANAGED TO GET A TRACER ONTO SAWACHIKA!!
NAGAYAMA, TRACE HER OVER THE PC!!
ONCE I BAG HER, I'LL BE BACK!
EH? AH... GOT IT! TANAKA-KUN, DO YOU KNOW HOW TO USE THIS?
YEAH...
PEEP
I FOUND HER! SHE'S RUN-NING RIGHT IN FRONT OF CLASS 1-F!
ROGER!!
SOMY
HEY! THIS IS GETTING BAD!!
ARE THERE MORE OF THE ENEMY NOW THAN BEFORE?!
WE'LL NEVER HOLD OUT!
HANAI SHOULD BE HERE BEFORE LONG!! HANG IN THERE UNTIL THEN!!
JUST A LITTLE FARTHER! IF WE COULD BUILD A BARRICADE JUST A LITTLE FARTHER DOWN...
KIN
MAKE SURE IT'S THE BEST CAFÉ EVER, OKAY?
EH

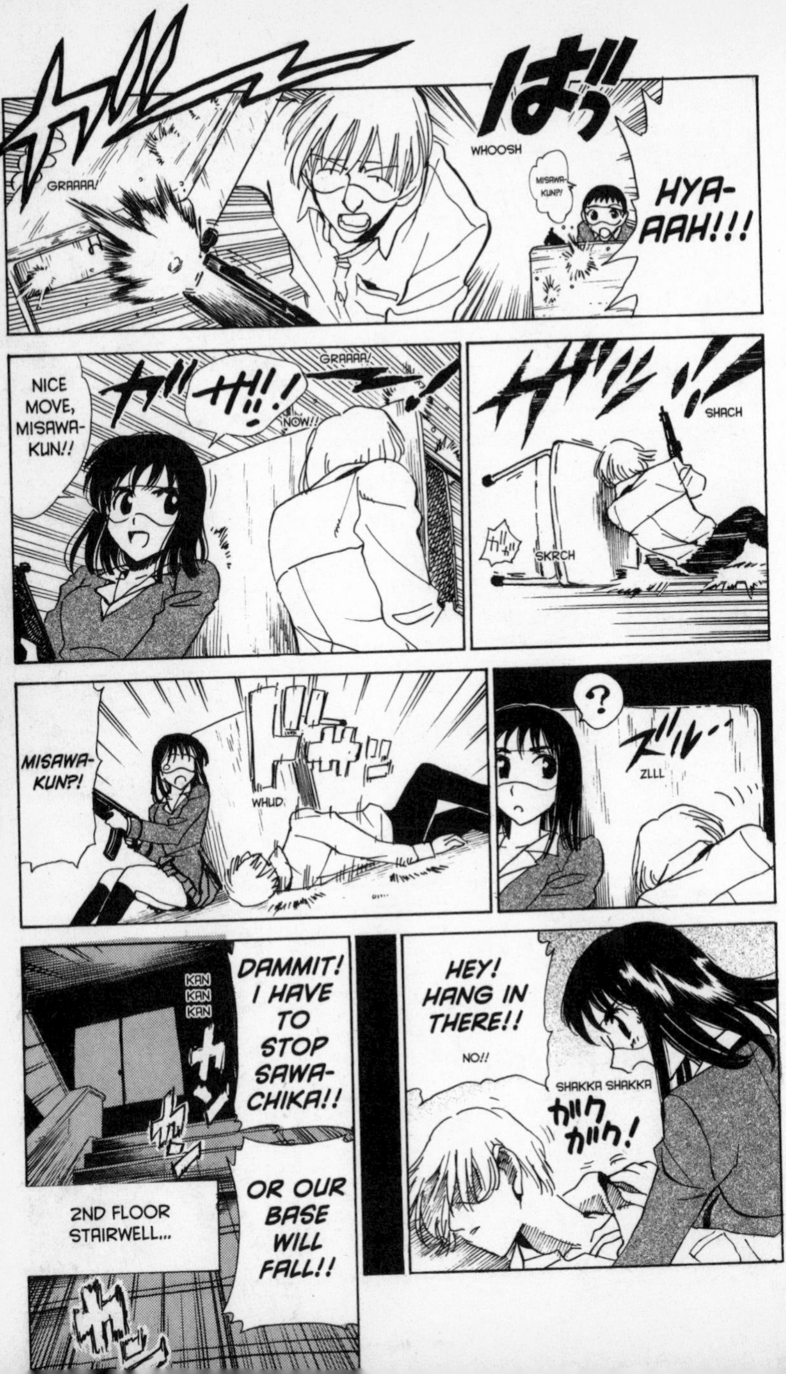
HYA-AAH!!!
MISAWA-KUN?!
WHOOSH
GRAAAA!
SHACH
SKRCH
GRAAAA!
NOW!!
NICE MOVE, MISAWA-KUN!!
ZLLL
WHUD
MISAWA-KUN?!
HEY! HANG IN THERE!!
NO!!
SHAKKA SHAKKA
DAMMIT! I HAVE TO STOP SAWA-CHIKA!!
KAN KAN KAN
OR OUR BASE WILL FALL!!
2ND FLOOR STAIRWELL...

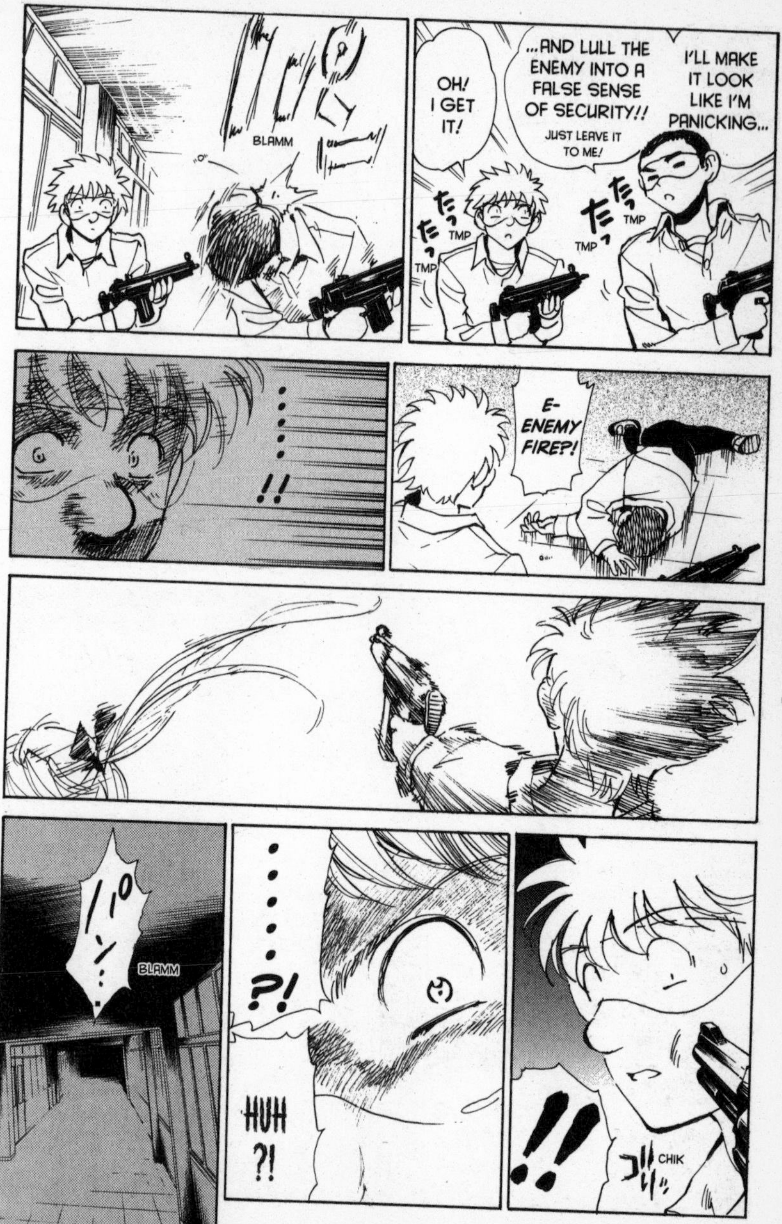
I'LL MAKE IT LOOK LIKE I'M PANICKING...
...AND LULL THE ENEMY INTO A FALSE SENSE OF SECURITY!!
JUST LEAVE IT TO ME!
OH! I GET IT!
TMP
TMP
TMP
TMP
BLAMM
"O"
E- ENEMY FIRE?!
......!!
!!
CHIK
......?!
HUH ?!
BLAMM

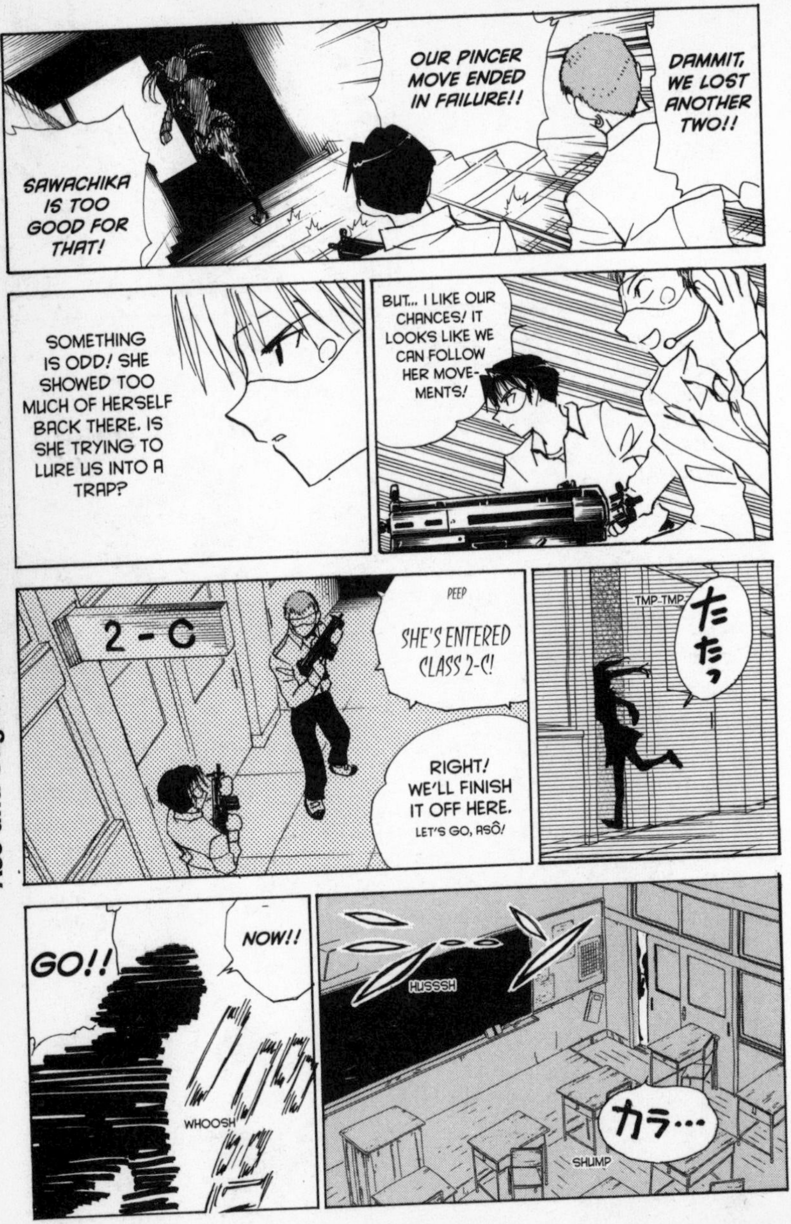
DAMMIT, WE LOST ANOTHER TWO!!
OUR PINCER MOVE ENDED IN FAILURE!!
SAWACHIKA IS TOO GOOD FOR THAT!
BUT... I LIKE OUR CHANCES! IT LOOKS LIKE WE CAN FOLLOW HER MOVE-MENTS!
SOMETHING IS ODD! SHE SHOWED TOO MUCH OF HERSELF BACK THERE. IS SHE TRYING TO LURE US INTO A TRAP?
たたっ
TMP-TMP
PEEP
SHE'S ENTERED CLASS 2-C!
2-C
RIGHT! WE'LL FINISH IT OFF HERE.
LET'S GO, ASÔ!
HUSSSH
カラ…
SHUMP
NOW!!
GO!!
WHOOSH

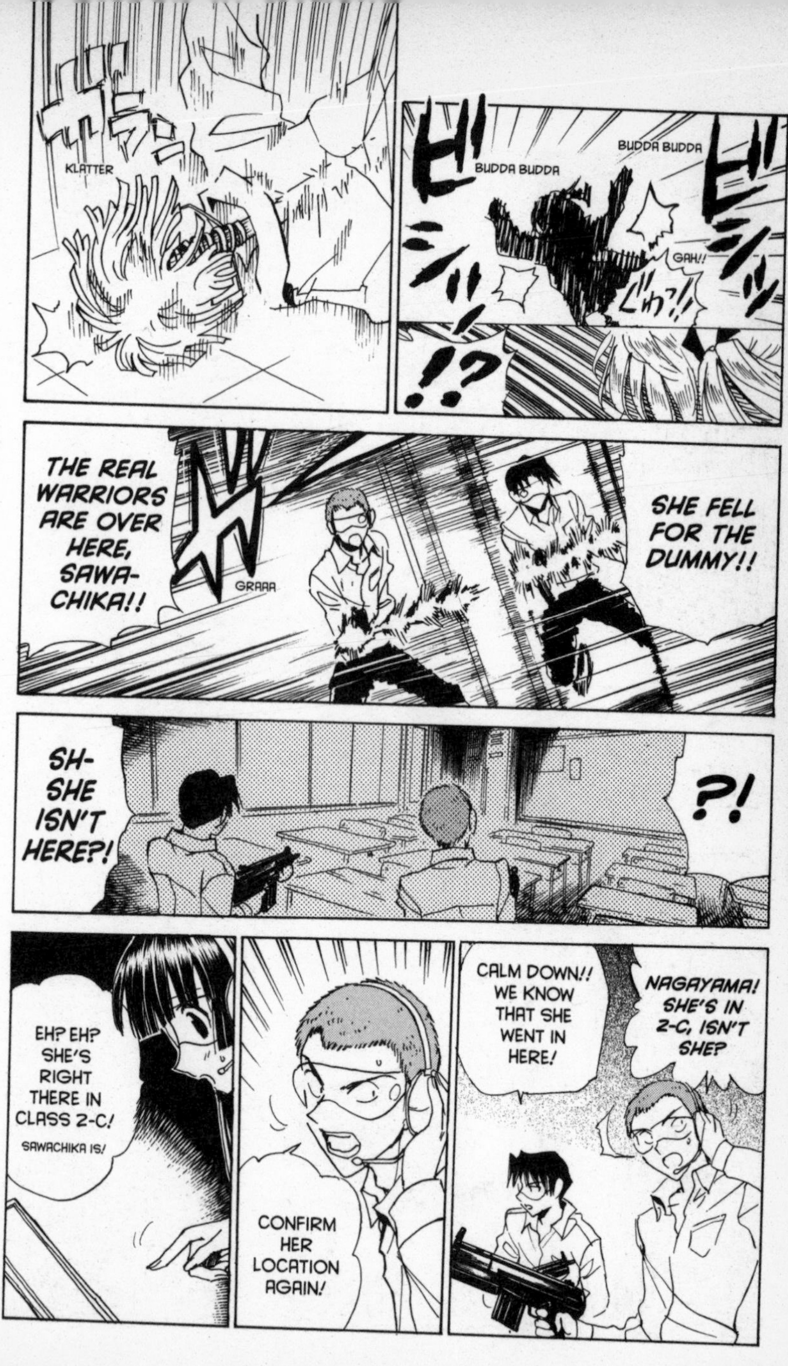
BUDDA BUDDA
BUDDA BUDDA
GAH!!
!?
KLATTER
SHE FELL FOR THE DUMMY!!
THE REAL WARRIORS ARE OVER HERE, SAWA-CHIKA!!
GRAAA
?!
SH-SHE ISN'T HERE?!
NAGAYAMA! SHE'S IN 2-C, ISN'T SHE?
CALM DOWN!! WE KNOW THAT SHE WENT IN HERE!
CONFIRM HER LOCATION AGAIN!
EH? EH? SHE'S RIGHT THERE IN CLASS 2-C!
SAWACHIKA IS!

They're Pretty Good.

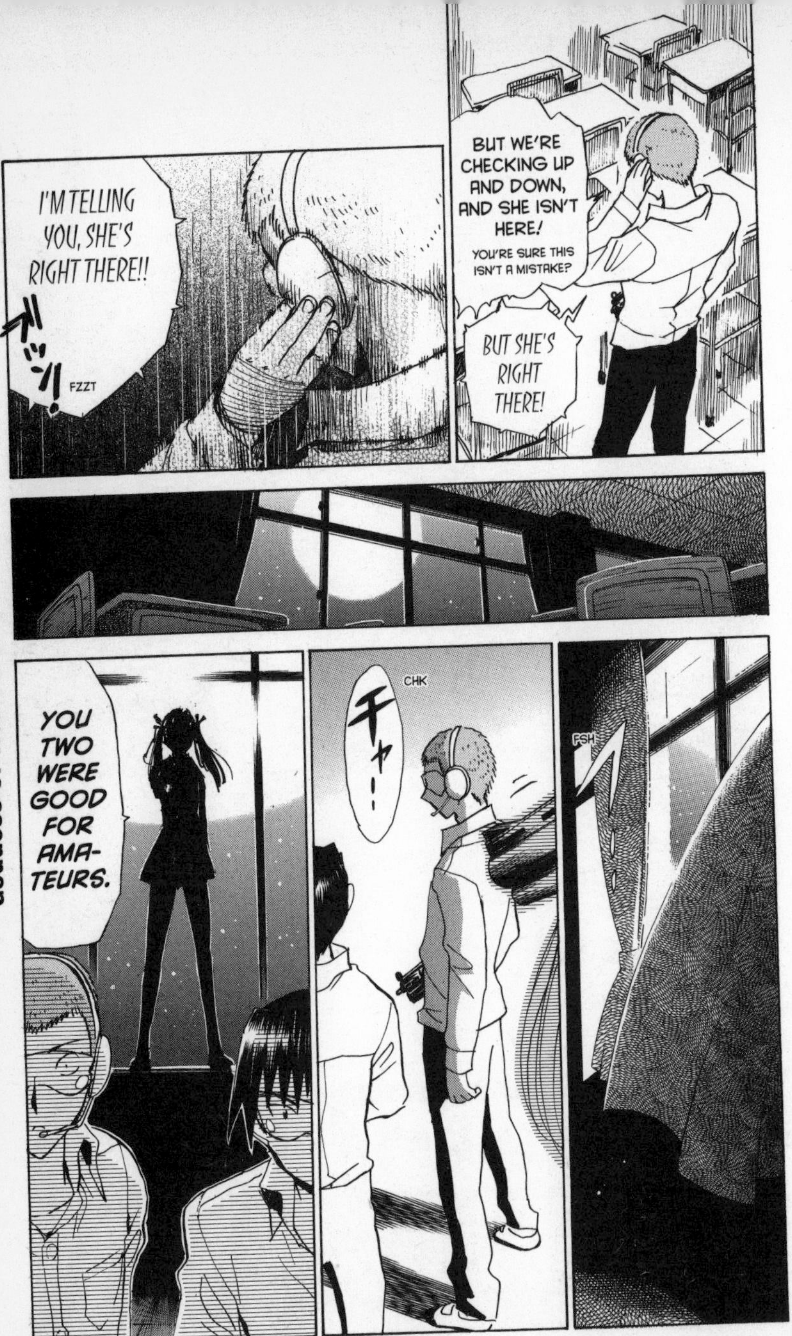
BUT WE'RE CHECKING UP AND DOWN, AND SHE ISN'T HERE!
YOU'RE SURE THIS ISN'T A MISTAKE?
BUT SHE'S RIGHT THERE!
I'M TELLING YOU, SHE'S RIGHT THERE!!
FZZT
FSH
CHK
チャ!
YOU TWO WERE GOOD FOR AMA-TEURS.

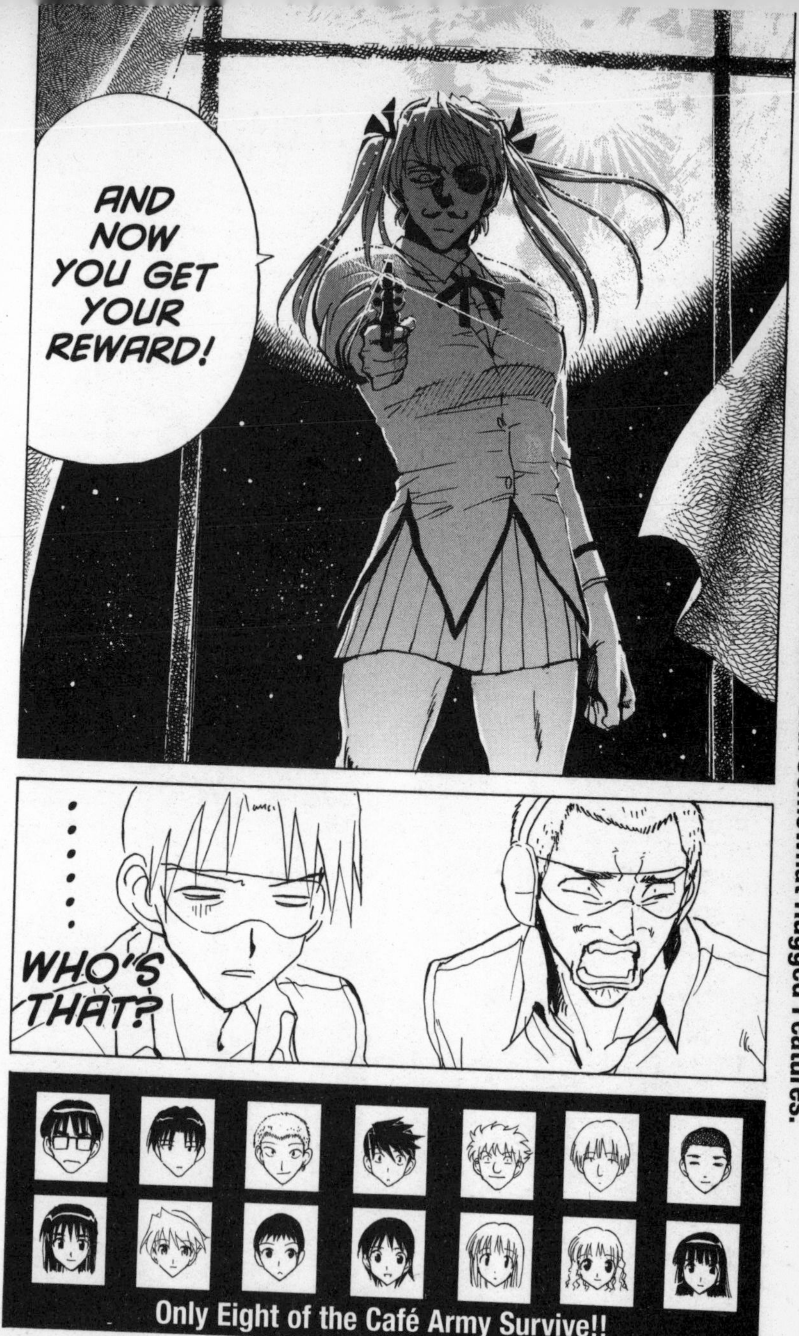
AND NOW YOU GET YOUR REWARD!
......WHO'S THAT?
Only Eight of the Café Army Survive!!

Sawachika Eri: 16 Years Old. Somewhat Rugged Features.

106 ....Fin

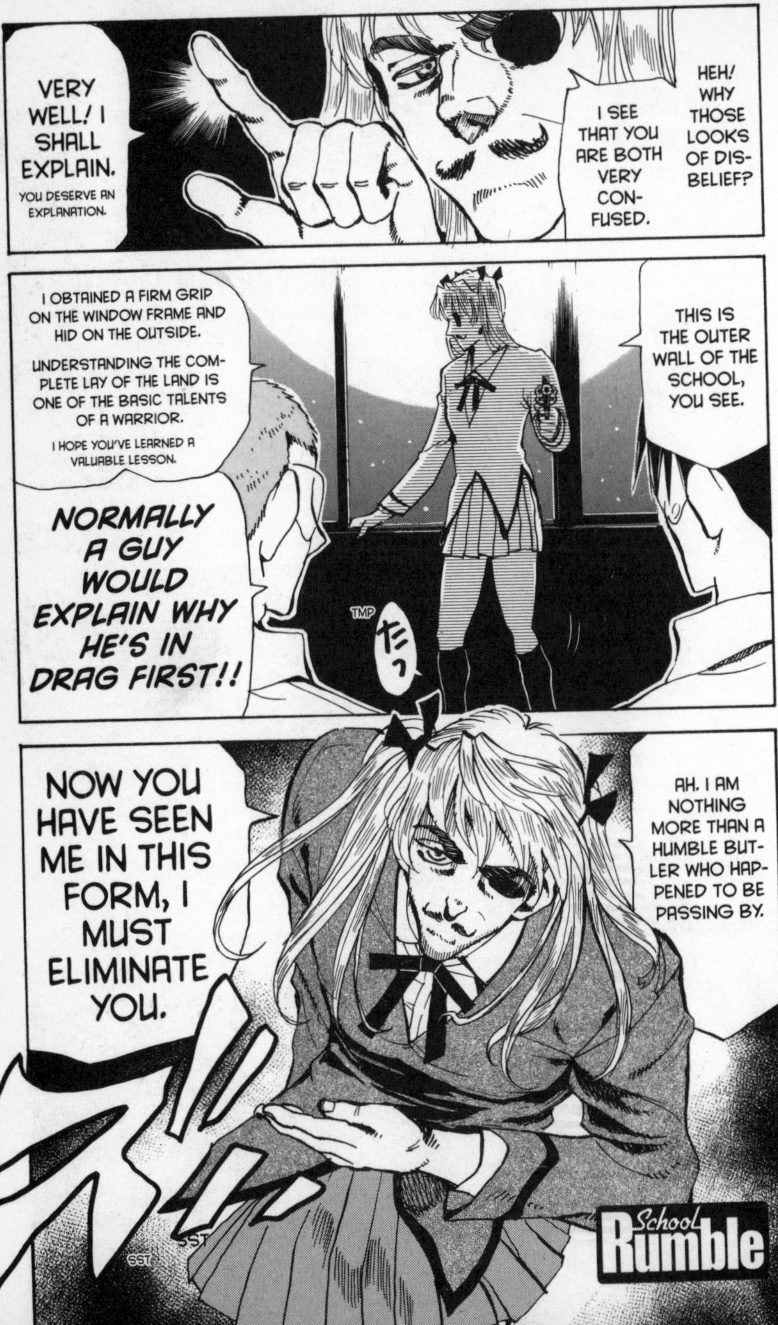
HEH! WHY THOSE LOOKS OF DIS-BELIEF?
I SEE THAT YOU ARE BOTH VERY CON-FUSED.
VERY WELL! I SHALL EXPLAIN.
YOU DESERVE AN EXPLANATION.
THIS IS THE OUTER WALL OF THE SCHOOL, YOU SEE.
I OBTAINED A FIRM GRIP ON THE WINDOW FRAME AND HID ON THE OUTSIDE.
UNDERSTANDING THE COM-PLETE LAY OF THE LAND IS ONE OF THE BASIC TALENTS OF A WARRIOR.
I HOPE YOU'VE LEARNED A VALUABLE LESSON.
TMP
たっ
NORMALLY A GUY WOULD EXPLAIN WHY HE'S IN DRAG FIRST!!
AH. I AM NOTHING MORE THAN A HUMBLE BUT-LER WHO HAP-PENED TO BE PASSING BY.
NOW YOU HAVE SEEN ME IN THIS FORM, I MUST ELIMINATE YOU.
SST
School Rumble

#107 WHISPERS IN THE DARK

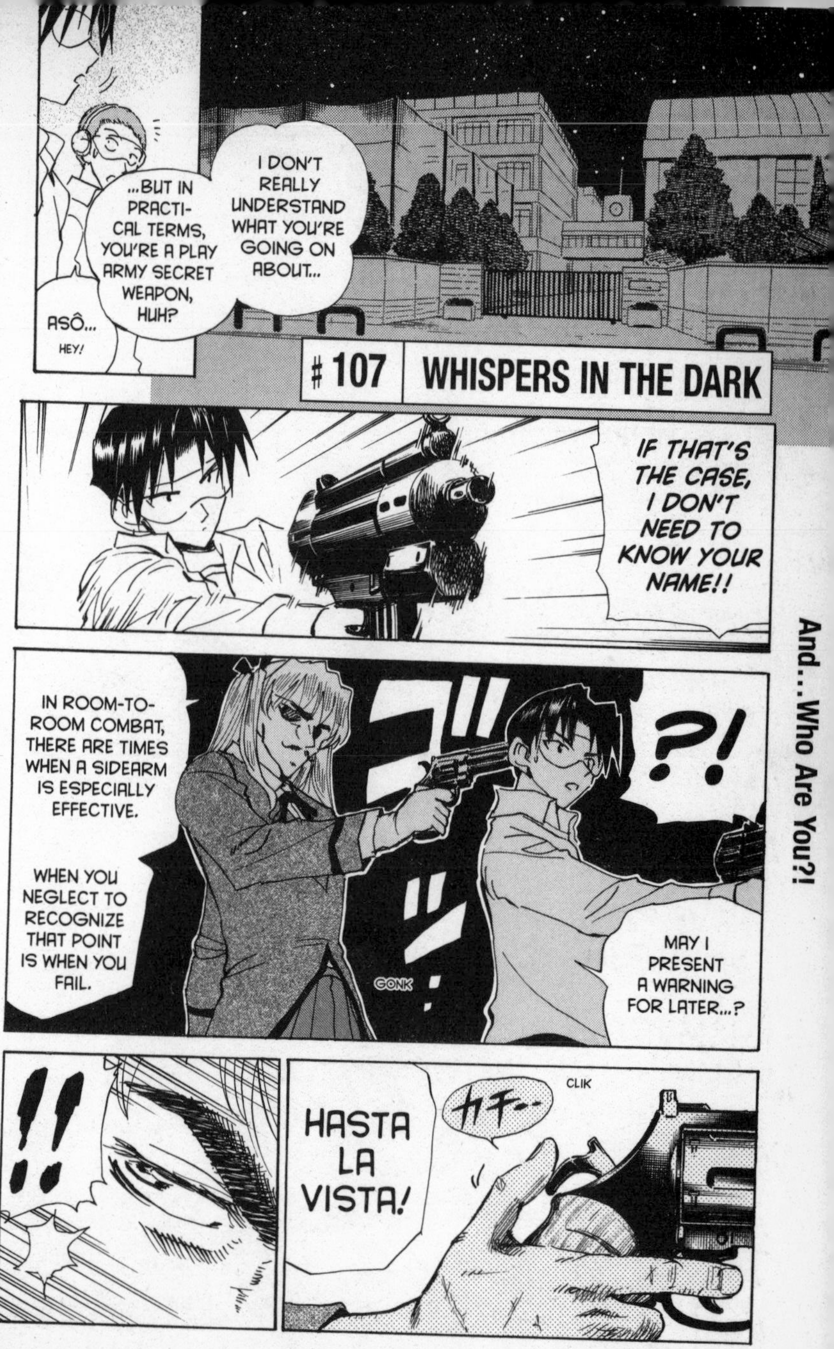
I DON'T REALLY UNDERSTAND WHAT YOU'RE GOING ON ABOUT...
...BUT IN PRACTICAL TERMS, YOU'RE A PLAY ARMY SECRET WEAPON, HUH?
ASÔ...
HEY!
IF THAT'S THE CASE, I DON'T NEED TO KNOW YOUR NAME!!
?!
MAY I PRESENT A WARNING FOR LATER...?
IN ROOM-TO-ROOM COMBAT, THERE ARE TIMES WHEN A SIDEARM IS ESPECIALLY EFFECTIVE.
WHEN YOU NEGLECT TO RECOGNIZE THAT POINT IS WHEN YOU FAIL.
GONK
CLIK
カチー
HASTA LA VISTA!
!!

And...Who Are You?!

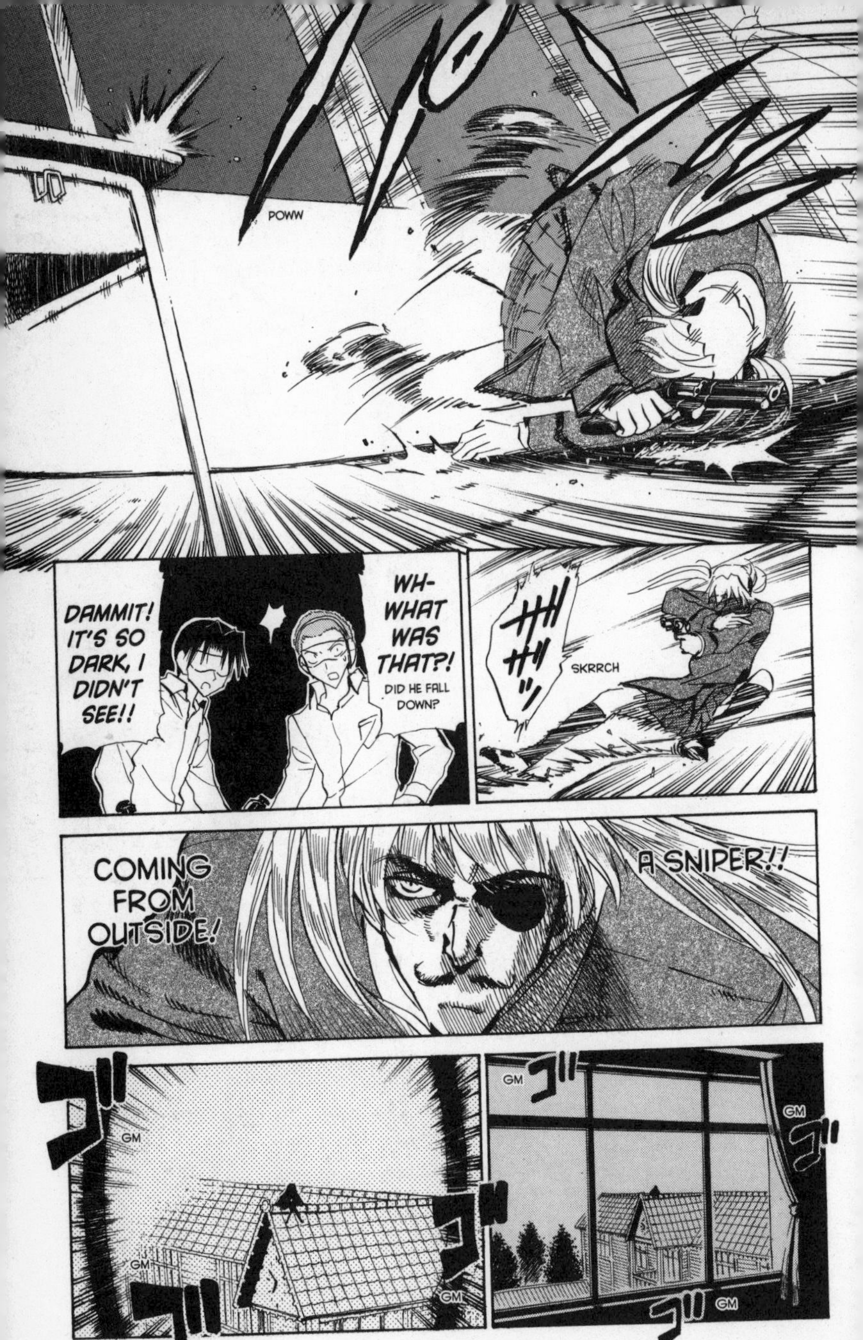
POWW
SKRRCH
WH-WHAT WAS THAT?!
DID HE FALL DOWN?
DAMMIT! IT'S SO DARK, I DIDN'T SEE!!
A SNIPER!!
COMING FROM OUTSIDE!
GM
GM
GM
GM
GM
GM

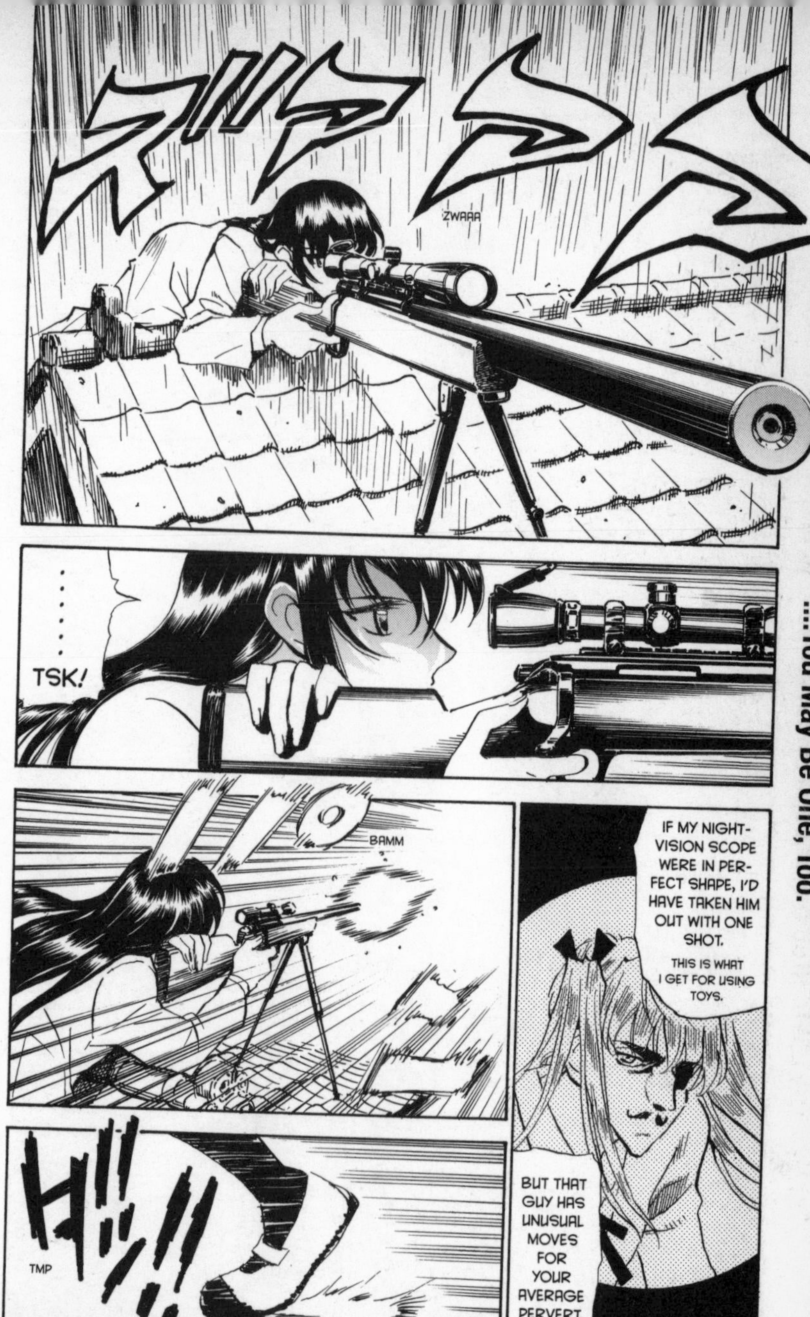
ZWAAA
....
TSK!
IF MY NIGHT-VISION SCOPE WERE IN PERFECT SHAPE, I'D HAVE TAKEN HIM OUT WITH ONE SHOT.
THIS IS WHAT I GET FOR USING TOYS.
BUT THAT GUY HAS UNUSUAL MOVES FOR YOUR AVERAGE PERVERT.
BAMM
TMP

Forgive The Late Introduction. Nakamura, the Sawachika Household Butler.

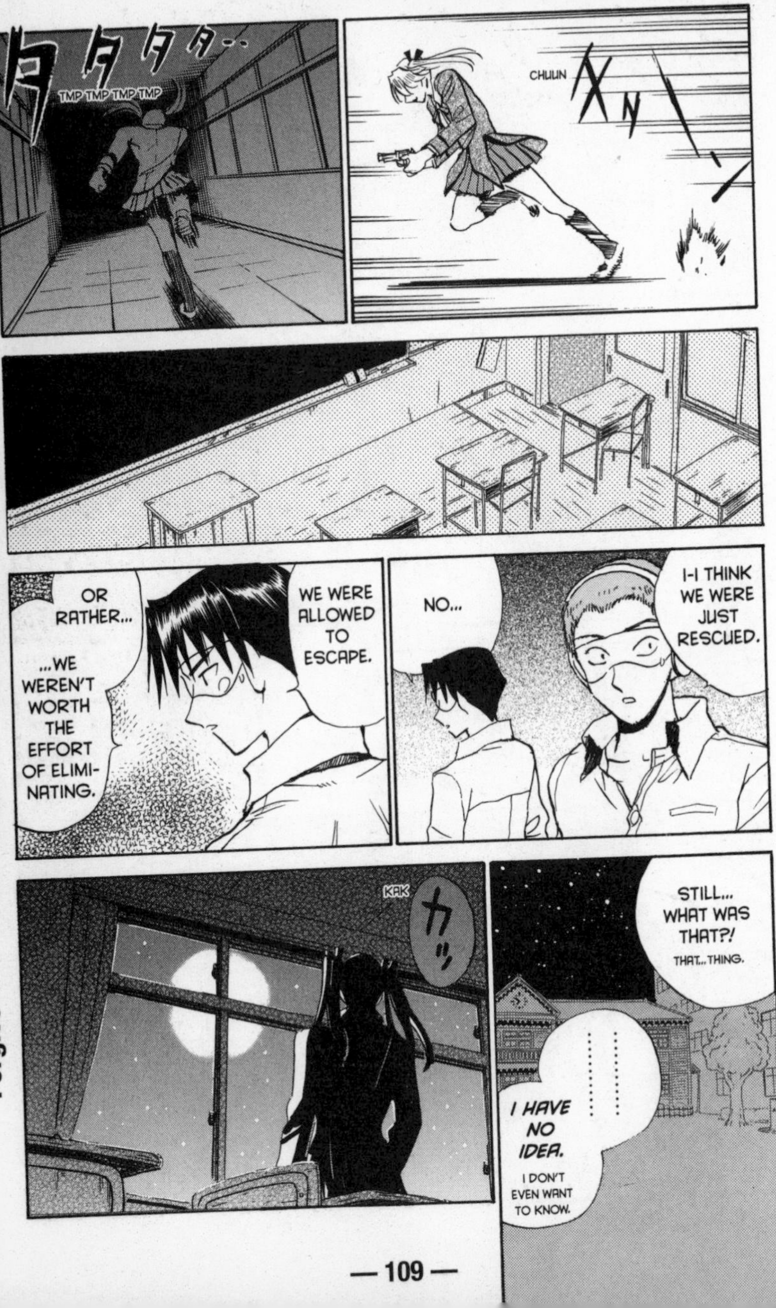

CHUUN
チュン
タタタタ…
TMP TMP TMP TMP
I-I THINK WE WERE JUST RESCUED.
NO...
WE WERE ALLOWED TO ESCAPE.
OR RATHER...
...WE WEREN'T WORTH THE EFFORT OF ELIMINATING.
STILL... WHAT WAS THAT?!
THAT...THING.
......
I HAVE NO IDEA.
I DON'T EVEN WANT TO KNOW.
KAK
カッ

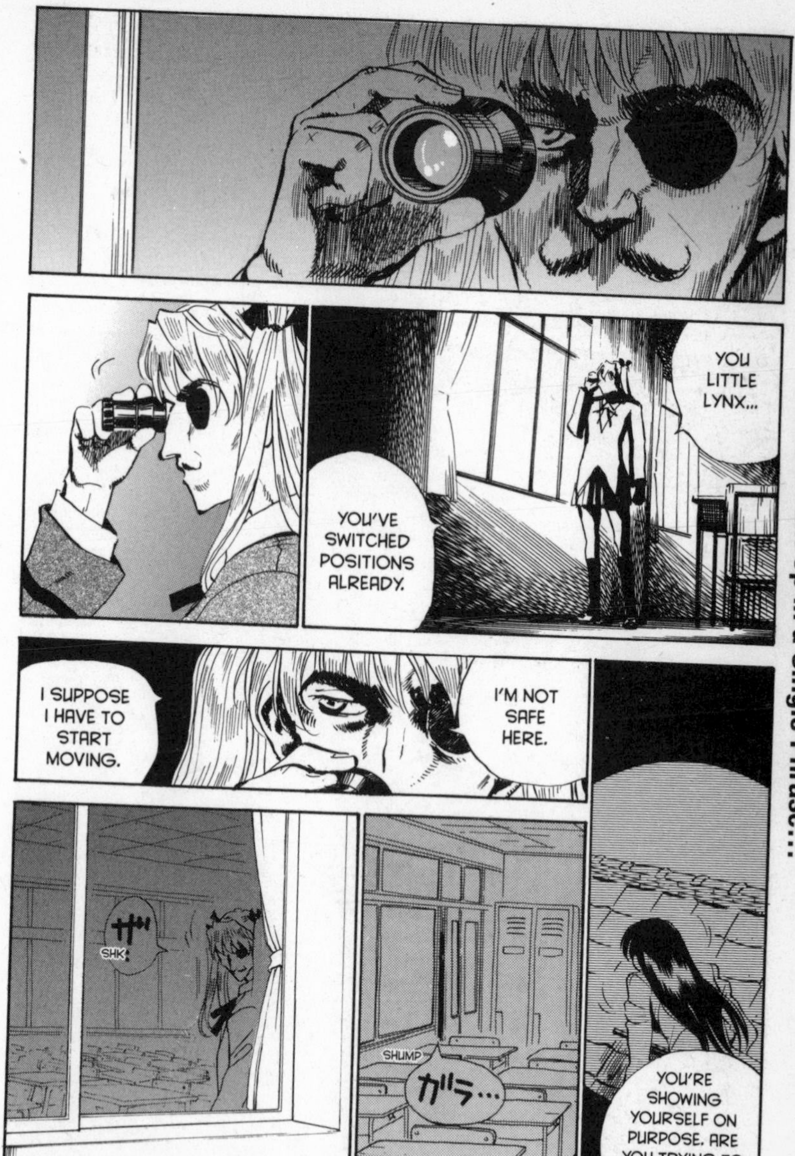
YOU LITTLE LYNX...
YOU'VE SWITCHED POSITIONS ALREADY.
YOU'RE SHOWING YOURSELF ON PURPOSE. ARE YOU TRYING TO THROW ME OFF MY GAME?
I'M NOT SAFE HERE.
I SUPPOSE I HAVE TO START MOVING.
ガラ…
SHUMP
ザ
SHK

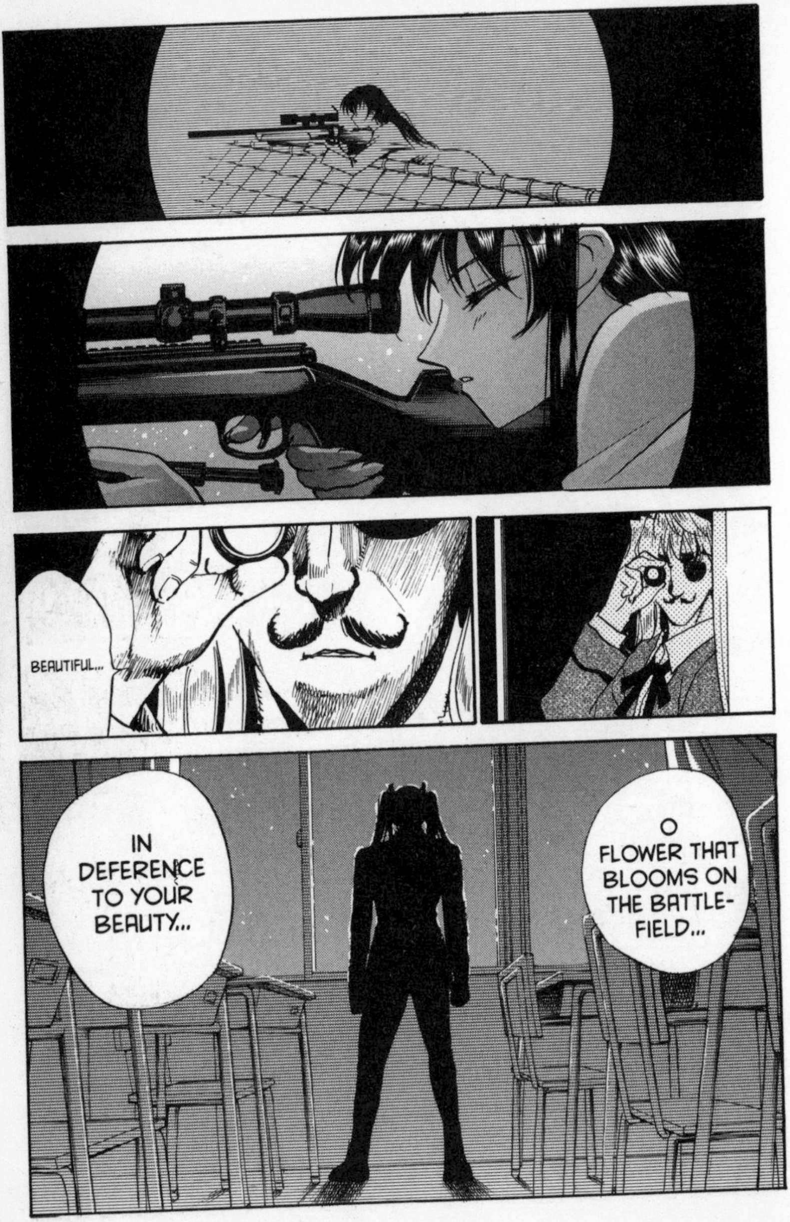
BEAUTIFUL...
O FLOWER THAT BLOOMS ON THE BATTLE-FIELD...
IN DEFERENCE TO YOUR BEAUTY...

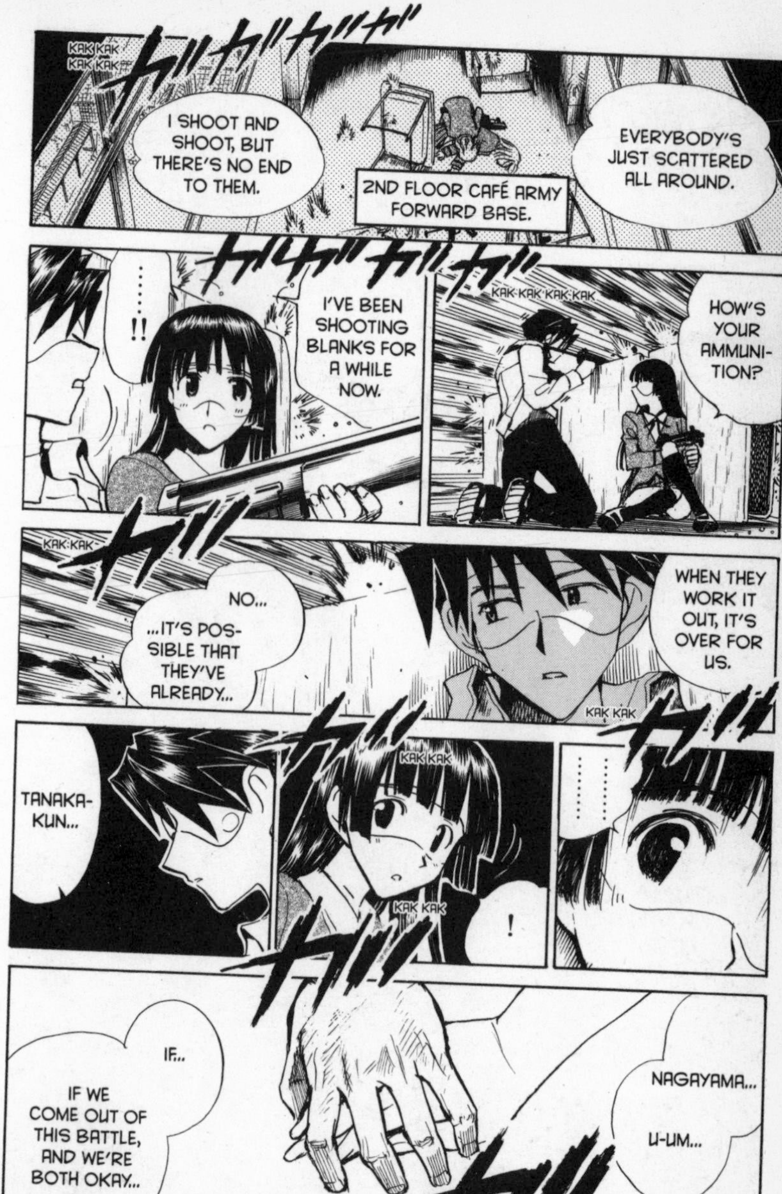
EVERYBODY'S JUST SCATTERED ALL AROUND.
2ND FLOOR CAFÉ ARMY FORWARD BASE.
I SHOOT AND SHOOT, BUT THERE'S NO END TO THEM.
KAK KAK KAK KAK
KAK KAK KAK KAK
HOW'S YOUR AMMUNITION?
I'VE BEEN SHOOTING BLANKS FOR A WHILE NOW.
......!!
WHEN THEY WORK IT OUT, IT'S OVER FOR US.
KAK KAK
NO...
...IT'S POSSIBLE THAT THEY'VE ALREADY...
KAK KAK
......
......
!
KAK KAK
KAK KAK
TANAKA-KUN...
NAGAYAMA...
U-UM...
KAK KAK
IF...
IF WE COME OUT OF THIS BATTLE, AND WE'RE BOTH OKAY...

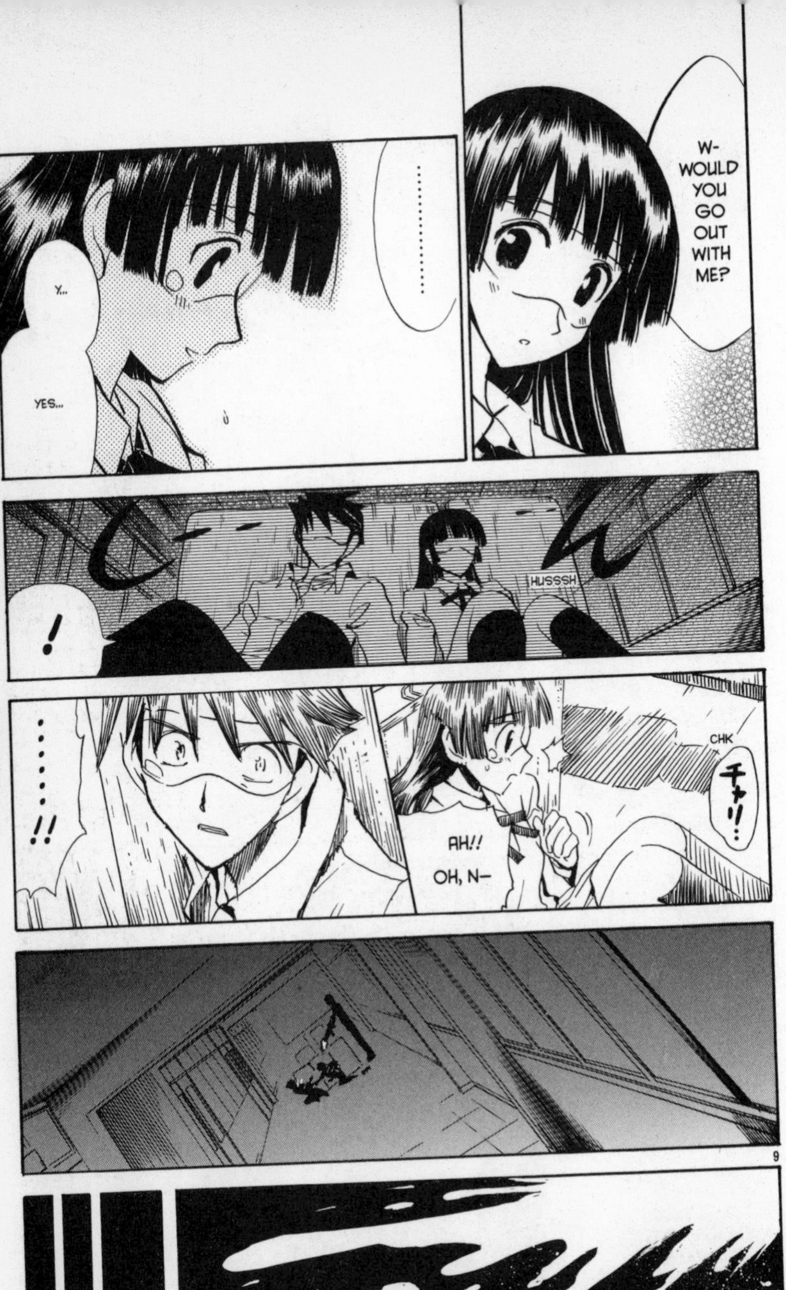
W- WOULD YOU GO OUT WITH ME?
......
Y...
YES...
HUSSSH
!
CHK
チャリ!..
AH!!
OH, N—
......!!

Turmoil.

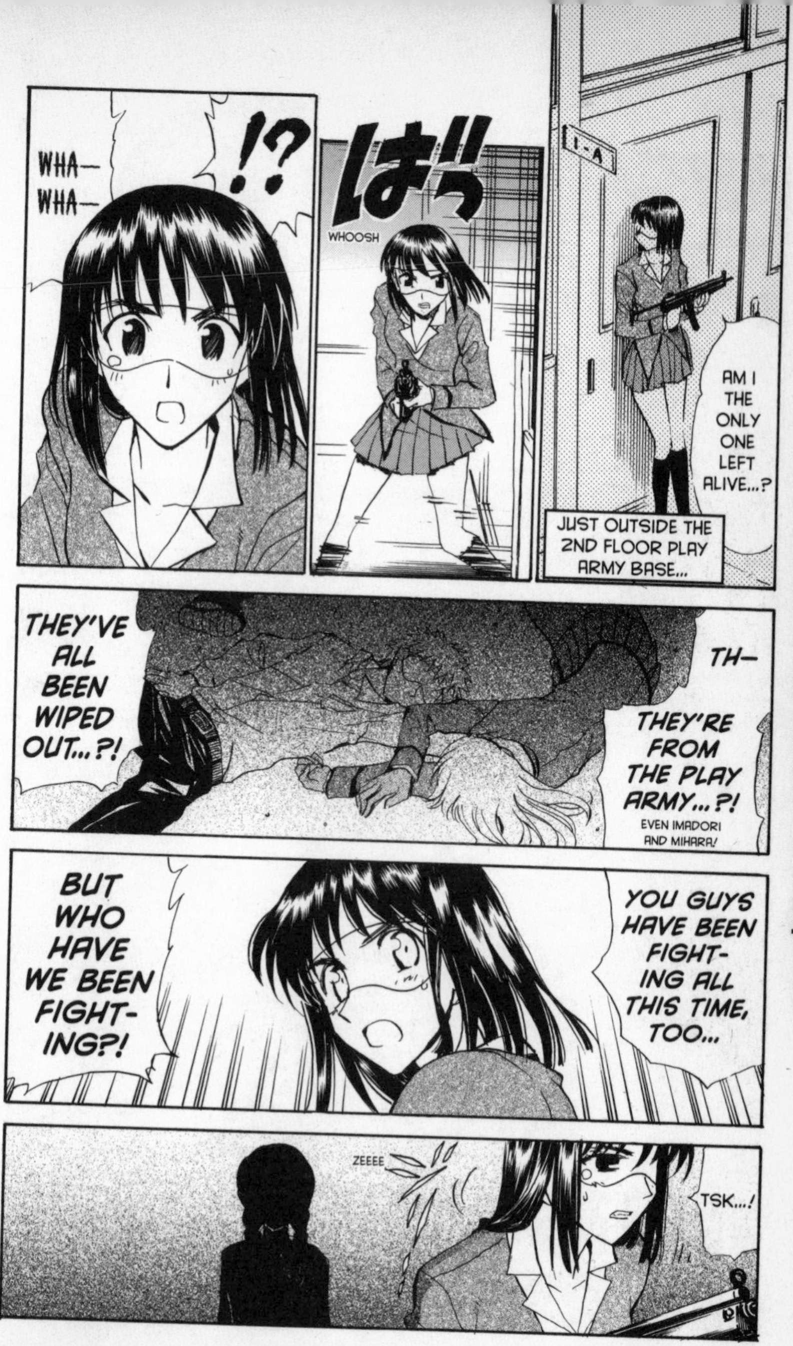

AM I THE ONLY ONE LEFT ALIVE...?
JUST OUTSIDE THE 2ND FLOOR PLAY ARMY BASE...
はっ
WHOOSH
!?
WHA— WHA—
TH— THEY'RE FROM THE PLAY ARMY...?!
EVEN IMADORI AND MIHARA!
THEY'VE ALL BEEN WIPED OUT...?!
YOU GUYS HAVE BEEN FIGHT- ING ALL THIS TIME, TOO...
BUT WHO HAVE WE BEEN FIGHT- ING?!
TSK...!
ZEEEE

The Location of Imadori's Hand: Suspicious.

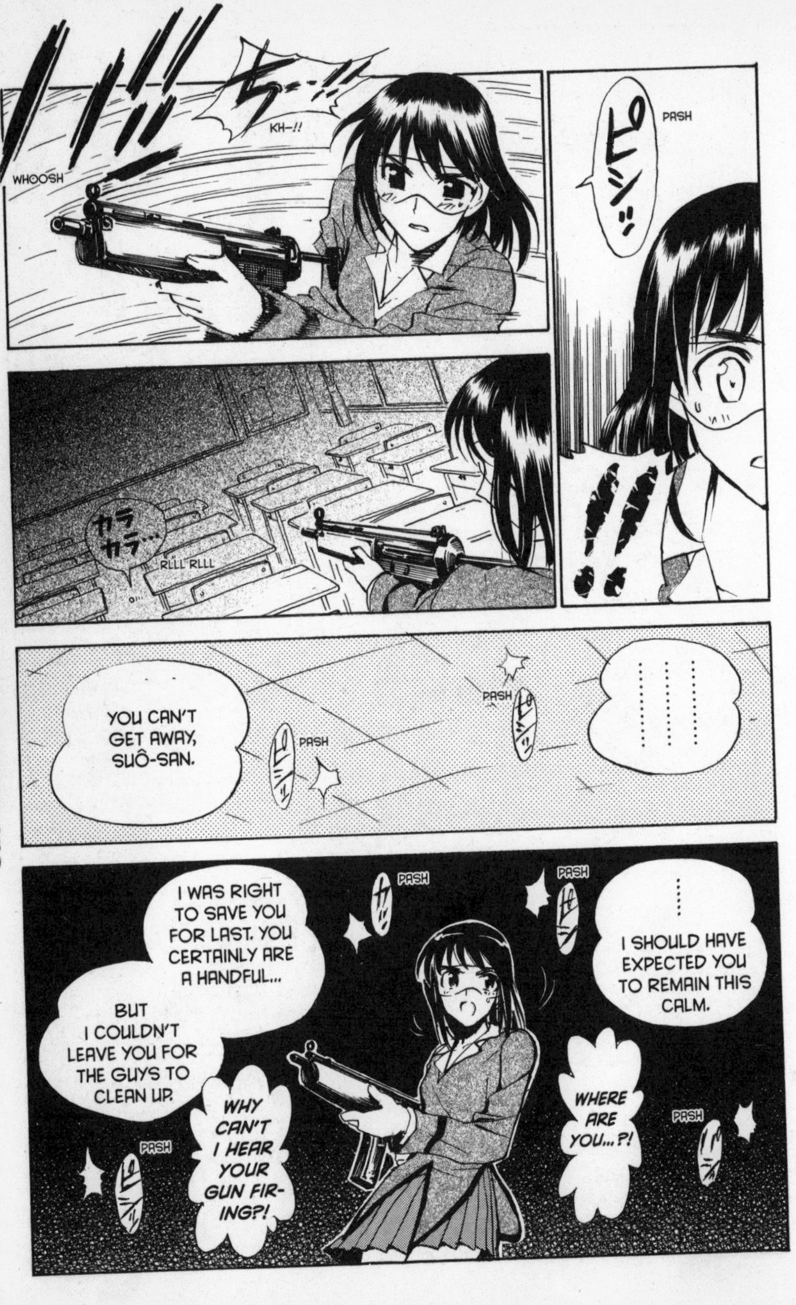
PASH
!!
KH-!!
WHOOSH
カラカラ…
RLLL RLLL
……
PASH
PASH
YOU CAN'T GET AWAY, SUÔ-SAN.
…
I SHOULD HAVE EXPECTED YOU TO REMAIN THIS CALM.
PASH
PASH
I WAS RIGHT TO SAVE YOU FOR LAST. YOU CERTAINLY ARE A HANDFUL...
BUT I COULDN'T LEAVE YOU FOR THE GUYS TO CLEAN UP.
PASH
WHERE ARE YOU...?!
WHY CAN'T I HEAR YOUR GUN FIRING?!
PASH

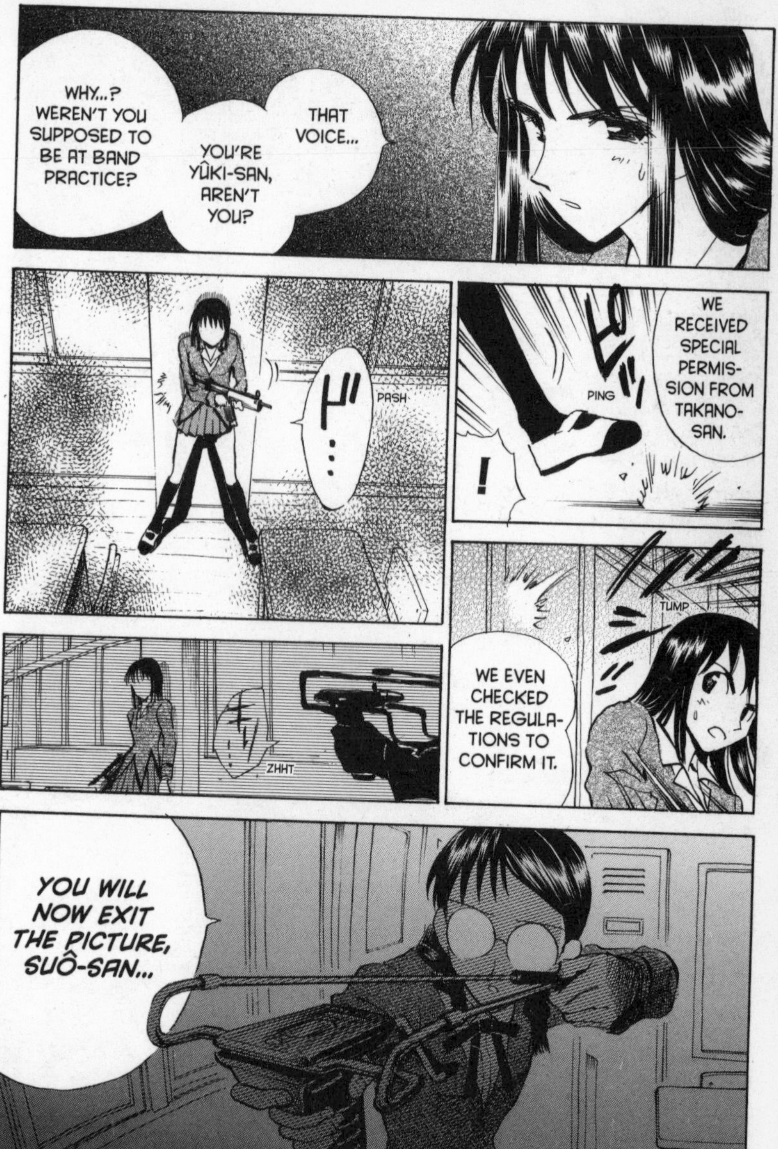
THAT VOICE...
YOU'RE YÛKI-SAN, AREN'T YOU?
WHY...? WEREN'T YOU SUPPOSED TO BE AT BAND PRACTICE?
WE RECEIVED SPECIAL PERMIS-SION FROM TAKANO-SAN.
PING
!
PASH
TUMP
WE EVEN CHECKED THE REGULA-TIONS TO CONFIRM IT.
ZHHT
YOU WILL NOW EXIT THE PICTURE, SUÔ-SAN...

Scary.

 # 107 . . . . Fin

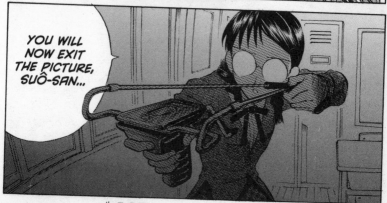

#108 TRULY, MADLY, DEEPLY

CAFÉ ARMY: HANAI, SUÔ, ASÔ, SUGA.
PLAY ARMY: HARIMA, TSUKAMOTO, SAWACHIKA (THE REAL ONE).
BAND ARMY: KARASUMA, FUYUKI, ICHIJÔ, SAGANO, YÛKI.
NOW, ONLY 12 STUDENTS SURVIVE!!

Mai-chan Went Home Already.

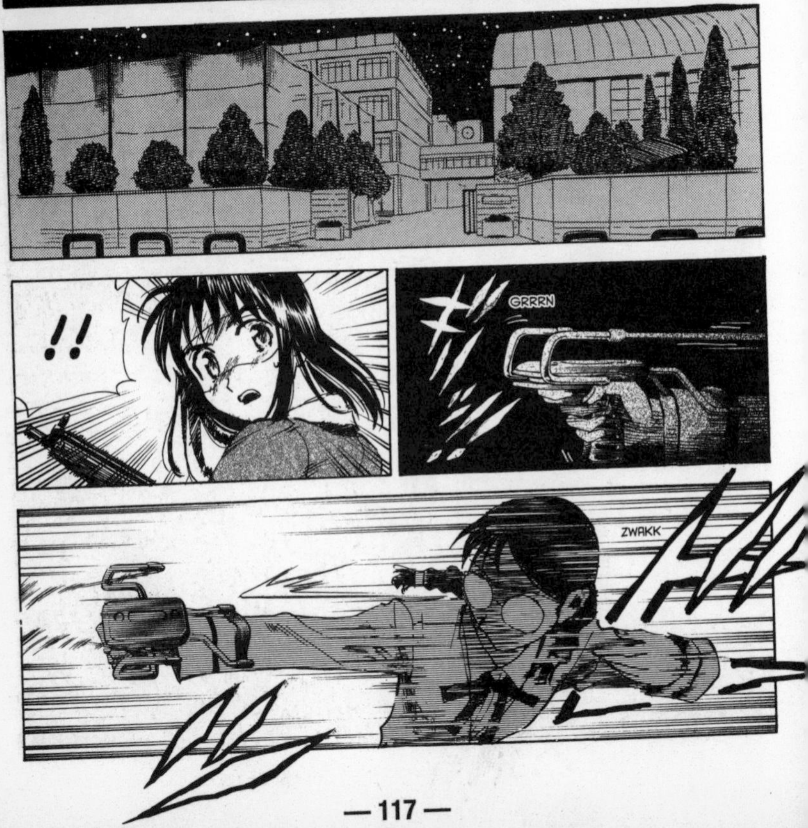
GRRRN
!!
ZWAKK

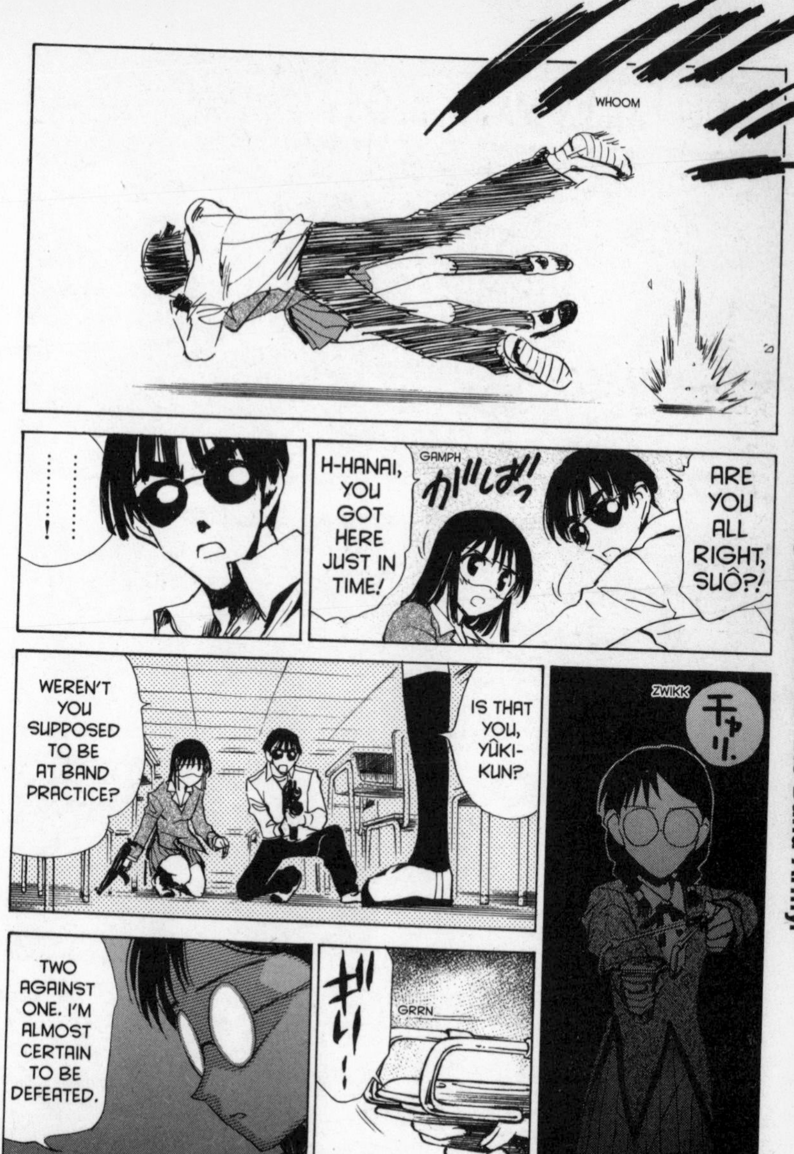
WHOOM
ARE YOU ALL RIGHT, SUÔ?!
GAMPH
H-HANAI, YOU GOT HERE JUST IN TIME!
......!
ZWIKK
IS THAT YOU, YÛKI-KUN?
WEREN'T YOU SUPPOSED TO BE AT BAND PRACTICE?
GRRN
TWO AGAINST ONE. I'M ALMOST CERTAIN TO BE DEFEATED.

Yûki Tsumugi: Assassin of the Band Army.

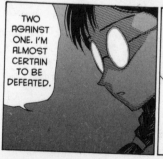

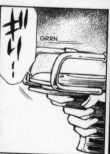

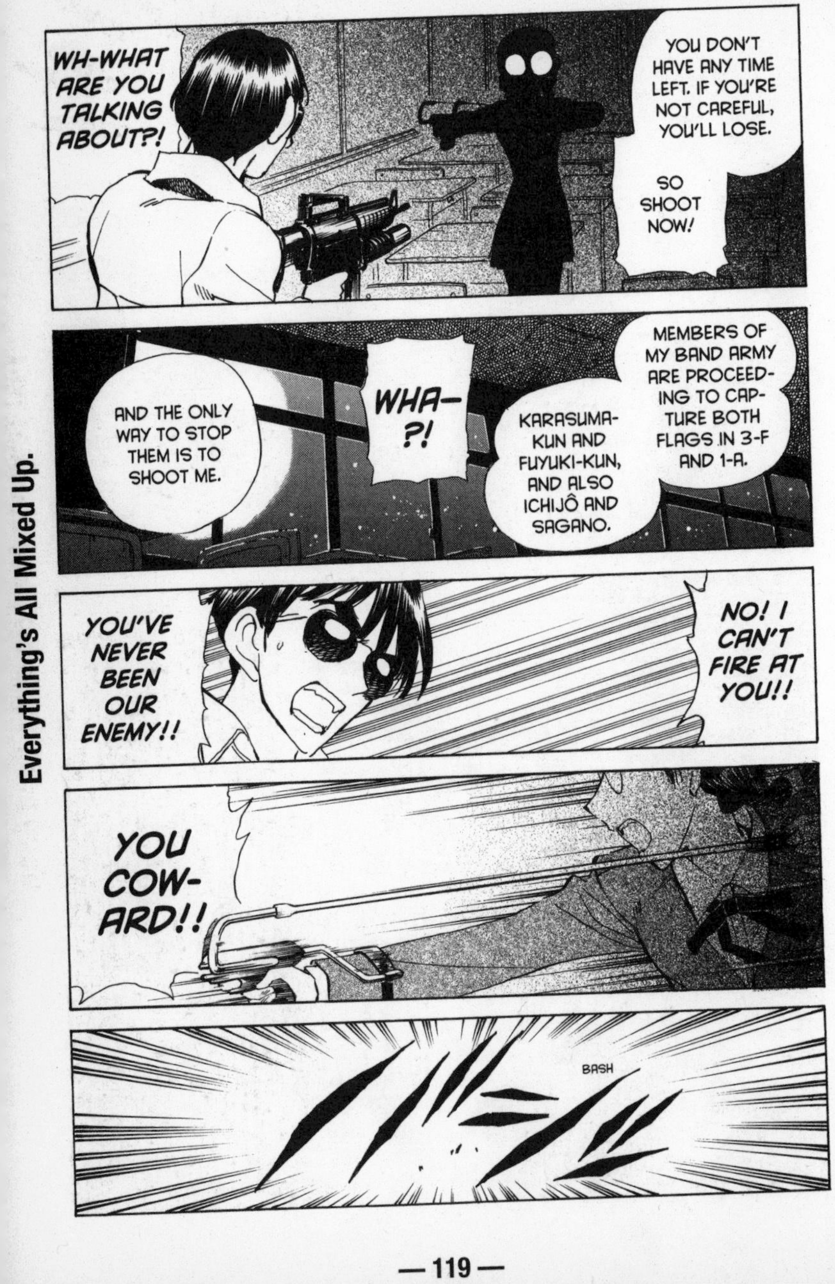
YOU DON'T HAVE ANY TIME LEFT. IF YOU'RE NOT CAREFUL, YOU'LL LOSE.
SO SHOOT NOW!
WH-WHAT ARE YOU TALKING ABOUT?!
MEMBERS OF MY BAND ARMY ARE PROCEEDING TO CAPTURE BOTH FLAGS IN 3-F AND 1-A.
KARASUMA-KUN AND FUYUKI-KUN, AND ALSO ICHIJÔ AND SAGANO.
WHA-?!
AND THE ONLY WAY TO STOP THEM IS TO SHOOT ME.
NO! I CAN'T FIRE AT YOU!!
YOU'VE NEVER BEEN OUR ENEMY!!
YOU COWARD!!
BASH

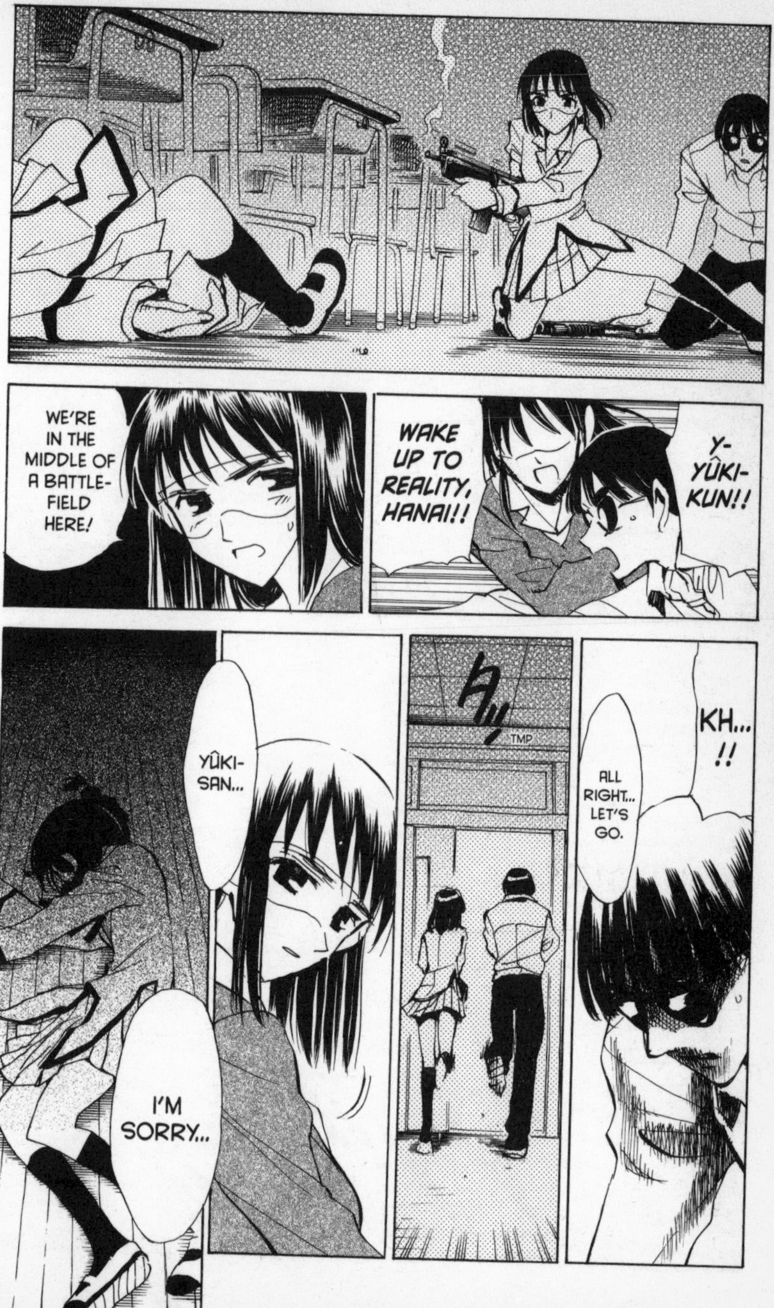
Y-YÛKI-KUN!!
WAKE UP TO REALITY, HANAI!!
WE'RE IN THE MIDDLE OF A BATTLEFIELD HERE!
KH... !!
ALL RIGHT... LET'S GO.
TMP
YÛKI-SAN...
I'M SORRY...

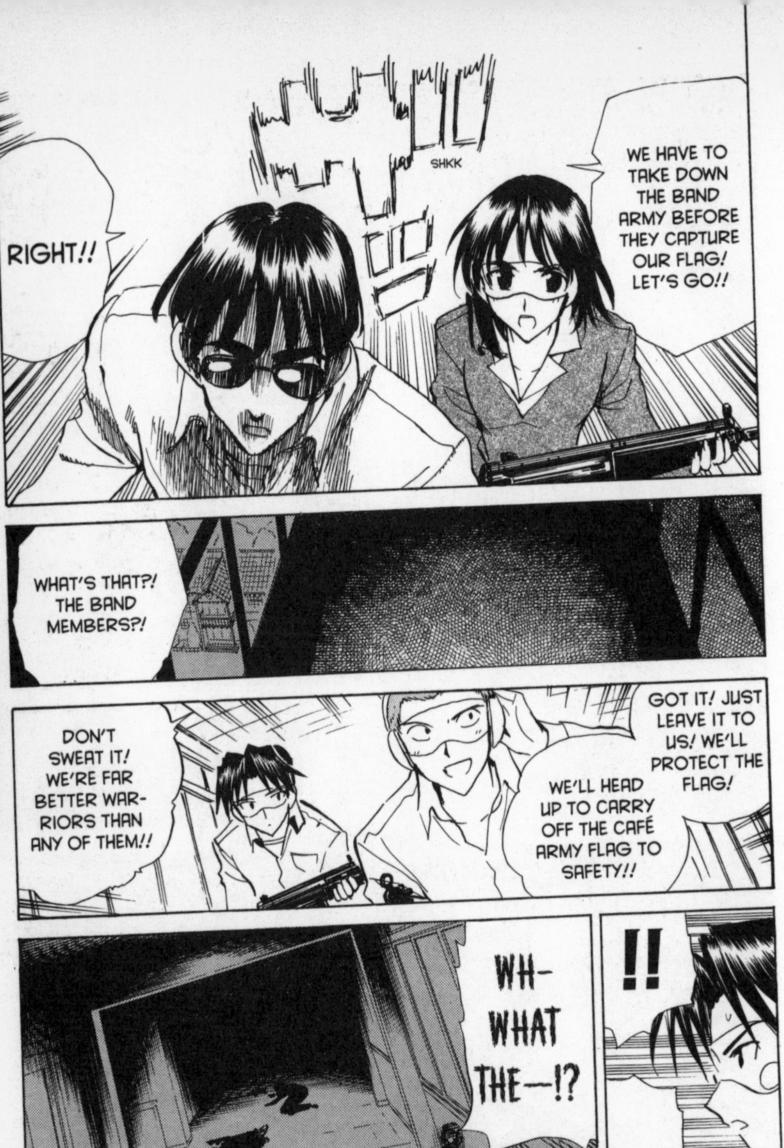
WE HAVE TO TAKE DOWN THE BAND ARMY BEFORE THEY CAPTURE OUR FLAG! LET'S GO!!
SHKK
RIGHT!!
WHAT'S THAT?! THE BAND MEMBERS?!
GOT IT! JUST LEAVE IT TO US! WE'LL PROTECT THE FLAG!
WE'LL HEAD UP TO CARRY OFF THE CAFÉ ARMY FLAG TO SAFETY!!
DON'T SWEAT IT! WE'RE FAR BETTER WAR-RIORS THAN ANY OF THEM!!
!!
SUGA! LOOK!
WH-WHAT THE—!?

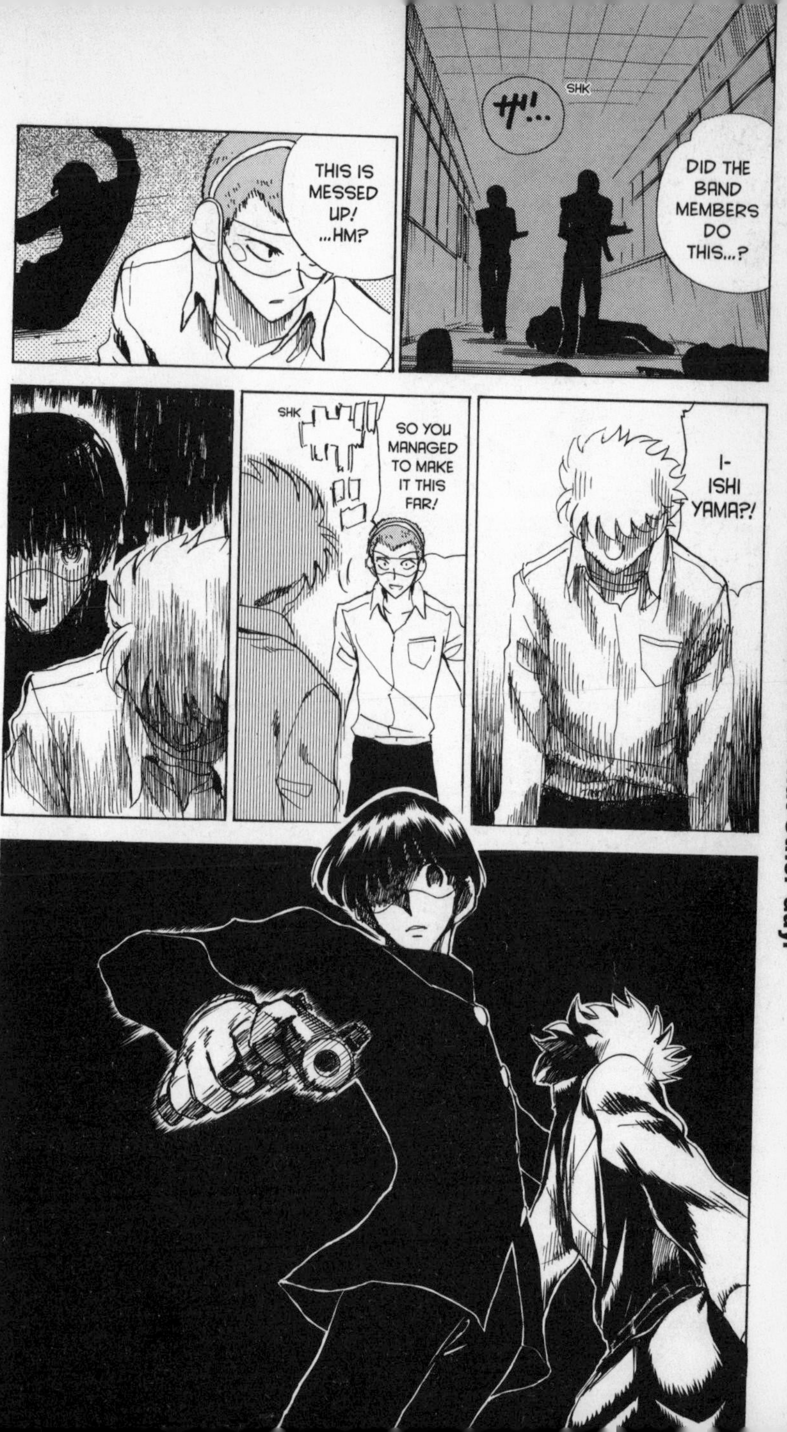
SHK
DID THE BAND MEMBERS DO THIS...?
THIS IS MESSED UP! ...HM?
I-ISHI YAMA?!
SHK
SO YOU MANAGED TO MAKE IT THIS FAR!

Also Known As: That Other Guy.

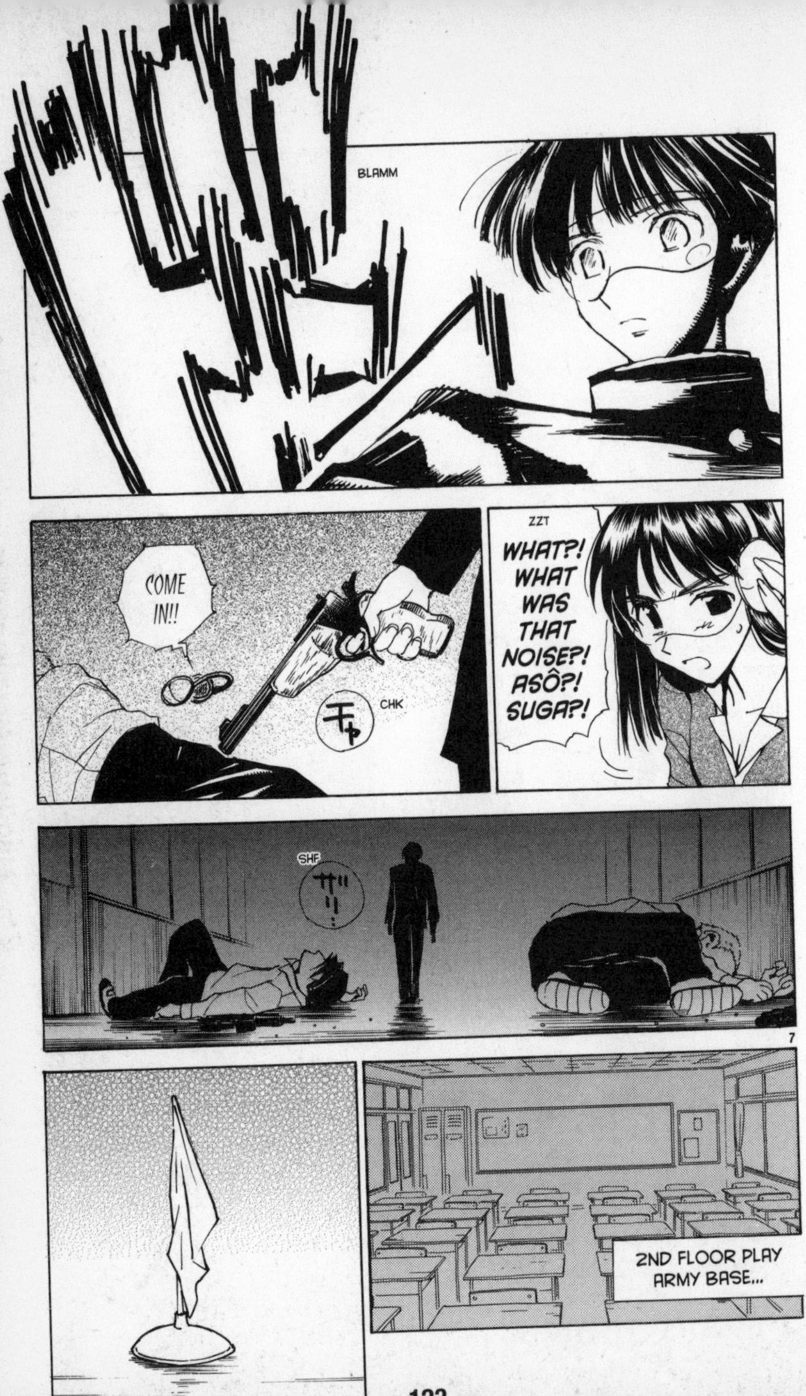
BLAMM
ZZT
WHAT?! WHAT WAS THAT NOISE?! ASÔ?! SUGA?!
COME IN!!
CHK
SHF
2ND FLOOR PLAY ARMY BASE...

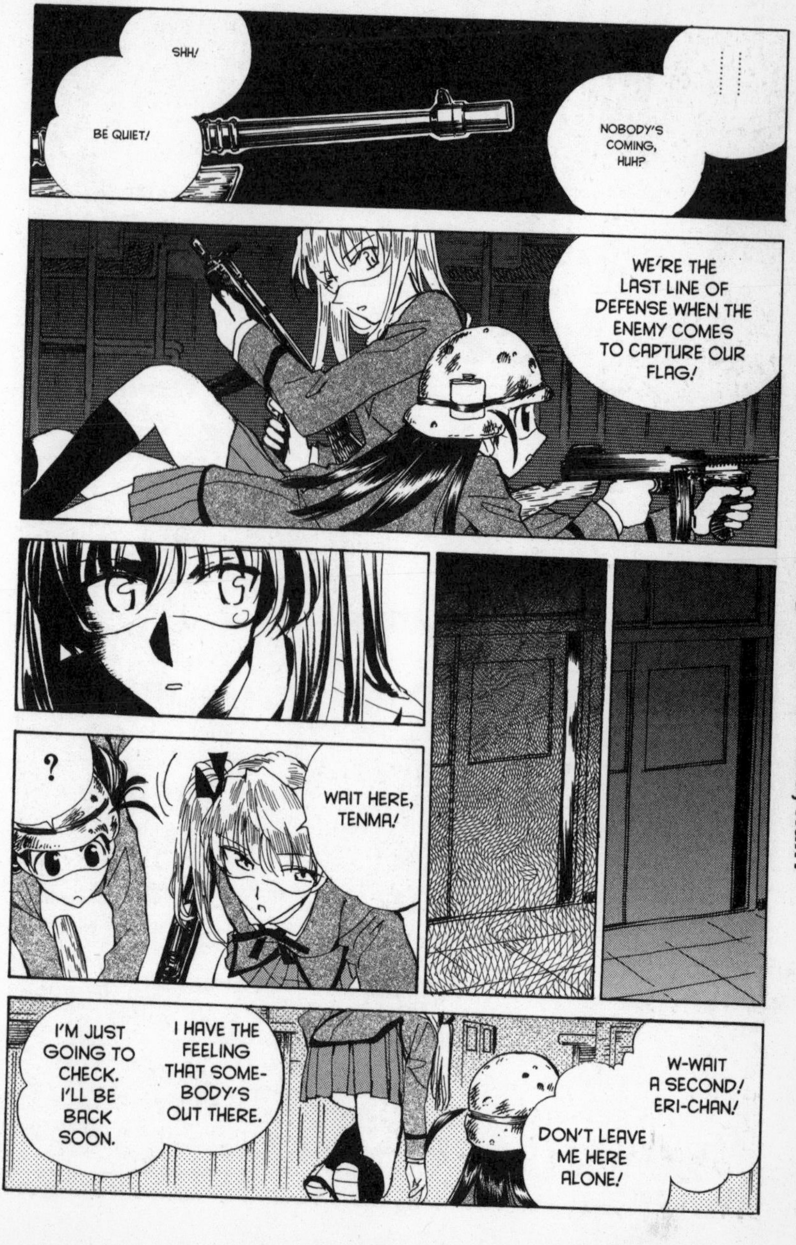
......
NOBODY'S COMING, HUH?
SHH!
BE QUIET!
WE'RE THE LAST LINE OF DEFENSE WHEN THE ENEMY COMES TO CAPTURE OUR FLAG!
?
WAIT HERE, TENMA!
W-WAIT A SECOND! ERI-CHAN!
DON'T LEAVE ME HERE ALONE!
I HAVE THE FEELING THAT SOME-BODY'S OUT THERE.
I'M JUST GOING TO CHECK. I'LL BE BACK SOON.

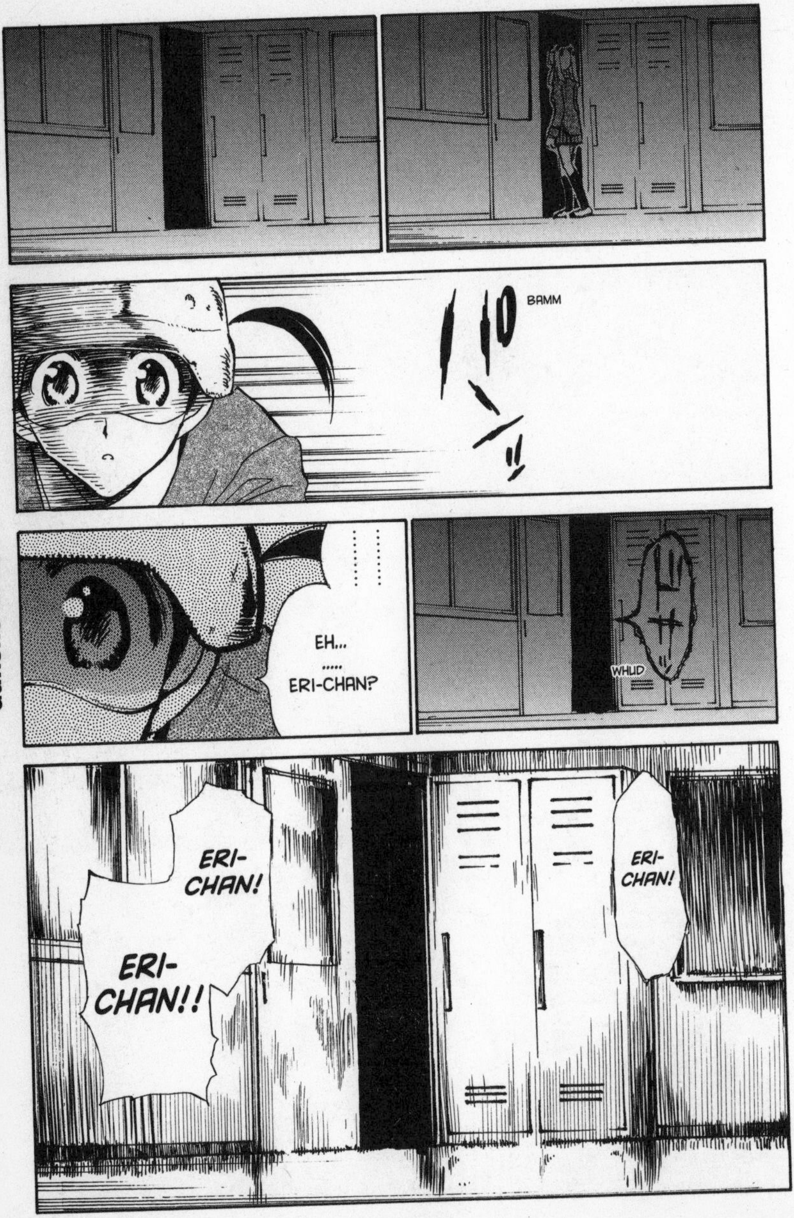
BAMM
WHUD
......
EH... ..... ERI-CHAN?
ERI-CHAN!
ERI-CHAN!
ERI-CHAN!!

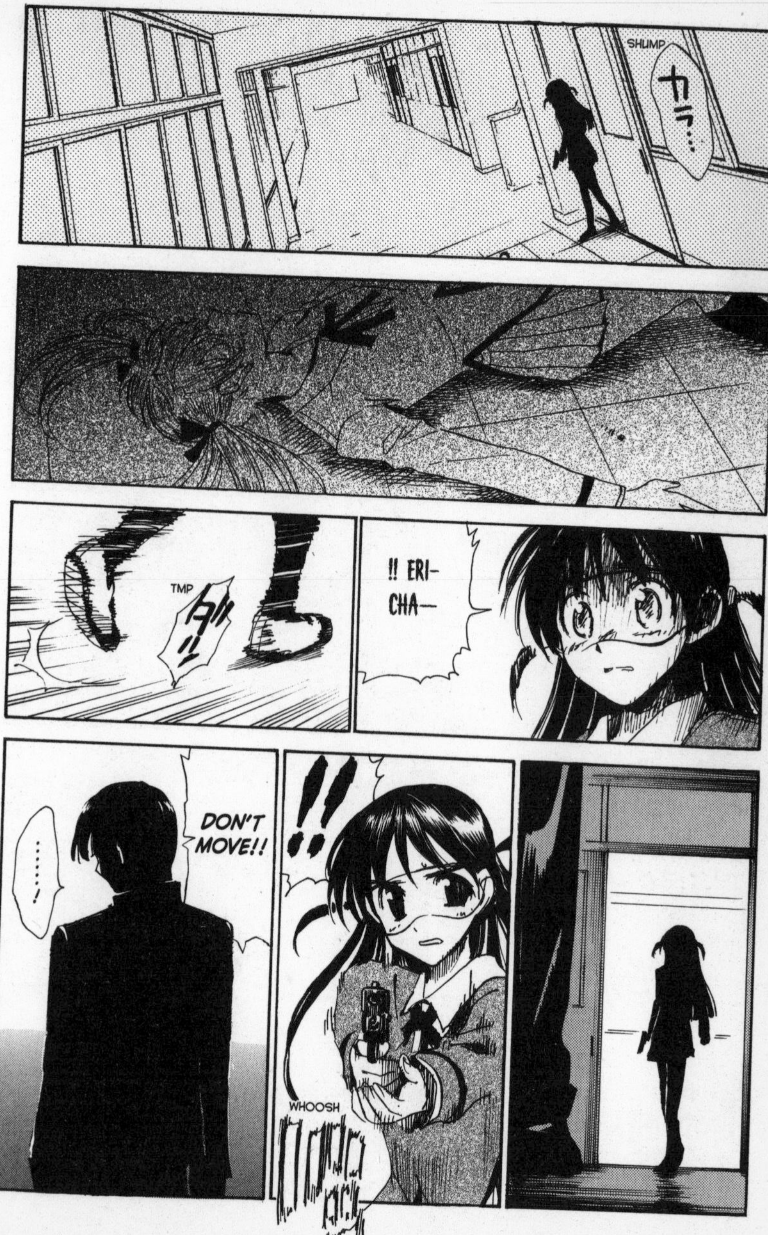
SHUMP
カラ…
!! ERI-CHA—
TMP
タッ!!
!!
DON'T MOVE!!
WHOOSH
......!

Sawachika Eri: KIA

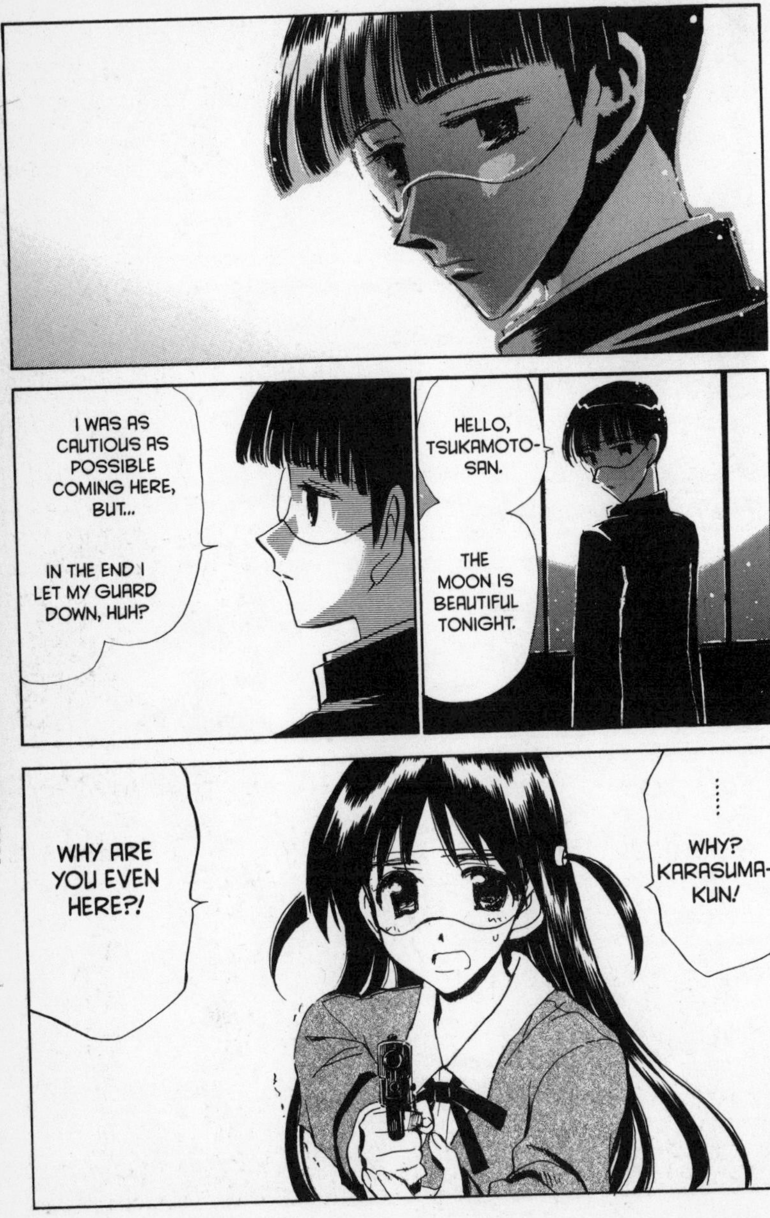
HELLO, TSUKAMOTO-SAN.
THE MOON IS BEAUTIFUL TONIGHT.
I WAS AS CAUTIOUS AS POSSIBLE COMING HERE, BUT...
IN THE END I LET MY GUARD DOWN, HUH?
......
WHY? KARASUMA-KUN!
WHY ARE YOU EVEN HERE?!

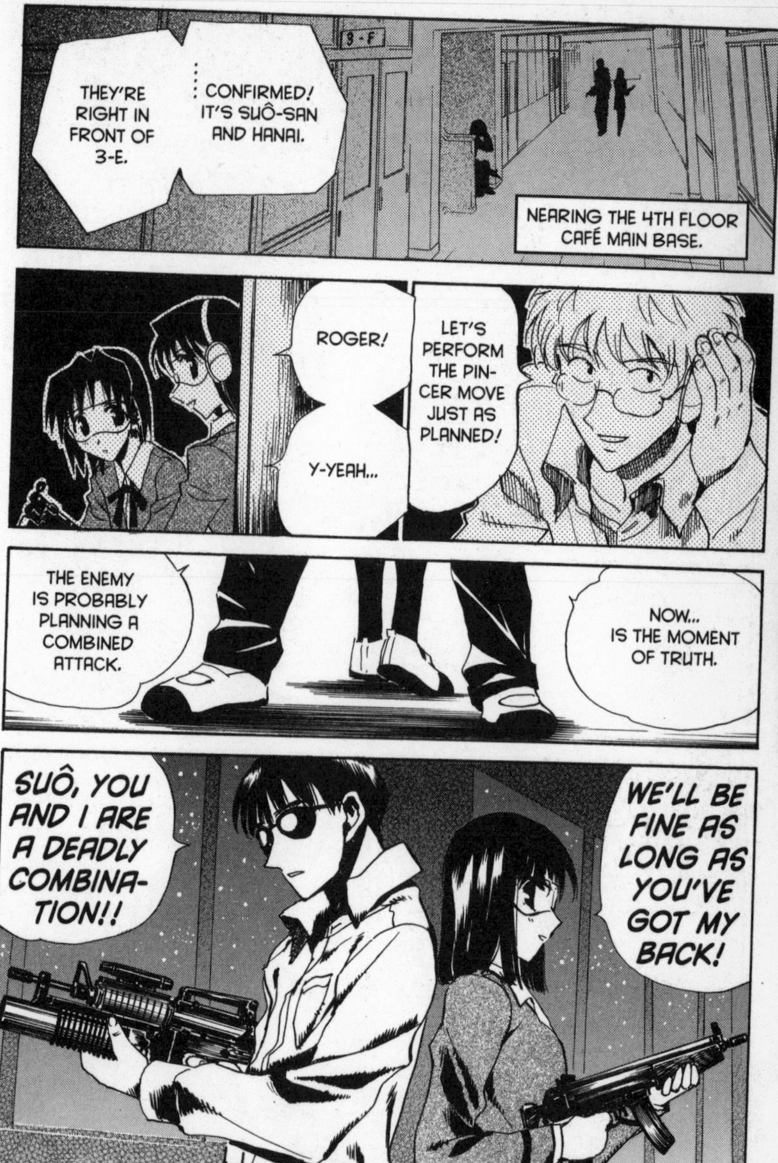

⋮ CONFIRMED! IT'S SUÔ-SAN AND HANAI.
THEY'RE RIGHT IN FRONT OF 3-E.
NEARING THE 4TH FLOOR CAFÉ MAIN BASE.
LET'S PERFORM THE PIN-CER MOVE JUST AS PLANNED!
ROGER!
Y-YEAH...
NOW... IS THE MOMENT OF TRUTH.
THE ENEMY IS PROBABLY PLANNING A COMBINED ATTACK.
WE'LL BE FINE AS LONG AS YOU'VE GOT MY BACK!
SUÔ, YOU AND I ARE A DEADLY COMBINA-TION!!

Mighty Warriors Both.

108 . . . . Fin

♭21 NUIT DOCILE

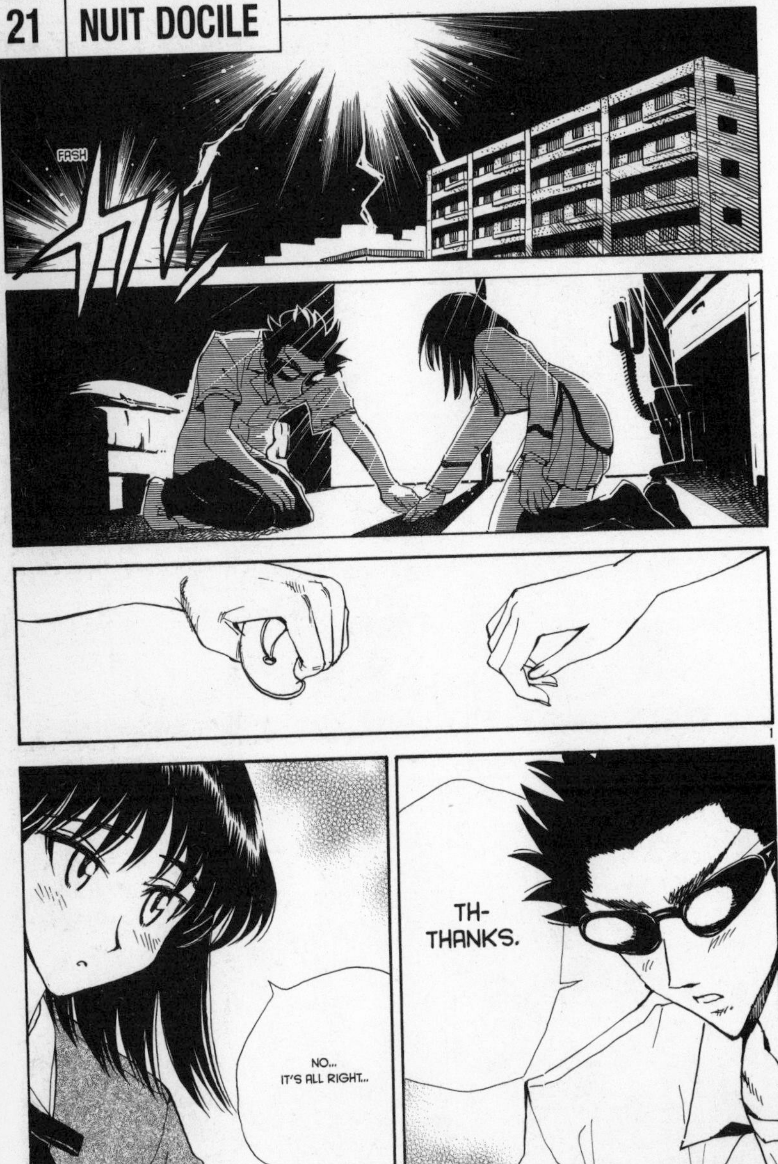
FASH
TH-
THANKS.
NO...
IT'S ALL RIGHT...

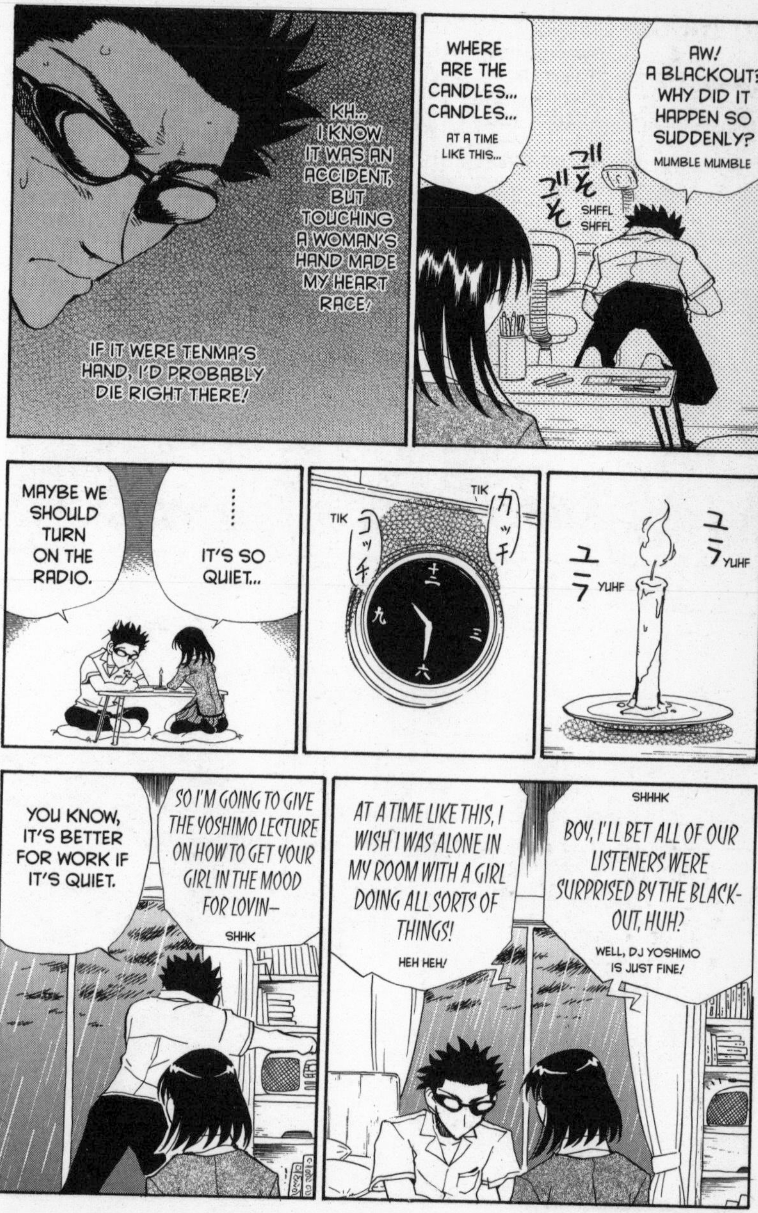
AW! A BLACKOUT? WHY DID IT HAPPEN SO SUDDENLY?
MUMBLE MUMBLE
WHERE ARE THE CANDLES... CANDLES...
AT A TIME LIKE THIS...
ごそ ごそ
SHFFL SHFFL
KH... I KNOW IT WAS AN ACCIDENT, BUT TOUCHING A WOMAN'S HAND MADE MY HEART RACE!
IF IT WERE TENMA'S HAND, I'D PROBABLY DIE RIGHT THERE!
ユラ YUHF
ユラ YUHF
カッチ TIK
コッチ TIK
......
IT'S SO QUIET...
MAYBE WE SHOULD TURN ON THE RADIO.
SHHHK
BOY, I'LL BET ALL OF OUR LISTENERS WERE SURPRISED BY THE BLACK-OUT, HUH?
WELL, DJ YOSHIMO IS JUST FINE!
AT A TIME LIKE THIS, I WISH I WAS ALONE IN MY ROOM WITH A GIRL DOING ALL SORTS OF THINGS!
HEH HEH!
SO I'M GOING TO GIVE THE YOSHIMO LECTURE ON HOW TO GET YOUR GIRL IN THE MOOD FOR LOVIN—
SHHK
YOU KNOW, IT'S BETTER FOR WORK IF IT'S QUIET.

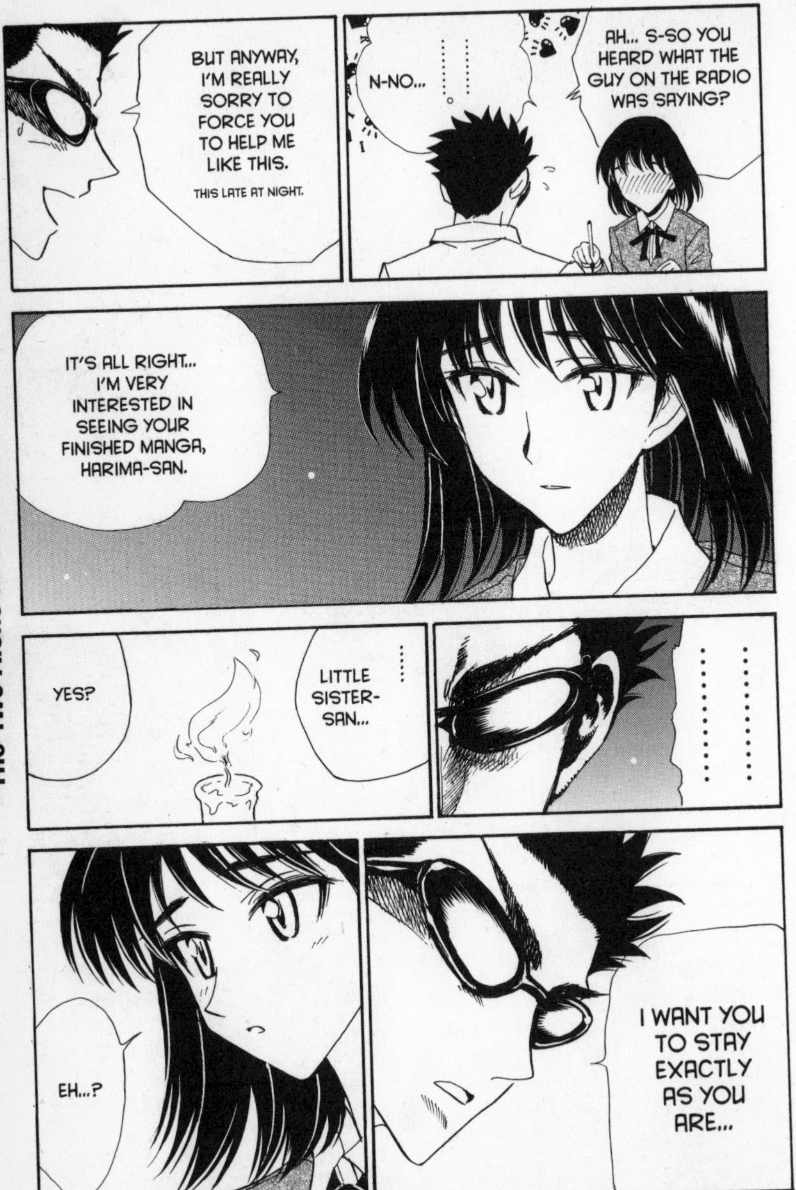
AH... S-SO YOU HEARD WHAT THE GUY ON THE RADIO WAS SAYING?
N-NO...
BUT ANYWAY, I'M REALLY SORRY TO FORCE YOU TO HELP ME LIKE THIS.
THIS LATE AT NIGHT.
IT'S ALL RIGHT... I'M VERY INTERESTED IN SEEING YOUR FINISHED MANGA, HARIMA-SAN.
LITTLE SISTER-SAN...
YES?
I WANT YOU TO STAY EXACTLY AS YOU ARE...
EH...?

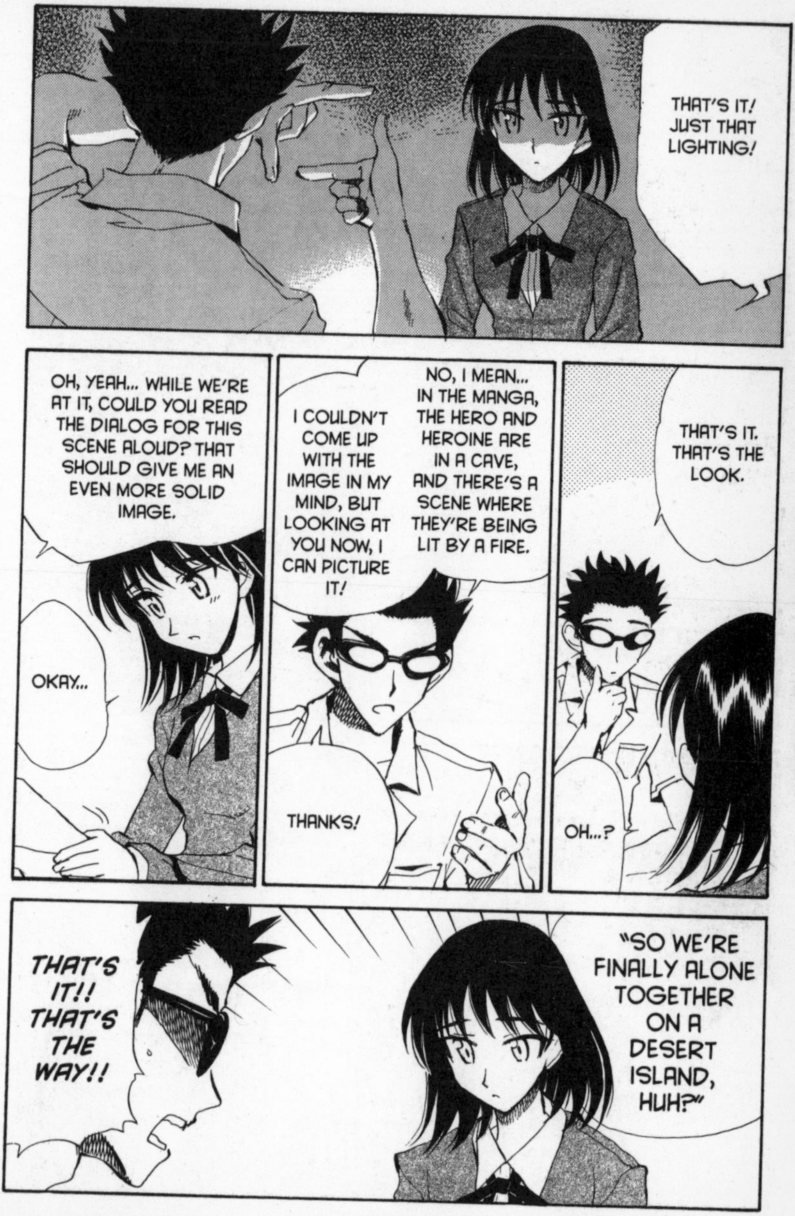
THAT'S IT! JUST THAT LIGHTING!
THAT'S IT. THAT'S THE LOOK.
OH...?
NO, I MEAN... IN THE MANGA, THE HERO AND HEROINE ARE IN A CAVE, AND THERE'S A SCENE WHERE THEY'RE BEING LIT BY A FIRE.
I COULDN'T COME UP WITH THE IMAGE IN MY MIND, BUT LOOKING AT YOU NOW, I CAN PICTURE IT!
THANKS!
OH, YEAH... WHILE WE'RE AT IT, COULD YOU READ THE DIALOG FOR THIS SCENE ALOUD? THAT SHOULD GIVE ME AN EVEN MORE SOLID IMAGE.
OKAY...
"SO WE'RE FINALLY ALONE TOGETHER ON A DESERT ISLAND, HUH?"
THAT'S IT!! THAT'S THE WAY!!

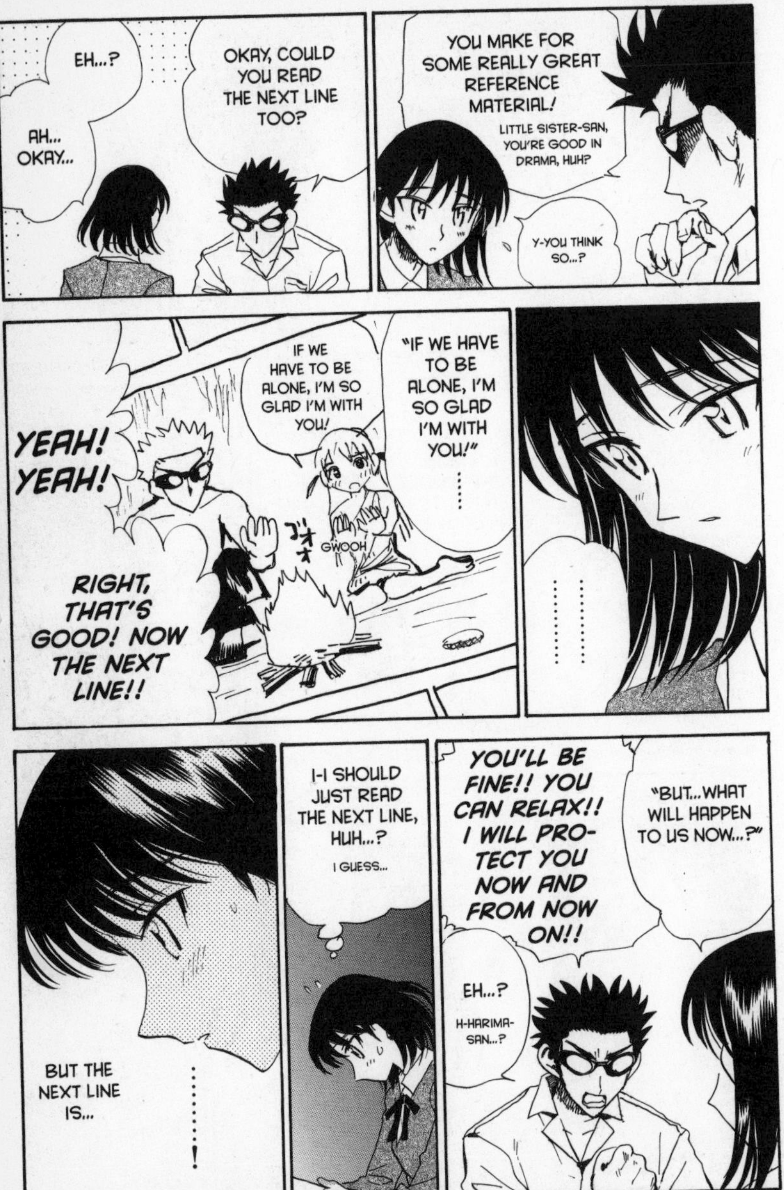
YOU MAKE FOR SOME REALLY GREAT REFERENCE MATERIAL!
LITTLE SISTER-SAN, YOU'RE GOOD IN DRAMA, HUH?
Y-YOU THINK SO...?
OKAY, COULD YOU READ THE NEXT LINE TOO?
EH...?
AH... OKAY...
......
"IF WE HAVE TO BE ALONE, I'M SO GLAD I'M WITH YOU!"
......
IF WE HAVE TO BE ALONE, I'M SO GLAD I'M WITH YOU!
YEAH! YEAH!
ゴオオ
GWOOH
RIGHT, THAT'S GOOD! NOW THE NEXT LINE!!
"BUT...WHAT WILL HAPPEN TO US NOW...?"
YOU'LL BE FINE!! YOU CAN RELAX!! I WILL PRO-TECT YOU NOW AND FROM NOW ON!!
EH...?
H-HARIMA-SAN...?
I-I SHOULD JUST READ THE NEXT LINE, HUH...?
I GUESS...
......!
BUT THE NEXT LINE IS...

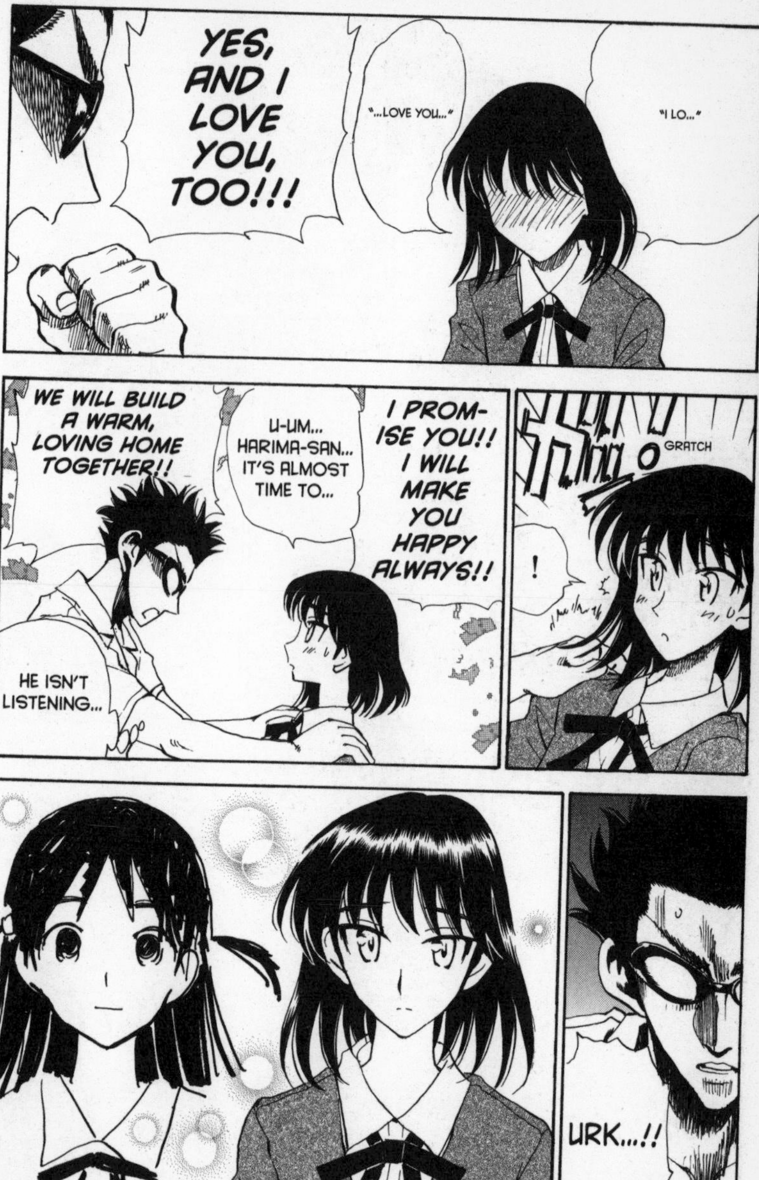
"I LO..."
"...LOVE YOU..."
YES, AND I LOVE YOU, TOO!!!
GRATCH
!
I PROM-ISE YOU!! I WILL MAKE YOU HAPPY ALWAYS!!
U-UM... HARIMA-SAN... IT'S ALMOST TIME TO...
WE WILL BUILD A WARM, LOVING HOME TOGETHER!!
HE ISN'T LISTENING...
URK...!!

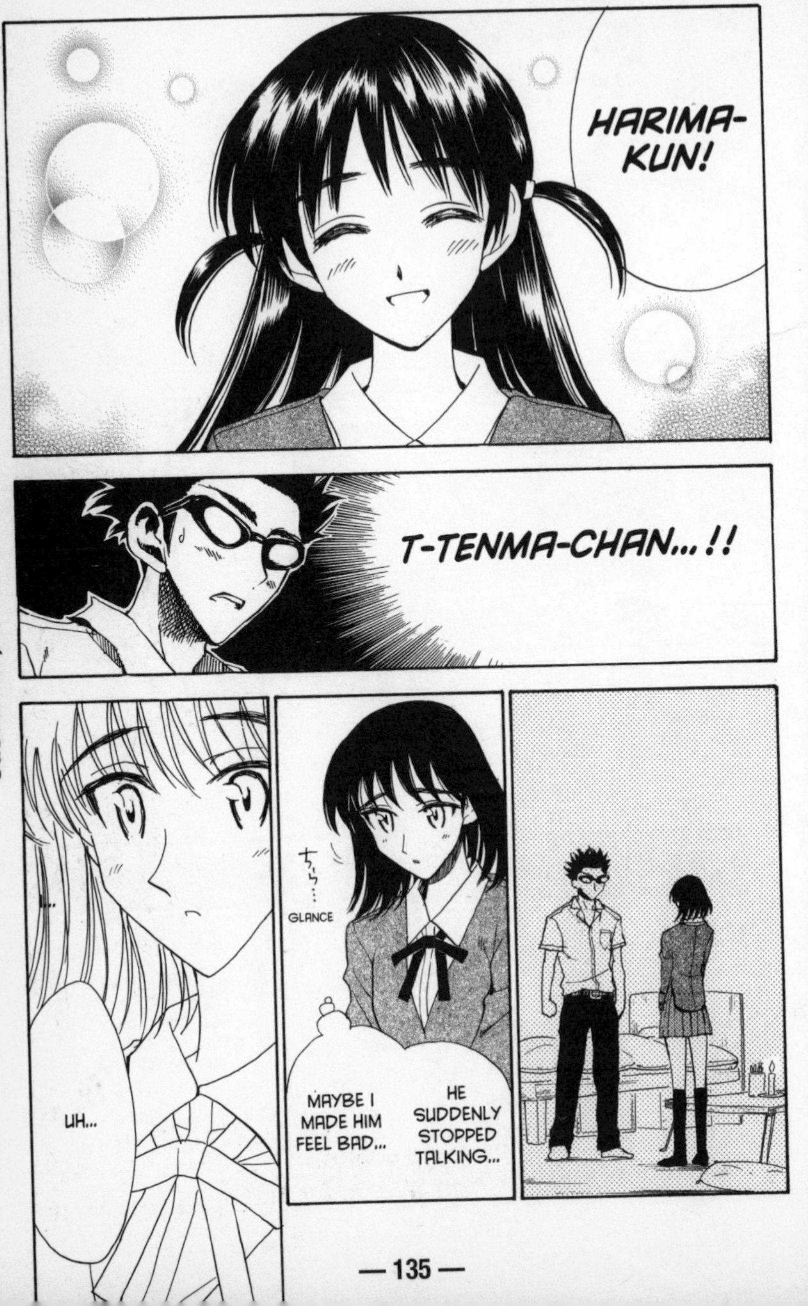
HARIMA-KUN!
T-TENMA-CHAN...!!
ちら…
GLANCE
HE SUDDENLY STOPPED TALKING...
MAYBE I MADE HIM FEEL BAD...
...
UH...

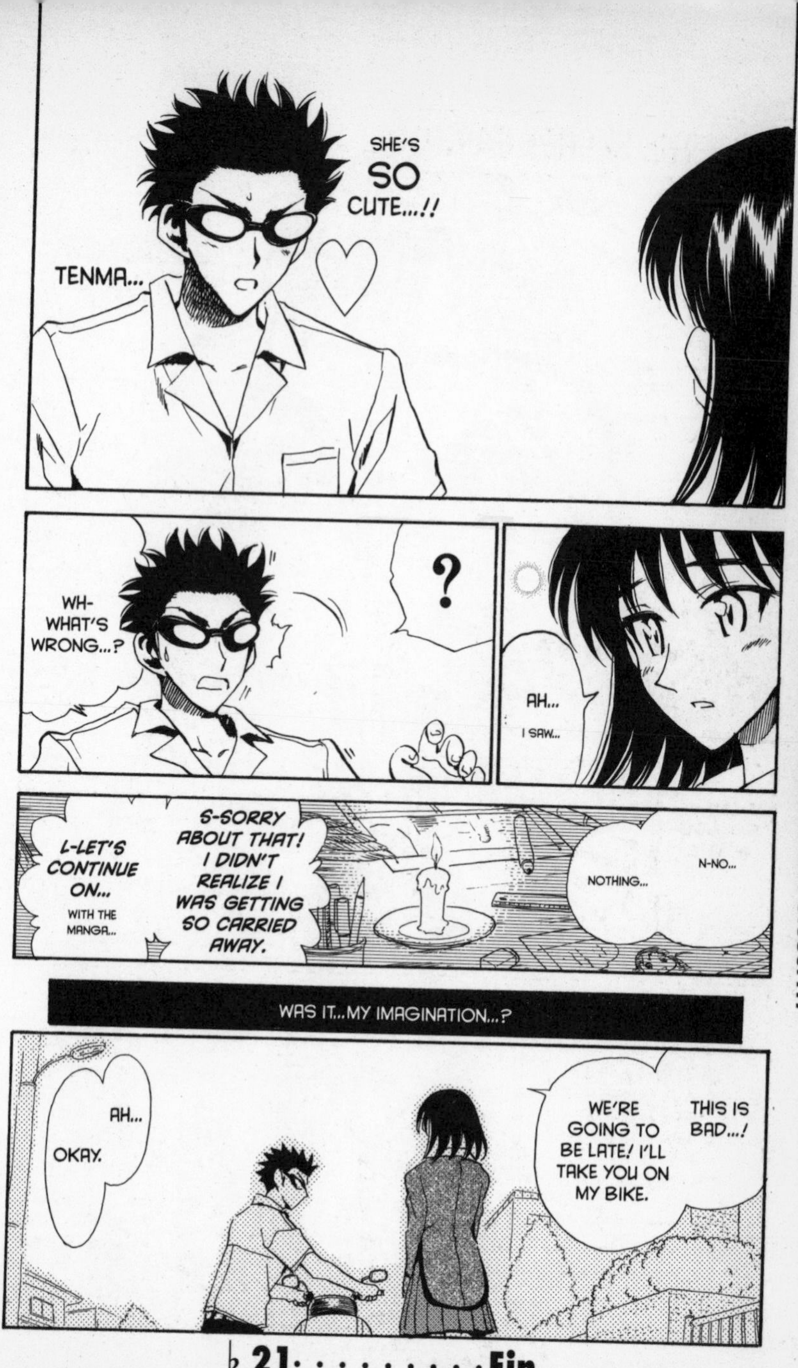
SHE'S SO CUTE...!!
TENMA...
AH...
I SAW...
?
WH-WHAT'S WRONG...?
N-NO...
NOTHING...
S-SORRY ABOUT THAT! I DIDN'T REALIZE I WAS GETTING SO CARRIED AWAY.
L-LET'S CONTINUE ON...
WITH THE MANGA...
WAS IT...MY IMAGINATION...?
THIS IS BAD...!
WE'RE GOING TO BE LATE! I'LL TAKE YOU ON MY BIKE.
AH...
OKAY.

♭21· · · · · · · · ·Fin

♭22 THE SECRET GARDEN

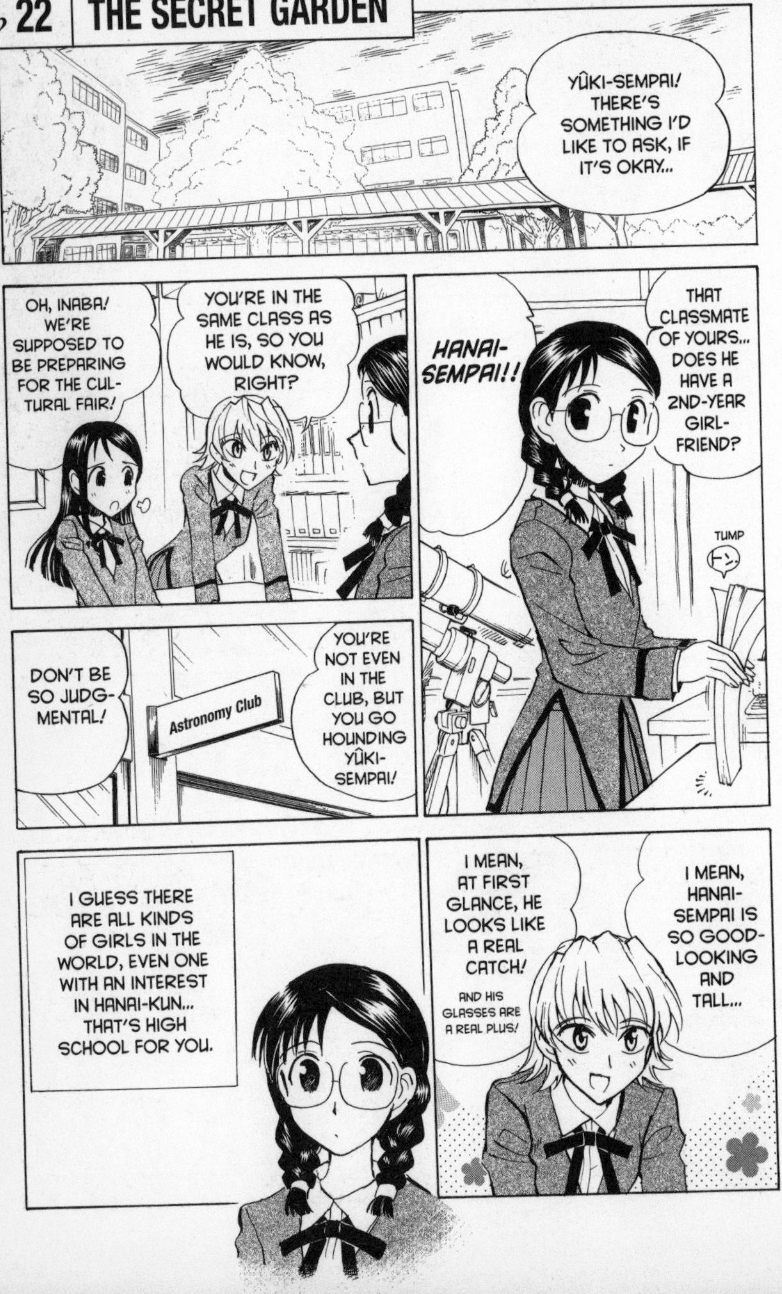

YÛKI-SEMPAI! THERE'S SOMETHING I'D LIKE TO ASK, IF IT'S OKAY...
THAT CLASSMATE OF YOURS... DOES HE HAVE A 2ND-YEAR GIRLFRIEND?
HANAI-SEMPAI!!
TUMP
YOU'RE IN THE SAME CLASS AS HE IS, SO YOU WOULD KNOW, RIGHT?
OH, INABA! WE'RE SUPPOSED TO BE PREPARING FOR THE CULTURAL FAIR!
YOU'RE NOT EVEN IN THE CLUB, BUT YOU GO HOUNDING YÛKI-SEMPAI!
Astronomy Club
DON'T BE SO JUDGMENTAL!
I MEAN, HANAI-SEMPAI IS SO GOOD-LOOKING AND TALL...
I MEAN, AT FIRST GLANCE, HE LOOKS LIKE A REAL CATCH!
AND HIS GLASSES ARE A REAL PLUS!
I GUESS THERE ARE ALL KINDS OF GIRLS IN THE WORLD, EVEN ONE WITH AN INTEREST IN HANAI-KUN... THAT'S HIGH SCHOOL FOR YOU.

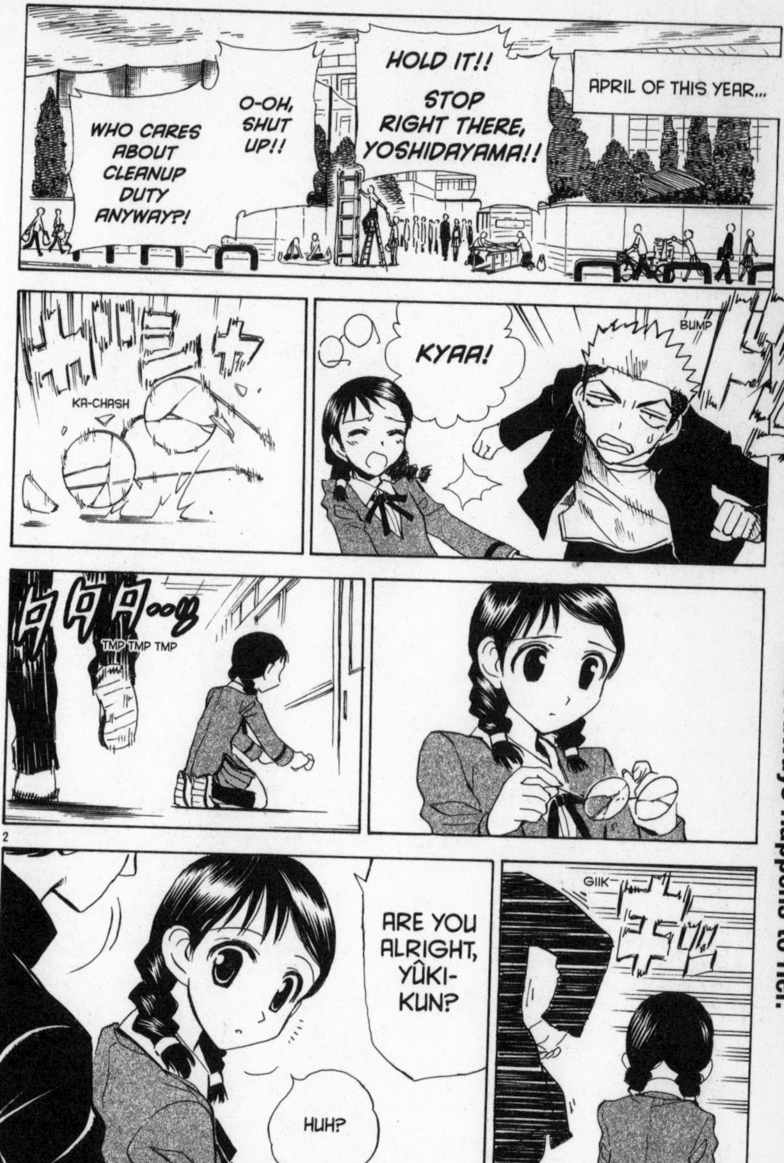
APRIL OF THIS YEAR...
HOLD IT!!
STOP RIGHT THERE, YOSHIDAYAMA!!
O-OH, SHUT UP!!
WHO CARES ABOUT CLEANUP DUTY ANYWAY?!
BUMP
KYAA!
KA-CHASH
TMP TMP TMP
2
GIIK
ARE YOU ALRIGHT, YÛKI-KUN?
HUH?

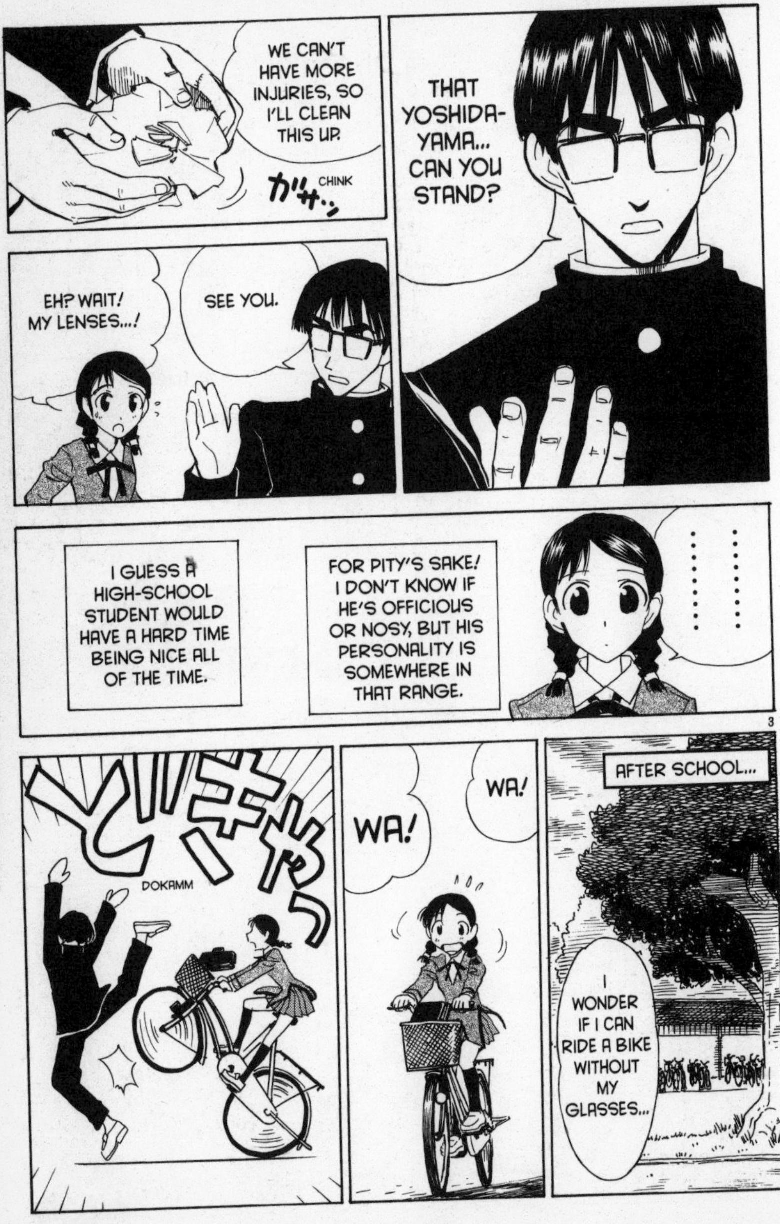
THAT YOSHIDA-YAMA... CAN YOU STAND?
WE CAN'T HAVE MORE INJURIES, SO I'LL CLEAN THIS UP.
ガサッ
CHINK
SEE YOU.
EH? WAIT! MY LENSES...!
......
FOR PITY'S SAKE! I DON'T KNOW IF HE'S OFFICIOUS OR NOSY, BUT HIS PERSONALITY IS SOMEWHERE IN THAT RANGE.
I GUESS A HIGH-SCHOOL STUDENT WOULD HAVE A HARD TIME BEING NICE ALL OF THE TIME.
3
AFTER SCHOOL...
I WONDER IF I CAN RIDE A BIKE WITHOUT MY GLASSES...
WA!
WA!
DOKAMM

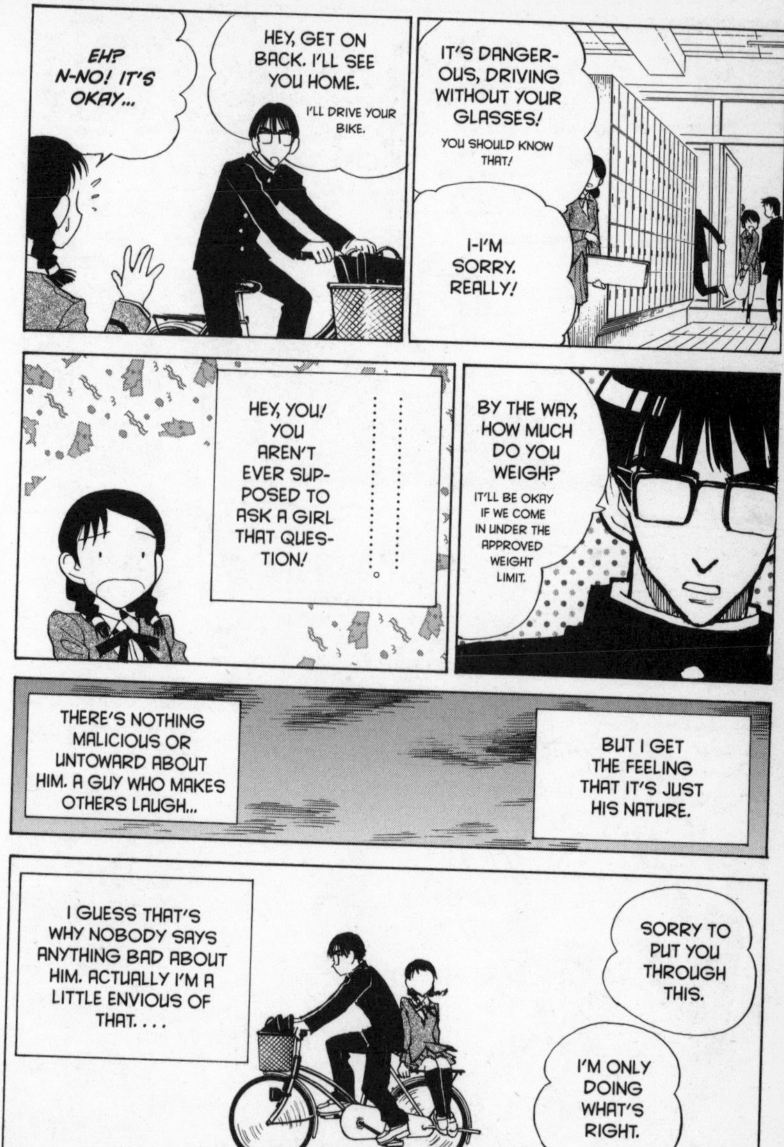
IT'S DANGER-OUS, DRIVING WITHOUT YOUR GLASSES!
YOU SHOULD KNOW THAT!
I-I'M SORRY. REALLY!
HEY, GET ON BACK. I'LL SEE YOU HOME.
I'LL DRIVE YOUR BIKE.
EH? N-NO! IT'S OKAY...
BY THE WAY, HOW MUCH DO YOU WEIGH?
IT'LL BE OKAY IF WE COME IN UNDER THE APPROVED WEIGHT LIMIT.
HEY, YOU! YOU AREN'T EVER SUP-POSED TO ASK A GIRL THAT QUES-TION!
THERE'S NOTHING MALICIOUS OR UNTOWARD ABOUT HIM. A GUY WHO MAKES OTHERS LAUGH...
BUT I GET THE FEELING THAT IT'S JUST HIS NATURE.
SORRY TO PUT YOU THROUGH THIS.
I'M ONLY DOING WHAT'S RIGHT.
I GUESS THAT'S WHY NOBODY SAYS ANYTHING BAD ABOUT HIM. ACTUALLY I'M A LITTLE ENVIOUS OF THAT. . . .

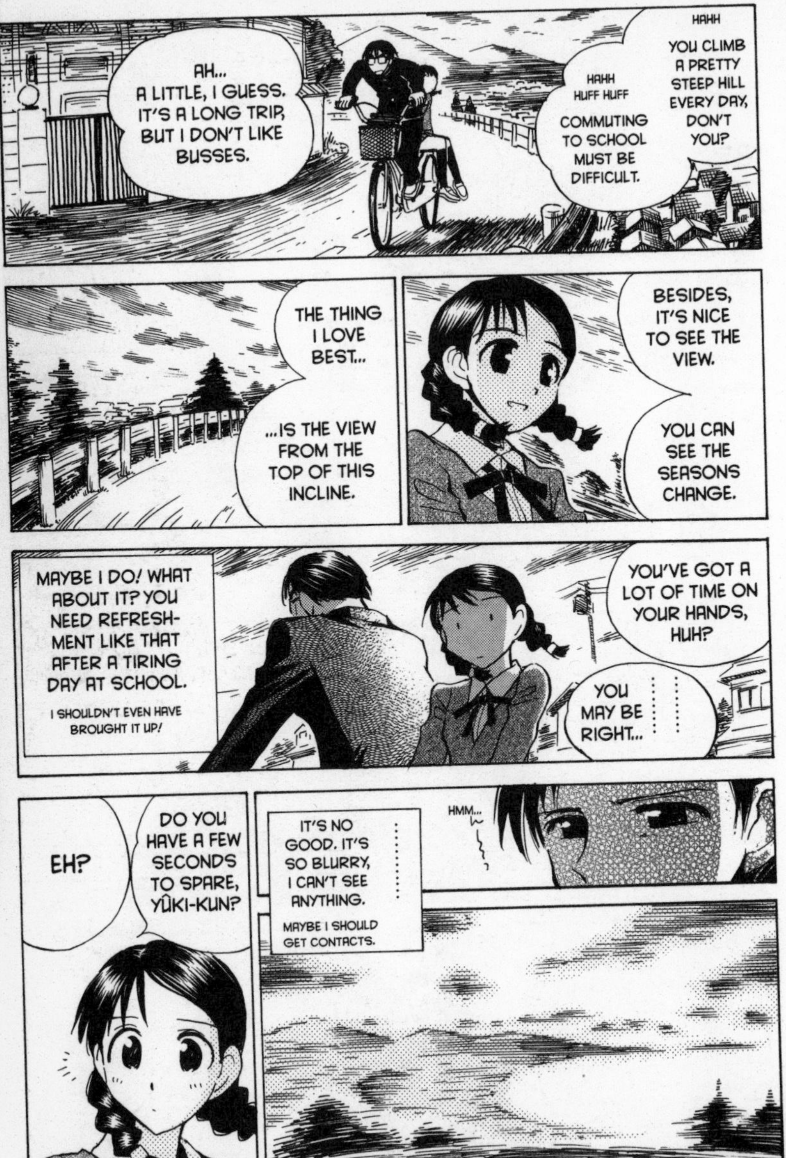
HAHH
YOU CLIMB A PRETTY STEEP HILL EVERY DAY, DON'T YOU?
HAHH HUFF HUFF
COMMUTING TO SCHOOL MUST BE DIFFICULT.
AH... A LITTLE, I GUESS. IT'S A LONG TRIP, BUT I DON'T LIKE BUSSES.
BESIDES, IT'S NICE TO SEE THE VIEW.
YOU CAN SEE THE SEASONS CHANGE.
THE THING I LOVE BEST...
...IS THE VIEW FROM THE TOP OF THIS INCLINE.
YOU'VE GOT A LOT OF TIME ON YOUR HANDS, HUH?
YOU MAY BE RIGHT...
MAYBE I DO! WHAT ABOUT IT? YOU NEED REFRESHMENT LIKE THAT AFTER A TIRING DAY AT SCHOOL.
I SHOULDN'T EVEN HAVE BROUGHT IT UP!
HMM...
IT'S NO GOOD. IT'S SO BLURRY, I CAN'T SEE ANYTHING.
MAYBE I SHOULD GET CONTACTS.
DO YOU HAVE A FEW SECONDS TO SPARE, YÛKI-KUN?
EH?

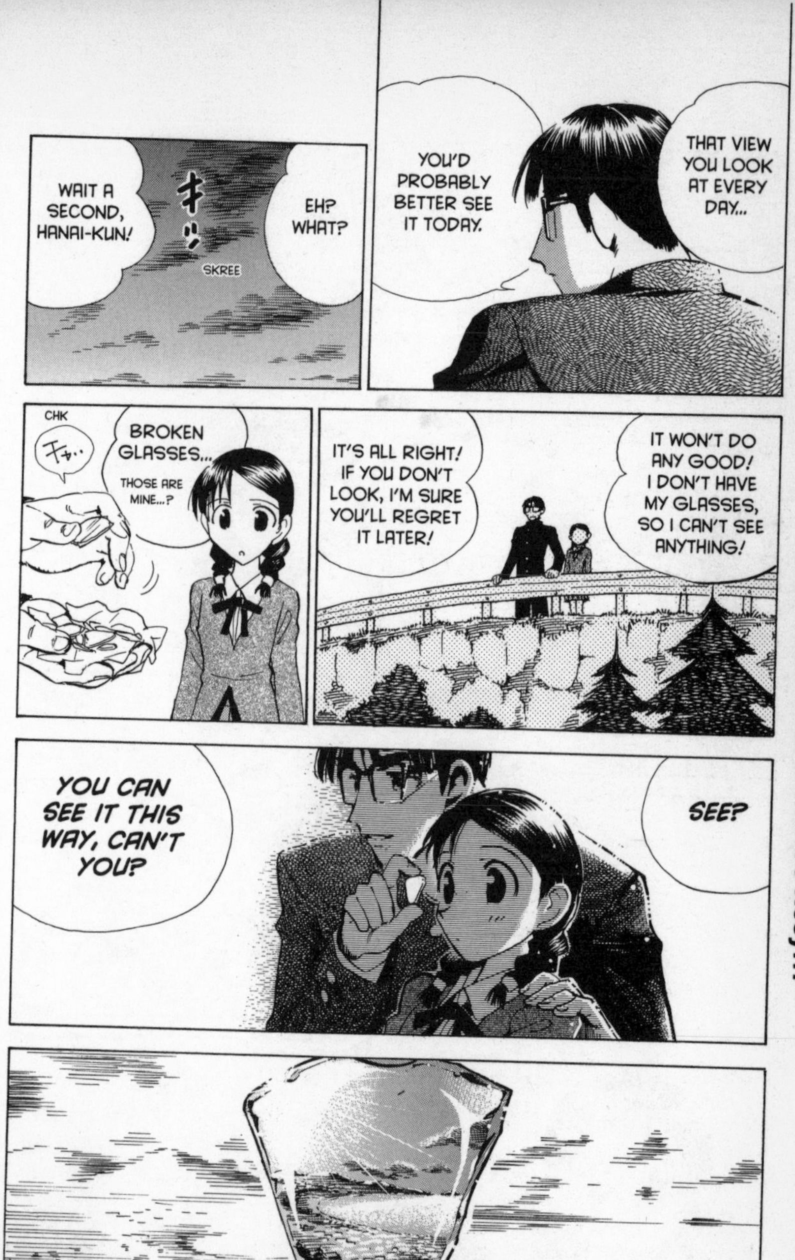
THAT VIEW YOU LOOK AT EVERY DAY...
YOU'D PROBABLY BETTER SEE IT TODAY.
EH? WHAT?
SKREE
WAIT A SECOND, HANAI-KUN!
IT WON'T DO ANY GOOD! I DON'T HAVE MY GLASSES, SO I CAN'T SEE ANYTHING!
IT'S ALL RIGHT! IF YOU DON'T LOOK, I'M SURE YOU'LL REGRET IT LATER!
BROKEN GLASSES...
THOSE ARE MINE...?
CHK
SEE?
YOU CAN SEE IT THIS WAY, CAN'T YOU?

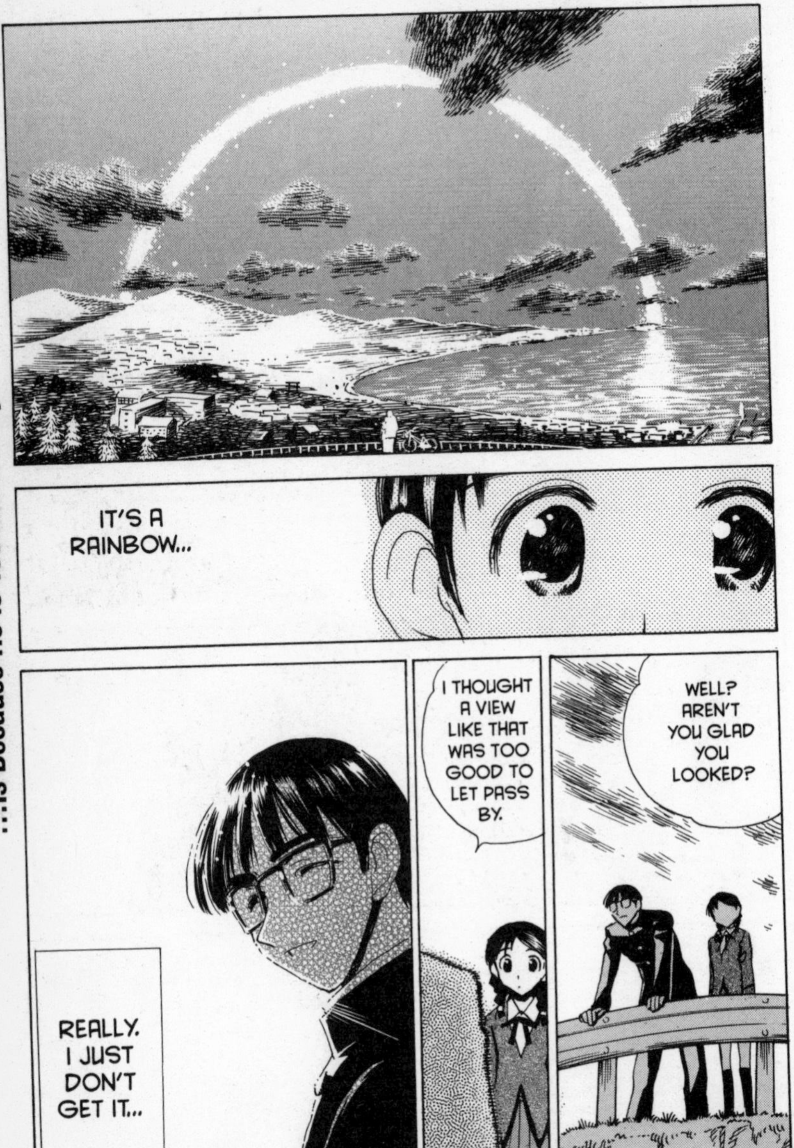
IT'S A RAINBOW...
WELL? AREN'T YOU GLAD YOU LOOKED?
I THOUGHT A VIEW LIKE THAT WAS TOO GOOD TO LET PASS BY.
REALLY. I JUST DON'T GET IT...

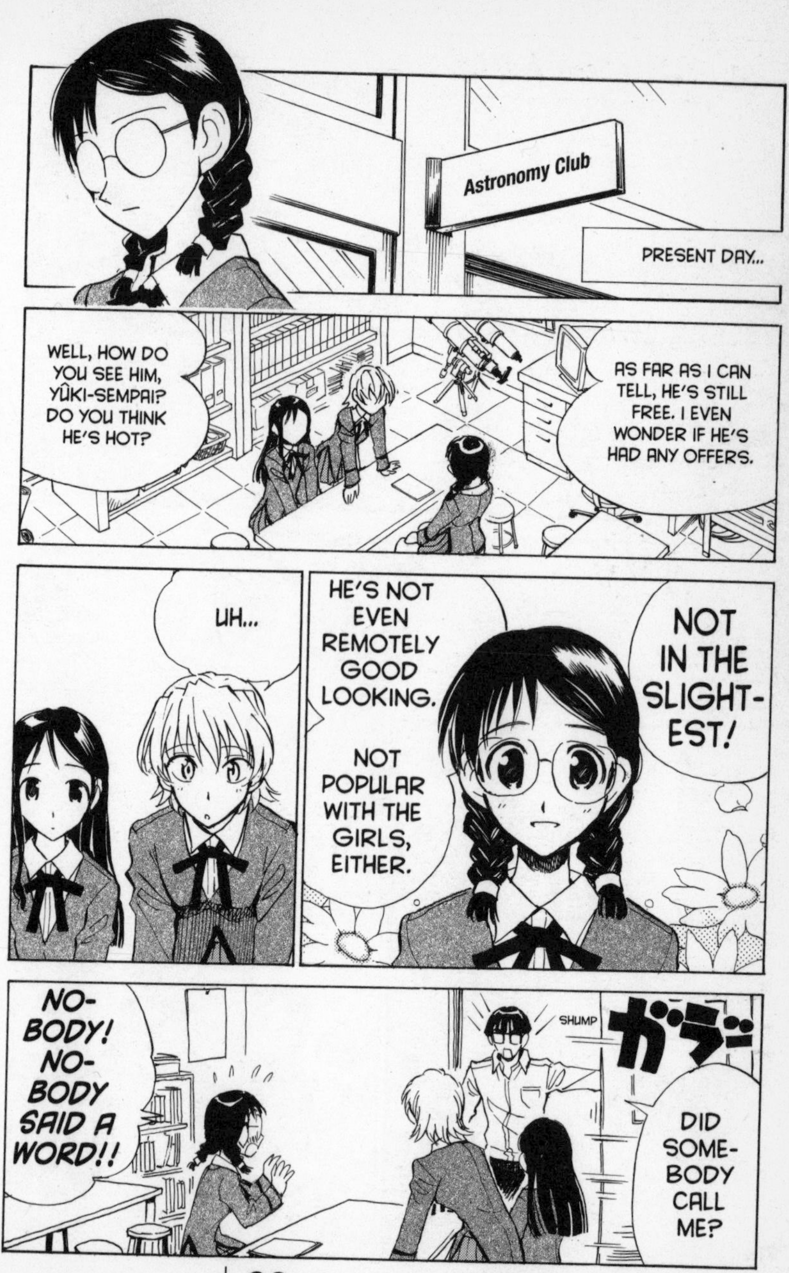

Astronomy Club
PRESENT DAY...
AS FAR AS I CAN TELL, HE'S STILL FREE. I EVEN WONDER IF HE'S HAD ANY OFFERS.
WELL, HOW DO YOU SEE HIM, YÛKI-SEMPAI? DO YOU THINK HE'S HOT?
NOT IN THE SLIGHT-EST!
HE'S NOT EVEN REMOTELY GOOD LOOKING.
NOT POPULAR WITH THE GIRLS, EITHER.
UH...
ガラッ
SHUMP
DID SOME-BODY CALL ME?
NO-BODY! NO-BODY SAID A WORD!!

♭23 CALIFORNIA MAN

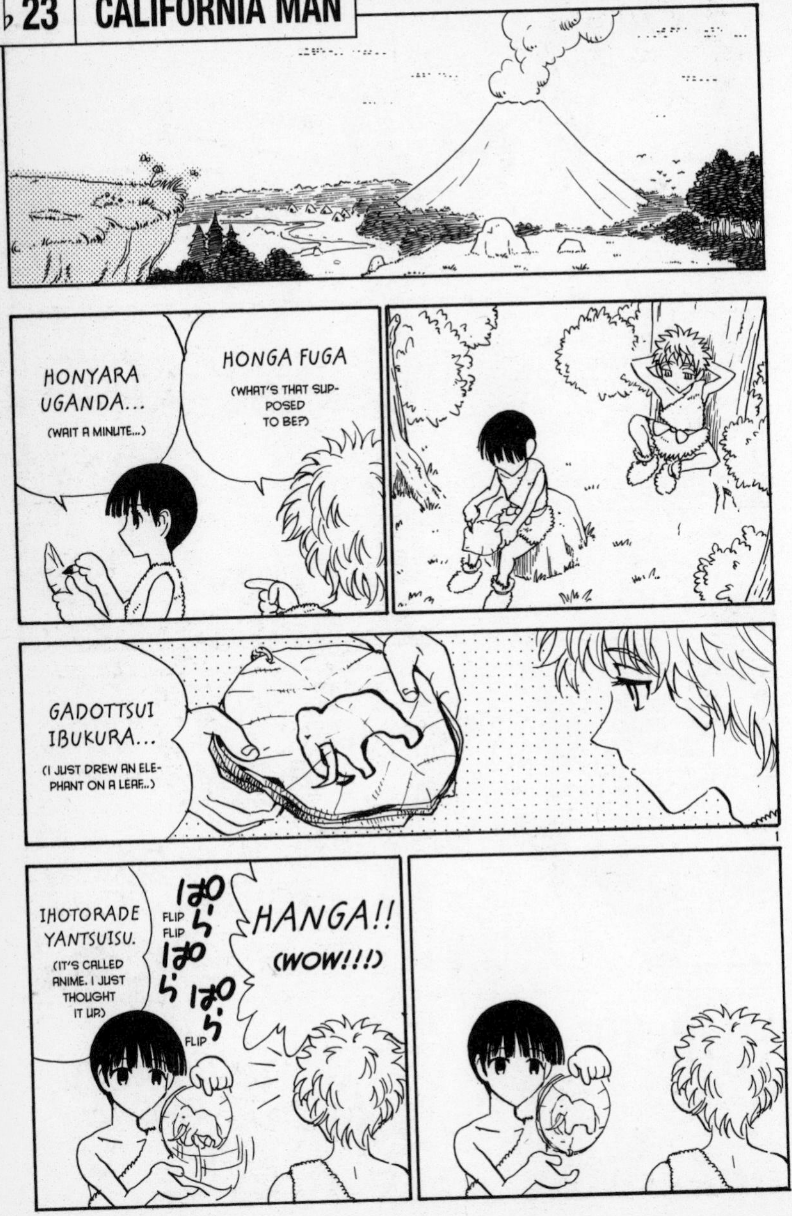

HONGA FUGA
(WHAT'S THAT SUP-POSED TO BE?)
HONYARA UGANDA...
(WAIT A MINUTE...)
GADOTTSUI IBUKURA...
(I JUST DREW AN ELE-PHANT ON A LEAF...)
1
HANGA!!
(WOW!!!)
ぱらぱらぱら
FLIP FLIP FLIP
IHOTORADE YANTSUISU.
(IT'S CALLED ANIME. I JUST THOUGHT IT UP.)

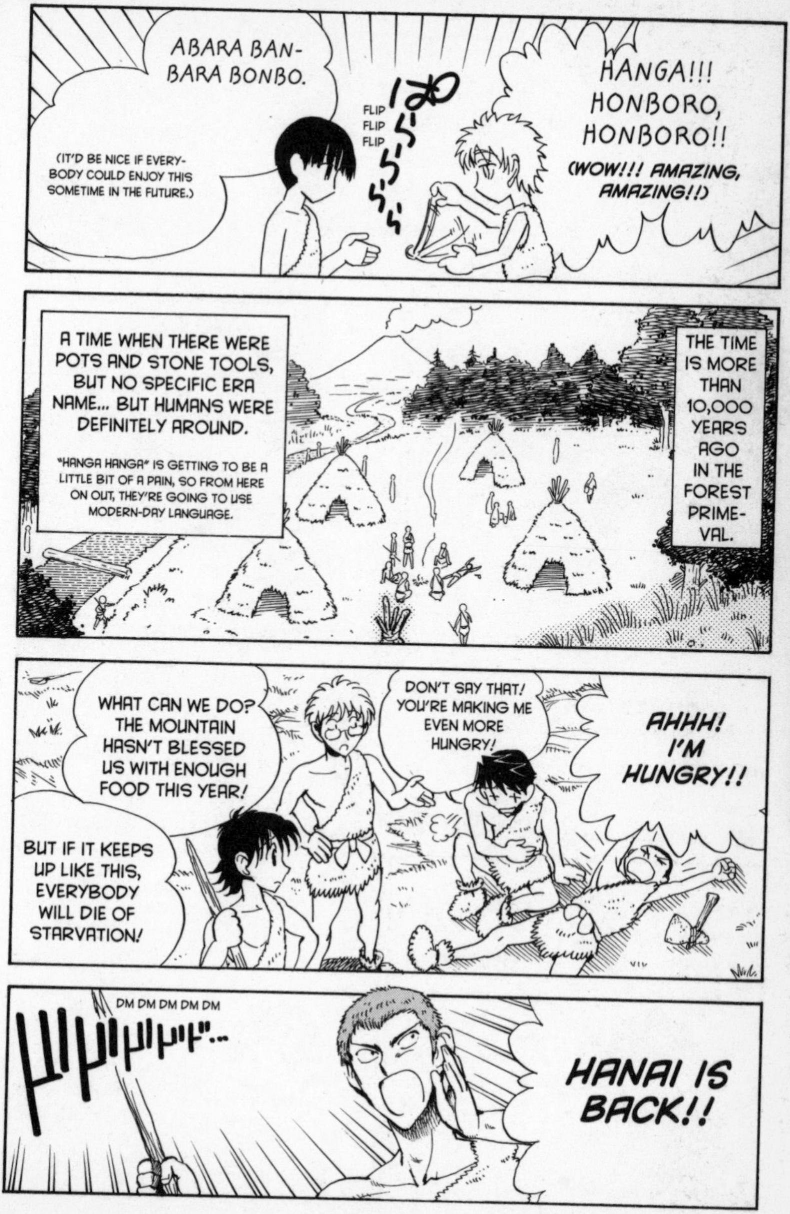
HANGA!!! HONBORO, HONBORO!!
(WOW!!! AMAZING, AMAZING!!)
ぱらららら
FLIP FLIP FLIP
ABARA BAN-BARA BONBO.
(IT'D BE NICE IF EVERYBODY COULD ENJOY THIS SOMETIME IN THE FUTURE.)
THE TIME IS MORE THAN 10,000 YEARS AGO IN THE FOREST PRIMEVAL.
A TIME WHEN THERE WERE POTS AND STONE TOOLS, BUT NO SPECIFIC ERA NAME... BUT HUMANS WERE DEFINITELY AROUND.
"HANGA HANGA" IS GETTING TO BE A LITTLE BIT OF A PAIN, SO FROM HERE ON OUT, THEY'RE GOING TO USE MODERN-DAY LANGUAGE.
AHHH! I'M HUNGRY!!
DON'T SAY THAT! YOU'RE MAKING ME EVEN MORE HUNGRY!
WHAT CAN WE DO? THE MOUNTAIN HASN'T BLESSED US WITH ENOUGH FOOD THIS YEAR!
BUT IF IT KEEPS UP LIKE THIS, EVERYBODY WILL DIE OF STARVATION!
HANAI IS BACK!!
ドドドドド…
DM DM DM DM DM

I Christen Thee: Primeval Rumble.

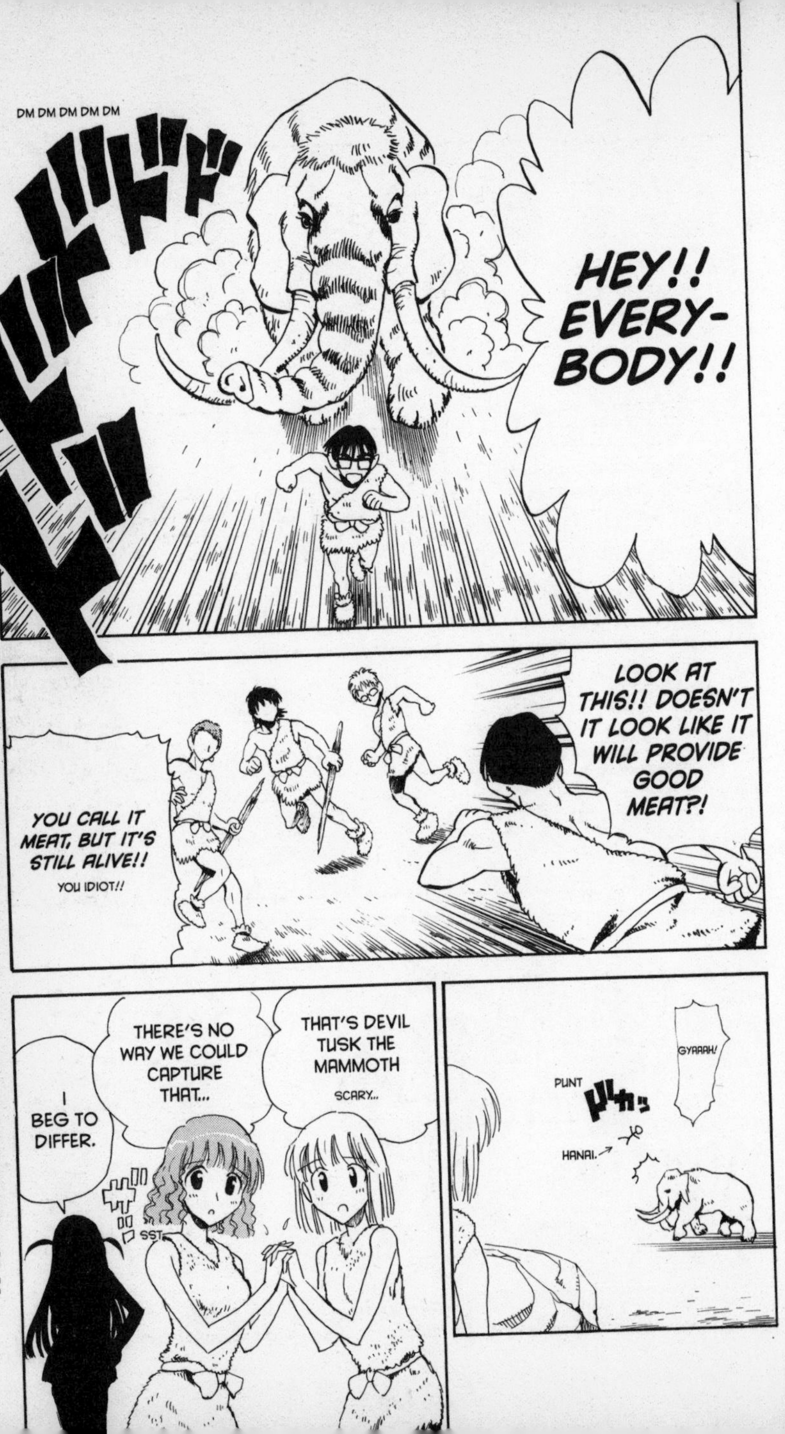
HEY!! EVERY-BODY!!
DM DM DM DM DM
LOOK AT THIS!! DOESN'T IT LOOK LIKE IT WILL PROVIDE GOOD MEAT?!
YOU CALL IT MEAT, BUT IT'S STILL ALIVE!!
YOU IDIOT!!
GYAAAH!
PUNT
HANAI.
THAT'S DEVIL TUSK THE MAMMOTH
SCARY...
THERE'S NO WAY WE COULD CAPTURE THAT...
SST
I BEG TO DIFFER.

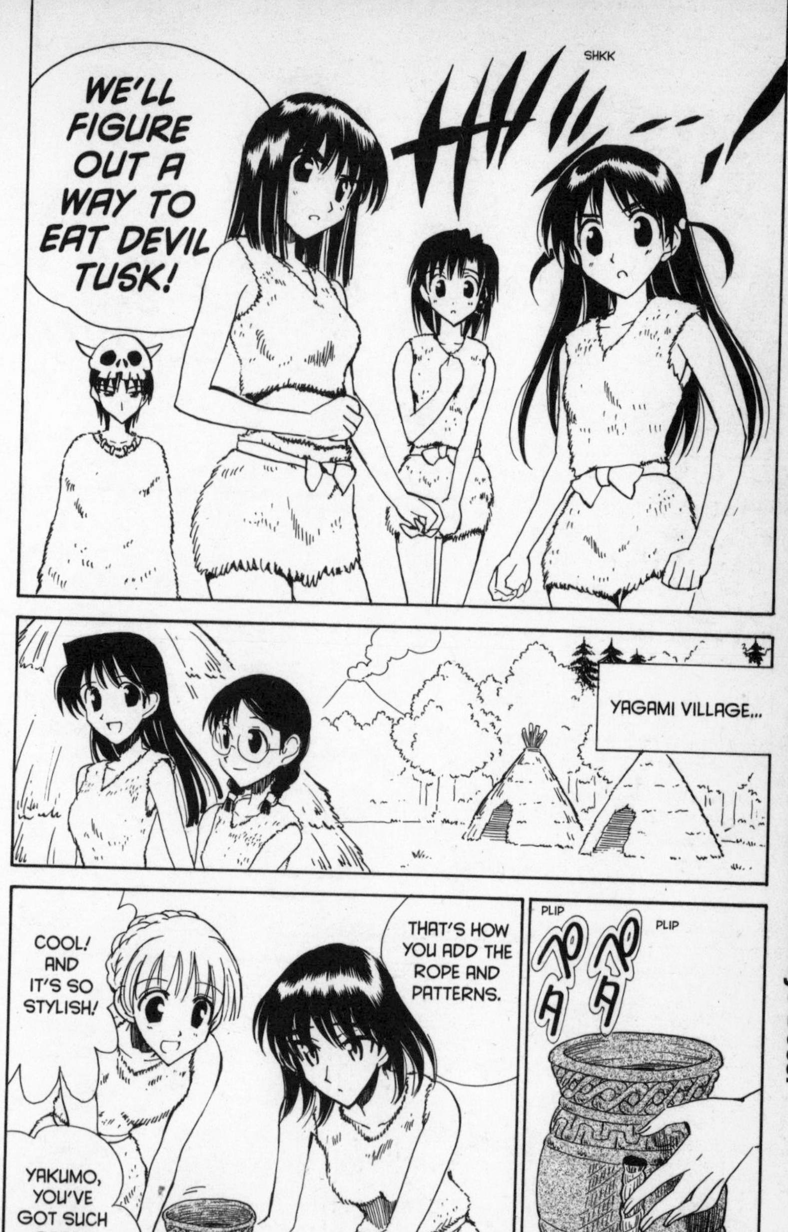
WE'LL FIGURE OUT A WAY TO EAT DEVIL TUSK!
SHKK
YAGAMI VILLAGE...
PLIP
PLIP
THAT'S HOW YOU ADD THE ROPE AND PATTERNS.
COOL! AND IT'S SO STYLISH!
YAKUMO, YOU'VE GOT SUCH GREAT FASHION SENSE!

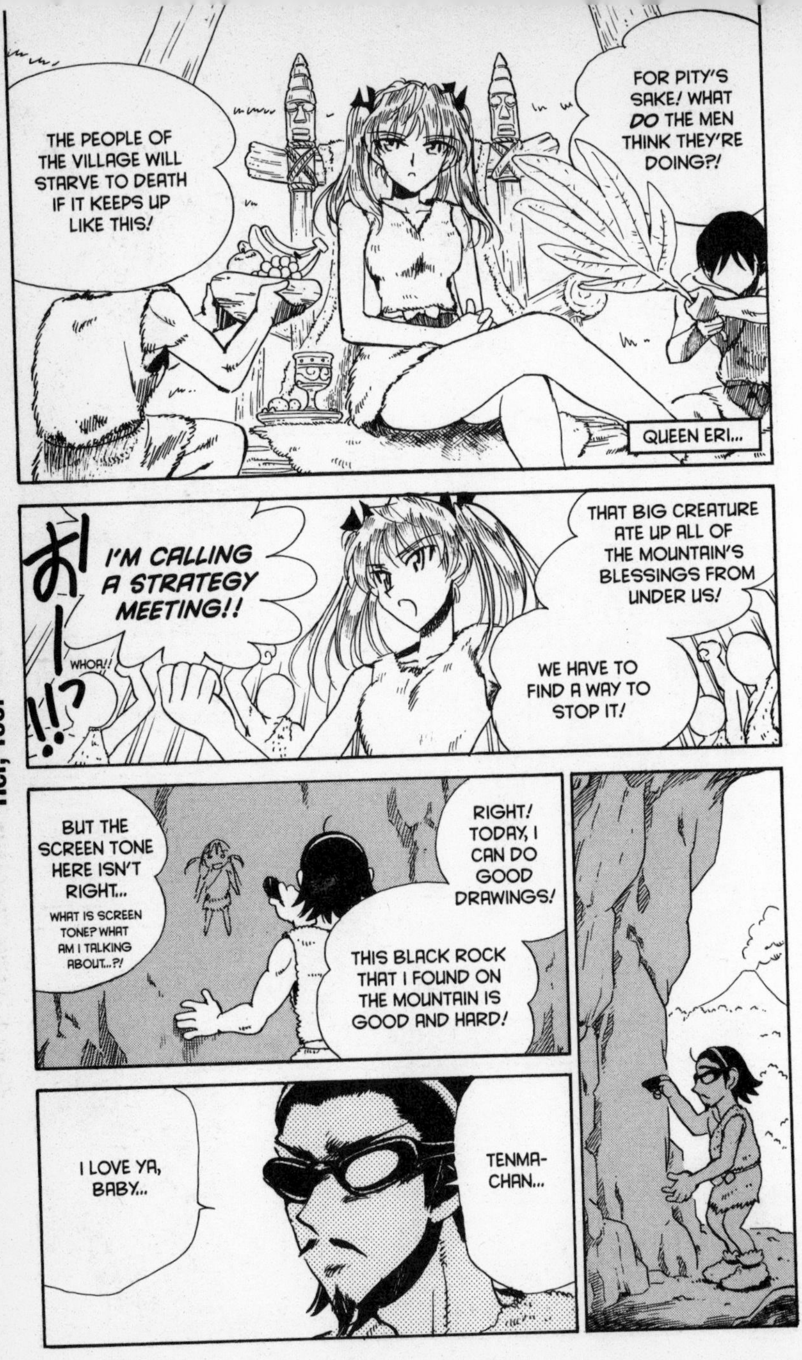
FOR PITY'S SAKE! WHAT *DO* THE MEN THINK THEY'RE DOING?!
THE PEOPLE OF THE VILLAGE WILL STARVE TO DEATH IF IT KEEPS UP LIKE THIS!
QUEEN ERI...
THAT BIG CREATURE ATE UP ALL OF THE MOUNTAIN'S BLESSINGS FROM UNDER US!
WE HAVE TO FIND A WAY TO STOP IT!
I'M CALLING A STRATEGY MEETING!!
おー!!
WHOA!!
RIGHT! TODAY, I CAN DO GOOD DRAWINGS!
THIS BLACK ROCK THAT I FOUND ON THE MOUNTAIN IS GOOD AND HARD!
BUT THE SCREEN TONE HERE ISN'T RIGHT...
WHAT IS SCREEN TONE? WHAT AM I TALKING ABOUT...?!
TENMA-CHAN...
I LOVE YA, BABY...

No Matter the Era, He's Never Popular.

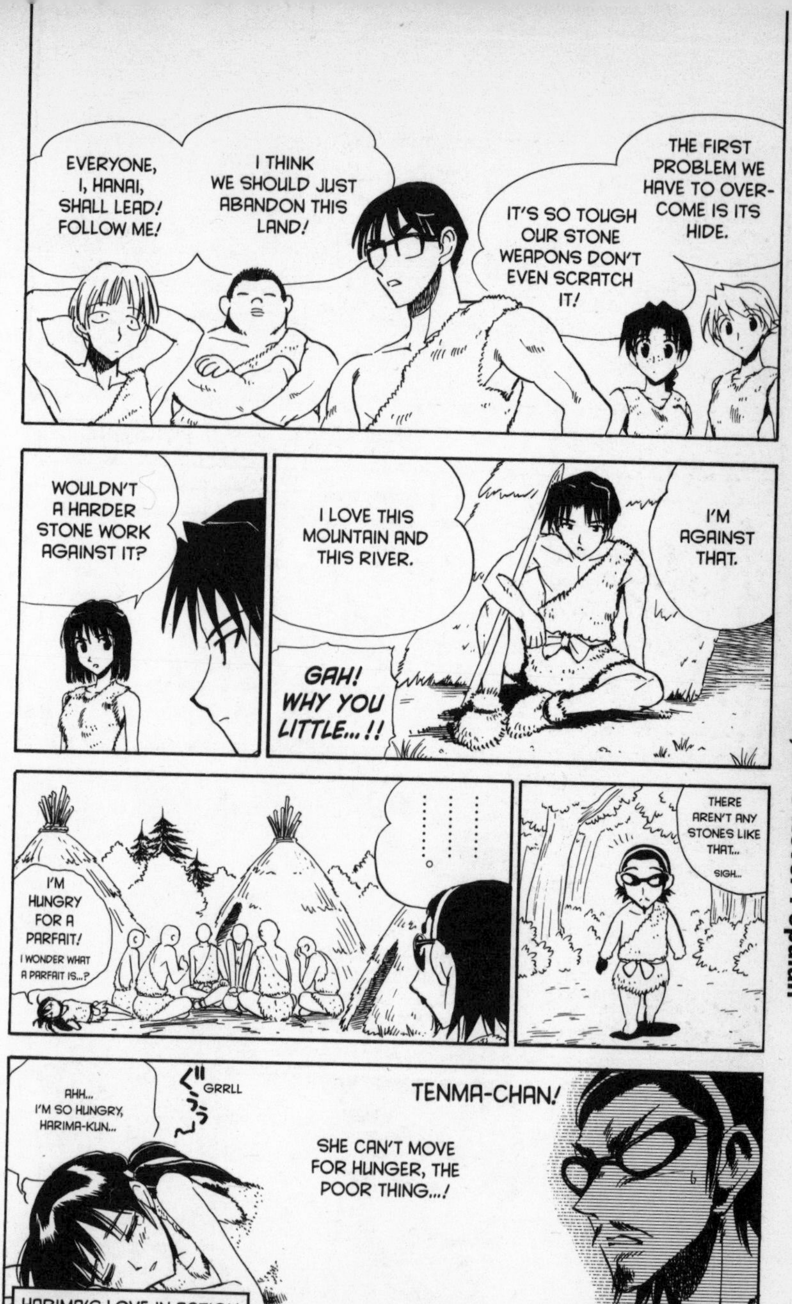
THE FIRST PROBLEM WE HAVE TO OVER-COME IS ITS HIDE.
IT'S SO TOUGH OUR STONE WEAPONS DON'T EVEN SCRATCH IT!
I THINK WE SHOULD JUST ABANDON THIS LAND!
EVERYONE, I, HANAI, SHALL LEAD! FOLLOW ME!
I'M AGAINST THAT.
I LOVE THIS MOUNTAIN AND THIS RIVER.
GAH! WHY YOU LITTLE...!!
WOULDN'T A HARDER STONE WORK AGAINST IT?
THERE AREN'T ANY STONES LIKE THAT...
SIGH...
......
I'M HUNGRY FOR A PARFAIT!
I WONDER WHAT A PARFAIT IS...?
TENMA-CHAN!
SHE CAN'T MOVE FOR HUNGER, THE POOR THING...!
GRRLL
AHH... I'M SO HUNGRY, HARIMA-KUN...
HARIMA'S LOVE IN ACTION.

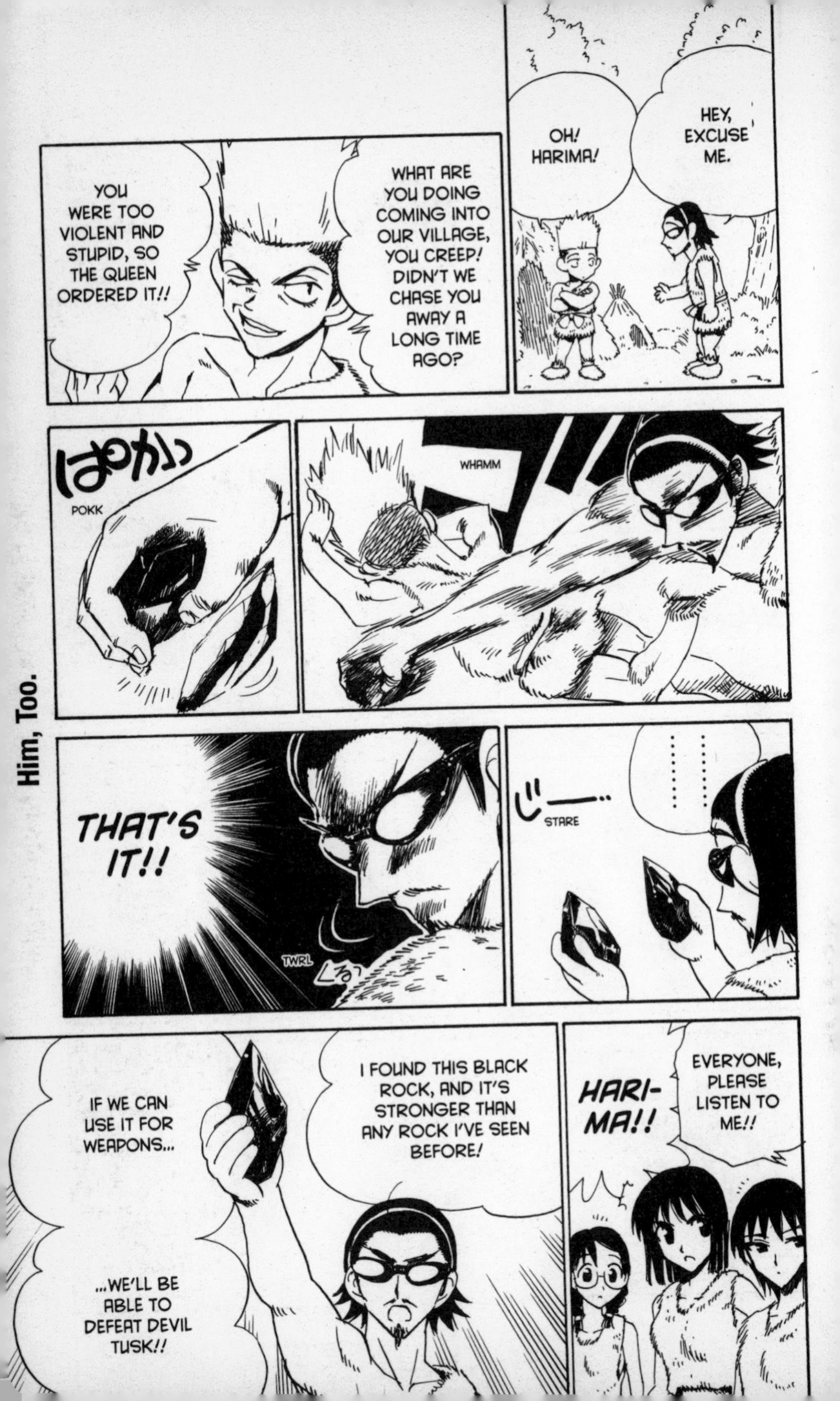
HEY, EXCUSE ME.
OH! HARIMA!
WHAT ARE YOU DOING COMING INTO OUR VILLAGE, YOU CREEP! DIDN'T WE CHASE YOU AWAY A LONG TIME AGO?
YOU WERE TOO VIOLENT AND STUPID, SO THE QUEEN ORDERED IT!!
WHAMM
ぱかっ
POKK
......
じー
STARE
THAT'S IT!!
くるっ
TWRL
EVERYONE, PLEASE LISTEN TO ME!!
HARI-MA!!
I FOUND THIS BLACK ROCK, AND IT'S STRONGER THAN ANY ROCK I'VE SEEN BEFORE!
IF WE CAN USE IT FOR WEAPONS...
...WE'LL BE ABLE TO DEFEAT DEVIL TUSK!!

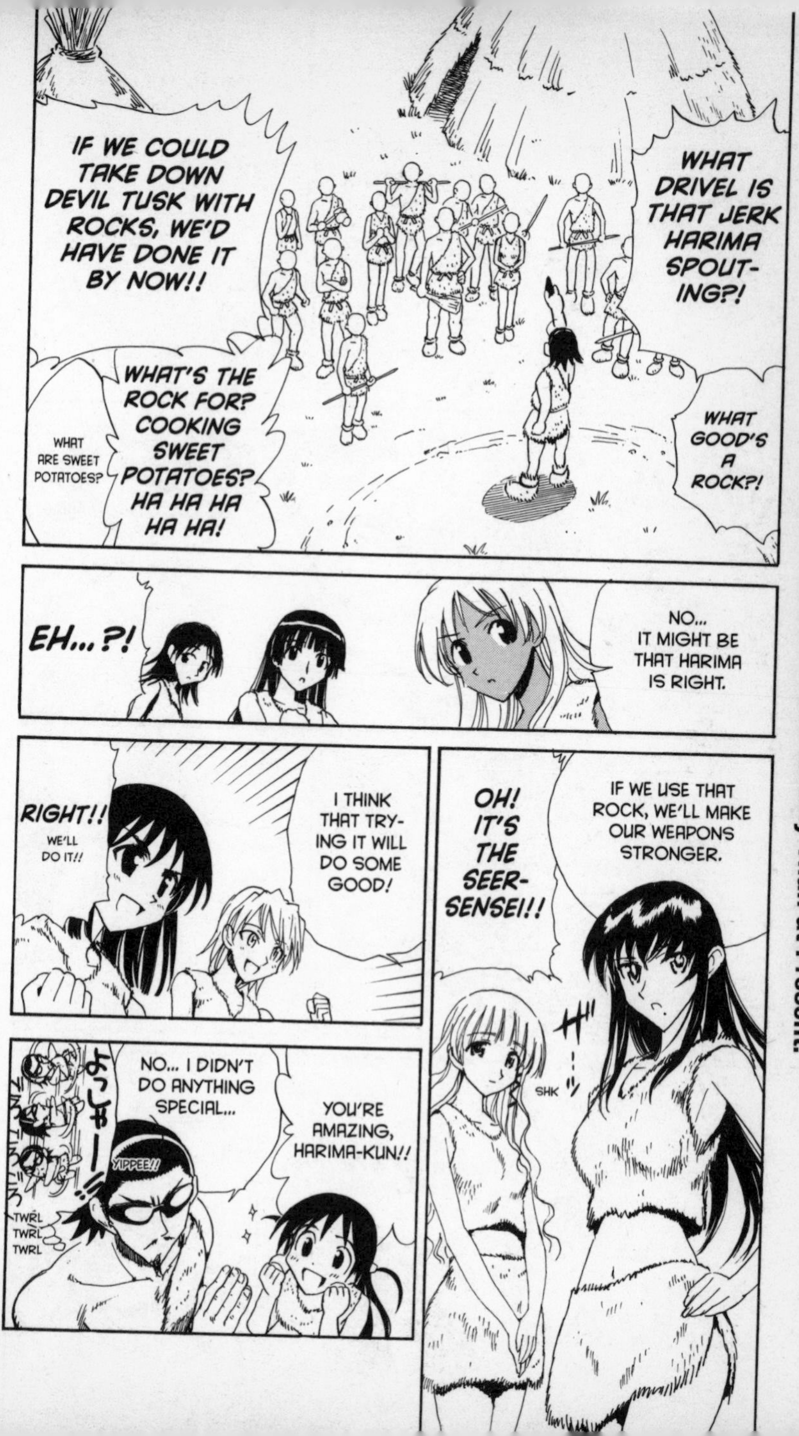
WHAT DRIVEL IS THAT JERK HARIMA SPOUTING?!
WHAT GOOD'S A ROCK?!
IF WE COULD TAKE DOWN DEVIL TUSK WITH ROCKS, WE'D HAVE DONE IT BY NOW!!
WHAT'S THE ROCK FOR? COOKING SWEET POTATOES? HA HA HA HA HA!
WHAT ARE SWEET POTATOES?
NO... IT MIGHT BE THAT HARIMA IS RIGHT.
EH...?!
IF WE USE THAT ROCK, WE'LL MAKE OUR WEAPONS STRONGER.
OH! IT'S THE SEER-SENSEI!!
SHK
I THINK THAT TRYING IT WILL DO SOME GOOD!
RIGHT!!
WE'LL DO IT!!
NO... I DIDN'T DO ANYTHING SPECIAL...
YOU'RE AMAZING, HARIMA-KUN!!
よっしゃー!!
YIPPEE!!
TWRL
TWRL
TWRL

Harima: Treated More Harshly Than at Present.

His Thinking Has Never Changed.

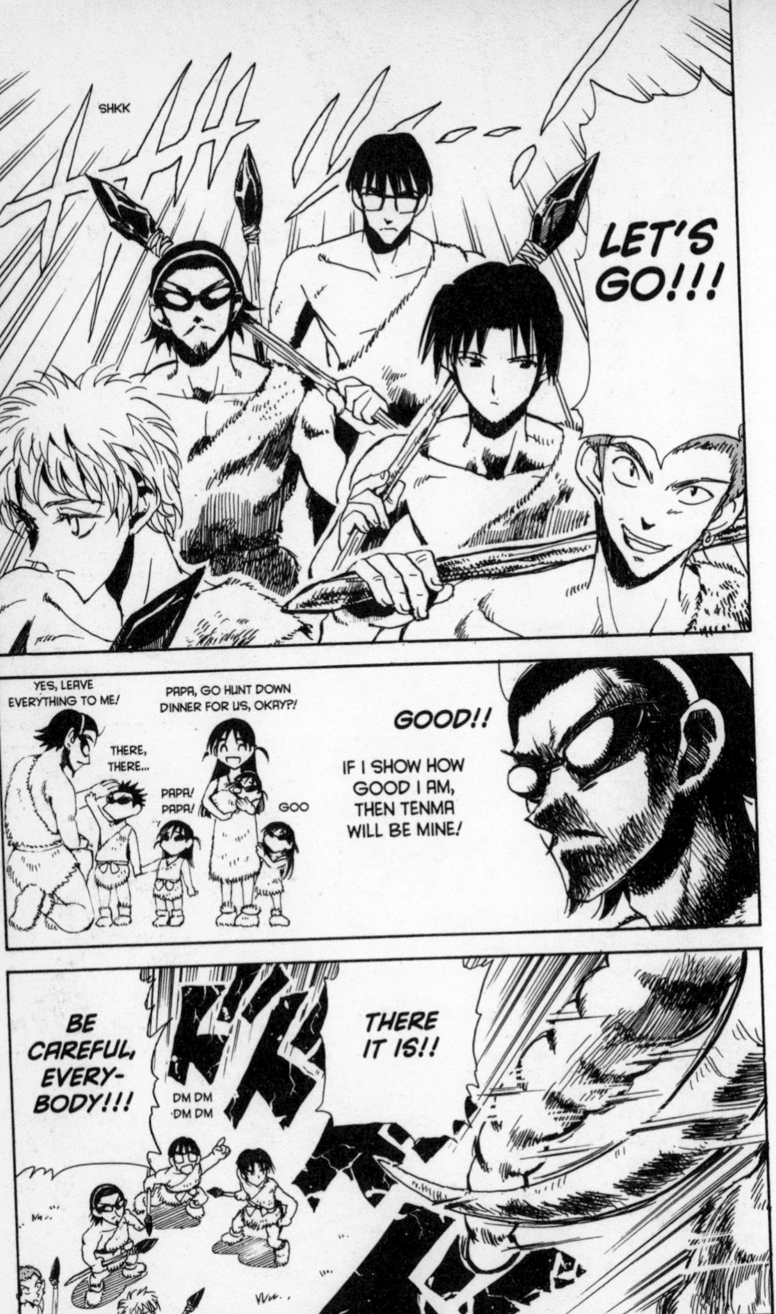
LET'S GO!!!
SHKK
GOOD!!
IF I SHOW HOW GOOD I AM, THEN TENMA WILL BE MINE!
PAPA, GO HUNT DOWN DINNER FOR US, OKAY?!
YES, LEAVE EVERYTHING TO ME!
THERE, THERE...
PAPA! PAPA!
GOO
THERE IT IS!!
BE CAREFUL, EVERY-BODY!!!
DM DM DM DM

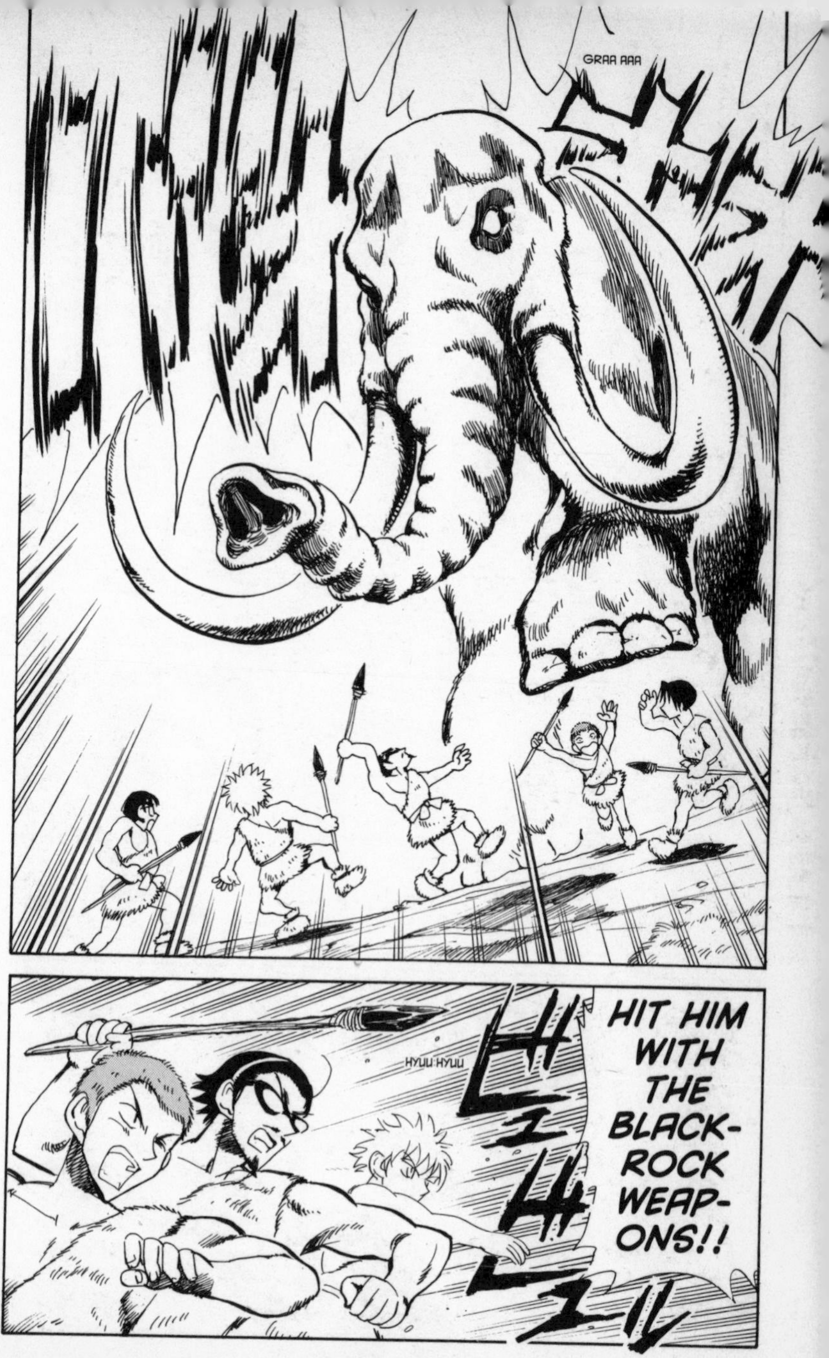
GRAA AAA
HIT HIM WITH THE BLACK-ROCK WEAPONS!!
HYUU HYUU

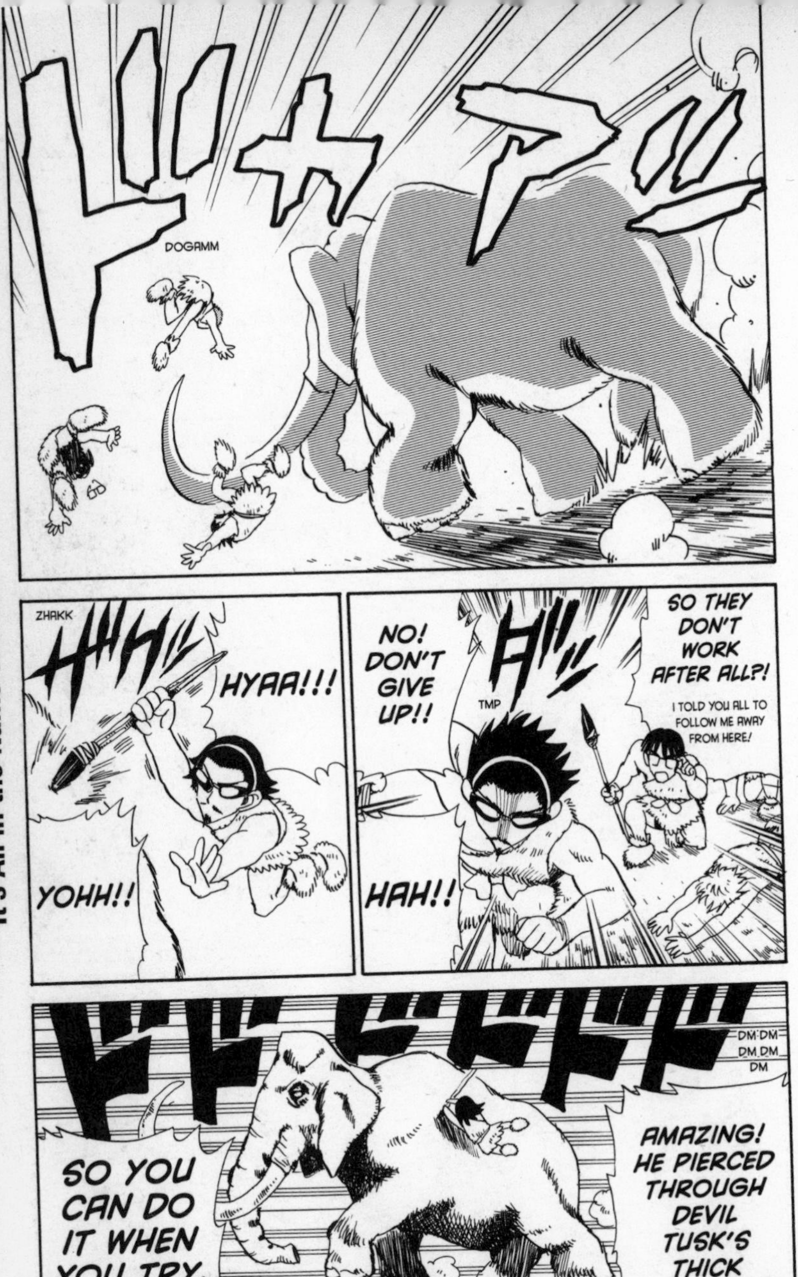
DOGAMM
SO THEY DON'T WORK AFTER ALL?!
I TOLD YOU ALL TO FOLLOW ME AWAY FROM HERE!
NO! DON'T GIVE UP!!
TMP
HAH!!
ZHAKK
HYAA!!!
YOHH!!
DM DM DM DM DM
AMAZING! HE PIERCED THROUGH DEVIL TUSK'S THICK HIDE!!
SO YOU CAN DO IT WHEN YOU TRY, HARIMA!!

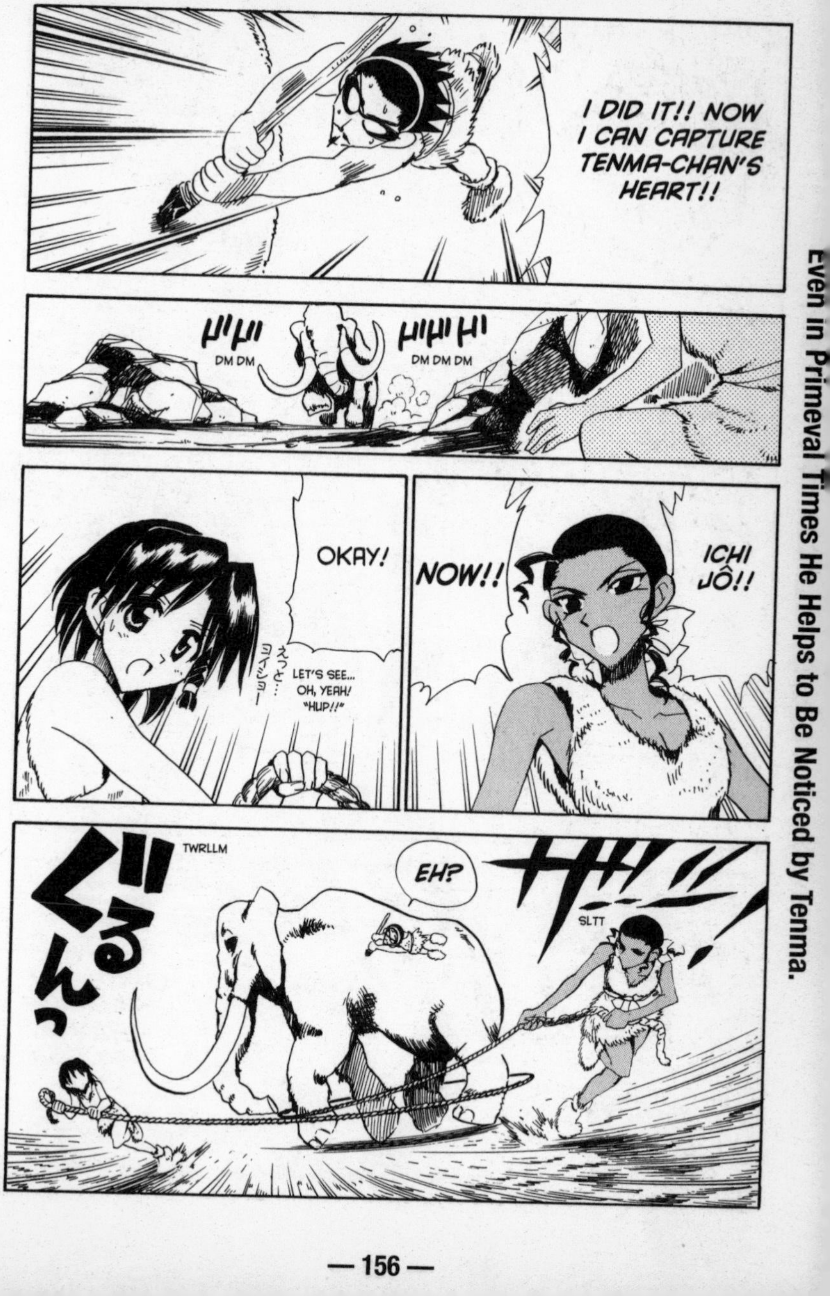
I DID IT!! NOW I CAN CAPTURE TENMA-CHAN'S HEART!!
DM DM DM
DM DM
ICHI JÔ!!
NOW!!
OKAY!
えっと…ヨイショー
LET'S SEE... OH, YEAH! "HUP!!"
SLTT
EH?
TWRLLM

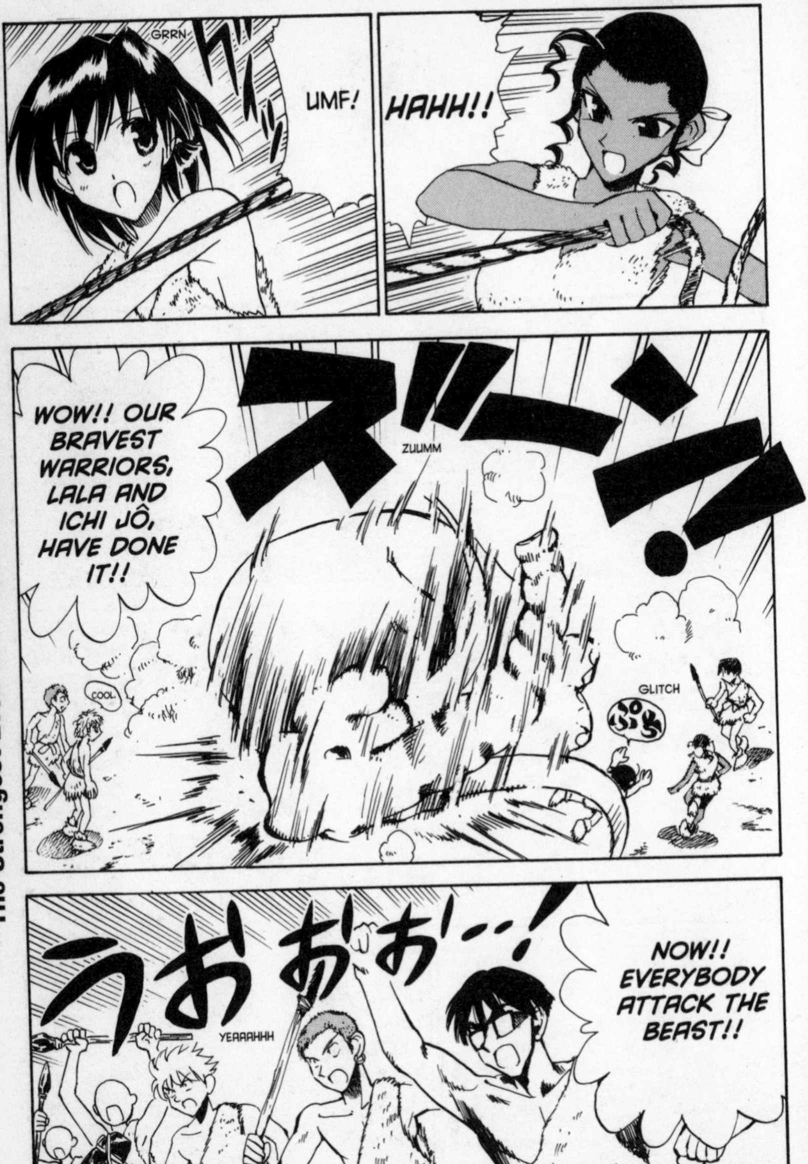
HAHH!!
GRRN
UMF!
ZUUMM
WOW!! OUR BRAVEST WARRIORS, LALA AND ICHI JÔ, HAVE DONE IT!!
GLITCH
COOL
NOW!! EVERYBODY ATTACK THE BEAST!!
YEAAAHHH

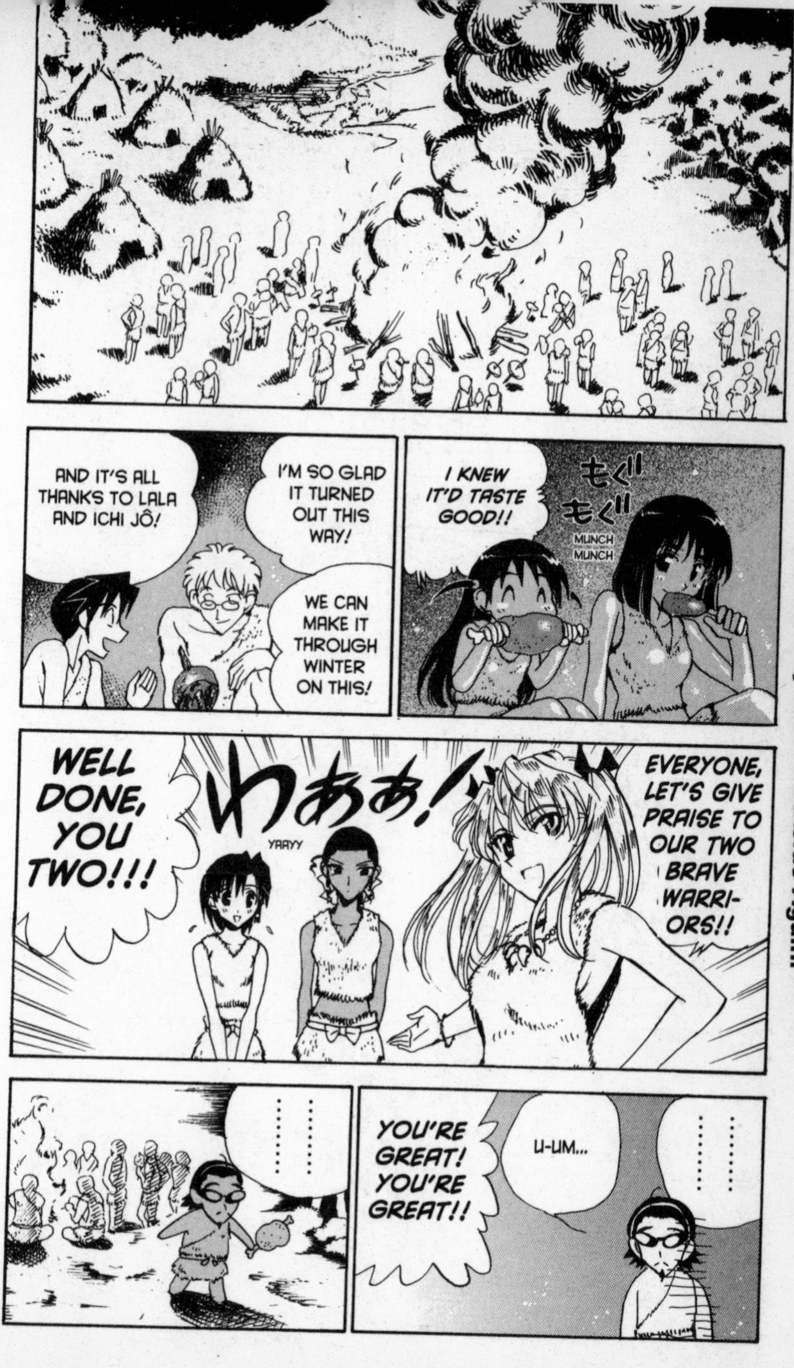
I KNEW IT'D TASTE GOOD!!
もぐもぐ
MUNCH MUNCH
I'M SO GLAD IT TURNED OUT THIS WAY!
AND IT'S ALL THANKS TO LALA AND ICHI JÔ!
WE CAN MAKE IT THROUGH WINTER ON THIS!
EVERYONE, LET'S GIVE PRAISE TO OUR TWO BRAVE WARRI- ORS!!
わあぁ!
YAAYY
WELL DONE, YOU TWO!!!
......
U-UM...
YOU'RE GREAT! YOU'RE GREAT!!
......

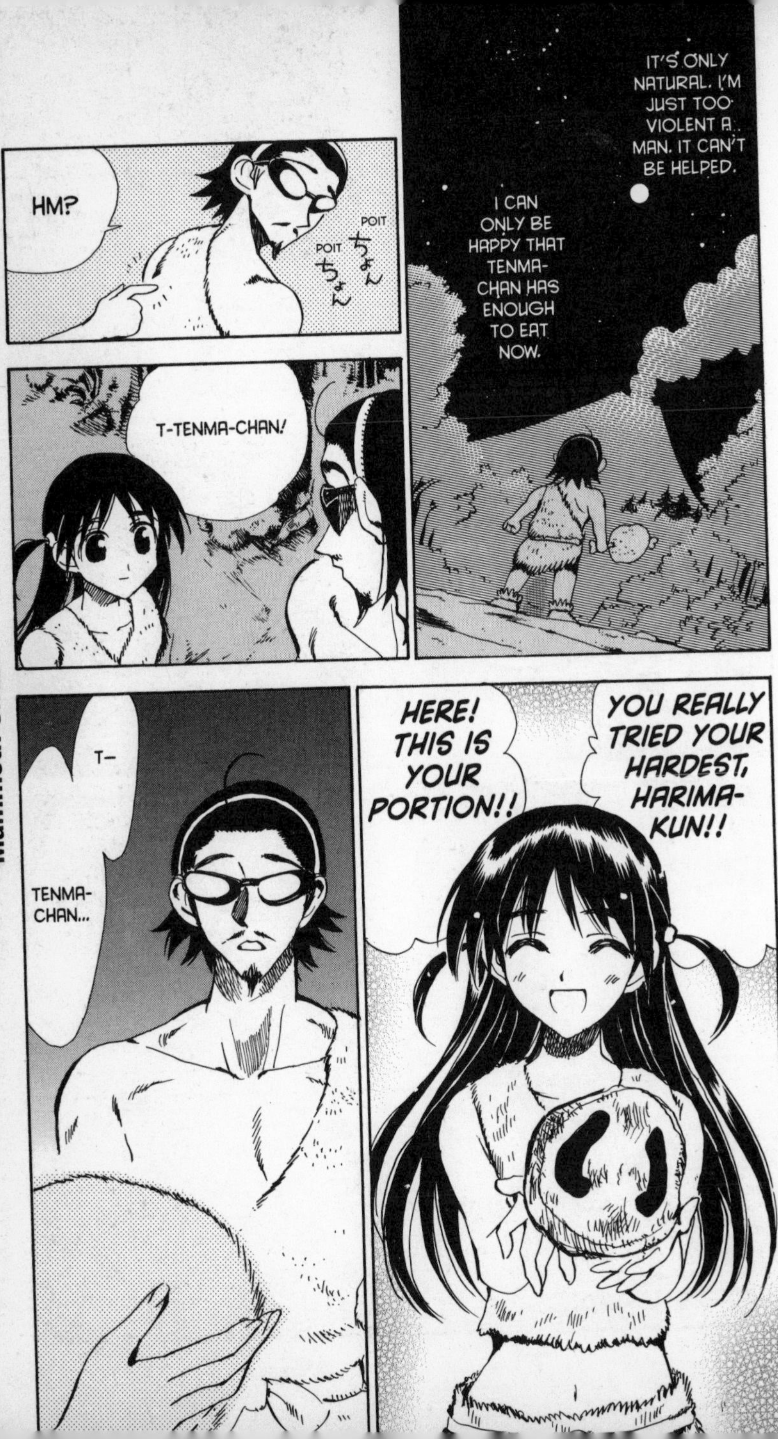
IT'S ONLY NATURAL. I'M JUST TOO VIOLENT A MAN. IT CAN'T BE HELPED.
I CAN ONLY BE HAPPY THAT TENMA-CHAN HAS ENOUGH TO EAT NOW.
HM?
POIT
ちょん
POIT
ちょん
T-TENMA-CHAN!
YOU REALLY TRIED YOUR HARDEST, HARIMA-KUN!!
HERE! THIS IS YOUR PORTION!!
T-
TENMA-CHAN...

Mammoth Snout.

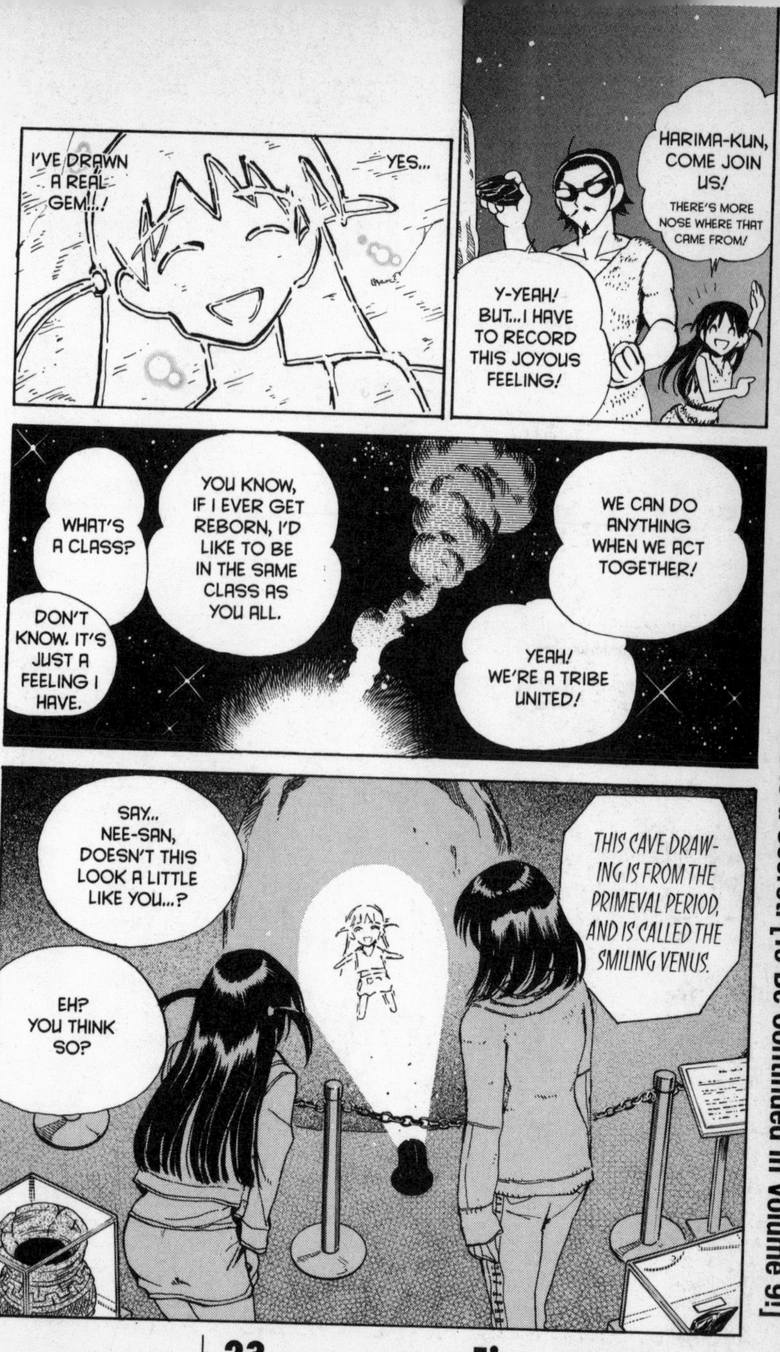
HARIMA-KUN, COME JOIN US!
THERE'S MORE NOSE WHERE THAT CAME FROM!
Y-YEAH! BUT...I HAVE TO RECORD THIS JOYOUS FEELING!
YES...
I'VE DRAWN A REAL GEM...!
WE CAN DO ANYTHING WHEN WE ACT TOGETHER!
YEAH! WE'RE A TRIBE UNITED!
YOU KNOW, IF I EVER GET REBORN, I'D LIKE TO BE IN THE SAME CLASS AS YOU ALL.
WHAT'S A CLASS?
DON'T KNOW. IT'S JUST A FEELING I HAVE.
THIS CAVE DRAWING IS FROM THE PRIMEVAL PERIOD, AND IS CALLED THE SMILING VENUS.
SAY... NEE-SAN, DOESN'T THIS LOOK A LITTLE LIKE YOU...?
EH? YOU THINK SO?

What happens to Tenma and Harima After This Is a Secret. [To Be Continued in Volume 9!]

♭23 . . . . Fin

TO LIVE LIKE A TURTLE

By Nijô Jô

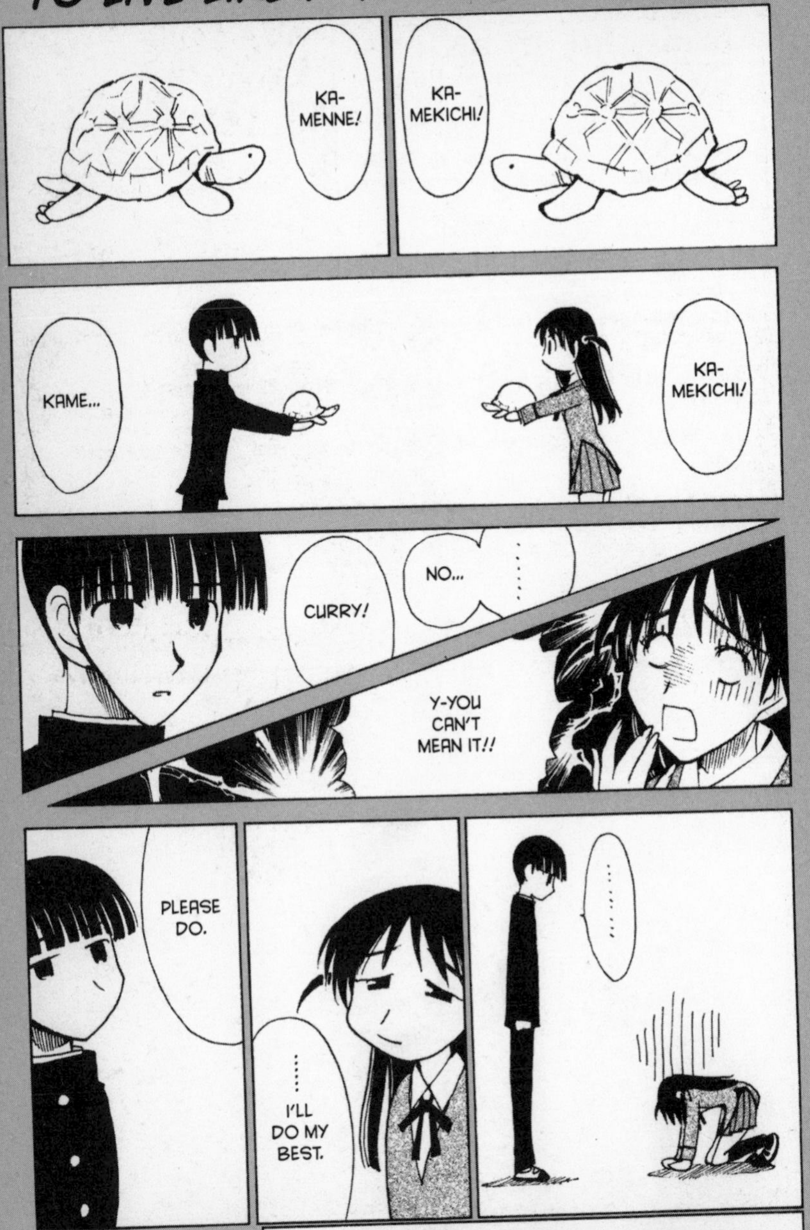

KA-MEKICHI!
KA-MENNE!
KA-MEKICHI!
KAME...
......
NO...
CURRY!
Y-YOU CAN'T MEAN IT!!
....
...... I'LL DO MY BEST.
PLEASE DO.

THE END

Original Bonus Manga Number 3

About the Creator

Jin Kobayashi was born in Tokyo. *School Rumble* is his first manga series. He has answered these questions from his fans:

What is your hobby?
Basketball

Which manga inspired you to become a creator?
Dragon Ball

Which character in your manga do you like best?
Kenji Harima

What type of manga do you want to create in the future?
Action

Name one book, piece of music, or movie you like.
The Indiana Jones series

Translation Notes

Japanese is a tricky language for most Westerners, and translation is often more art than science. For your edification and reading pleasure, here are notes on some of the places where we could have gone in a different direction in our translation of the work, or where a Japanese cultural reference is used.

Zabuton Cushions, page 6

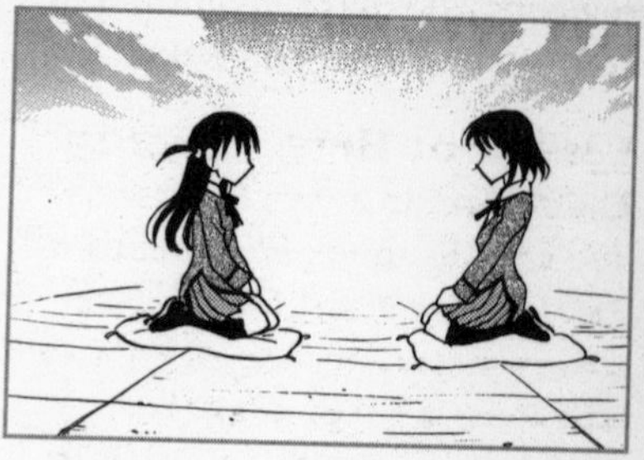

Before most Japanese homes had Western-style furnishings, floors were covered with *tatami* mats. Even now, nearly every home has at least one *tatami* room used for receiving guests, among other purposes. Tatami mats are made of rushes tightly bound into long rectangles. They have a bit of "give" to them so that not a lot of added padding is necessary when sleeping or sitting down. *Zabuton* cushions, about three feet square and two to three inches thick, were made for use on *tatami* mats. Pulling out a *zabuton* when one is to have a serious talk is a part of Japanese culture.

Suke-san, Kaku-san, page 12

A *jidai-geki* called "Mito Kômon" has been running so long, the actor playing the main character has changed four times due to old age. Mito Kômon (whom Tenma resembles in the panel) is an elderly uncle of the Shogun. He and his henchmen wander the land to right injustices caused by ambitious and greedy people. About fifty minutes into each show there is a large brawl, and out comes the Shogun's family seal, proof of Mito Kômon's relationship with the head of state. With that the bad guys bow down, knowing they can't

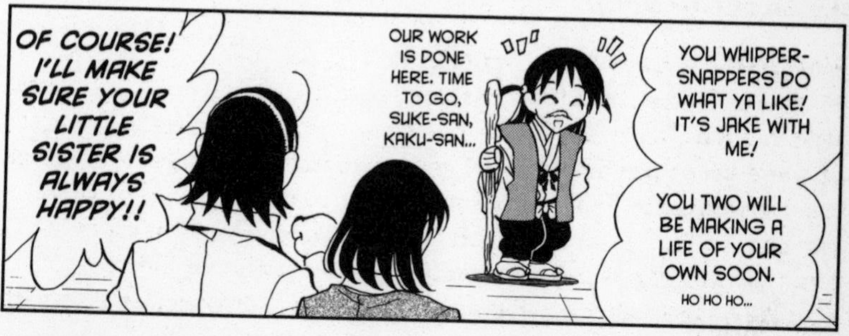
YOU WHIPPER-SNAPPERS DO WHAT YA LIKE! IT'S JAKE WITH ME!
YOU TWO WILL BE MAKING A LIFE OF YOUR OWN SOON.
HO HO HO...
OUR WORK IS DONE HERE. TIME TO GO, SUKE-SAN, KAKU-SAN...
OF COURSE! I'LL MAKE SURE YOUR LITTLE SISTER IS ALWAYS HAPPY!!

stand against the Shogun's power. Although there are quite a few regulars who make up Mito Kômon's little band, the two main loyal servants are Suke and Kaku.

I Just Got Here, page 15

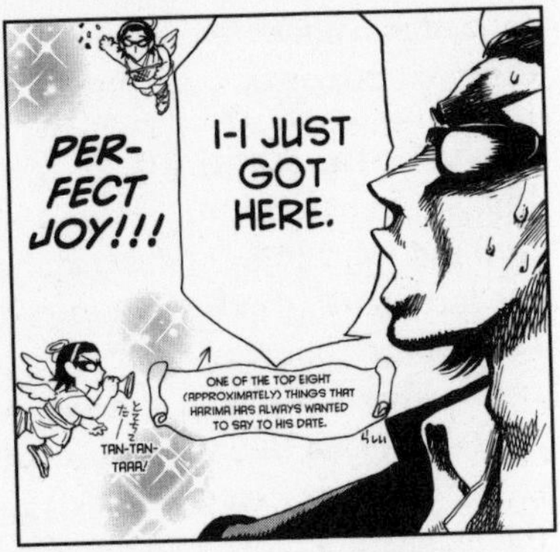

I-I JUST GOT HERE.
PER-FECT JOY!!!
ONE OF THE TOP EIGHT (APPROXIMATELY) THINGS THAT HARIMA HAS ALWAYS WANTED TO SAY TO HIS DATE.
TAN-TAN-TAAA!

The second to arrive for a date will usually apologize for getting there late and ask if the person has been waiting long. No matter how long the wait might have been, the gallant thing to say is *Ima kita tokoro*, which means that he or she got there only a few short minutes before the date did. The phrase appears in romances all the time.

All the Way into Tokyo, page 17

Most of the suburban areas around Tokyo are fully functioning towns unto themselves. Unless suburban residents work in Tokyo, many of them hardly ever travel there. The Tokyo trip is for special occasions such as concerts or other special entertainment, or for shopping for hard-to-find items.

Crepe Shop, page 17

These thin flour pancakes rolled with jam and other fillings have been a hit with Japanese tastebuds since the Meiji Era at the turn of the twentieth century.

Shadow Is Light . . ., page 31

Much like Western students assigned to read Shakespeare, Japanese students must learn and memorize classic Japanese literature. Most of these books are hundreds of years old, and the Japanese language has evolved quite a lot in the intervening years. The present word for "shadow," *kage*, actually refers to the image that light creates, and therefore the word (especially in classic Japanese literature) actually means light rather than darkness. Eri, who is unfamiliar with Japanese word origins, sees the two as opposites.

Cultural Fair, page 43

In addition to the athletics festival, nearly every school also has a cultural fair for which each class, club, team, or other official school group must provide some form of entertainment. Most common are food stalls, but activities also include haunted houses, museum-like displays, puppet shows, music, and dance performances.

Hanafuda, page 49

Did you think that Nintendo started with Donkey Kong? No, Nintendo was in business making a card deck called Hanafuda in the late 1800s. Cards were introduced to Japan in the 1500s, when Portuguese sailors brought their 48-card decks with them to Japan. Card games have been somewhat popular ever since, but during the Edo Period (1603–1868), small cards were created with 12 suits representing the months, each suit having four cards imprinted with the image of a flower that matches the month. Because the cards (fuda) are printed with flowers (hana), they were called Hanafuda, and they become one of the primary gambling devices of twentieth-century Japan. Nintendo was (and still is) the primary manufacturer of Hanafuda.

A Place in the Sun, page 86

"A Place in the Sun" was written by Ron Miller and Bryan Wells for Stevie Wonder. In 1966 it reached number 9 on the U.S. pop charts, and since then it has been covered by everyone from the Supremes to Engelbert Humperdinck. It has also been recorded (in Japanese) by Miki Imai, Keison, and Kiyomi Suzuki for the Japanese market.

The Hanging Bridge Effect, page 112

I can't describe it half as well as Takano Akira did on page 135 of Volume 1. But for those who have joined us late: When one is in a frightening situation, one gets a breathless, heart-drumming feeling, and if a member of the opposite sex is present, one can confuse those feelings for love.

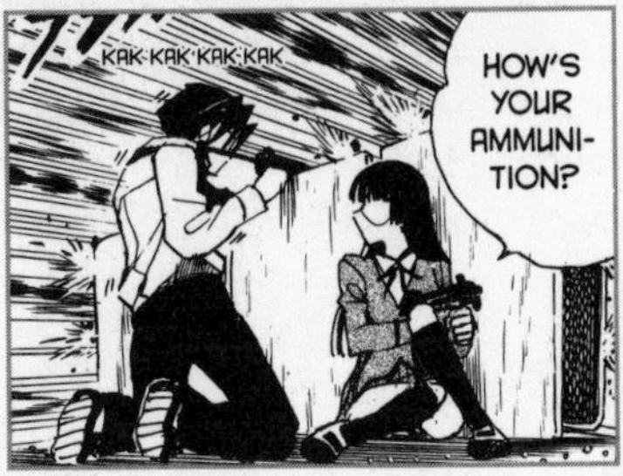
HOW'S YOUR AMMUNI-TION?
KAK KAK KAK KAK

Clean-up Duty, page 146

Although there are janitors in Japanese schools, the primary work of keeping the classroom clean falls to the students who use the room as their homeroom. The jobs are divided equally among the students, but there are always a few students who are willing to work very hard to get out of the relatively easy clean-up duty assigned to them.

Sweet Potatoes, page 152

Yakiimo is a baked sweet potato that is sold by street vendors and is a popular treat in the fall and winter months in Japan.

Kamekichi Kamenne, page 161

Kame is the Japanese word for turtle, and in this one-page manga, the two turtle's names are Kamekichi ("kichi" means happiness and is often the second kanji in men's names) and Kamenne (the "nne" ending is actually the French female name ending, which the Japanese know very well from the legend of Jeanne d'Arc).

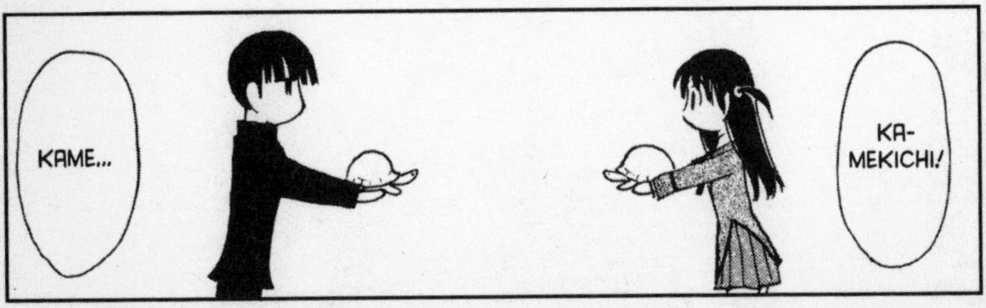
KA-MEKICHI!
KAME...

Watch out! It's Volume 9!

School Rumble

On sale from Del Rey Manga, April 15, 2008

TOMARE!

[STOP!]

You're going the wrong way!

Manga is a completely different type of reading experience.

To start at the *beginning*, go to the *end*!

That's right! Authentic manga is read the traditional Japanese way—from right to left. Exactly the *opposite* of how American books are read. It's easy to follow: Just go to the other end of the book, and read each page—and each panel—from right side to left side, starting at the top right. Now you're experiencing manga as it was meant to be!